# The Real Nick and Nora

# The Real Nick and Nora

Frances Goodrich and Albert Hackett,
Writers of Stage and Screen Classics

David L. Goodrich

**Southern Illinois University Press**
Carbondale and Edwardsville

Library of Congress Cataloging-in-Publication Data

Goodrich, David L.
  The real Nick and Nora : Frances Goodrich and Albert Hackett,
writers of stage and screen classics / David L. Goodrich.
    p. cm.
  Includes bibliographical references and index.
    1. Goodrich, Frances. 2. Hackett, Albert. 3. Authorship — Collaboration —
History — 20th century. 4. Dramatists, American — 20th century — Biography.
5. Screenwriters — United States — Biography. 6. Married people — United States
— Biography. I. Title.

PS3513.O53515 Z68 2001
812'.5209 — dc21
[B]
ISBN 0-8093-2408-3 (alk. paper)                                2001020700

The paper used in this publication meets the minimum requirements of American
National Standard for Information Sciences—Permanence of Paper for Printed Library
Materials, ANSI Z39.48-1992. ⊚

For
Patty and Adele
and for
Frances and Albert's nieces,
Madeleine Noble and Frances Hall,
and their nephew Maxwell Huntoon

# Contents

# Illustrations

# Acknowledgments

**D**uring my work on this dual biography of the married screenwriter-playwrights Frances Goodrich and Albert Hackett, I had the help of many people in many places.

Spouses are often thanked last in the acknowledgments ("And, finally, without the help of ———, this book would never have been written"), but I begin with Patty. She winced only occasionally when hearing the stories related here repeated for the hundredth time; with great patience, she offered warm encouragement, useful comments, and many creative thoughts.

Much help also came from other family members: my daughter, Adele Donham; my sister, Madeleine Noble; my brother-in-law, John Noble; my cousins Frances Hall, Maxwell Huntoon, Grace Lee, and Chris Havens; and Albert's widow, Gisella Svetlik. I am grateful to all of them.

Still more family members will be found in this book: Frances and Albert exchanged frequent letters with my parents and other relations; quoting that interplay makes those voices seem alive again.

The most valuable single source for someone researching a book dealing with a century of American popular entertainment is the Billy Rose Theatre Collection at the New York Public Library for the Performing Arts. The richness of its magazine and newspaper clippings is amazing, and its staff is marvelously helpful. In particular, I want to thank Christine Karatnytsky, Rod Bladell, Don Fowle, David Bartholomew, Dan Patri, Christopher Frith, Brian O'Connell, Ed Sager, Louis Paul, and Jeremy Megraw.

In 1962, Frances and Albert gave their professional papers, including correspondence, clippings, script drafts, final scripts, and "miscellany," all of them filling thirteen large boxes, to the Wisconsin Center for Film and Theater Research. Harold Miller, Joanne Hohler, Robert C. McKay, and William E. Beaudreau helped me to draw on that rich material.

Through all their years as playwrights, Frances and Albert had their New York–based friend Leah Salisbury as their theatrical agent (and although they had other agents in Hollywood, they always paid commissions to her from their earnings there). The extensive, often very personal, correspondence between the Hacketts and Salisbury is at the Rare Book and Manuscript Library at Columbia University. I thank Kevin O'Connor, Henry Rowen, SueYoung Park, and Anne Simms for help in consulting it.

At the Brownell Library, in Little Compton, Rhode Island, I received excellent help from Beth Dolembeske, Lynne Borges, and Karen Corrigan. I also owe many thanks to the staff of the Osterville, Massachusetts, Free Library: Barbara Conathan, Lorraine Felt, Linda Dalrymple, Melissa Petza, Jean Haggerty, Connie Marr, Joan Melchiono, and Cindy Roach.

Other librarians and archivists who generously offered time and aid include Kathy Mortenson and Kathleen Glynn at the Falmouth, Massachusetts, Public Library; Samuel A. Gill and Kristine Krueger, the Academy of Motion Picture Arts and Sciences; Karen Mix, Mugar Memorial Library, Boston University; Nancy Dean, Kroch Library, Cornell University; Sara S. Hodson, the Huntington Library, San Marino, California; Jim Carr, Margaret Adams Archives, Dennis, Massachusetts; Christine Bocek, Los Angeles Public Library; Terry Korpitka, Historic Northampton; Raymond Wemmlinger, The Players Club; Kay Bost, DeGolyer Library, Southern Methodist University; Gerise Herndon and Cathy Henderson, the Harry Ransom Humanities Center of the University of Texas at Austin (Pierre Lamarche also helped me greatly); Teri Bond Michael, UCLA School of Theater, Film, and Television; Ned Comstock, University of Southern California Library; Nancy S. MacKechnie, Vassar College Library; and Jennifer King, American Heritage Center, the University of Wyoming.

I owe much to the following five "men of letters." I got encouragement and good advice from three long-time friends who are smart, highly accomplished editors: Corlies Smith, Sam Vaughan, and Ashbel Green. The widely read author and movie history expert Pat McGillgan offered many valuable tips on research and gave useful comments on an early version of the manuscript. Professor Lawrence Graver of Williams College, the author of the definitive book on the subject, steered me carefully through the thorny theatrical history of *The Diary of Anne Frank*.

Many of Frances and Albert's friends and coworkers gave much time and effort, recalling memories in face-to-face and telephone interviews, answering written questions, and writing letters. I'm indebted to them all, especially (in no particular order) to the ones named here. Gloria Stuart Sheekman, one of the Hacketts' closest friends and, as of the year 2000, the oldest actor to be nominated for an Oscar, sent often-funny "inside" words from California. From Uzes, France, Dr. Patrick Woodcock sent wonderfully detailed letters vividly describing his long friendship with Frances and Albert in Bel Air and London. In London, I had a pleasant afternoon with another of the Hacketts' English friends, Frith Banbury, the director of the production of *The Diary of Anne Frank* in that city. In New York, I had an equally pleasant afternoon with Garson Kanin, the director of the play's Broadway production, and his wife, the actress and author Marian Seldes (once my schoolmate), and received many lively recollections and a rewarding file of Hackett-Kanin memos and letters. Elizabeth Frank (no relation to Anne), the winner of a 1986 Pulitzer Prize for her biography of the poet Louise Bogan, shared sandwiches and childhood memories of the Hacketts, plus insights into 1950s–1960s Hollywood life. Other warm memories came during fine talks with Al and Dolly Haas Hirschfeld, who knew the Hacketts "forever" in many places and in the company of many mutual friends. After Dolly's death, Louise Kerz Hirschfeld offered generous aid. I am deeply grateful to Al for allowing me to use his splendid drawings of Myrna Loy and William Powell and of seven members of the original Broadway cast of *The Diary of Anne Frank.*

    The list of others who gave me welcome help, suggestions, recollections, and factual material in correspondence and sometimes lengthy interviews includes Sam Adams, Lisa Aronson, Janice Aubrey, Margie Barab, Mary Ellin Barrett, Avis Berman, Lois Berman, Patricia Bosworth, Margaret Brooks, David Brown, Matthew J. Bruccoli, Rosemary Chodorov, Mary Marshall Clark, Gerta Conner, Joan Copeland, John S. Copland, Anna Crouse, Ormonde de Kay, Byron Dobell, Stanley Donen, Sarah Douglas, Mrs. Michael Durney, Fredrick Eberstadt, Allan B. Ecker, Barbara Epstein, Julius Epstein, Peter Filichia, Patty Havens Finn, Gary Giem, Madeline Gilford, Ruth Goetz, Bo Goldman, Tammy Grimes, Mary Rodgers Guettel, Philip Hamburger, Kitty Carlisle Hart, Philip V. Havens, Jack Heiner, Jimmie Hicks, Foster Hirsch, Chantal Hodges, Celeste Holm, David D. Huntoon, Anne Jackson, Michael Janeway, Diane Johnson, Barbara Kerr, Wendy Kesselman, Terry Kingsley-Smith, Barbara S. Kraft, Dr. Veljko Krstulovic, Mr. and Mrs. Ring Lardner Jr., Lynn Lane, Karen Lerner, David Lloyd, Leila Hadley Luce, William Ludwig, Deirdre Marsters, Jay Martin, Dorothy McHugh, Faith McNulty, Joan Mellen, Phyllis Meras, David Middleton, Joseph Mitchell, Patricia Neal, Nick and Jo Nickerson, John Oblack, Harriet O'Keeffe, Dr. Kathy Panama, Douglas M. Parker, Cynthia Patten, Abby Perelman, Adam Perelman, Mr. And Mrs. Nat Perrin, Charlton Phelps, Hal Prince, Maurice Rapf, Flora Roberts, Florence

Rome, Judith Goetz Sanger, Nora Sayre, Richard Schickel, Nancy Rica Schiff, Floyd Scholz, Jessica Silvers, Joan Castle Sitwell, Robert H. Smith Jr., A. M. Sperber, Alan Stamm, Dorothy Stickney, George Stoutamyer, Blanche Sweet, Tory Moore Tennaro, Gene and Sylvia Thompson, Alice Trillin, Catherine Turney, Sally Dixon Wiener, and Billy Wilder.

I also owe a large debt for splendid help to John Thornton, an agent of talent, patience, and good humor.

Keyboard wizard Marilyn Penney performed a miracle, squeezing my many words onto two tiny disks, and I'm forever grateful.

I'm also deeply grateful to many efficient, cheery-sounding (we never met face-to-face) people at Southern Illinois University Press, including, in no special order, Jim Simmons, Elizabeth Brymer, Rick Stetter, Carol Burns, Larry Townsend, Barbara Martin, Dan Seiters, Kristine Priddy, and Jonathan Haupt. My thanks go, as well, to that fine Montana copy editor Shana Harrington.

In these acknowledgments, I may have left out some individuals I should have included. I offer them my apologies. If there are errors on the pages that follow, they are mine, not those of the people named here.

In addition, I gratefully acknowledge various copyright holders for permission to reprint the following previously published material:

"A Playwright's Cradle Days," by Albert Hackett, *Variety*, January 4, 1961, p. 7.

"Reminiscences of Albert and Frances Hackett," 1983, Columbia University Oral History Research Office Collection.

"Reflection on Ice-Breaking" by Ogden Nash. Copyright © 1930 by Ogden Nash. First appeared in *The New Yorker*. Published by *The New Yorker*. Reprinted by permission of Curtis Brown, Ltd.

Filmography from *Backstory: Interviews with Screenwriters of Hollywood's Golden Age* edited by Patrick McGilligan. Copyright © 1986, The Regents of the University of California, University of California Press.

Excerpts from the letters of S. J. Perelman from *Don't Tread on Me: The Selected Letters of S. J. Perelman*. Copyright © Adam and Abby Perelman. By permission of Harold Ober Associates.

Two letters written by Frances Goodrich and Albert Hackett, one to Carson McCullers and one to Ogden Nash. Harry Ransom Humanities Research Center, The University of Texas at Austin.

# The Real Nick and Nora

# Introduction

**A** few minutes before curtain time, October 5, 1955, at the Cort Theater, on 48th Street, east of Broadway. Every seat is filled; many in the sophisticated, chattering audience are in evening gowns or black tie—this is a major theatrical event, the opening night of a controversial new play, *The Diary of Anne Frank*. Hidden in the very last row of the topmost balcony, dry mouthed and twitching (their words), are Frances Goodrich and Albert Hackett, the play's authors. Goodrich, sixty-five, and Hackett, fifty-five, married for twenty-four years, playwright-screenwriters famed for their many movies during Hollywood's Golden Age, including *The Thin Man*, *It's a Wonderful Life*, and *Easter Parade*, are deeply anxious about how the critics and the audience will react tonight. Their play, based on Anne Frank's journal, is serious and conscience-stirring; it deals with the horrors of the Holocaust and is essentially heartbreaking; it's been said that people will never sit through it. Writing it has been by far the greatest challenge of their career and has captured their deepest feelings. Now, they recall (again, their words) the two stressful years they've devoted to the project, the eight versions they've written, the many miles they've traveled, the many people who've helped them.[1] After the final curtain falls, they will walk through the warm night air to Sardi's restaurant, where, with the cast, the director, and the producer, they will attend the traditional opening night party, sitting beneath caricatures of grinning theater greats, bantering about nothing, waiting with fast-pounding hearts for the reviews.

To get to that balcony on that tension-filled evening, Frances and Albert had followed intriguing, sometimes pleasant, sometimes difficult paths. She was born into a comfortably fixed, upper-middle-class family and, after college, went on the stage, where she had modest success and met her first husband. After a disastrous second marriage to a famous man, she wrote a play—which started her collaboration with Albert. His background was markedly different: at age six, after his blue-collar father died, he was put on the stage to help pay the rent, and by the time he and Frances married, in 1931, he had become a well-paid comic performer. In Hollywood, the Hacketts wrote many other films that are now engraved on America's popular culture, including the two most famous Jeanette MacDonald–Nelson Eddy musicals, *Naughty Marietta* and *Rose Marie;* an adaptation of Eugene O'Neill's only comedy, *Ah, Wilderness!;* two more Judy Garland musicals (in addition to *Easter Parade*); and, for Spencer Tracy, *Father of the Bride* and its sequel. The writer-director Garson Kanin called them "an enchanting couple; they were the writers that producers and directors used to kill to get."[2] Through the years, they worked with or befriended many highly talented people, among them S. J. Perelman, F. Scott Fitzgerald, Irving Berlin, Lillian Hellman, Dashiell Hammett, Billy Wilder, Charles Brackett, Ogden Nash, Fredric March, Dorothy Parker, Nathanael West, Vincente Minelli, Ira Gershwin, Al and Dolly Hirschfeld, and James Cagney. They were known for their wit and high spirits and the pleasure of their dinner parties; they were key activists in the bitter battles against the film producers to create the Screen Writers Guild; they waged some memorable fights with their bosses; they defeated a job-threatening, right-wing attack on their patriotism. Perhaps most important, in the world of show business, which isn't famed for such qualities, they were noted for their modesty, integrity, and decency. "The nicest people I ever knew," one of their peers said; another called them "the most beloved couple in Hollywood."

I'm the Hacketts' nephew. My earliest detailed memory of them is a summer evening fifteen years before *The Diary'*s opening night. Age ten, I was in their room in a country inn in the pleasant Green Mountain town of Rochester, Vermont (usually based in Los Angeles, they'd joined my parents in picking me up after summer camp). The room was large, simply furnished, and homely; the Hacketts had glamorized it with the scent of perfume, a card table set up for gin rummy, and a brightly gleaming silver cocktail shaker. Frances was then fifty, of medium height and a bit overweight, stylishly dressed and subtly made up, with brown eyes and brown bangs. She had a handsome, strong-nosed profile; listening to my boyish babble, she watched me carefully, smiling often; she spoke with a faintly actressy accent, saying "darling" and "lovely" a lot. Albert was two inches taller and slightly built, with short-cropped brown hair and horn-rimmed glasses. He, too, was good-looking, and somehow elfin, with smaller features and laugh lines on his cheeks. He delivered his off-beat, self-mocking quips with many chuckles, a wide-eyed, innocent look, and precise pronunciation ("news" was "nee-use," not "nooze"). The two of them were talking with my parents with what sounded like great wit and sophistication—which made them seem a lot like Nick and Nora Charles, the glamorous, wisecracking, widely loved *Thin Man* couple they'd helped to create. As I got to know the Hacketts better in later years, I sensed even more strongly their resemblance to Nick and Nora—hence the title of this book.

After that Vermont meeting, I saw Frances and Albert occasionally at family gatherings. In 1959, I drove through France and Switzerland with them. He sometimes called her "Madam," or "the madam," or "the lady I'm traveling with"; she called him "Hackett" and navigated with a pocket compass. After 1962, when they moved from California to New York, my wife and I were invited to wonderful dinner parties, where they entertained their famous friends. As I grew closer to them, I saw that they were intensely loyal to family and friends, supported liberal causes, and were outspoken and always ready to praise talent and damn incompetence. Frances had no taste for "woman's traditional role" and was more assertive than Albert, whom she called "gentle"; on the surface, she was practical, even managerial—but she had a deeply emotional, even sentimental, streak. Albert was loved for his spontaneous wit—but underneath, tough childhood experiences had made him cautious and skeptical.

The Hacketts seldom discussed their separate lives before their marriage, and many who knew them later assumed they'd "always been together," but in fact they'd had great luck in finding each other. After their partnership began, they stayed constantly, tightly, side by side, fighting often while working hard ("We *yelled* at each other—our office sounded like a bear pit"), but always managing to reconcile their differences. That closeness carried over into other areas: their feelings and decisions about politics, the arts, living arrangements, money and what to do with it, commitments to causes. Adding their acting years onto their writing years, the Hacketts embody a colorful, two-perspective history of pre-TV American popular entertainment, encompassing vaudeville, nickel-and-dime melodrama, silent films, the earliest "talkies," and drama, comedy, and musical comedy, both on Broadway and in Hollywood. The projects they worked on as writers, and their involvement in social and political developments, reflected the evolving pattern of life in America.

When I started researching this book, I wondered what its main theme would be—and then I realized that three subjects were repeated again and again.

The first was the fun that Frances and Albert shared, particularly in the 1930s, during Hollywood's Golden Age, when the place was jam-packed with people of wit, charm, and even genius. Not all of their Hollywood hours were golden, and they had periods of depression and even (in Frances's words) "a lovely nervous breakdown," but mostly they enjoyed that hectic, creative, historic period. The Hacketts had an enormous talent for friendship; they were—everyone said it—entertaining, witty, great to be with.

The second theme was professionalism. Self-taught as writers, drawing on their acting experience, Frances and Albert knew that solid scripts were the key to successful productions, and *pushed* themselves. Their professionalism enabled them to move from lightweight comedies to musical comedies, then to comedies with deeper undertones, and finally into a totally different area, capping their career with *The Diary of Anne Frank,* in which one of the twentieth century's most-admired, best-loved voices spoke to the world.

The third theme is character. It's often said that nice people don't win in show business, but Frances and Albert were unquestionably winners, and over and over they were described as kind, warm, generous, gracious, wonderful—as people of extraordinary goodness. Hearing this, sensing that too much virtue might be dull, I began searching for flaws and hidden scandals. I found adventure and conflict and drama in the Hacketts' separate, premarriage stories, but concerning the happy years after, the praise continued. Katherine Cornell called them "most adorable"; another person said they were "the most devoted and friendliest couple in a town noted neither for its monogamy nor affability";[3] a third found them "effortlessly amusing and insightful. . . . After living and working together for over fifty years, the Hacketts' clear enjoyment of and affection for one another is nothing short of inspirational."[4]

At Sardi's, on the opening night of *The Diary of Anne Frank,* the tension burst when Frances and Albert read unanimously splendid reviews and heard cheers of triumph. The play went on to win every major award, including the Pulitzer Prize, and is still performed often today, sending its message around the world. "Every notice good," Frances wrote. "Walking on air!"[5] Some time later, she recalled that writing the play had sparked in her and Albert "a deep spiritual satisfaction which no other work, in all of our years, has ever given us."[6]

Because writers like the Hacketts aren't stars or household names, they're seldom written about. That's unfortunate: many have lived highly interesting lives. Also rare nowadays are accounts of loyal, loving couples — so in two ways this book explores fresh ground. It tells the story of two extrasmart, intriguing, funny people, from markedly different backgrounds, who joined forces, grew in skill and discernment and stature, and built a marital and creative partnership that has been called unique, remarkable, and extraordinary.

Frances, in her teens, in the Nutley house—as usual, with a book.
Author's collection.

Frances *(right)* in *Arms and the Man*, 1911, at Vassar, where she acted and directed. Her graduation yearbook motto was "Silence! We're rehearsing!" Special Collections, Vassar College Libraries, Poughkeepsie, New York.

Frances, the actress, hoping to appear on Broadway. White Studio;
Billy Rose Theatre Collection, The New York Public Library for the
Performing Arts; Astor, Lenox and Tilden Foundations.

Frances, the Broadway actress, early in her marriage to Robert Ames, 1917.
A photo retoucher has evidently given her a subtle nose job. White Studio;
Billy Rose Theatre Collection, The New York Public Library for the
Performing Arts; Astor, Lenox and Tilden Foundations.

Robert Ames, Frances's husband for six years. He was a success on Broadway and in the movies and was sometimes called a "heartbreaker." Billy Rose Theatre Collection, The New York Public Library for the Performing Arts; Astor, Lenox and Tilden Foundations.

Frances, the actress, around the time she met Hendrik Willem van Loon, 1925. Wisconsin Center for Film and Theater Research.

Hendrik Willem van Loon, the internationally famous author, whom his son called "a prodigious, infuriating, magnetic personality," photographed fifteen years after his and Frances's brief marriage. AP/Wide World Photos.

Albert at age nine onstage with the flamboyant Olga Nethersole in *The Writing on the Wall*, 1909. Albert started acting at age six. Billy Rose Theatre Collection, The New York Public Library for the Performing Arts; Astor, Lenox and Tilden Foundations.

Albert with actor Walter Hampden. Albert couldn't recall the actress or the play, which, he said, probably never got to Broadway. Billy Rose Theatre Collection, The New York Public Library for the Performing Arts; Astor, Lenox and Tilden Foundations.

Albert as a teenage actor.
Academy of Motion Picture
Arts and Sciences.

Albert around the time he and Frances first met. Wisconsin
Center for Film and Theater Research.

Albert in Hollywood, 1930, with unidentified cast members, during the filming of Sam Goldwyn's *Whoopee!* Albert repeated his successful stage role. Courtesy of *Vanity Fair*, Condé Nast Archive.

Albert *(standing)* in the hit comedy *Up Pops the Devil*, which he and Frances wrote before they were married. The artist was Al Hirschfeld, who later became the Hacketts' close friend. Billy Rose Theatre Collection, The New York Public Library for the Performing Arts; Astor, Lenox and Tilden Foundations.

# Frances Goodrich Has Hubby Now, Not Just a Pal

**By DORIS FLEESON.**

Intent on secrecy and in very much of a hurry, Frances Goodrich, actress, ran up to the Municipal building yester- day and took unto herself — and n o t com- panionately this time, either — her second hus- band.

He is Arthur M a u r i c e Hackett, a n d like his prede- cessor, Hendrik Willem V a n Loon, a man of letters. It was so se- cret that t h e couple didn't e v e n bring along any wit- nesses. So the ceremony w a s performed i n t h e municipal chapel by Depu- ty City Clerk Mc C o r m i c k with only half a hundred reporters and photographers present.

**Arthur M. Hackett**

**He's Handsome and Young.**

"O dear, this is such a surprise!" the excited and very glad little ac- tress exclaimed. "Why, I haven't even told my mother yet. This was really meant to be a secret."

But Frances proved better at picking her man than she did her spot, for Hackett is handsome and much nearer her own age than the Dutch - American historian, Van Loon, who left her in 1929 to re- marry Helen Criswell, his second wife.

Right after the ceremony the couple separated to go to their re- spective apartments, a few doors apart on East 55th St., to pack their trunks for a quick getaway to Hollywood last night.

**Companionate? Forget It.**

Hackett, author and playwright, is going to direct a picture, "Up Pops the Devil," his own and his wife's handiwork, which they have sold to Paramount.

Asked if she intended to carry out her former ideas of companion- ate marriage with Hackett, Miss Goodrich merely laughed and said, "Let's not talk any more about that."

# UP POPS CUPID AS DRAMATISTS GET MARRIED

### Frances Goodrich, Twice Wed Before, Made Mrs. Albert Hackett in City's Chapel

Up pops romance.

It popped up yesterday when Frances Goodrich, actress and writer, and Albert Hackett, actor and writer, who collaborated on that recent success, "Up Pops the Devil," popped into the Municipal Building and were married.

Miss Goodrich will be remem- bered as the third wife of Hendrik Willem Van Loon, author, and prior to that, the second wife of Robert Ames, actor. This time, by happy coincidence, she has mar- ried both an actor and a writer. It is Hackett's first marriage.

**MEANT TO HIDE IT.**

The bridal was to have been one of those secret affairs, with none the wiser until this morning, when the couple would be on their way to Hollywood. They are going there to supervise the moving pic- ture production of their play.

But they were recognized when they appeared at the Municipal Building, even though Hackett gave his name as A. Maurice Hackett. He is thirty and lives at 55 E. 55th St. Miss Goodrich is thirty-six, and lives at 360 E. 55th St.

**PLANS KEPT HIDDEN.**

They were married in the City Chapel by Deputy Clerk McCor- mick, with two office attendants as witnesses.

They departed at once, refus- ing to make known their plans.

Hackett's brother is Raymond Hackett, an actor on moving pic- tures. His step-father, Arthur Jonnson, was one of the first of the screen actors and his mother, Florence Hackett, a well-known actress.

Headlines announced the Hacketts' marriage February 1931. Obviously, Frances didn't like being caught by the camera. Billy Rose Theatre Collection, The New York Public Library for the Performing Arts; Astor, Lenox and Tilden Foundations.

Myrna Loy, William Powell, and Asta in *The Thin Man*, 1934, the Hacketts' first hit film, drawn by Al Hirschfeld, 1998. Frances acted with Powell in her twenties, and the Hacketts later befriended Loy. © Al Hirschfeld

Albert in the hit comedy *Mr. and Mrs. North*, which opened on Broadway in January 1941. It was his last acting job. Billy Rose Theatre Collection, The New York Public Library for the Performing Arts; Astor, Lenox and Tilden Foundations.

Seven members of the original Broadway cast of *The Diary of Anne Frank*, 1955, drawn by Al Hirschfeld. *Left to right:* Gusti Huber, Lou Jacobi, David Levin, Joseph Schildkraut, Eve Rubinstein, Jack Gilford, and Susan Strasberg. © Al Hirschfeld.

In 1956, in the Bel Air house, Albert showing how he acted out lines and scenes during their writing. Courtesy of University of Southern California, on behalf of the USC Library Department of Special Collections.

Frances and Albert with George Stevens and Millie Perkins, the director and star of the film version of *The Diary of Anne Frank*. Courtesy Ann Huntoon.

At a movie awards ceremony in New York, January 1982, Albert, gripped by Lauren Bacall, with his old pal Jimmy Cagney. AP/Wide World Photos.

Frances and Albert in their New York apartment a few months before Frances died. She was ninety-two but told the photographer (who wrote that "being with this couple is like watching a comedy team") that she was eighty-seven. © Nancy Rica Schiff 1983.

# 1

## Frances, the Lawn Child

She was born on December 21, 1890, in Belleville, New Jersey, then a pretty village on the Passaic River, where, her mother wrote, "sturgeon leapt and lawns ran down to shining waters." She had an older sister; a brother, another sister, and another brother (my father) followed. When she was two, the family moved to nearby Nutley, an equally pleasant village within easy distance of New York on the Erie Railroad and Hudson River ferries. In Nutley, there were green fields, tree-lined roads, big, comfortable houses, and another stretch of the clear, unspoiled Passaic. "It was lovely," Frances once said. "All around us were woods, and every spring the woods were full of wildflowers." The social center was the Field Club, featuring archery, outdoor teas, amateur theatricals, dances, and children's parties; the neighbors included businessmen, lawyers, doctors, architects, artists, writers, and well-to-do dilettantes.

One of the leaders of the Nutley community was Frances's father, Henry Wickes Goodrich, who'd been born in Brooklyn in 1860, the son of William Winton Goodrich, an eminent admiralty lawyer and for a time presiding justice of the Appellate Division of the New York State Supreme Court. Henry was compact and fair-haired, with a neatly trimmed Vandyke beard; he went to Amherst and Columbia Law School, then joined his father's New York firm. Henry did all right as a lawyer, but his real loves were directing amateur play productions and reciting poetry to groups of children in his big, turreted house. He marched in suffragette parades and served as president of Nutley's Board of Education, and he had imagination: during visits to museums, so his five children could "better appreciate color," he had them face away from the pictures, then bend over and look upside down between their legs. Henry enjoyed good company and brandy and cigars, and belonged to clubs in Nutley, Newark, and the summer colony in Little Compton, Rhode Island. His favorite club was The Players, in New York. Many members were actors and artists; Henry spent long hours on the piazza, placing modest bets on the color of the next passing horse or pair of ladies' stockings.

Frances's mother, Madeleine Christy Lloyd, was born in New York City in 1862, the daughter of a grim-looking, rigidly Calvinistic, Dutch Reformed minister named Aaron. She was small, slender, and quiet, but underneath were practicality, a strong will, and wry humor. She was never without a book and was passionate about the novels of Henry James. Madeleine, who was always close to Frances and gave her boundless career encouragement, had three brothers and a sister.

Frances never knew her uncle David Demarest Lloyd—he died just before she was born. One of the editors of the *New York Tribune,* he wrote plays that were performed in New York and other cities; the ads for one, *The Woman Hater,* said it was "as full of laughs as a shad is of bones."

John Crilley Lloyd was a gentle, humorous, tidily dressed coffee merchant, known as "the inventor of the Yuban blend," and a lifelong bachelor. Like others in the family, Frances enjoyed his company but probably found him reserved and conventional.

Frances's only maternal aunt, Caroline—called "Caro"—was always plainly dressed and had dark, almost-fierce-looking eyes. She went to Vassar, then briefly taught school. In Paris, she married a flaky-sounding "philosophical anarchist" and professional genealogist from Newburyport, Massachusetts, named Lothrop Withington. Caro divorced him, evidently because he turned out to have another wife in England; he drowned in the sinking of the *Lusitania.* Caro later married a New York jeweler and joined the Communist Party; when she died, in 1940, she was one of the three female co-owners of the *Daily Worker.* Caro's radicalism caused many family arguments; Frances loved her dearly but didn't buy her far-left convictions.

Frances's third uncle, Henry Demarest Lloyd, was a lawyer, journalist, editorialist, and author. His 1894 book, *Wealth Against Commonwealth,* exposing the machinations of the Standard Oil Company, has been cited often as a muck-raking classic; he himself was called one of his era's "great champions of social and economic justice." His friends included Clarence Darrow, Eugene Debs, Booker T. Washington, and Jane Addams; Robert Louis Stevenson said he was a "very capable, clever fellow."[1] As a child, Frances visited his handsome, forty-room Little Compton house (his wife was rich), where she was bossed around by a German fräulein. All her life, Frances recalled and respected her Uncle Henry's progressive ideas.

Frances went to a private grade school in Nutley, then to Passaic Collegiate School, and on to Vassar. At Vassar, then one of America's best all-female colleges, she joined various clubs and was elected to class committees. Her greatest love, probably inherited from her father, was directing plays; her graduation yearbook quote was, "Silence there, please! We're rehearsing." She also loved acting but didn't always get the best roles; she once wrote to her mother, "I'm afraid you don't realize how inconsolable I am about losing that part. The *star* part . . . And I've lost it after such a fight. . . . I clenched my fists and yelled." All her life, Frances protested when people were treated unfairly—and her letters from Vassar showed that: she complained about college officials who "can't argue and won't listen to justice. . . . It's a horrible feeling to realize you're in the right but that there are two women with all the authority in their hands, one woman a doddering idiot who only has enough craftiness to lie, lie, lie!" Another villain was the college doctor: "I know she has done more harm than good. . . . The medical department . . . is rotten at its core." (Frances was always suspicious of doctors: "Medicine always seems to work the wrong way with me. Perhaps because I distrust it." Albert once said that, to prevent colds, she should avoid drafts: "I think I'll put her in a bell jar.")

Frances could also be outspoken about family matters. Once, learning that her teenage brother Lloyd (my father) wanted to become a painter, she decided that would be risky and loudly told their parents to "Nip it in the bud!" Years later, Frances and Lloyd agreed that she'd been right: instead of painting, he became an art historian and museum director and did as well in that field as she did in hers. Although Frances could be feisty and petulant, she also had a softer, self-aware side. "This childlike, silly harangue," she once wrote to her mother, "although it has no doubt shocked your literary taste . . . has relieved me. . . . I find that the only thing that will console me is a box of oranges. . . . I must have them."

Frances's parents were listed in the *Social Register*, and many of her college friends "came out." She did, too, but nobody in the family now knows when or where, because she almost never mentioned her debut—probably because it had bored her. After graduating from Vassar in 1912 (most of her classmates wore white dresses during the ceremony, but Frances later boasted that she wore red), she studied briefly at the New York School of Social Service and kept up her interest in acting. After performing in a comedy at The Players, she was invited to join two friends in a vaudeville act, but her father said no. "I said, 'You're ruining my life, you're ruining

my life,'" she recalled, "so he went to The Players Club and found somebody, and got me into a stock company."[2]

The Northampton (Massachusetts) Players had been formed in 1912
with the advice of serious theater-world people, including Harvard professor George Pierce Baker, and had fine directors. The company, whose
motto was "of the people, by the people, for the people," performed in the
Academy of Music, an imposing, city-owned building on Main Street with
Louis Comfort Tiffany windows and one thousand seats in the orchestra,
orchestra circle, and balcony. Most of the actors lived in nearby hotels.
Frances worked often in Northampton from 1913 through 1916, appearing, usually as the ingenue, in at least twenty different productions. Most
were comedies, with titles like *In the Vanguard, A Pot o' Broth, Nearly Married,* and *The Dawn of a Tomorrow,* and they're forgotten today, but their
authors included Arthur Wing Pinero, J. M. Barrie, and William Butler
Yeats. Frances also appeared in *Hamlet* as the Player Queen; Horatio was
played by William Powell. Years later, in Hollywood, Powell's career got
its greatest-ever boost from *The Thin Man,* which was scripted by the Hacketts, and he said to Albert, "Your wife? I was with her in the Civil War."
For Powell, the Northampton experience was unhappy: he was often the
company villain but never got, he said, even "an enthusiastic hiss."[3] Also
in the company was a "juvenile" actor named Robert Downing Ames.

Bob Ames was a year older than Frances, blond, and good-looking. The
son of a Hartford, Connecticut, insurance executive, he'd worked as a
ticket seller in a Hartford theater in his teens and had started acting there
at age twenty. An associate of the actor-manager Henry Miller spotted him;
after minor parts in Miller road shows, he went to Northampton to get
more experience before going to Broadway. By the time Frances met him,
he was twenty-four, had married and divorced a woman from Fall River,
Massachusetts, and had two children who lived with their mother.

Frances was now twenty-three, energetic, and attractive: photos show
a well-dressed, demure young lady, who is obviously proud of her profile.
So far, her life had been sheltered: at home, traces of Calvinism lingered;
at Vassar, sharp-eyed deans had kept watch (one of her sisters, who also
went there, said it was like being "mewed up in a nunnery"). During her
seasons in Northampton, she and Bob Ames were constantly together, acting in the same plays. Ames was intriguingly different from the gently
reared Ivy Leaguers Frances had grown up with in Nutley and Little
Compton: he was a hard-working member of a glamorous profession (of

*her* profession). Also, other women were attracted to him—a newspaper article called him a "heartbreaker." In later years, thanks to his presence, looks, and talent, he did well on the stage and in films, playing featured roles as the husband or lover of Pola Negri, Ina Claire, Mary Astor, Vilma Banky, and Gloria Swanson.

In the fall of 1916, Ames moved to Broadway in a Henry Miller hit, *Come Out of the Kitchen,* a sentimental comedy, starring Ruth Chatterton, about a temporarily broke family who pose as servants in their own Virginia mansion while it's rented to rich Northerners. Four months later, Frances made her Broadway debut in the same show, as one of the Northerners' houseguests. The play had elaborate sets and aggressive publicity: the chintz wall coverings in the mansion's drawing room reportedly had been "aged" by applying coatings of alcohol, shellac, and buttermilk; a dinner, prepared backstage by a "real cook of the old mammy school imported from Virginia" was served onstage. Frances's part was small, and she got no special mention in the reviews, but one critic said the play was acted by "an agreeable company of charming people, who know their business."

"Charming people" fit Frances neatly. Both on and off the stage, charm came to her so naturally, one observer wrote, that she "tended to deprecate it." By now, she was well-trained as an actress, and until she and Albert started writing full-time, she appeared in many different shows—but never in major roles. The problem may have been her intelligence, which she couldn't tune out completely; perhaps it kept her personality from reaching the audience. The playwright George Kelly once told her, "Do less—it will make the audience think you're better than you are." Her fellow actors called her "adequate but not interesting" and "seemingly insecure in her womanhood," and she agreed, once saying flatly, "I wasn't very good." That seems exaggerated: performers who *truly* aren't very good don't work as often as she did.

Being under Henry Miller's management in plays like *Come Out of the Kitchen* was fine, Frances said: "You had no contract because it wasn't necessary. . . . You could count on 52 weeks of work out of the year because you were one of the company."[4] Obviously, being together with Robert Ames in Northampton and New York—where Frances lived in an East 28th Street hotel—was also fine: the two fell in love, and on May 3, 1917, they were married. Frances's father, a strong supporter of Nutley's Grace Episcopal Church, had helped pay for its good-looking murals, but—probably because Ames was divorced—the ceremony wasn't held there but instead in the big, rambling, book-filled house at 187 Nutley Avenue, where a moose head loomed eerily over the piano. A few days later, the newly-weds left on a California-bound tour with the rest of the *Come Out of the Kitchen* company.

Frances's marriage to Bob Ames lasted six years and was clouded from the start, mainly by his drinking, which ultimately helped to kill him at age forty-two. Another problem was that their careers often separated them: for example, between January and June 1918, Frances toured with a *Come Out of the Kitchen* company to Detroit, Toledo, Washington, Syracuse, Brooklyn, Rochester (twice), and Baltimore; during those five months, Ames was with the company for approximately two. In addition, Ames evidently didn't like being married to an actress: he once said that "one prima donna in a family is quite enough."

In late 1919, apparently trying to stabilize her marriage, Frances quit the stage; describing this time, she wrote, "For a year, I've been a parasite, doing nothing."[5] At home, in their East 45th Street apartment, she was probably a fine hostess—she always did well in that department—but, having grown up with servants, was hopeless in other areas. She often said, almost sounding proud, "I can't cook," and she hated tasks like washing curtains and mopping kitchens. Several times, she brought Ames to Little Compton to visit her family. My father recalled that he was pleasant and was an avid golfer who made his own clubs; Frances's aunt Caro wasn't as kind, referring to him as "poor Bob."

Frances and Robert Ames were divorced in 1923. Later, he was married and divorced two more times. His third wife was the beautiful, sweet-voiced Vivienne Segal, who starred in such shows as *No, No, Nanette* and *Pal Joey;* about her, Ames griped, "For three years I was more or less of a lackey, pushing elevator buttons and waiting for her to get dressed for ap-pointments."[6] His fourth wife, a New York socialite named Muriel Oakes, once described what happened when he drank—"liquor made him sulky, bad-tempered, and irritable"—and said he was often cruel to her when she pleaded with him to "climb on the water wagon."

Although their marriage was unhappy, Frances and Ames remained friendly afterward—at least on the surface. The year after their divorce, they both appeared in the out-of-town tryouts of a "golf comedy" called *Kelly's Vacation*. Frances had a minor part; Ames, the leading man, showed off his swing by hitting drives into the wings, but even so the play failed to reach Broadway. Three years later, when Frances was in Chicago act-ing in another play, and Ames was there with his brand-new, fourth wife, Miss Oakes, all three checked into the same hotel—and were joined by a young New York nightclub hostess named Helen Lambert, who told the newspapers she was suing Ames because he'd promised to marry her. The tabloids loved this, running headlines like "Triangle Surrounds Ames," and "Wife, Ex-Wife, Would-Be Wife, All Under One Roof." Miss Lambert's lawyer declared that the suit would "teach Ames that he cannot play with the hearts of women at will." Tracked down by reporters, Frances said that although Ames owed her back alimony, she wasn't suing and was so pleased with his recent marriage that the first thing she expected to do was hunt up Ames and his wife and have dinner with them.

Frances may have stayed Ames's friend right after their breakup, but in later years, she sometimes had trouble recalling how long they'd been married, and she criticized his habits: "He was a good actor, but a drunk. . . . He went into pictures and did well. But he was a drinker."[7] Plainly, these comments came from painful disappointment; Frances was highly emotional and had once felt passionately about Ames, whom she'd met when she was young and inexperienced and who had been, it's safe to say, the "first man in her life." Ames's alcoholism may have influenced her relations with other men. Her second husband, Hendrik Willem van Loon, was a teetotaler, and perhaps that added to his attraction. When she married Albert, everything was, she said, "lovely. . . . He drinks moderately. He's not against it, and he's not an alcoholic. He is a writer *and* an actor. So it's a very pleasant combination. None of the others were pleasant."[8] (Later, Frances had more experiences with alcoholics: many of the Hacketts' friends and coworkers drank too much, perhaps because of "artistic temperament" and the pressures of show business.)

Following *Come Out of the Kitchen*, Frances appeared, in New York and on the road, in three more Henry Miller productions starring Ruth Chatterton and sometimes Miller himself. The first two, *A Marriage of Convenience* and *Perkins*, didn't please the critics, but then came a successful revival of *Daddy Long Legs*, a comedy that told the story of a girl (Miss Chatterton) who started off in an orphan asylum and ended up "an author of repute." In December 1922, Frances appeared in *Fashions for Men*, by Ferenc Molnar; when it moved to Chicago, she shared an apartment with its twenty-two-year-old star, Helen Gahagan, who had recently been called "ten of the twelve most beautiful women in the world." The two remained friends after Gahagan married the actor Melvyn Douglas and went into California politics, where Richard Nixon notoriously smeared her as a "radical" during a senatorial campaign. Frances's next part was in *Chains*, described as "the most intelligent American play of the season." Again, Gahagan had

the lead, playing a pregnant, unmarried woman who refuses on principle
to marry the child's father, named Harry. Frances played Harry's mother,
"a Victorian-minded lady whose outlook is blurred by the fine print of the
etiquette book," and was praised for her "fine characterization."

When Frances, age thirty-three, was in Chicago in May 1923, in the touring company of *Chains,* she and Albert, age twenty-three, met for the first
time. It would have been interesting if they had felt instant attraction—
but, in fact, nothing special happened, except that Albert made a bad impression. A friend of his, Paul Kelly, later a star in films and plays, was
appearing as Harry, Frances's son. One evening, Albert came backstage,
and from Kelly's dressing room, Frances recalled, she heard "this voice
going on and on. I thought, that's a fresh, fresh guy." (Hearing the "fresh
guy" comment some years later, Albert replied, probably with a grin,
"That was a characterization I was using.")[9]

Touring in plays like *Chains* and *Fashions for Men* may have bred
Frances's lifelong love of travel. In the summer of 1924, she went to Spain
with Vassar friends and one day got into a sunny corral and waved a cape
at a fractious young bull, with many mustachioed, hat-wearing Spanish
males (and no women) looking on. In September 1924, she was back in
Chicago playing a "lady in distress" in the touring company of a "suave
and well-mannered" mystery-melodrama called *In the Next Room.* The
next year, 1925, brought major changes. At age sixty-five, Frances's father
died. She must have been hit hard—she had always been close to both of
her parents. (Happily, her mother lived to be ninety-six). In a memorial article, Henry was recalled as "a man of buoyant, optimistic temperament
with a wide variety of sympathies and enthusiasms. . . . Bodily sufferings
neither daunted his courage nor altered the gaiety of his laugh."[10] Also in
1925, Frances first met Hendrik Willem van Loon.

"A prodigious, infuriating, magnetic personality"; "an international charmer
and domestic dragon"; "a human machine of compelling energy"; "an indefatigable interpreter of human accomplishments"; "in the pageant of the
American good life, one of the most outstanding characters for more than
two decades"—all of these things were said about Hendrik Willem van
Loon, the brilliant, witty, homely, giant-sized (six-three, 290 pounds),
Dutch-born author of *The Story of Mankind* and thirty other books popu-
larizing human history and thought, which sold millions of hardcover
copies and were translated into over twenty languages around the world.
Frances first met him on Sunday, July 19, 1925, at a luncheon party in the

lively, arts-minded town of Westport, Connecticut. (Van Loon once said that in Westport there was "more adultery per square bed . . . than in any place east of the Rockies"; the painter Guy Pène duBois wrote that in those days Westport "exceeded the riotousness of New York. There gin and orange juice ruled the days and nights. . . . Work was an effort made between parties.")[11] Frances was now thirty-five, unattached, attractive, and pleased by her career: she'd just finished a long run in *The Show-Off*, by George Kelly, once described as "the finest comedy ever written by an American." ("I have no babies . . . no cats, no dogs, and no husbands," she wrote during the run, "but I'm in a play I'm proud to be in.") In contrast, van Loon, eight years older, was lonely, unhappy, and going through the breakup of his second marriage. Frances's first meeting with Albert didn't change her life, but when she met van Loon, she suddenly became the object of an obsessive, unrelenting pursuit.

Van Loon's campaign began the day after the Westport meeting, with an invitation mailed special delivery: "I do feel rather ashamed of yesterday's silly story feats and in order to offer a suitable explanation will you let me burn the sacrificial lamb at Mr. Ritz' Chinese garden on Thursday at one. . . . It is my intention to show you I kin do something beyond telling stories."[12]

They had lunch, and soon van Loon was writing things like

I have for forty years waited for one woman. When she would come, I knew that I would drop everything and would follow her. . . . I found Her. . . . She wore a purple hat and a little coat with red flowers embroidered all over it and she had lovely hands and not a ring on them.

and

The year has 365 days, 25 years have 365 times twenty, that makes five times five, that makes 7,725 letters . . . which you will get during the next twenty-five years. . . . Of course you might say, "Sir, how dare you write to me? Stop it. I say stop it," and I would answer, "Frances . . . why don't you lift up your pretty eyes unto the moon and tell the poor dumb critter it must not shine through your window (and, Oh, to be the moon)."

and

You have asked me . . . often to . . . fall in love with someone else. . . . I shall be looking. If only it were not always your damn face, your damn eyes, hair, ears, nose, arms, breasts (must you drag them in says Frances, yes my darling I must but drag is not quite the word).

Today, letters like these (and there were hundreds more, sometimes three a day, plus telegrams, flowers, and many costly gifts) seem adolescent, even absurd—so why did Frances wind up marrying their author? The answer is, "For several reasons . . ."

First, there was van Loon's ardent, flattering persistence over the next twenty-eight months—if ever there was a *really determined* man, he was it. Also, at this time Frances was often lonely, particularly when she was performing on tour. In the fall of 1925, when she was in Boston, van Loon, visiting Holland, sent her a Rembrandt etching. Her initially wary thank-you note wound up revealing her feelings: "Your beautiful etching came. I say 'your' advisedly, because of course I shall never accept it. It is reposing in the hotel safe. . . . I haven't had a letter from you in ten days. . . . We expect to be here six or seven weeks. . . . I am so lonely I could die."

In addition, van Loon was accomplished, stimulating, sophisticated. Born in Rotterdam, he had a Ph.D. in history, had taught at Antioch and Cornell, had worked in Europe and the United States as a journalist and editor, and was well into the creation of the books, often illustrated with his own quirky pen-and-ink drawings, that brought him riches and international fame. The books included *America, Tolerance, Van Loon's Lives,* and *The Story of the Bible.* They were highly readable and as charming and ebullient as their author: "When van Loon writes," one reviewer said, "you get plenty of history and plenty of van Loon." He was unbelievably energetic; his friends included eminent people in academia, journalism, the arts, and politics (Franklin D. Roosevelt called him "my true and trusted friend"). Also, he was quotable: "[As a child] I studied Cicero and Virgil . . . which had been written to catch little Dutch boys in grammatical errors"; "All art is born of a kick in the pants. Art is the medium . . . by which genius gets even with life"; "Somewhere in the world there is an epigram for every dilemma."

All of this—the reputation, the connections, the wit, the obsessive attention—surely had an effect on Frances; also, there was a cautious fondness between her widowed mother and van Loon. He was kind and attentive to Madeleine, inviting her to dinner, taking her to the theater. "It is refreshing to have someone around with a brain," she once wrote (perhaps with Bob Ames in mind). At the same time, Madeleine had reservations. She once proudly told van Loon about her French Huguenot ancestors, who had come to New York in 1663; peering through his horn-

rimmed spectacles, he replied loftily, in his thick accent, "Dukes do not emigrate." Madeleine knew that, despite the "van" in his name, he was in
no way ducal, and she found his condescension-plus-pretension hilarious;
"Dukes do not emigrate" quickly became a Goodrich family joke.

Early on, van Loon said he was going to get divorced and marry
Frances, but she had strong doubts and resisted for over two years. According to a biography written by his son, Gerard, van Loon once made
"an explicit pass" during a carriage ride through Central Park, which
Frances "gracefully sidestepped." Another time, he persuaded her to invite him to Little Compton, where, Gerard wrote, "they could go swimming together . . . and he would . . . be vouchsafed a coveted glance at her
little feet. 'You may buy all the pretty dresses you want,' he wrote, 'and all
the lovely things that shall make your loveliness the greater, but your feet,
dear Heart, belong to me and they shall be garbed so fittingly that flowers shall grow where you tread the ground.'" During this visit, van Loon
violated the Beach Club's dress code. In those days, men put on short-
sleeved tops that extended down to form a kind of jock strap, then buckled on trunks. One day, van Loon strode out of a changing room (perhaps
blinking madly in the sunlight without his glasses) and steered his wal-
ruslike 290 pounds toward the surf wearing only the undergarment—and
was swiftly sent back to finish dressing.

In his book, Gerard van Loon said that Frances tried hard to discour-
age Hendrik, telling him to "go away and find other women and go on a
series of debauches" and describing the many men who were then in love
with her, but this only made him more determined than ever. Van Loon
led a messy, mixed-up life, lying to his wife and Frances, scurrying fre-
netically around Europe and the United States, overworking, and often
consulting doctors about nervous disorders, but in his wooing of Frances,
he stayed steady and consistent, despite many angry breakups. Gerard
wrote that Hendrik had set out to "bulldoze" Frances into marriage; my
mother said that Frances once told her, "I have no choice—the only way
to solve this is to marry him." In the spring of 1927, Hendrik returned from
a stay on the Riviera and renewed his program of beating Frances down;
she escaped temporarily in a touring company. He gave her a pigskin traveling case marked with the letter B—standing, he said in a note, for both
"Beloved" and "Bitch"; this caused Frances to erupt and send a reply intended to cut their ties forever. Van Loon went briefly to Europe but by
early June was back in New York, arranging for his wife's Mexican divorce
and again flooding Frances with letters.

The divorce came through in September; on October 11, Frances and van
Loon were married in a civil ceremony by their friend Louis Browne, a
rabbi and college professor, and the author of van Loon–style books on history and religion. Thanks to van Loon's celebrity, newspaper reporters
asked about the marriage and were told it would be "companionate": the
van Loons wouldn't actually live together but would keep their separate
apartments—which were forty-eight blocks apart.

If the marriage to Ames was clouded from the start, the arrangement
with van Loon was doomed from the start. Evidently, Frances—with sur-
prising naïveté, considering her sophistication later in life—trusted that
she and her spouse would remain "truly companionate"; it seems equally
obvious that *he* expected that sooner or later her feelings would soften, and
they would become "truly married." Those differing attitudes created all
kinds of problems, and there were many others. The two were deeply in-
compatible, with totally different backgrounds, feelings, and opinions. He
liked living flamboyantly and wanted to show Frances off in the city's
grandest gathering places; she preferred a less showy style. Frances's
friends still included Robert Ames, whom van Loon disliked intensely.
When van Loon introduced Frances to *his* friends, she was cool and interrupted van Loon's conversation (when his friends commented, he forced
a smile and replied, "But isn't she beautiful?"). Among the people who
sensed the (mainly sexual) tension was Madeleine: she said the situation
was "perplexing and disquieting. . . . Neither seems happy, and what in
thunder they married for, I cannot imagine." Newspaper reporters continued to probe and got conflicting stories: van Loon said that since he was
a writer and his wife was on the stage, "we have found that living apart
is a very pleasant system, as my typewriter is going all day long while she
is sleeping," and Frances said that her routine would interrupt her husband's work, "as my telephone is ringing all day long." In the midst of all
this, burglars broke into Frances's apartment and stole clothes, jewelry,
and furs—plus her typewriter, which led to the thieves' arrest when detectives spotted them taking it into a pawnshop.

Years later, with "extraordinary, superhuman candor," Frances told
Gerard van Loon that her behavior during those months had been "exe-
crable." At one point, bowing to pressure from friends, she wrote to van
Loon suggesting they "try living together. . . . I'll go anywhere you want,
live with you at your apartment, have you live here. . . . Please let me
know what will make you happy"—but by then the situation was unsal-
vageable. Four months after he and Frances had taken their vows, he left

for Italy; ultimately, he rejoined his second wife. Before that, he wrote to Frances:

> I just did not happen to be the man you were in love with or apparently ever could be. . . . You were just as charming and pleasant to me as you were to almost any stranger. . . . Gawd-allmighty how I annoyed you. How I annoyed you when I assumed the attitude of the husband-protector and how I made you miserable when I tried to be the husband-lover. How, my dear poor child, I just made you feel uncomfortable all the time. . . . Did we ever laugh at the same joke? And I used to try and be funny. How damn ghastly it must have been to you and what a pretty mess of my own distilling.

Frances and van Loon were divorced in the fall of 1929, but they stayed in touch, and there was fondness on both sides. "Won't you come and see me?" she wrote. "I cannot bear the thought of any enmity between us." He replied that he felt "neither hatred nor hard feeling—nothing but the somewhat painful consideration that in some ways I am not as bright as the world tries to make me out and the recollection of the most charming and lovely woman who ever enriched [my] life." Respecting him and his achievements, Frances saved all of his letters and gave them to Gerard van Loon when he was writing about his father.

On October 17, 1927, Frances opened in *Skin Deep,* an inept comedy about domestic strife between musical geniuses; it vanished after eight performances. On December 26, she opened in *Excess Baggage,* a comedy about domestic strife between vaudeville performers; this time, the reviews were favorable. The play starred Miriam Hopkins and Eric Dressler and featured the comedian Frank McHugh. Madeleine wrote that she appeared in "one act only, but in two scenes, so that she has a chance to wear two gorgeous costumes. She looks very foreign . . . like a Polish tragedienne." Ten other plays opened on Broadway the same night— an all-time record; *Excess Baggage* was the most successful, running for 216 performances. With steady money coming in, Frances started saving—and also, like many others in that heady time, speculating in the stock market ("probably will lose," Madeleine commented). Frances had thought of traveling in Europe during the coming summer but instead decided to go to Elitch's Gardens, outside Denver, in those days the country's oldest, most prestigious summer theater. To prepare, she bought a wardrobe: "I went to sales. I knew all the plays we were going to do, and I knew what my parts would be because I'd seen them in New York—I was second woman."

Now age thirty-seven, Frances was always carefully made up and beautifully dressed: when she wasn't buying clothes for the stage, she patronized the better stores and offstage wore pearls, hats with veils, and white gloves, a dress style she kept most of her life. Thanks in part to her stage training, she moved gracefully and spoke charmingly; the writer Emily Kimbrough once reported, "Frances has one of the loveliest speaking voices to be heard. It is modulated, cultivated, which means there is no regional accent except in a word she uses often. Though her environs are no nearer the deep South than the outskirts of New York, she says 'dawlin.'"[13] By now, Frances had become a "one-match-a-day" smoker and sometimes had heavy coughing fits. She would doubtless have disliked being called "sophisticated," but some people probably thought of her that way: after all, she'd acted on Broadway for a decade, and the newspapers had reported often on her marriages to two successful, glamorous men.

Between acting, visits to Nutley, and a full social life, Frances had few spare hours. Nevertheless, she'd written a play, titled *Such a Lady*, which she called a "comedy about a very nice woman, about 35, pretty and conscious of it. Selfish and unconscious of it. She has never forgotten that she was once a belle." Frances knew the play needed work, so she asked "that fresh guy," Albert Hackett, for help. That step, of course ultimately had splendid, life-altering consequences. She probably took it partly because, having seen Albert from time to time in recent years, she knew that he, too, was an aspiring writer, with a natural gift for comedy, a wealth of theatrical experience, and charm as great as her own. Also, she must have been attracted to him—then twenty-seven, enjoying a fine acting career, he was slender, dark-haired, and good-looking. In addition, the life he'd led probably intrigued her: she'd been born into comfort, but for the man she was now interested in, things had been very different.

# 2

## Albert, the Nickelodeon Child

During an interview when Albert was eighty-two, an oral historian from Columbia University asked him about his birthday—February 16, 1900—and his parents' names.

"I was born," he replied, "on Eighty-Fourth Street and Park Avenue, which is very elegant now, but was then called Goat Hill. My mother's name was Florence Spreen. . . . My father's name was Maurice Hackett. His name is my middle name—I'm Albert Maurice Hackett. Those were the only two parents I had. I think."

At that point, Albert probably flashed his wide-eyed, innocent look.

The look must have changed with the next question: "Did your father die when you were small?"

"When I was about five years old," Albert answered. "He died in Denver. He was tubercular [and was sent there by a charity in the hope of being cured]. My mother was 21 with three children, staying with my grandmother, who was a seamstress or dressmaker. And word came, everything was going fine. So on a charity ticket, my mother took the three of us. My sister was 18 months older than I, and my brother was two years younger." (Albert later recalled that on the train to Denver, he and his brother were "entranced by the liquid soap in the lavatory.")

"We went out there," Albert continued, "and found instead of everything being fine, he was in the euphoric condition of a tubercular, and he was dying. He was in a Salvation Army place. . . . And so we had to get another charity ticket to bring us back to New York.

"Shortly after that, his body came back, and there was a great discussion as to what would happen to my mother and these three children. One part of the family said, 'Put them in an orphanage,' and somebody else said, 'Put them on the stage,' and that's how we got on the stage."

"Had your mother been an actress before?" the interviewer asked.

"She had been in a school play."

"And that's the only————?"

"That's the beginning of her career."

Albert's casual style in this interview was typical: his youthful years were hard, and in the theater he picked up a smiling, ironic attitude; in his soft-voiced, somewhat shy but witty way, he didn't simply tell jokes but related droll anecdotes and made quick asides with professional, deadpan delivery.[1]

Albert's mother, Florence Gertrude Spreen, was born in either Rochester or Buffalo, New York—exact records aren't available—and moved to New York City at age fifteen; a short time later, she married Maurice, who'd been born in Geneseo, New York. Albert once said that Maurice's father, Martin, was born in Ireland, and after coming to the United States worked as a ditchdigger. Before he got tuberculosis, Maurice worked as a store clerk and perhaps also as a streetcar conductor. What's noteworthy in all of this family history is that nowhere, on either side (except for Florence's school play), was there any trace of theatrical experience—and yet, not only did Albert build an acting career for himself, but so did his mother, brother, and sister. Concerning the way Florence and her children found survival on the stage, one of Albert's friends commented, "Albert never forgot being poor. . . . I think he understood that very poor people can be very courageous and make something out of life that other people can't."[2]

The four Hacketts, Albert told me, got started in the theater without training, thanks to "actors' agencies." He continued, "There were lots of them then; Packard's was one of the biggest. People said, 'The kids are cute. They'll be fine—just tell them what to do.' At that time, if you had a child and were trying to find a place for him other than prison"—here, I got the innocent look—"someone would suggest an agency, which would tell the parents how to [get] him on the stage. The mothers had to go along with the children, to dress them and take care of them—so the mothers could also get involved in acting."

For Florence, who was attractive and always beautifully dressed—thanks, no doubt, to her mother, the dressmaker—the theatrical connection opened a new life. Walk-ons and bit parts were followed by larger roles; ultimately, she played in vaudeville and in road companies—sometimes with her children—and in silent films, in which she was "equally convincing and satisfying as a self-centered society butterfly or a grief-crazed fishwife." She also appeared in a series of plays in Manhattan that Albert called "the 'Uns'"—*The Unloved Wife, The Unwed Mother,* and so forth. The matinees were just for women, on Thursdays, the maids' day off. Albert said that when he was around twenty-one, his mother sneaked him into a box during a performance of *The Unloved Wife*. He recalled that his mother said, "Don't watch the play, it's very bad—watch the audience." "The moment the curtain went up," he went on, "[the audience] started to cry. . . . The place was dripping with tears." Albert's mother played the lead, and one of the other characters asked if her husband beat her. When she replied, "No," she was asked, "Well, what *is* it?" and answered, "I don't know, he's just strange."[3]

Lines from melodramas like "the *Uns*" stuck in Albert's memory, and years later he salted his conversation with bits like "You see, our lives will be different from now on" and "Tell them I deny everything!" He also occasionally used what sounded like vaudeville slang: "Put the sleeve on"; "hot-footed it out of there"; "just keeping the air alive" (which evidently meant "making small talk").

All three of Florence's children were bright, energetic, and good-looking. The eldest, Janette, became a dancer-choreographer in vaudeville. In the 1920s, with her first husband, Harry Delmar ("He looked good," she once said, "though he wasn't much of a dancer"), she had a twenty-minute "flash act" (it's been said that these "looked like a big flash for short dough") featuring eight chorus girls. "There were lots of headdresses," Albert remembered. "Janette designed the costumes and wrote the words and music and starred. They played the Palace, and I went to applaud." Reviewers praised Janette's dancing ("topflight vaude dancer") and her figure ("lovely, well-formed"). She and Delmar were divorced, and she continued performing, doing butterfly dances and shag dummy routines with other partners, including Cesar Romero. In 1930, she married John Steel, a tenor best known for first singing "A Pretty Girl Is Like a Melody" in the 1919 *Ziegfeld Follies*. When vaudeville collapsed, Janette worked as a dress designer and as a hostess on ocean liners.

Florence, Janette, and Albert all had talent, but the most accomplished performer was Raymond. He and Albert acted together a number of times and were always close. When Raymond was five, he told an interviewer he had a "funny joke" about Albert: "He was in a melodrama and he was supposed to play dead, and all the time . . . he was chewing gum. . . . Nobody noticed it but me."[4] By age six, playing in *The Awakening of Helena Ritchie*, Raymond was a carefully coached, established child star with few of the affectations of stage youngsters. In his teens, he often acted on the road; at age twenty-three, he and Humphrey Bogart played "rented lovers with just the proper touch of diffidence" in a farce called *The Cradle Snatchers;* at age thirty-two, he appeared opposite Lillian Gish in Dumas's *Camille:* "He is a fine romantic actor. . . . He has the purity appropriate to

Miss Gish's vestal Camille, and he is tense and handsome." Raymond also worked as a featured player in such 1929 and 1930 films as *Madame X*, *The Trial of Mary Dugan*, *Footlights and Fools*, and *The Sea Wolf*, alongside Lionel Barrymore, Edward Everett Horton, Gloria Swanson, Dorothy Gish, and other stars.

Raymond was married twice, the second time to bright, beautiful Blanche Sweet, the ex-wife of the director Marshall Neilan. She'd started acting on the stage and in vaudeville; one of D. W. Griffith's leading ladies, she appeared in 121 silent pictures and three "talkies." Blanche was once called "one of the two most famous moving picture stars in the world—the other one being Mary Pickford." After Raymond died, in 1958, she moved to New York. She lived to be ninety and for a time was forgotten—but later a documentary was made about her life, and the Museum of Modern Art held a retrospective of her films. In New York, Frances and Albert saw Blanche often. She was feisty and loved a drink and a joke. One stormy Christmas night when she was well into her eighties, after a family dinner she rejected my pleas to take a taxi home, fell asleep on the Lexington Avenue bus, overshot her stop, crashed down several times on the ice while walking back, and the next morning called and cheerily related her adventures, adding that she'd given the driver hell for not waking her.

In 1960, Albert wrote an article for *Variety* describing his first stage role, in 1906, at age six, and parts of his childhood career:

> Fifty-five years ago, when *Variety* was starting, I was starting. I was playing in *Lottie the Poor Saleslady, Or Death Before Dishonor* [in New York]. *Variety* has changed a lot since. So have I. I was playing a little girl. I don't remember much about my part except that I died in the second act. As the curtain came down . . . I would struggle out from under the leading lady who had collapsed with grief on top of me, and rush offstage. There, someone would adjust feathery wings over my long nightgown, lift me onto a kitchen table. I would clasp my hands in prayer. A lantern slide would project moving clouds onto a drop behind me and, on cue, an oval cutout would open and the audience would see me winging my way to heaven. Cheers and whistles and I was through—[but] not completely, as I used to help [backstage]. I used to hold a smoke pot in the fire scene. I also rolled buckshot on a drum head in the storm scene. . . .
>
> [Touring] company carpenters were always my friends. . . . One made a large black bag for me to put my Flexible Flyer in, so I could

carry it on the train with me. . . . One season I played 300 one-night stands. I remember main streets and stage doors and dressing rooms that are completely unrelated. Poughkeepsie, N.Y., is very vivid and yet very vague to me.

The morning of the day we were to play there, we went in to see if there was any mail. The Smith Brothers had their factory there. For publicity they sent every member of the cast a package of cough drops. I had a fine time. I not only ate my own box but several other boxes that had been thrown away. From then on things are vague. I remember people working over me trying to get me to wake up; a doctor standing beside me in the wings; going on and getting my lines out and drawing a blank again. [Another source says that Albert passed out onstage and fell behind a table, and his fellow actors had to ad lib until they could get the curtain down and revive him.]

I remember one time going along a main street. . . . I remember horses and cars, a few parked automobiles . . . and the Nickelodeon. This is what my sister and I were looking for. . . . They were playing a Biograph picture with Mack Sennett. . . . [There was] a small ticket booth with "Admission 5¢" painted in large gold lettering. My sister and I were about of a size except that she made two of me whenever there was a situation.

The office girl looked down through the opening in the glass. . . . My sister spoke up. "May I see the manager, please?"

The girl stood up to see us better. "You mean Mr . . . ?"

My sister said, yes, the manager. The girl put a little wooden cover before the wicket and went into the dark theater. . . . The manager appeared and looked down at us puzzled. "You want to see me?" he asked.

"Do you recognize the profession?" asked my sister.

The manager was more puzzled than ever. . . . "Profession? What profession?"

"We are playing at the Grand Opera House in *The Travelling Salesman* . . ." My sister did not have to say another word. The manager's face lit up in recognition. "Oh, you want to see the show?" he exclaimed. "Go on in. Go in. Glad to have you." And in we went.[5]

For Albert and his mother and siblings, life on tour sometimes held unexpected twists. Once, when they were in a remote midwestern town in a less-than-great show, an actress warned Florence that the producer (the actress was sleeping with him) planned to depart, leaving the cast stranded. Florence waited until payday, collected their wages, and then took off with the children; Albert later said that the actress's help made him realize, early in life, that he could trust women. Sometimes, Albert was the only child in a touring company and had no roommates. He told a friend that during those lonely nights, he "practiced dying": falling out of bed with a moan or expiring with a gasp with his head on the pillow. He was constantly concerned about making money to help the family, and at one point, when he couldn't get an acting job, he worked as an errand boy on Wall Street — but when he brought his earnings home, he was told that, compared to acting, that was a waste of time.

In 1907, Albert again performed as a girl, in a revival of *Rip Van Winkle*, by Dion Boucicoult. "To add to the confusion," he said later, "my sister played a boy in the same play. It was years before we got our sexes straightened out." In 1908, the two of them appeared, as a newsboy and a boot black, in a vaudeville sketch called *After the Play* ("cute little youngsters. . . . The sketch will be all right . . . if these two Hackett children are retained"). In 1909, Albert was cast as the son of Olga Nethersole, a flamboyant, English-born actress, in *The Writing on the Wall*, a drama about the sometimes-lethal living conditions in New York City tenements; his mother had the role of his aunt. The following year, he had no acting job. There was no one at home to take care of him because his mother and brother and sister were all on the road, so he was, as he later joked, "sent to a convent."

Mount Saint Dominic Academy, in Caldwell, New Jersey, founded in the 1880s, though indeed run by Dominican Sisters, wasn't a "convent," but an economically managed school for boys and girls: $20 per month covered room, board, and tuition. The boarders, who lived in a grim-looking building called the Mother House, were charged 15¢ for a haircut and 25¢ for a bottle of cod liver oil. The school — ironically, it was about seven miles from Frances's large, comfortable Nutley house, which she was then visiting during Vassar vacations — wasn't exactly Dickensian, but it was very different from the cozy, bustling apartment that Albert, age ten, was used to, and he was homesick. Starting in June 1910, he spent almost a year there, and he once said, "It was awful. I had the feeling of being deserted." His grievances included the fact that his mother once sent him a copy of *Treasure Island*, but for some reason he didn't get it: "Instead, they gave me a book called something like *Joe the Bootblack*." Another problem was that the school seemed harsh and boring compared to the theater. In his *Variety* article, Albert wrote that at night, whenever there was an electric storm the nuns would get all the boys up out of their beds and into the hall. There we would kneel and pray. When the lightning flashed and the thunder boomed it was like old times to me and I'd fall to sleep, to be wakened by a whack on the head and an order to pray. They seemed to be afraid of thunder and lightning. The only thing bad about it that I knew was it could ruin a performance if you weren't careful. Particularly thunder—you had to hold back a line sometimes 'til the noise was over, or even say the line again.

Albert's experiences at "the convent" may explain his later dislike of what he called "the Catholic point of view." Around the time he was there, his mother, while appearing in a play titled *The Burglar and the Lady,* married a member of the company, Arthur V. Johnson, and moved to Philadelphia, where Johnson was an actor-director with the Lubin Film Company.

Six-foot-two, dark-haired, handsome, in his midthirties at the time, previously one of D. W. Griffith's principal leading men, Arthur V. Johnson has been called "the first matinee idol of the silent films." Albert had never really known Maurice, his father ("My memory of him is very vague. I daresay that when he was ill [with tuberculosis], people were frightened of having children around him"), and he found Johnson "wonderful, just wonderful. . . . Once we went to Coney Island or somewhere like that, and he carried me on his shoulders. He said, 'I'm going to teach you to swim.' Well, you know, that [made him] a great hero for me.

"I remember [once], we were doing a scene in a picture," Albert went on, "and he looked at me, and said, 'Don't stand like that, take a grip on the stage, stand there so that no one can push you over.' [Years later], I was talking to Jim Cagney, and he said, 'I think your stepfather was one of the best actors I ever saw,' so I told him this thing about 'take hold of the stage,' [and] it impressed Cagney."[6] (Indeed, Cagney repeated Johnson's dictum often—including in his autobiography, where he called it "treasured advice" —and through the years it became a cliché among performers.)

From Arthur Johnson, Albert acquired the habit of reading Shakespeare: "He always had a complete book of Shakespeare's plays. . . . When I went off on the road . . . I also had a complete book of Shakespeare's plays; that was my reading. I didn't have much of an education, and reading Shakespeare isn't easy, but I stayed with it. . . . I had a feeling that some of it would rub off on me, as I hoped some of my stepfather would rub off on me."[7]

Sadly, this man whom Albert loved and admired, and who filled an emotional need, didn't remain in his life: he and Albert's mother separated within a few years for reasons that aren't fully known—although Albert once commented that Johnson was "always drunk." In the meantime, Albert and Raymond had exciting experiences, acting, sometimes in knicker-bockers, at the Lubin Studio outside Philadelphia.

At that time, most silent film companies—Edison, Vitagraph, and others—operated in the New York area and had their own companies of salaried players, rather like theatrical stock companies. In Philadelphia, the stars of the Lubin Company were Albert's stepfather and Florence Lawrence. "I was very young then," Albert said. "It was practically like working in a barn. They set up anywhere, and just banked the lights around. . . . Since the films were silent, seldom did they have to have any quiet. Two or three companies would be shooting at once. There was no pandemonium, they just said, 'Quiet, everybody,' but the man said, 'I've got to build this thing,' and kept on sawing. Still, it was relatively quiet, so you could hear when they said, 'All right, come on in. All right, look at her. Now, start to cry'—or whatever.[8]

"It was wonderful for us at the studio," Albert went on, "because there were cowboys . . . men who had been with the Buffalo Bill shows and things like that. Outside of Philadelphia, at a place called Betzwood, they would keep the horses, where they did Westerns . . . and Civil War stories, with battle scenes. The wonderful thing for us was to get out there . . . around 40 miles from Philadelphia. They would put an ad in the papers saying 'Extras Wanted, $3 a day.' They would give these men uniforms, ask 'Who rides a horse?' and everybody said they could ride. They'd give them horses, run them through this thing once just to get the idea of what the battle was like—not shoot off any cartridges or anything—then pull them back and say, 'All right, let's go. Now you can shoot those guns.'

"They'd mine these fields. Then when the men went on for the battle scene, they were plunging, with these things blowing up—well, it was scandalous, what was going on! The horses would go crazy, and these farmers didn't know how to ride these Western horses. Some horses and riders didn't come back at all, they said. They started when the explosions started, and never came back. Three dollars a day. It was just glory, that was all it was."[9]

Discussing his early acting years, Albert often mentioned various laws en-
acted thanks partly to the Society for the Prevention of Cruelty to Children,
which he called "the Gerry Society," a reference to Elbridge T. Gerry, the
organization's leader. He had mixed feelings about the society: its activities sometimes kept child actors like himself, Raymond, and others from
working, but at the same time, its goals were worthy, and in the end, he
and other children benefited. "The Gerry Society," he once said, "demanded that child actors go to school and prove that they were being
taught." His year at "the convent" and a period with a tutor in Philadelphia had started his education; when his mother's marriage to Arthur
Johnson broke up and the family moved back to New York ("When we got
on that train to leave Philadelphia," he once recalled, "it felt like the end
of the world"), he was enrolled at the Professional Children's School.

Today, the Professional Children's School is sizable and sophisticated,
with many famous graduates and a seven-story building, but then it was
only three years old, with a handful of child-actor students in a few rooms
on West 46th Street. Albert once said that in those days, life was a "scramble" for acting children enrolled in regular schools. While they worked on
the road, they had to interrupt their education; while performing in New
York, they couldn't attend classes on matinee days; and if they went looking for work, they again had to skip classes. "The PCS," he said, "[met this
need. You could] work in the theater and get an education. . . . You had recognized teachers and classes, and when you went on the road, your ex-
amination papers were sent to you and sent back and corrected. . . . It was
a wonderful, protective thing for the kids." He was always grateful to the
school and stayed connected, making cash donations to building drives
and attending fund-raising parties. He once wrote an article about the
place and quoted a cheer written by a member of the class of 1916:

> Tutti Frutti Punch and Judy
> The PCS will do its duty.
> Don't you worry—don't you fret
> The PCS will get there yet![10]

While he was at the Professional Children's School, Albert occasionally
took time off to look for acting jobs. "It was difficult," he said. "[I would
work] in anything . . . a small part that ran for three or four days in a silent
picture, that sort of thing. If you got something that lasted ten days, that
was really making it." He once posed for the slide for an illustrated song;

these were projected onto the screen between the reels of a film, while the piano player led the audience in singing. Albert's poses involved "something about a birthday. My song didn't catch on, but my sister posed for one called 'I'm Tying The Leaves So They Won't Fall Down, So Nellie Won't Go Away.' There was a scene of a boy tying the leaves on a tree, because the doctor had said that when the leaves fell down, Nellie would die." (Repeating material like that, Albert stayed deadpan—except for a tiny gleam of amusement in his eyes.)

During this time, Albert lived with his mother, his grandmother—Mrs. Spreen—and his brother and sister in a "little railroad apartment" on West 64th Street. His grandmother made the costumes for Janette's vaudeville act in the apartment, and Raymond and Albert shared a bedroom, where the headdresses and costumes were put at night. "We had to fight our way through these things to get to bed, and the next day they would be sewn with beads and things." Albert's grandmother—who at one time quit dressmaking to work as a cook on a New York–based fishing boat and brought fish home for the family—was someone he loved deeply: when he was ninety-five, delirious and approaching death, he kept asking, "Where's my grandmother?"

Albert got back on the Broadway stage in mid-January 1916, in *Just a Woman*, a melodrama in which a loyal wife, after helping her husband to succeed, "learns that money begets only misery"; one critic called the show "low-grade piffle." Later that year, he was in a touring company of *Peter Pan*, starring the great Maude Adams. "I was playing the part of John," he said. "John always had the honor of trying Miss Adams's wire—when she came in, she flew to the mantel, then back down again—so they gave me a harness, and hooked me up, and I flew to the mantel, and as I did, my knees buckled under me, and I started to collapse: they'd given me a girl's girdle. . . . They picked me up from the floor. . . . It was so embarrassing."[11]

In 1917, Albert appeared in movies, filmed in the New York area, called *The Boy Who Cried Wolf* and *Knights of the Square Table*. The United States was, of course, at war by then, and Albert could have enlisted, but "it never occurred to me. I knew a lot of boys were enlisting, but I had no desire to be a soldier. . . . I was trying to get a job, to help pay the rent." Instead of serving in the army, Albert entertained it, traveling with a vaudeville troupe through the South, playing in towns near army camps in a sketch, *Children of France,* about a French boy and his sister who get caught sneaking secrets through the German lines. "The youthful French spies," a review said, "who carelessly walk around carrying German maps in their wooden shoes, are given a slight idea of German 'kultur' when a Teuton captain nonchalantly remarks, 'Take 'em out and shoot 'em.' Albert Hackett gives a particularly good interpretation of a supposedly frightened and guileless youth."

*Children of France*, Albert said later, was "dreadful; how we won that war, I don't know." However, there were compensations: "Fred Allen was on the bill for ten days; I didn't let him out of my sight. . . . He had just started as a juggler, and at the finish of his act he was doing some trick, and we were all set up behind him, a full stage with big shell-holes. . . . He had something on his chin that he was juggling, and he got a big hand, and went off, and the lights went out and on came a picture of George Washington, so they applauded that; on came the lights and he bowed again, then Abraham Lincoln, then Woodrow Wilson—finally he came backstage crawling on the floor, exhausted from bowing—it was glorious!"[12]

Frances had made her Broadway debut in 1917 in *Come Out of the Kitchen*; Albert was in the silent film version, released in May 1919. One critic wrote, "Good support is furnished by . . . the gifted Albert M. Hackett." Also released in 1919, with Albert in another supporting role, was *Anne of Green Gables*, starring Mary Miles Minter. The following year, he was in *Away Goes Prudence*, starring Billie Burke. Then he got back on the stage, touring in a comedy by Alice Duer Miller, *The Charm School*, as Tim, one of a pair of spoiled twins who "toil not and have never seriously considered spinning." He had to speak many of his lines—"We want to marry an heiress," for example—in tandem with his brother, Jim. When *The Charm School*'s tour ended, in Chicago, he decided, at age twenty, to go to Hollywood and look for work.

"Fortunately," Albert recalled, "I landed there when my sister was playing [in one of the theaters]. . . . I was able to put the sleeve on her to pay my hotel bill. When she left, after five days, I had just a certain amount of money, and I was going around on streetcars to studios. It was awful rough. . . . Once, I got a call [from a studio]. To get there, I had to take a streetcar from Hollywood, where I had a room, into Los Angeles and another out to [the studio. By the time I got there], they said, 'It's all been settled.'"

One week, a friend lent Albert her bungalow. By then, he said, he "was going a little bit crazy, I think. I didn't know how to eat, and I didn't have much money, and I was stupid. I felt . . . that the most nourishment was in cream. Well, I would drink cream and then be ill all over the place. . . . It was a dreadful time."[13]

Albert's first Hollywood visit may have been an ordeal, but it finally produced a solid part: he played Mabel Normand's brother, Billy O'Dair, in *Molly O'*, a 1921 Mack Sennett picture that told the story of an Irish ditchdigger's daughter who falls in love with a "prominent doctor" and gets kidnapped in a dirigible. "The job lasted about six weeks," he said, "and then I hotfooted it back to New York." There, in *Up the Ladder*, a comedy about an upwardly mobile Wall Streeter and his family, he played the broker's son and got fine notices: "priceless legs and feet that speak." Also in the cast were Paul Kelly and Humphrey Bogart; after the play closed, the three of them performed in a vaudeville sketch. Albert ultimately forgot what the sketch was about, but he remembered an act on the same bill, Swayne's Rats and Cats, featuring rats dressed in jockey outfits: "The cats would stand there and the rats would run under one and jump over the next. [Then they had] a cat way up on a pedestal and a man waiting below . . . for the cat to jump. [One time] the drum was going, [and the cat was just sitting] there, cleaning itself. . . . It didn't remember the cue. The man stepped into the wings, and he had a blowpipe, and . . . putty. He took a bite of putty and blew it out and hit the cat, then he came back onstage and the drum rolled again, and the cat jumped down into his arms—that was the finale."[14]

Around this time, Albert went with Paul Kelly to a church in mid-Manhattan. After the service, the two spoke with the priest, and Albert said he thought "they should engage an *actor* on Sundays to read [the sermons]. . . . I said, 'I see people going to sleep, but there's so much good stuff you could [do].' . . . He said, 'People have heard these things again and again.' . . . I said, 'You hear things on the stage again and again.' . . . He showed me a book [of sermons]. . . . I said, 'Which one?' He said, 'Any one.' I opened it, and I said, 'Look at the *meat* in that speech'—and he took the book away from me and said, 'I think you better go.'"[15]

Albert's friend Paul Kelly was the son of a Brooklyn bar owner and had nine brothers and sisters; like Kelly, three became child actors. In 1927, in Hollywood, Kelly got into an argument with an actor named Ray Raymond over his relations with Raymond's wife and hit him so hard that Raymond died the next day. Kelly was convicted of manslaughter and served twenty-five months in San Quentin; he later married Raymond's widow. During this tragedy, Albert stayed loyal. "After he'd gone to jail," he once said, "Paul made a big hit in a play called *Bad Girl*. Then I think Columbia signed him up. But when they announced that Paul Kelly was going to be in pictures, the women's clubs [said] they would not go to see Paul Kelly. . . . So [the studio suggested he should] change his name. Paul [said] his name was Paul Kelly, and that was his only name. So they let him go. . . . Finally Zanuck signed him up under his own name, and he made it. It was a wonderful, wonderful thing—he faced it through. By this time I believe people began to believe Paul wasn't really so guilty."[16]

Albert was in three silent films released in 1922 and 1923. One of them, *The Country Flapper*, starred Dorothy Gish as a flirtatious village girl named Jolanda. Albert and Raymond played brothers, and a critic found "much food for chuckles in a diverting battle between [the Hacketts] for the privilege of talking to Jolanda, while the girl proceeds to walk off with another rival." In mid-1923, Albert joined Beulah Bondi and Spencer Tracy and others in the highly regarded Stuart Walker Company, which put on plays in Indianapolis and Cincinnati. In *The Dummy*, cast as a slangy Bowery teenager who helps "deteckatives" catch a kidnapper, he scored a "triumph. . . . Cheek, humor, plausibility, dialect, and youth's illusions—he had them all." The company didn't always do well: concerning another play, an observer commented, "[Of the nine actors] only Lucille Nickolas and Albert Hackett seemed to be at all sure . . . what it was all about."

In the Stuart Walker Company, Albert honed his skills and learned which roles suited him; considering his build and height, they didn't include romantic leads. *Nice People* had a scene depicting a dance. "Young girls," he recalled, "were saying, 'I wish Scotty would come, he's the only one I can dance with' and 'When he takes me in his arms, I think he's going to crush me.' Well, they were awfully tall, those girls. . . . As I came onstage, one of them said, 'Here comes Scotty now'—and I never heard such a laugh in my life! Then, in the second act, I led this girl into a summer house on her family's estate. I had a flask, and I gave her a drink, and I kissed her, and then I said, 'Has anyone ever kissed you like that before?' Well, that laugh was even bigger—it just ripped the place to bits! From then on, I said that line quietly, out of the corner of my mouth."[17]

While he was in the Stuart Walker Company, Albert traveled to Chicago to see Paul Kelly and made his "fresh guy" impression on Frances. Also, a Cincinnati radio station broadcast a one-act play he'd written. For several years, both at home and on the road, even during his worst cream-drinking days in California, he'd been putting words on paper, hoping to get them published or performed. "Apparently," he said, "I always wanted to be a writer. I got a little Corona typewriter when I was around 15. . . . I began by writing children's verse; the magazines sent it back promptly."[18] Finally, Franklin P. Adams published two poems in his widely read newspaper column, *The Conning Tower*. Albert said that although he wasn't paid, appearing there felt like "a very big day." In his twenties, he also wrote vaudeville sketches that didn't sell—but one time he got advice from a successful sketch writer, Edwin Burke, who later became a leading screenwriter.

"I told him," Albert recalled, "'How wonderful that you're going to read my script,' and he said, '*I'm* not going to read it—*you're* going to read it.' I read the first line, and he said, 'I don't know anything.' Then I read the second line, and he said, 'I still don't know anything.' I read the third line. . . . [He kept saying that], and I finally got the point: I hadn't said who the people were, or where they were. . . . I think I must've read four or five pages before he said, '*Now* I know something.' . . . I thought that was wonderful. . . . That always stayed with me: 'I don't know anything.' It's the only thing I can say about play-writing."[19] (Frances once made an equally succinct comment on writing: while slashing the air with her hand like a sword, she said, "The main thing is, *cut, cut, cut!*"—meaning that, in films, dialogue should be swift because the camera does so much of the work.)

Albert's Cincinnati radio play had only three performers, including himself, and its title and story have been lost, but having it produced must have encouraged him. In October 1923, he opened in New York in *The Nervous Wreck*, written by the prolific, highly successful Owen Davis. Subtitled *A Farcical Adventure in the Far West*, starring Otto Kruger and dealing with comical Easterners visiting Arizona, full of "backfiring motors, barking dogs, exploding pistols, klaxons . . . and shattering crockery," it was a major hit. Albert played Chester Underwood, a "young saphead" who wore knickers and "golfing hosiery" and murmured to girls, "Don't you like me? I'm kind of keen on you." Audiences and critics *did* like him: "an unusually fine actor"; "deserves special mention." He stayed on through *The Nervous Wreck*'s long run in New York and on the road; in 1928, 1929, and 1930, in New York and on tour, he was in *Whoopee*, the Ziegfeld stage musical version of the play starring Eddie Cantor; and in 1930 he went to Hollywood to make *Whoopee*'s movie version, produced by Samuel Goldwyn. As he said years later, *The Nervous Wreck*, in all its different forms, wound up giving him "quite a career."

In the summer of 1925 (the summer that Frances met van Loon), Albert acted at the Lakewood Theater, outside Skowhegan, Maine. Started in 1901, sitting beside Lake Wesserunsett ("Some of the oldest inhabitants," a joke went, "still can't spell it"), Lakewood had one of the country's better stock companies; that year, it included Dorothy Stickney and Howard Lindsay, who became Albert's lifelong friends and later got married and starred in the hit comedy *Life with Father*. That fall, Albert opened in New York in *Twelve Miles Out*, a melodrama about Prohibition-era bootleggers and hijackers, playing the heroine's dissolute younger brother. During an intermission, a reporter found him backstage strumming "Paddlin' Madeline Home" on a ukelele, and Albert complained, thinking of his youthful looks, "I'll be playing juveniles when I'm eighty." "When you're eighty," the reporter replied, "you'll *want* to play juveniles."

In the spring of 1926, Albert took a two-month vacation in Europe, going over on the *Aquitania* and touring England, France, Belgium, Germany, and Switzerland. This wasn't his first trip outside the United States—a few years before, he'd gone on a Caribbean cruise with Raymond—but being able to afford this particular holiday must have pleased him greatly: the *Aquitania*, with its first-ever swimming pool and electric elevators, was that time's most fashionable and luxurious liner, famed for its food, service, and glamorous passenger list.

In later years, Albert enjoyed the other vacations—and the well-cut clothes and the cars and houses—that his efforts brought him, but, perhaps because of his childhood poverty, he was always a bit insecure about money; more than once, he joked that his only real interest in receiving mail was looking for checks. His lifelong frugality was well-known. Once, he kiddingly announced that his birthday present to a fellow writer was going to be a box of paper clips, but someone pointed out that, because of his reputation, people might think the clips were a serious present. Another time, asked if success had changed his lifestyle, he replied, deadpan, that he'd bought an electric pencil sharpener. Frances also cared about money—to her, it spelled independence—but because her childhood had been easier, she wasn't as anxious as he. Occasionally, she teased him about the differences in their backgrounds: when Albert was talking about going to nickelodeons as a little boy, she commented, "I didn't do that— that was for *street* children. I was a *lawn* child."[20] (Albert could also tease: once, meeting the timid, pleading stare of a less-than-bright female poodle, he declared, "Inside there is someone Frances went to Vassar with.")

Albert was now attractive, articulate, and successful. He was constantly in the company of exciting, highly desirable women and must have been drawn to some of them, and surely some returned his feelings. However, I never heard him talk about the women in his early life. Evidently, he and an actress named Ruth saw a lot of each other at one time, and once, at the wedding of some friends, she suggested that, since the minister was *right there*, perhaps they should also get married. Albert declined; soon after, she married someone else, but she and Albert remained friends.

In the summer of 1926, Albert again acted at Lakewood; in February 1927, he returned to Broadway in *Off Key*, a flop about a troubled marriage, starring Florence Eldridge ("Mister Hackett is an uncommonly deft and inventive comedian"). In the Chicago production of a hit called *Crime*, starring Chester Morris, he played the fiancé of seventeen-year-old Sylvia Sidney. Two bad Broadway plays followed; in the second, *Mirrors*, a "flashy exposé of wanton life," he was again paired with Miss Sidney, and a critic said they deserved praise for their efforts. Despite those efforts, *Mirrors* folded early in 1928, but Albert had plenty to keep him busy. For one thing, the aspiring writer Frances Goodrich had asked for help in revising the play she'd written, and that was proving interesting. Also, he'd signed on as part of the company at Elitch's Gardens, outside Denver—and Frances would be there.

# 3

## Working, Fighting, and Living Together

**A**s the decades passed, Frances and Albert forgot the characters and plot of Frances's play *Such a Lady*, but Frances had a clear memory of Albert's revisions: "He tore it to bits and destroyed it. . . . I had the idea of a very nice woman, and Albert turned her around to be an absolute bitch. . . . Curious, wasn't it? . . . We never sold it, but a producer [Winthrop Ames] read it and said it was not for him, but he hoped to see anything else we wrote." About his revisions, Albert said, "It's a wonder we were still speaking after that."[1]

Battles like that were a frequent feature of the collaboration that started in 1928 and flourished for thirty-four more years, until 1962, when the Hacketts' last movie was released. Three of their five plays were originals; the other two, like many of their films, were adaptations of books. Four of their screenplays—for *The Thin Man, After the Thin Man, Father of the Bride,* and *Seven Brides for Seven Brothers*—were nominated for Academy Awards but didn't win; however, Frances and Albert later won several prizes that many people rank above Hollywood's Oscars.

Starting with *Such a Lady*, Frances and Albert never worked alone again or collaborated with others—except once, when Albert was away, and Frances tried working with a woman. It wasn't a success: "I had to be very polite so as not to hurt her feelings. I'd say, 'My dear, this is just delightful, but don't you think it might be a little easier to speak if you wrote it a bit more colloquially?' It took so much time being polite that we got very little work done."[2]

Frances and Albert's acting experience helped in their writing. Pacing up and down, with Albert sometimes bounding about on springy knees, they would play a scene, seeing if it worked, discussing its content and where it was going, testing how tight it was and what "held" and what didn't. "Having been an actor for so long," Albert once said, "I was always playing a scene—standing up, and opening the door, and going out into the hall, and coming in again—all that silly sort of thing, but that was the only way I could *feel* the scene. . . . I think that made a difference, that we had both been playing things, and could say, 'That's a hard line to play.' . . . We wrote a good colloquial line."³

After acting out a scene, the Hacketts sat down at typewriters, and each wrote a draft. Then they exchanged the drafts and began to "criticize freely"—but it was more than just criticism. "*Scream* is more like it," Frances said. "Albert is a very, very gentle human being, and I am the one who screamed. I never knew there could be such battles over little words." Once, when Albert suggested a line, Frances yelled, "Over my dead body does that go in!" so loudly that she lost her voice. "For three days," he said, "we couldn't work, because I couldn't hear what she was saying." Another time, he was the harsher one: "He said to me," she recalled, "'If you think that's good, you should be *scared.*' You couldn't say anything worse than that, could you? Quietly, he said it. Didn't lose his voice at all. . . . That one is emblazoned on me." When a writing session was done, peace was restored: "Someone [who] had an office next to us [in the 1930s, on the MGM lot] said it was like being near a bear pit—but at twelve o'clock [time for lunch], we came out laughing and joking." When a scene was finished, Frances and Albert couldn't tell whose ideas were whose—"except," Frances said, "once in a while I knew a certain line was Albert's, because it was so good."⁴

"Dying is easy," the old joke goes. "What's hard is playing comedy." As the Hacketts' screaming shows, *writing* comedy is also hard—but evidently it was inevitable that comedy would become their main means of expression: Albert had a gift for spontaneous funny remarks plus a flair for delivering clever lines on stage, and Frances was also attuned to life's absurdities, could concoct amusing ideas and dialogue, and had performed mostly in comedies. After they'd become well-known, they were asked to adapt a book that Frances called "stark drama" for the stage. "Albert and I are not that kind of writers," she replied, "and we're lost without our little laugh and our little tear trickling down." Early on, they discovered that their abilities were complementary: her writing talent evidently wasn't as great as his, but she was better at organizing things, getting them to sit down and start working. Both of them had learned long ago that success demanded effort: "We have a capacity for hard work, and it has paid off." Even when they worked at home on their own projects, they kept strict nine-to-five hours: "People can set their watches by us." Working for a studio, they welcomed being in an office, because there were fewer distractions: "At home, you can see a plant that needs watering and lose your concentration." For both of them, writing was tough—particularly first drafts, which she called "horrors" and he called "the puking stage." At the start of their collaboration, their joint credits often listed him before her, and he suggested that they take turns being named first, "but the studio eventually decided," he said, "that G came before H. Someone once asked about putting Frances's name first, and she said, 'I'll be Goodrich long after I'm Mrs. Albert Hackett, so it doesn't matter to me where my name comes.'"

Frances and Albert have been called perfectionists who always took their craft far more seriously than themselves or their surroundings and— because of the variety of their scripts—the most eclectic screenwriting team that Hollywood has produced. Once they'd shown their skill, they seldom had to accept second-rate projects. They were once asked if either was better at writing dialogue for male or female characters, and Albert replied—probably with one of his wide-eyed looks—"We thought of everyone as being homosexual, so we never had to worry about that." The remark was typical of the style Albert brought to the collaboration. He was freer and looser than Frances, more "show biz," and his wisecracks were often earthy. The elegant actress Celeste Holm told me with a laugh that once, at a party he was hosting, Albert very politely asked if she wanted "gin, whiskey, or an enema."

Marriage-collaboration relationships like the Hacketts' are rare and, of course, have their own complex inner dynamics. Clearly, Frances and Albert were strongly attracted to each other, but as far as I know, they never talked to others about their intimate life, and if they exchanged love letters—which I doubt greatly; they just weren't like that—they've disappeared. In public, they weren't demonstrative—no hand-holding, no affectionate caresses—but when either spoke, the other concentrated intently. The only words of theirs that I've found describing the emotional side of their union are a note jotted by Frances, in almost "absent-minded" handwriting, on the back of a memo from their Hollywood agent, Bert Allenberg—"I can't think of us as not being married. It just seems as if we had to be married"—and a very different-sounding letter in which, after saying that she and Albert should think of their mutual career as "a lifetime of earning," Frances added that that would be correct "if I were sure that Albert and I would stick for a lifetime. But there are so many chances against that. I always figure that we are going to be married and writing together for just the length of the present contract, and that we can't look beyond that. So we are trying to save enough in these next months to have a little income for both of us, in case of a split."

That letter was written four years into a marriage that wound up lasting fifty years, until Frances's death. Perhaps she and Albert had recently fought harder than usual about their writing, or overwork had made her tired and pessimistic, or she was recalling her first two marriages. Almost certainly, her doubts were not caused by unfaithfulness. In the 1930s, Hollywood mores were easygoing, and the Hacketts were always far from prudish (concerning a woman who was sleeping with another woman's husband, Frances once told me, "She's trying to *comfort* him"), so it's reasonable to wonder if either was ever unfaithful, but there's no evidence of that. On the contrary, as one of their friends observed, "When you heard that the Hacketts were coming, you expected one person to walk through the door." However, it does seem that Albert was sometimes flirtatious. Another acquaintance reported that when Elizabeth Taylor was starting her career, Albert spotted her from his office window, walking across the MGM lot, carrying a pet hamster. "Albert rushed downstairs and told her how much he admired her pet, and she said, 'I *bet* you admire the hamster.' Albert used to tell that story on himself."[5]

Despite the frequent shouting in their office, Frances and Albert treated each other as equals in their work; however, he often deferred to her in other areas. Garson Kanin, their friend and the director of the New York production of *The Diary of Anne Frank*, once jocularly said he considered Frances a "tough baby." Frith Banbury, the director of *The Diary's* London production, said, "I always had the feeling that Frances drove the train—that she negotiated everything, and stage-managed everything. . . . I thought she was conscious of her age vis-à-vis his. . . . Frances was the driving force. . . . What used to amuse me was that she sometimes appeared to be a Helen Hokinson [fatuous, overly genteel] sort of lady, saying, 'darling, lovely, sweet,' but [she] had absolutely the sharpest eye you could have, and all of this was only a sort of layer—which is not to say that she wasn't absolutely sweet natured, but she saw straight through phoniness."[6]

In Hollywood story conferences, Frances was often the only woman in the room, and she had to uphold "the woman's point of view." "I'm always the only woman working on the picture," she told an interviewer, "and I hold the fate of the women [characters] in my hand. . . . Perhaps there isn't a 'woman's angle,' and I'm sentimental to think there is, but I am very sentimental. . . . I'll fight for what the gal will or will not do, and

I can be completely unfeminine yelling about it." ("Miss Goodrich," the interviewer commented, "is a charming, soft-voiced, brown-eyed lady with bangs, who would seem more at home behind a tea service than at a script conference, and the unfeminine yelling she describes with such pleasure is hard to visualize.") "We have a terrible time, Hackett and I," Frances went on. "We fight and scream and shout when we're working. Albert is nice, but I'm a loud-mouthed woman. But it's like having a baby—afterwards you forget all the horrible part. It's done, and it comes out all right, and you're delighted."

Except for occasional illnesses and a serious collapse in the late 1930s caused by overwork, most of their lives Frances and Albert enjoyed greater-than-average physical and mental strength—and they could overcome problems. The Christmas that Frances was eighty-seven, she and Albert and my parents came to dinner with me, my wife, Patty, and our daughter, Adele—then a student at Vassar—at our house in New York. Halfway through the meal, Frances suddenly looked alarmed: a piece of meat was blocking her windpipe. Adele tried the Heimlich maneuver; Albert pounded Frances's back; I called 911. As Frances grew more desperate, Patty ran outside and rang the doorbells of neighboring houses; miraculously, out of one came a young man who had recently performed the Heimlich maneuver on a woman in a restaurant in Chicago. He grabbed Frances, jerked hard, cracked a couple of her ribs (she didn't realize that until the next day)—and undoubtedly saved her life. As we all tried to calm down and forget the horror and terror, Frances said quietly to Adele, "If that's death, it isn't so bad." We suggested that Frances should recuperate on a bed, but her spirits had returned, and she said she'd lie down only if she could "stretch out on the dining table as the centerpiece." Later, as she and Albert were leaving, Frances announced that they were going to their old friend Dorothy Stickney's annual Christmas gathering. Albert talked her out of that, and she went home—and later sent a check to her rescuer's favorite charity.

Frances and Albert's unique talent for friendship was mentioned earlier. A friend of theirs said she felt there was a "mystery about how they were able to maintain such warm relations with people who were notoriously difficult and prickly—for instance, Lillian Hellman. Were they simply impervious to the splinters and rough edges in other people, or was there a sense of 'what we get into with people and what we don't'? Did they have a code of boundaries that didn't get crossed? Their involvement with humor and entertaining and enjoying other people was a wonderful quality, but you can't be that witty without having a dark side, and you can't be insightful without having a very good grasp of human motives and complications.

"It's unusual for people today," the Hacketts' friend went on, "to be humanly and professionally successful for an incredibly long time without compromising their principles and without being untrue to themselves, and they did that. But one wonders: how did it happen? Since the 1960s, we've all been raised with this new doctrine of confrontation and being 'straight.' . . . The Hacketts were evidently living examples of the benefits of an older code where one isn't confrontational, where you don't say to people, 'You've made me feel lousy, and I think you shouldn't be doing this'—the group therapy model of life. They apparently didn't have any of that, and perhaps they simply avoided sticky or dodgy situations."[7]

In 1933, after visiting New York, Frances and Albert returned to the West Coast on a liner called the *California*. From Havana, Albert sent me—I was three—a terrific-looking postcard showing the thirty-thousand-ton ship, saying, "I tried to get you on the telephone before I left to say goodbye—but your line was busy. Goodbye." I adored that postcard and carried it around until it nearly fell apart. To me, it shows how the Hacketts got on with children: they took trouble over them, treated them with warmth and humor. After they moved back to New York in 1962, every Thanksgiving their fifth- and sixth-floor apartment on Central Park West was visited by kids, nibbling cookies, glugging juice, and gawking at the balloons of the Macy's parade only a few feet away. The children of their nephew Maxwell Huntoon Jr. were sometimes there; Albert once said to Max, as a monstrous green dinosaur floated by, "Can you imagine waking up with a hangover and seeing that thing looking in your window?" Producer-director Hal Prince's offspring were also there; Prince called the Hacketts "real family people . . . born not only to be aunts and uncles, but parents and grandparents." They never did become parents; Frances, of course, was forty when they married. An interviewer once asked Albert what he'd say to a child if he had one, and he replied, "What could I tell a child? About anything? If it was a boy, I could tell it not to waste time with a ballet dancer—but that's about the only thing I could say to a boy. . . . But a girl? To know what to tell children—I wouldn't have any idea."[8] Later, when they steeped themselves in the personality of the adolescent Anne Frank, Frances became deeply attached and often wept when speaking about her—it has been said that, in a way, the pretty, sensitive, wonderfully talented Anne "became Frances's daughter."

Evidently, Frances and Albert were both self-conscious about the difference in their ages. According to a Hollywood friend of theirs, sometime in the 1930s, while Albert was trying on a coat in a fancy store on Wilshire Boulevard, a clerk asked Frances, "You're buying something for your son?" and she called out, "Hackett, come!" and they left and never went back.[9] In May 1936, when applying for a passport, Albert turned in one issued in 1926 and in a sworn statement admitted that in 1926 he'd cut three years off his age because he was then a juvenile actor and wanted to seem younger. He might have restored those three years to avoid legal difficulties—or perhaps he wanted his passport age to be closer to Frances's. In interviews, Frances sometimes chopped off a few years, and when she and Albert applied for their marriage license, she dropped four. Frith Banbury said he felt Frances was "nervous about Albert being that much younger than herself—he might have cast a roving eye.... She felt she had to entertain all the time for him.... In a way, Albert was the child—'We must keep the child entertained.'... There was a slight feeling that he might go off the rails if she didn't keep him fully occupied."

In one of Frances and Albert's best-known screenplays, *It's a Wonderful Life*, an angel shows the hero what life in his hometown would have been like without him. What would Frances and Albert's lives have been like without each other?

When their connection began, Frances, twice divorced, was approaching the age when her chances of getting married again—and of continuing to work on the stage—were growing slimmer. So far, she hadn't succeeded in her writing. Albert evidently had a promising acting career ahead of him; he, too, had writing hopes but also hadn't yet succeeded. Given their ambition, talent, and personalities, it seems likely that, separately, both would have had productive, satisfying lives . . .

Or perhaps not . . .

I never heard Frances or Albert use the word *fate* in connection with their life together, and despite having worked on *It's a Wonderful Life*, they surely didn't believe in angels . . .

But . . .

In the summer of 1928, at Elitch's Gardens, Frances and Albert continued plugging away in their spare hours at *Such a Lady;* ultimately, as Frances said, the heroine got turned into a bitch, and the play became "threadbare." Elitch's Gardens, home to stock companies and touring companies starring top-drawer performers, had been built in 1891 on the outskirts of Denver amidst striking mountain scenery (including, on clear days, Pike's Peak), adjoining an amusement park and elaborate flower gardens. The theater is no longer in business, but when Frances and Albert were there—she was second woman, he was the juvenile—it was lively and prosperous, with a dozen productions between June and August. The other actors included Fredric March and Albert's recent coworker Sylvia Sidney. Actors Equity then allowed summer stock pay as low as $50 a week, and Frances and Albert didn't do badly; she was paid $150, he got $200. March, the leading man, who once said that "it was considered a feather in the cap of an actor to have played a season at Elitch's," was highest paid, at $500; Sidney got $225.

Shows hoping to get to Broadway were sometimes tried out at Elitch's Gardens. That summer, in addition to previously produced plays with such titles as *The Baby Cyclone*, *The Torch Bearers*, and *Behold the Bridegroom*, the management put on *The "K" Guy*. The play titillated Denverites because Sylvia Sidney romped around in a bathing suit and an Egyptian dancing costume, but it lasted only a week when it finally reached New York. During those months, there were annoyances, and a whiff of scandal. The director, Melville Burke, who had directed Albert in the Stuart Walker Company, gave several parts that Frances coveted to his wife; that was distressing, particularly because some of the costumes Frances had brought from New York went unused. Also, the original leading lady, Miriam Hopkins, was replaced because she was getting a divorce: evidently Burke, a devout Catholic, had negative feelings about that. As a replacement, Burke hired an English actress, Isobel Elsom—but that created even worse problems. "She was a lovely actress," Frances recalled. "Lovely . . . but having thrown Hopkins out because she was getting a divorce, along comes Elsom and brings her lover. Right there in a little community, and they're living together in the place, and he's drunk all the time."[10]

Frances and van Loon were still married, and van Loon was jealous of Albert; he sometimes referred to him—a good deal younger and vastly more attractive physically—as "that little shoe clerk." (In later years, the jealousy vanished, and van Loon sometimes sent friendly greetings to Albert.) While in Denver, learning that van Loon had gone back to his second wife and was living with her in a fishing village in Holland, Frances decided to file for a divorce. To get it, she needed information on van Loon's living arrangements. Her mother was traveling in Europe; Frances cabled, asking her to hire a detective to do some spying. In Paris, Madeleine found a man named Leoni, who sent a non-Dutch-speaking colleague to Holland and, for $240 in francs, produced a totally useless document, about which Madeleine wrote, "I am, naturally, disappointed and rather taken aback by Leoni's report. . . . I wonder how he thought a detective who could speak nothing but French could get on in Holland. In the cathedral at Quimper, which is quite lovely, by the way, especially the exterior, there is a tremendous picture where is portrayed the gift to some local noble or prelate, of the Breton language miraculously, all at once! An angel is placing his finger on the gentleman's lips, and we understand immediately a flood of Breton idioms poured out. Perhaps that is what Leoni expected for his [colleague]. . . . I have thought of how [those] francs would re-roof the Nutley house, pay the Little Compton taxes . . ."

In late September 1928, Frances joined the Broadway cast of a hit, *Heavy Traffic*, starring Mary Boland, which dealt with "the rapid shiftings of the heart in the milieu of . . . the sensation-seeking idle rich"; one critic called it "a comedy of much well-tailored talk and worldly innuendo, which has to do penance for its sauciness by walking barefoot over a nettlesome plot." Not long after, Albert was also back on the stage, in *Whoopee*.

In this lavishly produced Florenz Ziegfeld musical—which had curious comedy turns, bizarre plot convolutions, and sudden burstings-into-song and starred the floating-eyed Eddie Cantor, who sometimes wore blackface—Albert didn't sing or dance. He again played the young, foolish-sounding Chester Underwood, who made his entrance riding in a big car with the horn blasting, crying out to Cantor, whose flivver was blocking his way, "I say, my man, that's a good old thing. Chase the bug off the road, will you?"—whereupon Cantor angrily twisted his nose. With its catchy title song, elaborate, colorful sets designed by the famous Joseph Urban, and gorgeous chorus girls, whose shoulders—and often a lot more— gleamed out through their costumes ("They smile while they dance, fresh, and unworried. . . . The more ornately beautiful ones . . . come out on horses to be admired"), the extravaganza was a smash. Albert particularly remembered a chorus girl named Kiki Roberts: "She was 'Legs' Diamond's girl—the gangster. Everybody took a shot at him—they were always picking bullets out of him." (Diamond, a racketeer and murderer and the owner of the Hotsy Totsy Club, on Broadway, survived four almost-fatal assaults; after he was finally killed, in December 1931, Roberts, whose real name was Marion Strasmick, had a vaudeville act. Dancing to banjo music, she was billed as "Kiki, the Gangster's Gal." Albert evidently remained intrigued by gangsters: he used to tell a story about a man who wandered into a church during a gangland funeral, saw an attractive young woman in the casket, and asked what she'd died of. "Gonorrhea." "But gonorrhea doesn't kill you." "It does if you give it to Big Louie.")[11]

In *Whoopee,* in addition to appearing as Chester Underwood, Albert was Eddie Cantor's understudy. He never had to play Cantor's part, but one day in late 1929, when the show was in Philadelphia, Cantor telephoned that he didn't feel well and wasn't going on in the matinee. "So then they called a rehearsal," Albert said years later, "and no one remembered the lines; Cantor had changed things so much and put his own jokes in. Finally, they said, 'Good luck, Mr. Hackett.' 'Dear God,' I thought, 'here I am and I have never even put on blackface before.' At that moment, Cantor came in, saying, 'All right, I'm here, kid.' So, thank God, we were spared that. Philadelphia's had lots of things happen to it, but they were spared that."[12]

While he was touring, Albert continued to work on *Such a Lady* with Frances, by mail; she once said, "Me in New York, Albert out on the road in *Whoopee,* and back would come my script. All was not good." When Albert returned, although *Such a Lady* hadn't worked out, and they were both busy performing, they soon started writing another play. With his brother and sister married and well launched on their careers, Albert was still living with his mother and grandmother, so he and Frances worked in her apartment, on East 55th Street.

Frances and Albert's new effort—another comedy, titled *Western Union, Please*—told the story of an eager but naïve chap who says he's going out to buy a loaf of bread, deserts his family for ten years to seek a fortune and adventure, then returns in the splendid uniform of a Western Union messenger (in those days, they *did* dress splendidly) to find he's been declared legally dead. Starring Donald Meek and Jean Adair, it had a weeklong tryout in August 1930 at the Lakewood Theater in Skowhegan but didn't get picked up for Broadway. (A few years later, the Hacketts revised it, and it was performed often in summer stock and by amateur groups; Frances once commented, "The play was good to us.") The temporary failure of *Western Union, Please* didn't deter Frances and Albert: they began writing a third play, which turned out to be their first hit, *Up Pops the Devil.*

These projects took time and hard work. Frances and Albert pared down their New York social life, skipping parties given by skeptical friends, who said they'd never get their work produced. A press release issued after the Hacketts had succeeded with *Up Pops the Devil* said these friends made cracks like "Why not have some fun? You'll never sell a play," and "What makes you think you can write? You never have before." Visiting Little Compton in the summer of 1929, Frances looked worn-out and one day spent four hours sleeping in an outdoor hammock. The following summer, after she had spent a lot more time with Albert, her mother felt she'd "sweetened and . . . developed a fine philosophy about everything." Apparently, by then Frances was recovering some of the self-confidence drained away by her relationship with van Loon; also, having worked together for many hours in the privacy of her apartment, by then she and Albert were probably more than just friendly collaborators. I once asked him about his feelings toward her at that time; his eyes lit up, and he said, "Well, she was a *girl* . . ."

These trips to Little Compton gave Frances a chance to see her mother and her brothers and sisters. Madeleine, now in her midsixties, was efficiently running the Nutley house and several properties in Little Compton. Living with her was Constance, the intellectual eldest sister, who'd graduated from Vassar in 1911 with honors, taught English literature there, earned a Ph.D. at Yale, then contracted Parkinson's disease; for the rest of her life, she was a semi-invalid addicted to reading. Years later, I sometimes drove her on her weekly visits to the Little Compton Library, where she returned roughly twenty books and borrowed another twenty. William, the next-youngest after Frances, had gone to Exeter and Stevens Institute of Technology and served in the Navy in World War I; he was in the real estate business and devoted many hours to studying his ancestry, which he proudly traced back to William Bradford, governor of the Plymouth Colony. He later married twice (his first wife died) and lived in a wing of the Nutley house. Next in line was Caroline: good-looking, witty, after Vassar she'd happily married Maxwell Carpenter Huntoon, a Providence manufacturer. The youngest sibling was Lloyd, my father. In 1930, he was starting the first of his many books on American art history; he later became director of the Whitney Museum of American Art, in New York.

Since Henry's death, Madeleine's finances had grown tight; in 1931, she started selling off real estate she owned in Little Compton and New Jersey. That fall, she wrote her will, plus a note to be read after she died, saying she wanted her five children to know "how happy you have all made me always; how rich and full my life has been, so that you never think of me with sadness. My one wish is that you will all be united in affection and helpfulness to each other in future years as you have always been in the past." Happily, Frances and the others did remain united—except about politics. As time passed, Will, a kind man but no great achiever, grew more and more conservative, until he even came to believe the lies of Senator Joseph McCarthy. This horrified his siblings, and there were arguments at family gatherings—which was probably what Will wanted: finally, he was getting some attention. Family loyalty was expressed often—for example, in 1965, when my father and his sisters helped to cover Will's heavy medical bills. Fortunately, this spirit of loyalty and family ties remains in most cases intact among Madeleine's grandchildren and great-grandchildren.

One subject Frances and her siblings never disagreed about was the delight they'd shared during Little Compton summers. When their parents first took them there, around 1903, the village was small and pristine—a town hall, a grange hall, a general-store-plus-post-office, a blacksmith shop, shingled houses, a tall-spired Congregational church. Surrounding it were cornfields and meadows stretching down to the ocean. After renting for a few summers, Henry bought a big, handsome house, with front-porch columns and a cupola looking out to the sea; nearby were a small golf-and-tennis club, sandy beaches, and a modest-sized harbor with a few fishing, lobstering, and pleasure boats. The beauty of the place attracted painters, including Worthington Whitteredge and Edwin Blashfield; most of the summer residents were upper-middle-class families from East Coast cities.

Some of Frances's strongest memories of Little Compton concerned the annual trip from Nutley, which was a real *event.* "In those days," my father once said, "[in addition to the five children and all the luggage], you had a full household . . . a cook, a maid, a hired man, a horse. . . . It [took] from three o'clock in the afternoon in Nutley, taking the Erie Railroad; then a ferry across the Hudson River; hansom cabs down to the . . . overnight boat to Fall River [Massachusetts]; then a train to Tiverton, Rhode Island; and then two-horse, four-seated wagons with our own horse fastened on behind, down to Little Compton about 13 miles away [where friends sent a strawberry shortcake to our house to welcome us]. . . . It was 21 hours, and my mother had to superintend all this, and she did it wonderfully. She was a very able person."[13] Evidently, Madeleine had to superintend because Henry didn't care for the confusion created by Frances, the other kids, the luggage, the cook, the maid, the hired man, and the horse; I was told that he used to go with the family as far as the Nutley train station, wave good-bye, and travel to Little Compton in solitary comfort a week later. In the meantime, Madeleine ran things with firmness and humor. For example, in July 1908, she wrote to Henry, who was still in Nutley, that she'd been mowing the lawn: "George [the gardener] as usual abandoned the work at the stroke of twelve, so I went out and in twenty minutes I had done more than he in two hours. I do not doubt that he was planning to spend his afternoon on that plot, but I have deprived him of that pleasure."

In June 1929, there was a break in Frances and Albert's writing of *Western Union, Please* while she acted in several productions at Albert's former haunt the Lakewood Theater. In *Upstairs and Down*—one critic called it "a poor play in bad taste"; it had lines like "When I had a husband, he was always about. Husbands used to be so adhesive"—Frances was carried onstage by Humphrey Bogart, then doing the charming, playboy roles that preceded his tough-guy image. "That was fun," she said years later. In the spring of 1930, there was another hiatus while Albert went to Hollywood for the filming of *Whoopee!*

One of the first Technicolor musicals, *Whoopee!*—the film's producers added the exclamation point—again starred Eddie Cantor and featured the beauteous Goldwyn Girls. About them, Goldwyn, a master of the artificial and notorious for his "casting couch," once said, "Every Goldwyn Girl [must] look as though she had just stepped out of a bathtub. There must be a radiant scrubbed cleanliness about them which rules out all artificiality."[14] The film was the first choreographed by the imaginative, later-famed Busby Berkeley, who placed the Goldwyn Girls not in a conventional chorus line—which would make them appear tiny onscreen, because the camera would have to pull impossibly far back to catch them all—but tightly together in geometric patterns, sometimes shot from above. *Whoopee!* gave Betty Grable her first featured role: in the opening scene, wearing a G-string, a leather halter, a Stetson hat, and two pistols, she yelled "What a wild man you are, Bill!" at a cowboy, lassoed him, and started the dancing. Albert did Chester Underwood again and had some thoughts about his future as an actor in the rapidly changing movie business: "I got a good look at myself, and I know I have a face maybe for behind the footlights, but certainly not up there on those big screens."[15] *Whoopee!* was a major hit and has since been called "the summation of filmed musical comedy, vintage 1930." It's still shown occasionally on TV—although nowadays it's offensive to several different groups, including blacks (Cantor in blackface), Jews, and Native Americans. Albert's performance can fairly be called adequate.

While he was in Hollywood, Albert made a new friend—and the relationship lasted for many, many years. Enjoying greater prosperity, he now had a car, and one day, driving home from the studio, he spotted James Cagney sitting on a bench, waiting for a bus. At the time, Cagney wasn't well-known, but Albert recognized him: "I'd seen him in plays and admired him—he was so good. . . . So I stopped, and I said, 'Are you James Cagney?' He said, 'Yes.' And I said, 'Well, I'm Albert Hackett,' and I took him home."[16]

Back in New York, Albert joined The Players, Henry Goodrich's favorite club. Bob Ames and Hendrik van Loon also belonged; at lunch there, someone once said to my father, "So you're Frances's brother—she's been married to three members!" Albert enjoyed telling a politically incorrect, perhaps apocryphal story about the place: "The Admissions Committee was discussing a candidate, and one of the committee men said, 'But he's homosexual,' and another said, 'I think we should take him in case one of ours dies.'"

Following the stock market crisis in October 1929, Frances lost some of her hard-earned savings and, according to a friend of theirs, phoned Albert and "asked him to meet her at a certain New York address, saying, 'I want to show you something.' He got there, and there was this long line in front of a bank, and Frances said, 'I just want you to see—that's my bank.' . . . It was the run on the bank when the crash came. . . . It struck Albert funny that she wanted to make sure he got a view of her money disappearing. . . . He enjoyed telling that story."[17]

Some of Frances and Albert's friends were young, wisecracking, bohemian writers and performers who lived in Greenwich Village walkups and drank a lot; the Hacketts' third play, *Up Pops the Devil*, which finally brought success, reflected that world. In the play, a couple—he's an aspiring writer, she's a dancer—get married after living together for a year. They agree that she'll work while he writes his novel, but he dislikes being "kept" and is jealous of her newfound admirer; they separate, then reunite (she's going to have a baby). The script was lightweight, with witty dialogue and no "message," except perhaps "It's ridiculous for men to be unhappy if their wives support them." It seems dated today, not only in its theme, but also because, as a Prohibition-era comedy, it was jam-packed with boozing and phone calls to bootleggers and people nursing hangovers. Originally, the main idea had been fairly serious: to show that if a man and woman lived together before marrying—which violated that time's moral code—after marrying they might be suspicious of each other. That version contained a key line spoken in anger by the hero, "Well you *did* live with me." When Frances and Albert realized that those words killed all sympathy for the hero, they began shifting toward comedy. While redrafting the script, they spent hours acting it, with Albert playing the male roles and Frances the female ones, and polished the dialogue as they went along.

Selling their creation wasn't easy: several producers rejected it, and one rainy day, after they left a producer's office, Albert threw the script out a taxi window in exasperation. Frances stopped the cab and picked the soaking-wet pages out of the gutter. Finally, in mid-July 1930, Lee Shubert, the most powerful—and feared—man in American theater, took it on, but not without some palaver. Frances and Albert had titled the play *Let's Get Married*, but Shubert insisted, despite considerable evidence to the contrary, that no play with "marry" in the title had "ever made a nickel." (Perhaps Shubert disliked the word because it reminded him of his own behavior: small, homely, and frozen faced, once called a "cadaver with a shot of adrenaline," he was married but was famed for having a different chorus girl sent every afternoon to a shabby room near his office. The Hacketts understood his power and deviousness: describing another Machiavellian producer, they wrote, "He out-Shuberts any Shubert.") New titles—*Too Many Friends, Everybody Welcome, Too Many Parties*—were tried, and then someone suggested the final one, which refers to the leading man's flirtation with a sexy, less-than-bright neighbor.

When casting for *Up Pops the Devil* began, it was hard to find someone to play the protagonists' best friend, Biney ("His only interest in life is parties; he always seems a little mussed"), so Albert took the part. The leads went to Roger Pryor and Sally Bates; Brian Donlevy had a supporting part. During rehearsals, all seemed fine: only a few revisions were needed. One eliminated a scene in which Biney, a theatrical stage manager, critiqued inept, rehearsing dancers, crying out things like "That's good, you're in time with everything except the music." Then, during a tryout in Asbury Park, New Jersey, as a newspaper article said, "the lines written in glee were received as though they contained the information that the audience was about to be dynamited." Night-long rewrites followed; during the next tryouts, in Atlantic City, Frances went to the lobby during an intermission and overheard a woman saying, "Never mind, Mama, when we get to New York, we'll see a good play." At the same time, Leah Salisbury, the Hacketts' agent, reported that, among show business folk, the rumors were good: "Not less than twenty people have stopped me on Broadway to say, 'I hear you have a hit.'"

*Up Pops the Devil* opened at the Masque Theater on September 1, 1930. Its competition was mostly revues, among them *Earl Carroll's Vanities* and *The Garrick Gaieties*, plus other comedies that also ignored the hard economic times afflicting many Americans. (On that day, the newspapers also shrugged off the hardships, focusing instead on a transatlantic flight by two French aviators, a $5 million North Atlantic sunken-treasure find, and the visit of Albert's favorite gangster, Legs Diamond, to a French spa to avoid the U.S. police.) *Up Pops the Devil* got fine reviews: "the most spontaneous offering of the season"; "some of the funniest lines heard in these parts for some time"; "Such wry pokes as *The New Yorker* takes . . . at the ribs of this giddy metropolis the authors . . . have sprinkled generously through their play." From Holland, Hendrik van Loon saluted Frances (but not Albert), cabling CONGRATULATIONS ON YOUR SUCCESS. Albert's performance, which involved many laconic asides, some lines delivered in a southern drawl, and the drunkenly inept packing of a trunk, was praised: "a good actor having an uncommonly good time"; "The evening's acting honors . . . belong to Albert Hackett." Despite his good notices, Albert had negative feelings about the play. He later recalled that when he switched from author to actor, he lost his perspective and could no longer see the play's weaknesses: "I went [onstage] and I never could tell what it was like after that." Later, after leaving the cast, he saw a performance and said to Frances, "'Why didn't you tell me it was as bad as this?' It was awful. The police should have stopped it."

*Up Pops the Devil* ran for 146 performances on Broadway; meanwhile, a production opened in Los Angeles, starring Raymond Hackett—in the leading role, not the supporting one Albert had played. In an opening-night telegram, Albert reminded his brother of a theatrical superstition: DON'T WHISTLE IN THE THEATER. Then Paramount bought the movie rights for $4,750, a comfortable sum in those days, and invited Albert to come to Hollywood as "dialogue director." The play's success, the movie sale, Albert's job offer—all of these combined to push Frances and Albert toward a decision, and at 11:30 on the morning of February 7, 1931, having paid a $2 fee, they were married in Manhattan's Municipal Building by a deputy city clerk, with two city office workers as witnesses.

The decision to marry had been hasty: "The movie money went to our heads," Albert joked. He had only enough time to buy a steel wedding band (he later gave Frances a gorgeous platinum, diamond-studded replacement). Trying to keep the ceremony secret, Albert gave his name as A. Maurice Hackett, but he and Frances were recognized, and reporters and photographers—one account said "half a hundred"—crowded around. They caught Frances wearing pearls and looking annoyed and wrote stories headlined "Up Pops Cupid As Dramatists Get Married" and "Frances Goodrich Has Hubby Now, Not Just a Pal." One reporter called Albert "young and handsome" and Frances an "excited and very glad little actress," and quoted her as saying, "Oh, dear, this is such a surprise! Why, I haven't even told my mother yet. This was really meant to be a secret." Asked if she "intended to carry out her former ideas of a companionate marriage with Hackett," Frances "merely laughed and said, 'Let's not talk any more about that.'" The next day (Frances must have recalled her just-married departure westward with Robert Ames), with Leah Salisbury and husband showering rice on them as they stepped aboard the train, Mr. and Mrs. Albert Hackett left for Hollywood.

# 4

## Hollywood 1931: A Hopeful Baptism

**W**hen Frances and Albert traveled to California in February 1931, they probably took the luxurious Twentieth Century Limited to Chicago, then a less fancy train to Los Angeles (the deluxe Super Chief wasn't yet in service). Arriving in Hollywood, they found a small, quiet town between the ocean and the mountains. There were no suburbs, shopping malls, or smog, and the scent of magnolias and gardenias was everywhere. In nearby Beverly Hills, there were only a few houses, and many bridle paths. Hollywood was then a narrowly focused, one-industry community; everyone knew everyone else and how much money everyone else was making. There were only a few decent restaurants and not much in the way of public entertainment ("No matter how hot it gets during the day," some people joked, "there's nothing to do at night"). Some inhabitants had created their own style: on Hollywood Boulevard, one observer said, the girls, famed for their beautiful faces, wore fur coats over lounging pajamas, slacks, or shorts, and dyed their hair in amazing colors; the men wore slacks, scarves, sandals, and jackets whose shoulders owed more to their tailors than to their physiques.

To the newly married Hacketts, their trip to "the Coast" was intriguing at first ("We have a little Ford roadster, and we drive about," Albert wrote) and must have seemed like a step toward opportunity, but it soon turned out to be dreary and unproductive. Although they'd written *Up Pops the Devil*, they went west not to do the screenplay—Arthur Kober, Lillian Hellman's ex-husband, acclaimed for his *New Yorker* stories about Bella Gross, a Bronx-born, husband-hunting "privitt sekretry," did it in collaboration with Eve Unsell—but because Albert had been hired as dialogue director. That job turned out to be pointless; equally distressing, Frances had no job at all.

Albert once said that being dialogue director was "a very silly thing," a hangover from the time sound was put into films. Hollywood directors didn't really understand dialogue then, so they got people from the theater to come and help. "Since I had played in the play," he added, "as well as having written it, they said, 'Come along and do the dialogue.' . . . In the cast of the picture, there were legitimate actors and actresses [including Norman Foster, Skeets Gallagher, and Carole Lombard], and no one had to tell them anything, except maybe to read a line a little differently, to get a laugh, or something of that sort. . . . I didn't do anything; I just sat there, and Eddie Sutherland, the director, would say, 'How did this thing play?' and I would show him what we did on stage. . . . [Eddie Sutherland was Louise Brooks's husband at one time.] He married a lot. Not in groups—one at a time. But he got around."[1] While he was "just sitting there," Albert learned some basics about the differences between the theater and films. "The picture," he said, "is more versatile. On the stage you have a butler and a maid discuss their employer and tell how selfish he is. On the screen you show the man in some selfish act. [On the stage,] you have to contrive to drag people on and off . . . sometimes unnaturally. In motion pictures you take the camera to the characters wherever they might be."[2]

To publicize *Up Pops the Devil*, Paramount's flacks concocted a wonderfully imaginative press release. "Albert Hackett," it asserted, "first became interested in writing when he was thrown out of a play several years ago. He was playing a boy role. . . . During a tense, dramatic scene his boyish treble cracked and squeaked. The audience howled. . . . The next year of uncertainty almost tore his heart out. Would he emerge as a tenor, a baritone, or a profound basso? While waiting he wrote poetry . . . [and] every kind of literature that can be written. . . . One day he started to write a play in collaboration with Frances Goodrich."

Albert's days on the set were often long, and when he got home, he often found an unhappy bride. "I had to get up at seven o'clock," he said, "to get to the studio at eight-thirty, to see the rushes or something like that, and then at the end of the day we were seeing the rushes again. . . . So I would get back to Frances about ten o'clock, and we'd go someplace to eat, and then I had to get up again at six or seven. . . . It was a scramble."[3]

Frances evidently didn't drive a car then and relied on Albert to get her around. (At one time, she did drive: in Little Compton, she once rammed the family Model T into a well, which troubled her greatly because her nephew Max Huntoon suffered a serious cut on the face.) Sitting at home alone didn't agree with Frances at all, especially because she wasn't working: all her life, she felt happiest when performing or writing. She did have one friend nearby, the beautiful, remarkable Ruth Chatterton, who was

then acting in pictures and later became a licensed airplane pilot and successful novelist, but basically she was "stuck there. . . . We had an awful
apartment—Oh, God, full of Spanish spears and draperies, and I'd wait at
night for [Albert] to come. I was used to a very different life."[4] Another
time, Frances said, "I couldn't stand it out there. . . . I was lonely." She
hated some of the parties she and Albert went to, where producers gathered together and talked shop, while the women talked "wives' talk." (According to Nora Johnson, the daughter of the screenwriter Nunnally
Johnson, at those parties nonworking Hollywood wives were "about as
welcome as venereal disease.") Gamely, Frances hid her unhappiness from
her family, writing her Aunt Caro, in Caro's words, "a nice letter, telling
us how very cheap living is there, and of all the lovely fruits."

Frances's term of solitary idleness was short. Although Albert had once
said he didn't have the face for "those big screens," through Myron
Selznick (producer David Selznick's brother and for many years Hollywood's leading agent), Albert was offered what Frances called "a very,
very [good], seven-year acting contract. . . . I said, 'You take it, I'm going
back to New York.'" Knowing how unhappy Frances was, not wanting
them to be apart, Albert sent a wire saying, "No, thank you very much,
love and kisses," and after eight weeks they returned east and settled into
Frances's apartment on East 55th Street. The film version of *Up Pops the
Devil* was released in May 1931 and got generally good reviews: "[Its] shining light . . . is Miss Lombard, whose sincerity . . . is surpassed only by her
exquisite beauty."

In May 1931, having recovered from their first Hollywood experience,
Frances and Albert visited Madeleine and Caro in Little Compton. Caro
roamed the seaside links in the dawn hours alongside "pompously parading seagulls" (her words), memorizing a speech she'd been invited to give
at her fiftieth Vassar reunion. Her garden brimmed with flowers (although
Caro was an avowed Communist, in those tolerant times she was a popular member of Little Compton's somewhat stuffy garden club). Among
those the Hacketts dined with were Frances's old friends Nicholas and Au-
gusta Maverick Kelley. Nicholas later became the top lawyer for the
Chrysler Corporation, which got him kicked out of the Socialist Party; Au-
gusta, a wit and a painter, was the granddaughter of Samuel Augustus
Maverick, whose unbranded calves, straying from his Texas ranch, gave
rise to the word used ever since to describe roving, casual individualists:
*mavericks*. While the Hacketts had been in California, a stage musical of *Up*

*Pops the Devil* had been put together. Titled *Everybody's Welcome,* it opened in October; its high moment came when Frances Williams sang "As Time Goes By," later revived as the theme song in the film *Casablanca.* The Hacketts weren't directly involved in *Everybody's Welcome*—"We just sat back and drew royalties"—so, back in New York, they started writing another play. (In 1938, *Up Pops the Devil* underwent yet another reincarnation when Bob Hope starred in the musical film version, *Thanks for the Memory,* singing the title number, which later became his "signature song.")

When Frances and Albert began work on their next comedy, *Bridal Wise,* New York showed terrible signs of the Great Depression—apple sellers on street corners, hundreds of unemployed people living in tents and tar paper shacks in Central Park—but the new offering, like *Up Pops the Devil,* was escapist entertainment and ignored the problems. This time, the witty lines were spoken not in Greenwich Village but in the Maryland fox-hunting country, where a well-off young couple, played by two of the day's better-known actors, Madge Kennedy and James Rennie, get divorced partly because he has grown overly fond of horses and another woman, marry other spouses, and then are reunited when their eight-year-old son gets thrown out of boarding school. The child is a loud-mouthed little horror, and his two brand-new stepparents dislike him instantly, but his parents realize that they love him, then realize that they also love each other.

When *Bridal Wise* was being tried out in Brooklyn in early 1932, Aunt Caro wrote to a friend that she'd heard it was "very risqué. . . . Madeleine is worried because all her respectable Nutley friends will be flocking in to see it if it ever reaches New York." All along, the play had a rocky career. During the Philadelphia tryouts, a critic said the plot was marked by "familiar situations and stock farcical devices." Also, the Philadelphia police, prodded by Albert's old nemesis, the Gerry Society, closed it because two cast members—playing the son and his best pal, who's black—were underage. "The funny thing was," Frances said, "Albert had been a child actor and the director, Frank Craven, a fine director, had been a child actor . . . and here the police are closing this, and we're saying, 'Look at them. They weren't stunted by it. They weren't deformed by being child actors. Take a look at them. They're doing okay.' But they closed it."[5] As a final insult, when the play opened in New York in May 1932, Frances and Albert's names were accidentally left off the program.

Its producers called *Bridal Wise* "as exciting and full of spills and thrills as a steeplechase, and as snappy and modern as this year's swimming

suits," and it got some enthusiastic reviews (including "very, very funny
. . . [by] two of our more facile and amusing dialogue-writers" — Robert
Benchley, in the *New Yorker*), but several critics panned it ("Mr. Hackett and
Miss Goodrich also wrote *Up Pops the Devil*. That was a better comedy.
. . . They do not appear to have cared much about what happened to this
one"). From the start, business was poor, and Frances and Albert took a
cut in royalties. Eventually, the play ran about six months, and it later did
well in stock. The Hacketts hoped the movie rights would be sold, but they
never were. Once, they *almost* were — and the failure infuriated Frances. In
a letter to Leah Salisbury, she said that Frank Craven was working at the
Fox studio, and executives there asked him if, to make the sale, "it would
be possible to . . . cut out the divorce and [cast two child actors the studio
favored] *and he said no*. It was at dinner that he told us [this], with other
people talking and laughing. It just made Albert and me dumb. The mis-
chief was done. There was nothing to be said. I believe that his idea is that
it would spoil our lovely little drama. So that's that. I suppose that he
thought his reputation was at stake . . . or something. I don't know. I was
wild. What does it matter what [the movie producers] do with the play?
They always do something. All I care about is selling it."

Shortly before *Bridal Wise* opened on Broadway, Frances and Albert got
an offer from Metro-Goldwyn-Mayer to return to Hollywood as a writing team; the pay was $750 per week for the two of them, a lot of money
in those depression days. Concerning the offer, which started them on a
course that changed their lives, Albert joked, "We figured out that we
spent the better part of a year writing and re-writing *Bridal Wise,* and made
exactly $3.50 a week. . . . So we were glad to go back to California and
begin earning a salary that was very gratifying indeed."[6] *Bridal Wise* was
the nadir of the Hacketts' earning power. From then on, their income in-
creased steadily until they were among Hollywood's highest-paid writers. Sometimes, their paychecks seemed unreal: "It doesn't matter to [the
studio] what you ask for, they'll pay it," Albert said. "It doesn't matter to
them. If they think you can make money for them, what you'll get paid is
of no consequence, in relation to what something good can bring in."[7]

# 5

## Entering Hollywood's Golden Age

Frances and Albert sometimes said they returned to Hollywood in 1932, having signed a six-month MGM contract, "just to make enough so we could go back to New York and write more plays," but in fact, for the next seven years, they worked almost exclusively on movies. It's not hard to see why. Although at first they had odd, sometimes disappointing experiences, they soon mastered the craft of screenwriting, formed a strong bond with a smart, enthusiastic producer, and started earning a lot. Also, they got close to many interesting friends and even learned to enjoy Southern California living—up to a point. Still another reason for staying must have been that Hollywood's Golden Age, then in full swing with all its energy, expertise, and promise, attracted and excited them.

Hollywood's Golden Age has been defined as the great period from the end of silent pictures to the collapse of the studio system with the arrival of television. In those years, the movie industry saw, on all levels, a flowering of artistry, an outpouring of glamour, and a dazzling display of vitality. The leader in all of this, the place where many of the most talented moviemakers worked, perhaps the greatest motion picture studio ever, was MGM. It occupied more than fifty acres in the dusty Los Angeles suburb of Culver City, facing a drugstore and three gas stations; it had a colonnaded facade, white sound stages and, later, a sleek, art deco administration building. A reporter once observed that "in operation, the plant presents the appearance less of a factory than of a demented university with a campus made of beaver board and canvas."[1]

MGM grossed many millions of dollars by putting out, in some years, forty or more pictures; the annual worldwide audience for those films has been estimated at a billion people. MGM was then dominated by the patriarchal—some said evil, overbearing, even reptilian—Louis B. Mayer and the brilliant, young Irving Thalberg, and it boasted that it beat the competition in all areas: its production facilities, the skill of its technicians, and the quality of the material its writers, directors, and producers worked on. And, of course, MGM had "more stars than are in heaven," including, to name just ten, Greta Garbo, Norma Shearer, Joan Crawford, Clark Gable, Jean Harlow, Judy Garland, Mickey Rooney, Spencer Tracy, William Powell, and Myrna Loy. The Hacketts wound up working on screenplays for eight of those ten; in the words of Ira Gershwin, a friend of theirs and an MGM lyricist, "Who could ask for anything more?"

Frances and Albert's odd experiences started a few days after they arrived at MGM. "Hollywood was jumping when we got there in '32," Albert told an interviewer. "I think there were 150 writers at MGM. Since we had just come out from New York, we were asked to go see a sick picture [*Prosperity*, starring Polly Moran and Marie Dressler]. We saw it in the projection room. Then we came to Thalberg's office and he said, 'Now, what did you think of it?'" (Albert's guess that MGM had 150 writers was exaggerated; the actual number was perhaps half that.)

"Well, sitting around a table," Albert continued, "were about sixteen people, most of whom we had never known before—Leo McCary, who directed it, and others . . . the biggest writers in the business, all called in to find out what was wrong with that picture. . . . Willard Mack was there, and Bayard Veiller, the man who wrote *The Trial of Mary Dugan*.

"'Well,' they said to us, 'what did you think of it?'

"We said we thought it was unspeakable. The production was bad, the writing was bad, the direction was bad. I don't know what else we said. There wasn't one person we let go free.

"Then there was this long, long silence. Finally Thalberg said, 'Have you any idea how you could fix this thing?'

"We said we'd go back to this little office we had, which was really a dressing room. They hadn't any offices left for writers by this time, there were so many. So we went back and worked liked badgers, writing an outline of what we thought the story was. We [took it] to the only friendly person we knew out there at that time, a writer named Zelda Sears. . . . When she read it, she burst out laughing. 'Why,' she said, 'you've written it back into just what it was to begin with. You see, I know, because I wrote the original story!' She was wonderful. She was grand. . . . Actually, we never worked for Mr. Thalberg. . . . This was the only time we were ever called in by him on anything. . . . We would meet him sometimes at a luncheon party or something like that, and he was always very nice, but we never got involved in anything of his."[2]

It's not known if the Hacketts' suggestions were followed, and they got no credits, but when *Prosperity* finally opened, it was called a "first-rate comedy—but don't forget your hanky" and "an antidote for Old Man Depression." Concerning the team-effort system used to generate screenplays then, Albert said that every script had several writers on it: "[The producers] would always welcome everybody coming in and taking a fling. . . . They'd spend a long time, wanting to make it good, and you were being paid, and you were asked to come in and push it along."

Another odd experience came when the Hacketts were assigned to a high-level producer, Paul Bern—who had written screenplays for famous directors and supervised the production of Garbo's MGM films—to do the screenplay of *Lost*, a story about a prostitute, which was to star Joan Crawford and Jackie Cooper. "We were not good at writing about prostitutes," Albert said. "We went to talk to [a Los Angeles policewoman] about prostitutes. She said they make the best mothers. . . . There was one who used to put her boy out on the fire escape when the men came in—pull the shades down, let him play out there, and have a fine time; it kept him healthy."[3]

Writing *Lost*, hoping to prove themselves, Frances and Albert ran into problems: "It is terribly hard work. . . . We are both so nervous and cross that we fight all the time. We shouldn't take so much trouble . . . but it is only to satisfy ourselves." To add to their difficulties, after they'd done "a simple scene," Bern called them in for a conference. "He said to us," Frances recalled, "'My secretary could do it better!' Then Albert read it for him, and he said, 'Well, why didn't you *write* it like that?' We said we did. [At that point we learned that, according to him] when you write 'Yes, I would like to go,' you add, 'Her face lights up, then she turns to him'— all this awful *dreck*. But that's what he wanted."[4] Writing to Leah Salisbury about this conference, Frances said, "I was perfectly furious. . . . He was so damnably rude. . . . I wanted to throw [the pages] in his face and leave."

Bern continued to criticize Frances and Albert's work after that meeting, which bothered them so badly that one day, meeting Fredric March, their friend from Elitch's Gardens, on the MGM lot, Frances told him, "'We hate that man. . . . It's just outrageous, the way he tears down what we do. . . . We're thinking of moving back to New York.' And Freddie said, 'Don't do that. He has in his family a history of suicide, and we're all concerned he'll commit suicide.'"[5] The Hacketts later recalled that remark vividly.

The Hacketts finished their screenplay on the day before Labor Day 1932 and delivered it to Bern, who told them he'd see them that night at a party at the home of March and his actress wife, Florence Eldridge. Bern didn't show up, which surprised the Hacketts. The next day, a newspaper reported that he had shot himself during the night because, rumor had it, he had problems making love to his recent bride, the "Blonde Bombshell" actress Jean Harlow. Since Bern's death, the question of whether he killed himself or was murdered has been rehashed often: in 1990, a seemingly well-researched book argued that he'd been done in by an ex-mistress; in 1993, another writer concluded, after equally diligent research, that the suicide theory was correct. At the time, the Hacketts were worried that concern over their screenplay might have added to Bern's stresses. Because of their unhappy work experience, they disliked him, but others felt differently and called him "worldly-wise and intellectual" and "probably the single most beloved figure in Hollywood." His death, Frances wrote, cast an "awful pall over the studio. . . . The scenario department called us . . . and the girl was crying so hard I couldn't understand her." Because of Bern's death—and perhaps because Crawford had never cared for the story—*Lost* lived up to its name and never went into production.

Around this time, Frances and Albert were offered other projects that didn't work out for them. One was the adaptation, for Marie Dressler and Wallace Beery, of three *Saturday Evening Post* short stories featuring earthy, lovable Tugboat Annie. "We practically have to write an original," Frances complained to Leah Salisbury. "All we have is the title and the boat." The Hacketts probably regretted not doing *Tugboat Annie,* because it was a major hit and landed Dressler on the cover of *Time.* Later, the Hacketts were given an original story by Edgar Selwyn, which Frances described in a letter to Salisbury, written at the office: "Egyptian locale. Sheiks, ladies in distress, dragomen, etc., for Ramon Navarro. We suffered all yesterday. A conference with [a producer] lasting two and a half hours. We worked all this morning, and then this afternoon [word came that] Thalberg did not consider that congenial work for us, and we were to quit it. . . . Thank Heaven. . . . It was all so false, all hooey. (I shall mail this at *home.*)"

When Frances and Albert first arrived in Los Angeles in early 1932, they lived briefly at the Roosevelt Hotel, then rented a house on Outpost Drive, in Hollywood. In a series of letters to Leah Salisbury, Frances described life there. The house, she said, was "nice, and plenty of room," but the furnishings were "terrible. All that bastard Spanish." They decided to get a housekeeper, "one of those [to whom] you say, 'We're bringing three people home to dinner,' and she does all the worrying," and hired a woman who'd worked for the Cagneys—but, Frances wrote, "after I had engaged her, Jim told me that her son had cleaned them out of liquor. So the other night we came home to find that we had been cleaned out, including . . . a big box of Amber cigarettes, two silver dollars, and the dice from our parcheesi set. So it must have been the kids, because they left all the tons of solid silver. So she goes tomorrow, and we get a man." A few weeks later, the Hacketts were robbed again, losing $400 worth of Frances's jewelry. "It is . . . very unpleasant to come home each night and look around for what they have taken. We have only our clothes left now."

On the positive side, Frances reported to Salisbury that she enjoyed the challenges at the studio: "I like it here. I like the work. Hope to God we make good . . . not for the option, but our pride. Also think that it will help us a lot on plots. Strengthen our weakest point." Added to that, there were "really nice times." One evening, the actress Catherine Willard gave a dinner party for them. The other guests were the Fredric Marches, the director John Cromwell and his wife, playwright-screenwriter-author Dwight Taylor and his wife, and the famed silent film star John Gilbert and his young, terrific-looking fiancée, Virginia Bruce. "We never did see Gilbert," Frances wrote. "He came in tight, went upstairs, and slept. Never did appear. I felt so sorry for poor little Virginia Bruce."

P. G. Wodehouse, who wrote screenplays in Hollywood in the 1930s, once remarked that in every studio there were "rows and rows of hutches, each containing an author on a long contract at a weekly salary. You see their anxious little faces peering through the bars. . . . There are authors on some lots whom nobody has seen for years. It is like the Bastille."[6] Wodehouse said he did better than the Bastille inmates; during one period, paid $6,000 a week for contributing to a script, he stayed at home working on a novel and only occasionally visited the studio to change a few words, such as "Well, I'm off" to "Pip, pip, I'm off, chaps."

Wodehouse's comments about other writers' working conditions were jokey but had a serious point: screenwriting could be rough. The Hacketts had New York friends who had "[come] back saying, 'It's awful out there' —but they had never actually done a picture." Realizing the importance of screen credits, determined to get some, Frances and Albert decided to hang on, and finally, in December 1932, were chosen to adapt a 1923 Broadway play by Martin Brown called *The Lady*.

Set in England, *The Lady* had a complicated, hackneyed plot: Sally, a servant girl who "always wanted to be a lady," marries "an aristocrat," who dies; she bears a son but is separated from him; eighteen years later, in a Paris bordello where she's the madam, her son (who hasn't recognized her) kills a man in self-defense; reunited at last during his trial, Sally and son vow to live together after he gets out of prison. At the play's end, Sally tells a newspaper reporter, "He's a *gentleman*, my son is a *gentleman*"; the reporter replies, "He's a gentleman because his mother was a lady."

Dismayed by this kind of dialogue, in their words "knowing nothing of English servant girls," the Hacketts turned Sally into an American chorus girl visiting England; Irene Dunne played the role. In the Paris bordello sequences, Sally had a new name, Madame Blanche, so the picture was titled *The Secret of Madame Blanche*. During the filming, Albert later wrote, "the director . . . had a hard job . . . [In one scene, the son] could not seem to get the proper hangover tone in his voice. The director solved it by putting a lettuce leaf down his throat."[7] One of the scenes featured heavy fog. "In those days," Albert said, "whenever you had a scene in England, it was hard for [Hollywood directors] not to put in fog—that's the only thing they knew about England, the fog. . . . We wrote in a couple of American chorus girls. . . . One of them said, 'Isn't the fog awful?' and the other said, 'Yes, a man tried to pick me up, and I turned around, and I couldn't find him.' . . . The director said we couldn't use it."[8] Another exchange between chorus girls was shortened. Standing backstage, hearing music from the orchestra pit, one girl said, "They're playing 'God Save the King.'" The producers made the Hacketts cut the next line: "What's the matter, is he sick?"

The script pleased MGM's executives, but the reviewers hated the finished picture: "Just another answer to what's wrong with the movies"; "You have seen its plot so often that you should know by now if you are fond of it." Theater owners were equally critical. "[We used to read] *The Motion Picture Herald*," Albert said, "and the people who owned the theaters would write in and say to other exhibitors how they did, playing a certain picture. One exhibitor wrote, 'Look out for this one, boys, it's a stinkola.' This was a time when they had block booking—if you wanted an MGM picture, one of the big ones, you had to take all of the MGM pictures, the stinkers as well."[9] Frances's concern was not for the exhibitors but for the star: "Poor Irene Dunne, poor Irene Dunne." Ironically, Miss Dunne felt otherwise. "Years later," Albert said, "we won an award for *Father of the Bride* . . . and [at the ceremony] Irene Dunne was giving us this award. . . . We were so embarrassed and ashamed to see her after that dreadful picture, [but] she laughed and said that she had a woman fan who wrote her all the time and said she was very good in this or that [movie], but the best thing she ever did was *The Secret of Madame Blanche*."[10]

During this period, studio employees worked six days a week, and writing *The Secret of Madame Blanche* put Frances and Albert under great pressure. "We have to be back [at the studio] every night for conferences," Frances wrote just before Christmas 1932. "Had to return at eight this morning to read a scene. We are punch-drunk. We still have that terrible final trial (murder in a French court!) to write, and we shall do it on Christmas and Monday so they can shoot Tuesday. We haven't had a minute to shop or see any Christmas cheer. No parties—no people at the house, no nothing. And we won't get it at all—except for Christmas dinner with the Cagneys." Frances and Albert often took turns composing letters; while they were working on *Madame Blanche,* Albert wrote in one, "I shall turn this over to Frances now. She is back from the ladies' room (her only diversion since we got put on [this job])."

During this time of misfires, Frances and Albert occasionally amused themselves on the MGM lot by, in his words, "going to watch Joan Crawford try to act." (Crawford, of course, gave many great performances, but she was then struggling in a flop—written in part by William Faulkner—called *Today We Live.*) The Hacketts' first projects had received mixed-to-negative reviews, but in the spring of 1933 they were assigned to *Penthouse,* a novel-length story by Arthur Somers Roche that had been serialized in *Cosmopolitan* magazine and dealt with a young lawyer who leaves corporate practice and gets involved with high-living gangsters while defending a friend accused of murder. The director was W. S. Van Dyke—and working with him was a big step forward.

Woodbridge Strong Van Dyke II was one of the many intriguing characters the movies attracted in those exciting days. Tall, lean, with a "knuckle-dented" profile and a wire-brush crew cut, Van Dyke had, like Albert, been put on the stage early to help a widowed mother with the rent: at age five, in curls and pinafore, he played the lead in *Ruth, the Blind Girl.* Later, after working as a miner, logger, and bit-part actor, he directed Westerns during the nickelodeon era and made films in Tahiti, Africa, and Alaska. Along the way, while directing such pictures as *Trader Horn* (1931) and *Tarzan the Ape Man* (1932), he became known as a "hard-bitten, hard-boiled man of the world with an understanding heart" and "One-Take Woody, Hollywood's fastest director." "Actors are bound to lose their fire if they do a scene over and over," he once said. "It's that fire that brings life to the screen."

While writing *Penthouse,* a "crime drama" that contained murder, machine gun fire, morphine needles, and pawn tickets falling out of purses,

Frances and Albert had conferences with Van Dyke where Frances—presumably in her usual ladylike tones—read aloud, Van Dyke critiqued, and a stenographer recorded the proceedings. ("Mrs. Hackett then read the scene in the speakeasy . . . and it was considered OK with the exception of the line, 'Would you like to dance?' and the action of the two girls going out. These things were eliminated. When Gazotti leaves Gertie with Durant she says: 'If she don't tell you all she knows, I don't know brunettes.' Durant replies: 'I may want to find out the things she doesn't know she knows.'")[11] The film starred Warner Baxter, Nat Pendleton, and Myrna Loy and was, Albert commented, Loy's "first picture without Mongolian makeup. She had been playing a lot of Fu Manchu stories before." (Loy was just getting away from roles in which she used an ethnic, "You touch me, I keel you" accent.) *Penthouse* was released in the fall of 1933 to fine reviews—"thoroughly exciting . . . tense and absorbing"; "There isn't a dull moment"—and the Hacketts' dialogue was called "snappy, fast . . . modern and sophisticated."

Among the publications that praised *Penthouse* was the *Hollywood Reporter*—and Frances and Albert quickly learned that there were strings attached. "[Hollywood] is a chiseling place," Frances wrote to Leah Salisbury. "A man from *The Hollywood Reporter,* which gave us a good notice, came [to our office] yesterday, and practically blackmailed us with the suggestion that if we didn't come across, we'd get a stinking notice on our next picture, so we had to put up $46 for an ad. And *Variety* has been at us all day for the same thing. And *The Film Daily*. It's a grand racket." The ad in the *Hollywood Reporter* ran across the bottom of the front page, with a bright-red background, and said "FRANCES GOODRICH, ALBERT HACKETT wrote the SCREENPLAY AND DIALOGUE for PENTHOUSE, MGM."

The warm reviews of *Penthouse* were a breakthrough—but Frances and Albert were still given some unimportant jobs. They worked on *I Married An Angel* ("We did an idea at the end") and on *The Hollywood Party* ("But of course these scraps won't get us any credit"). They also did "a little 'bootleg' work on *Stage Mother,* by which [the producers] mean that we are not officially on it, but they yell to us and we go over to the stage and hand them some fool line." At one point, Frances and Albert were called onto the set to write a scene for *Chained,* starring Joan Crawford and Clark Gable. An "unhappy wife story," a "typical 1930s hanky-rattler," *Chained* had costly sets and costumes ("ocean liners more glamorous than anything afloat, ski lodges on the scale of aircraft carriers . . . a fur coat so lavishly cloaking [Crawford's] figure that she appears to be the willing victim of rape by a mink-pack") but still did poorly, perhaps because Gable seemed bored, wishing he were in a different picture.

A more important job was *Fugitive Lovers,* in which Robert Montgomery, an escaped convict, woos Madge Evans, a Hollywood-bound showgirl, aboard a transcontinental bus, with the Three Stooges providing their usual grunts, growls, screeches, face slapping, and other bits of mayhem. Originally given the on-the-nose title *Overland Bus,* it was released in January 1934; Frances and Albert shared screenplay credit with George B. Seitz, the writer-director of serials, including *The Perils of Pauline.* The director was Richard Boleslavsky, a famed product of the Moscow Art Theater, who had directed such stars as the three Barrymores, Lionel, Ethel, and John. About Boleslavsky, Albert said, "If someone was supposed to do this, he'd do just the opposite. Just a dreadful man—arbitrarily changed everything. [*Fugitive Lovers*] was done fast and wasn't very good."[12]

Some reviewers shared Albert's negative view then, but when the movie was rereleased fifty years later, it was called "a little gem." In 1934, the promoters of the brand-new cross-country bus business must have hated the *Herald Tribune's* review, which said the movie presented "complete and devastating proof that a long distance journey by bus is the most unpleasant method of travel yet devised by the fiendish ingenuity of man. Unless the film is being cruelly unfair, a bus voyage is disfigured by dirt, discomfort, crowded quarters, low comics, escaped convicts, police interference, and very bad conversational gifts."

Through the years, many of Frances and Albert's films were first shown in super-deluxe movie palaces in New York's Broadway area. *Fugitive Lovers* opened in one of the grandest, the huge Capitol Theater, which had a majestic white marble staircase, fluted columns, rock-crystal chandeliers, a soaring dome decorated with classical bas-reliefs, and slatherings of silver leaf. The Capitol drew enormous audiences, who were treated to elaborate stage shows. Supplementing *Fugitive Lovers,* the Capital Grand Orchestra and the Capitol Ballet Corps presented the prison scene from *Faust* and a seven-episode number called "The Romance of a Rose." Like the other great movie theaters—the Roxy, the Paramount, Radio City Music Hall—the Capitol had a "grand concert" organ. The author Ben Hall wrote that these versatile instruments were "part one-man band, part symphony orchestra, part sound-effects department." When one ascended pompously out of the orchestra pit at intermission, it emitted a roar that made the marrow dance in one's bones. . . . The [organ] was as much a part of the movie palace as the electric lights that danced around the marquee, or the goldfish that swam in the lobby fountain. Inside the theater the music seemed to bubble up and soar into the darkness. . . . Far below, bathed in a rose spotlight, was the organist perched in the maw of the great golden console. A flick of the finger, and the chimes would call . . . a dramatic sweep of the hand and all would be silence. . . . [Then came] the crooning Vox Humana. . . . A quick kick at the crescendo pedal, a lightning jab at the combination pistons, and the mood would change to joy again—all glockenspiels, trumpets, tubas, and snare drums, as an invisible MacNamara's Band marched across the balcony.[13]

While working on *Fugitive Lovers* and the pictures for which they got no credit, Frances and Albert might have felt frustrated—but, in fact, good things were happening. They'd been associated with Van Dyke, one of Hollywood's top directors, and had met Hunt Stromberg, who was then on his way to becoming one of MGM's most successful and powerful producers. They later worked with Stromberg often and grew fond of him. Their talents had been noted, and on their next assignment, *The Thin Man*, they were again teamed with Van Dyke and Stromberg, and they quickened their pace, then took off. And in the meantime, they met some other interesting people . . .

When the Hacketts arrived in 1932, a potent aura of glamour surrounded the movie business, but Hollywood itself was in many ways a dull, inward-looking company town, with its energy centered around a single product and its social life linked directly to the industry hierarchy. "There was such a caste system in Hollywood," Frances once observed. "There was never anything like it. There were layers and other layers . . . and the lowest layer was the writers."[14] Albert added, "Out there we [saw] some actors we'd known from the theater . . . Jim Cagney, Freddie March, Frank McHugh, Chester Morris. Those people we had [acted] with or known for years.[15] [But] . . . when you wrote, [basically] the only people you knew were other writers. The stars all went to dinner with their producers . . . but seldom did they ever talk to writers. Writers were really less than the dust."[16]

The Hollywood caste system galled many writers. Ben Hecht said, "We were treated much like butlers, socially"; Michael Blankfort said, "The

main topic of conversation [among writers] was how stupid the producers and directors were. . . . The resentment was the resentment of the coal
miner who resents the boss because he's digging coal, he's getting all dirty.
The boss is nice and clean."[17] However, Frances and Albert's reaction was
far less bitter, because they enjoyed the people around them. During their
early Hollywood years, their friends included some of America's bright-
est, most original talents. "We had a wonderful [writers'] table there in the
MGM commissary," Frances said. "Just think of the people who were
there! Dashiell Hammett, Ogden Nash, Sid Perelman, Laura Perelman,
Dorothy Parker, Alan Campbell. . . . You know, it was a wonderful group."
The Hacketts had interesting times with those people: there were parties,
trips, shared causes, fights, reconciliations, bizarre encounters, and many
laughs. High on the list of those they stayed closest to, for the longest time,
were S. J. Perelman and his wife, Laura.

By the time Frances and Albert reached California, Sidney Joseph
("Sid") Perelman—born in Brooklyn in 1904, raised in Providence, Rhode
Island, an almost-graduate of Brown University (he flunked math; in 1965,
Brown gave him an honorary doctorate), the author of highly praised
magazine pieces and books, once described as "America's lampoonist lau-
reate"—had been in and out of the scene for a couple of years, mainly as
a writer for the Marx Brothers. Short, slight, mustachioed, always fastidi-
ously dressed, with owlish walleyes behind wire-rimmed granny glasses,
Perelman sometimes collaborated on screenplays with Laura. Although
Hollywood paid him well, Perelman hated it: to him, it was a "dreary in-
dustrial town controlled by hoodlums of enormous wealth," who had the
"ethical sense of a pack of jackals" and "foreheads only by dint of elec-
trolysis." Concerning Frances and Albert, his feelings were also strong: he
adored them.

"The Hacketts," the author Leila Hadley, one of Perelman's closest
friends, has said, "were the people Sid really loved. . . . They were like
cushions and pillows [for him]. . . . I would say they were the best friends
he had. . . . I often heard him say critical things about others, but never
about them."[18] As befits a writer, Perelman's affection often showed itself
in words. He gave the Hacketts signed copies of his books; in 1948, he
dedicated a best-selling book— *Westward Ha!, Or Around the World in Eighty
Clichés*—to them; through the years, he sent many funny, gossipy letters
(when Perelman's letters were published, several years after his death,
those to the Hacketts were outnumbered only by those to Leila Hadley).
In 1955, when Perelman was visiting Frances and Albert in Bel Air, he

wrote to Leila Hadley, "The Hacketts [are] phenomenons . . . incredibly
kind and generous people who do their work conscientiously, who take
just as dim a view as I do of this insane place but simulate good cheer, and
who continue to act with consideration and modesty."[19] Some years before, when he and Laura were living in Erwinna, Pennsylvania, he urged
the Hacketts to become neighbors: "How nice it would be if you could be
persuaded to buy a place in Pennsylvania. . . . There's nobody we'd rather
have living near us, you cunning things."[20] Another time, he wrote, "We
miss you, and this piece of paper constitutes a license to come stay with us
in the country forever. Honest to God and no kidding."[21]

While Frances and Albert remained in California, they saw the Perelmans often; after the Hacketts moved back to New York, in 1962, the four
met even more often, and the Hacketts gave a birthday dinner party every
year for Sid. He invited the two dozen guests; over the years, they included my parents; actresses Maureen Stapleton and Dolly Haas; writers
Leila Hadley, Philip Hamburger, Joseph Mitchell, Lillian Ross, Ruth Goetz,
and Israel Shenker; artists Ben Shahn and Al Hirschfeld (Haas's husband);
and critic Brooks Atkinson. The famously reclusive J. D. Salinger was once
invited and from his retreat in New Hampshire sent Frances and Albert a
characteristic note: "I thought there might be a chance of my getting to the
party, but a broken Jeep and other impediments will keep me here, I'm
sorry to say."

These celebrations didn't follow traditional lines: there were no presents
or candlelit cakes; nobody sang "Happy Birthday"; "people just mingled
and talked and felt honored to be there," Hamburger said. "The food was
always elegant and excellent, of course. . . . I do recall one particular party,
when Lillian Hellman approached me fiercely, and said, 'How come Sid
Perelman writes *you* postcards, and doesn't send any to me?' I was taken
aback by the savage tone."[22] Another regular at the parties, the painter
Gerta Conner, recalled that Perelman often invited a well-to-do diamond
merchant named Herman Elkon, who "fascinated Sid because he took
himself so seriously. Sid used him as a prototype in his writing. . . . He was
sort of a ladies' man and was always bragging about his conquests." Unfortunately, Elkon had a "very unattractive wife, who drank too much:
once they had to carry her out, and Sid was in hysterics. . . . The parties
were hilarious, with wonderful toasts—they were the best parties ever.
. . . They were the high point of the year for Sid."[23]

In addition to celebrating Perelman's birthdays, Frances and Albert worried about him. Their nephew Maxwell Huntoon recalled an evening in

the 1970s at the Hacketts' New York apartment when they learned that Perelman had developed pneumonia somewhere in China. "Frances," Max said, "twitched and gloomed during dinner and afterward told Albert, 'We've got to find out how he is.' They called a couple of people who didn't know where Perelman was, then tried to figure out how to get the phone numbers of hospitals in China. 'China's a big place,' Albert said. 'What about Peking,' Frances asked, 'or maybe Shanghai?' I don't remember how it ended, but there were a couple of calls to Information in China, and between Frances's deafness and the differences in language it would have been hilarious except that Frances and Albert were really concerned for their friend."

In one of the many letters Perelman sent to the Hacketts (a letter that wasn't published with the others), he commented on coping with his adolescent children during a visit to Martha's Vineyard:

You will be appalled and ashamed to hear that I've done almost no work. It seems that I'm in a gasoline conveyance almost every five minutes ferrying kids to some world-shaking appointment. Abby at the moment is deeply in love with a young man, aged 16, six feet three, and looking like a doorknob with a crewcut balanced on a wire coat-hanger supported by a broomstick. Adam has ants in the pants (or the non-pants, you know the Vineyard) for a butter-ball resembling a Wampas baby star. She has a 42-inch chest expansion and when she passes the sword-fishing fleet at Menemsha, the resultant whistles sound like a banyan tree full of mynah birds. Sex is rampant; I alone walk with downcast eyes, prim as a Puritan maid.

Through the Perelmans, Frances and Albert met Nathanael West, Laura's brother and the author of four fine novels, including *The Day of the Locust*, published in 1939, one of the harshest indictments of the Los Angeles scene ever written. According to Jay Martin, West's best biographer, West — who was then unhappily writing the screenplays of low-budget films at Republic Studios — probably named the hero of *Locust*, Tod Hackett, after Albert, "but he didn't base the character on him, he just used his name."[24] Albert liked West, a tall, husky, shy man then in his midthirties. Because he seemed to be slow-moving, he had been ironically nicknamed "Pep" at college, but Albert's description made him sound intense: "Pep was very warm, very friendly. Very interested in people. He listened to what you said in such a serious, absorbed way, it was like talking to a doctor." West was a passionate hunter and once took Albert duck-shooting. Albert wrote to Jay Martin in February 1967:

> Pep and I got together because of my interest in birds. Pep told of
> hunting wild doves, ducks, and geese, and wild swans flying over-
> head in the early mist. I was so excited by his stories that he asked me
> to come along. . . . A week or so later we set out in his car for some
> hunting club somewhere miles and miles to the north. We left Bur-
> bank at noon Saturday and got to the place about eleven o'clock at
> night. . . . We had driven three hundred miles. . . . We stayed at some
> tiny hotel. Got to bed about one A.M., were called at three A.M.,
> jumped into our clothes like firemen, had a cup of coffee and a slug
> of whisky, and off we drove with our guns (Pep's) and decoys to the
> shooting club. We spent from seven o'clock in the morning until
> eleven crouched down in barrels peering out watching for birds. . . .
> Whatever conversation there was was whispered. And it was all
> about birds. In fact there was very little conversation going up and
> coming back that was not about birds and hunting. . . . I don't re-
> member Pep ever talking to me about his books.

Albert didn't mention any kills made during those peculiar-sounding
hours, but there were some: he later said West didn't come when he and
Frances ate the birds. The Hacketts once gave West's career a boost by per-
suading MGM to buy a treatment he'd coauthored; unfortunately—and
typically, in West's ill-starred Hollywood experience—the film was never
made. In later years, West's books were highly praised, and he was called
"brilliant . . . America's first master of black humor . . . an American original, our Kafka from East 81st Street."

The Hacketts' friendship with some of those at the MGM commissary
writers' table—Ogden Nash, the Perelmans, Dashiell Hammett—was close
and ongoing, but their acquaintance with Dorothy Parker and her actor-
writer husband (and collaborator), Alan Campbell, was different.

Dorothy Parker, called "the wittiest woman in America," was small and
pretty but odd-looking with her black bangs and round, sad, dark eyes;
Sheilah Graham, the gossip columnist and author, thought she looked like
a "tired Renoir." Parker was, of course, a regular at the Algonquin Round
Table, and her quips have been repeated often: she was thrown out of a
Catholic school, she said, for insisting that "the Immaculate Conception
was spontaneous combustion"; as a copywriter at *Vogue*, she observed that
"brevity is the soul of lingerie"; after a notorious lesbian murderer sent her
victim's uterus to the victim's new lover in a suitcase, Parker was asked

what she might call that piece of luggage, and she replied, "A snatchel." Many people found Parker's tongue and personality too sharp, but a friend once called her "a Lady. . . . [She] was tiny, and had the softest, loveliest voice I ever heard. Her diction was impeccable, and, of course, her choice of words was precise." Concerning screenwriting, Parker wrote:

> When I dwelt in the East . . . I regarded it . . . with benevolent contempt. . . . I thought, "Why I could do that with one hand tied behind me and the other on Irving Thalberg's pulse." . . . Well, through the sweat and the tears I shed over my first script, I saw a great truth. . . . And that is that no writer, whether he writes from love or from money, can condescend to what he writes. What makes it hard in screenwriting . . . is the money he gets.
>
> You see, it brings out that uncomfortable little thing called conscience. You aren't writing for the love of it or the art of it or whatever; you are doing a chore assigned to you by your employer and whether or not he might fire you if you did it slackly makes no matter. You've got yourself to face, and you have to live with yourself. You don't— or at least, only in highly exceptional circumstances—have to live with your producer.[25]

The Hacketts met Parker in New York before going to Hollywood, and according to the playwright Ruth Goetz, from the start there was a bar to their ever becoming truly close: Frances and Albert weren't "political" enough. "When Dottie and I were members of the Communist Party," Mrs. Goetz said, "[the Hacketts] weren't political. Later, they worked for Spain—but Dottie and I gave the first party that was ever given for Spain, here in New York, and we had a lot of New York there . . . [including] the man who wrote *Man's Fate* [André Malraux] . . . raising money. . . . Dottie and I were in the Communist Party for about two years, and Dottie had no patience with anyone who didn't understand that the extreme left was the only way to go."[26]

For a time, at MGM, Frances and Albert and Parker and Campbell had neighboring offices. According to the author Marion Meade, when the door was open, the Hacketts could hear Dorothy and Alan composing dialogue out loud.

> "And then what does *he* say?" Alan asked.
> Dorothy's answer was soft but audible, "Shit."
> "Please don't use that word," Alan muttered. Turning back to his typewriter, he continued, "All right—and then what does *she* say?"

"Shit."
*"Don't use that word!"*[27]

Parker was often seen at fancy Long Island house parties and on choice French beaches, and her life seemed to be exciting and glamorous, but in fact it was sad: tormenting love affairs, heavy drinking, abortions, suicide attempts. In her forties, married to Campbell, she got pregnant—and announced the fact loudly. Frances found that pathetic: "She called [gossip columnists] Hedda Hopper and Louella Parsons to give them the scoop. In God's name! . . . And [she was] knitting for the camera!"[28] In the end, Parker miscarried. Her marriage to Campbell was rocky: they divorced after fourteen years, then remarried. She often bad-mouthed Campbell, saying he cheated his agent, struck her, and was, despite her pregnancy, homosexual. (Albert once heard her say, "What am I doing in Hollywood at my age and married to a fairy?") According to Sheilah Graham, early one Christmas morning during World War II, while Campbell was in the army, Parker knocked on the Hacketts' door, looking terrible, probably drunk, and proclaimed that, going through Campbell's checkbooks, she'd found that he'd spent $15,000 on a bracelet for Miriam Hopkins, the actress. This confused the Hacketts—hadn't Parker often insisted Campbell was gay? Later that day, she brought the Hacketts two framed photographs of Campbell and suggested they choose one as a gift; when they did, she gave both to them. After Campbell died, in 1963—some accounts say he killed himself—Parker began seeing an attractive young actor; Albert recalled that when a friend commented on his suntan, Parker replied, "Ah, yes, the hue of availability." After the Hacketts moved back to New York, in 1962, they talked to Parker about doing a stage adaptation of her famous short story *Big Blonde*. Nothing came of it; they said that Parker, living alone in the Volney Hotel, had become sad and reclusive. She died in 1967; one of her friends reported that years before, she'd drafted two epitaphs for her gravestone: EXCUSE MY DUST and THIS IS ON ME.

Another writer who put in time at MGM and disliked the work but liked the money was William Faulkner. At one point, Frances and Albert were given an office he'd recently vacated. They searched for any writing the famous man might have left behind, but "there was," Albert once said, "nothing except a large yellow pad on the desk. Faulkner had drawn a calendar and had circled every payday. But the only words he'd written on the whole pad were 'Boy Meets Girl.'"[29]

# 6

## The Thin Man

In *The Thin Man*, an eccentric New York inventor disappears; his mistress and a male informer are murdered; and an urbane, wise-cracking couple, Nick and Nora Charles, visiting from California—he's a good-looking, hard-drinking retired detective; she's beautiful and rich—finally unravel the mystery. The plot is confusing and not very interesting, but the movie has been called "probably the best-loved detective film ever made." The element that made it such a huge, enduring success was the interplay between Nick (William Powell) and Nora (Myrna Loy). They were one of the first *happily* married couples ever shown on the screen; as the author Ian Hamilton said, the banter between them

> is witty enough, line by line, but what makes it unusual is its deeply companionable spirit: the barbs and counterbarbs add up to a sort of ardently literate love talk, a sustaining of the relationship's vitality and edge—and its equality. . . . The Nick and Nora Charles partnership was Dashiell Hammett's invention [in his novel], but Albert and Frances Hackett knew it from within and added much that was their own. Film actors, it is said, liked to perform scripts by the Hacketts; for some reason, they always ended up getting praised for the *intelligence* of their interpretations.[1]

Another writer commented about *The Thin Man* that it wasn't "fanciful" to believe that only a devoted married couple like the Hacketts could have written it, and described Frances and Albert as "Hollywood's most playfully affectionate husband-and-wife team. They saw Nick and Nora, who treated each other as equals, as slightly idealized versions of themselves—suave, sensual, carefree, and witty."[2] A third author wrote, "If anyone could make marriage sexy, it was Loy and Powell. . . . They proved you could tie the knot and still have fun, but they were anything but settled down, what with the stimulus of murders to be solved and martinis to be drunk and a parade of low-lifes traipsing through their Park Avenue apartment, demanding a place at their seated dinners."[3] Frances and Albert were often asked if they'd put themselves into Nick and Nora; they gave different answers at different times: "Well, it was a very funny relationship, and we had a good time with [it]"; "You mention the physical attraction between husband and wife. . . . That was the situation Hammett had written into his book; we . . . went along"; "You do put a lot of yourself [into] scenes"; "The fun part was writing the husband-wife relationship." Some observers have said that the relationship between Hammett and Lillian Hellman closely resembled that between Nick and Nora, but that overlooks several facts: Hammett and Hellman were never married, they were often apart for long periods of time, they often fought bitterly over personal matters, and they were often unfaithful. In truth, the bond between the Hacketts was far more "Charles-like" than that between Hammett and Hellman.

*The Thin Man* was directed by "One-Shot Woody" Van Dyke. When Frances and Albert were first approached about the picture, they were hesitant; throughout their career, they were cautious about new projects, and there's a long list of seemingly attractive proposals they turned down because they felt the material was wrong for them. Concerning *The Thin Man*, Albert said, "Neither of us had ever read a mystery story, so we didn't know what to do. And Van Dyke said, 'I don't care anything about the mystery stuff—just give me five scenes between Nick and Nora. . . . Forget about the mystery, let that come in when you want.'" Frances was far more negative than Albert about the project—and, considering the film's enormous, decades-long popularity, her pessimism is ironic indeed. In late January 1934, she wrote to Leah Salisbury, "We're in a stew as usual. Trying to get a story out of *The Thin Man*. I doubt whether it will come through. I think that Stromberg will decide not to do it. I hope so. It strikes me as pretty run-of-the-mill. . . . It stinks!" In other letters, she added, "Albert and I do not believe it is a good script, or a good book, or a good story," and reported that they were "still slaving away at *The Thin Man*. If it would only make *me* thin, I could bear it."

Frances and Albert did the script in three weeks (Frances, years later: "My God, when I think what we used to do!"); Van Dyke shot it in somewhere between twelve and eighteen days (accounts differ). The first time Nick and Nora speak to each other, we're shown their teasing manner. It's a Christmastime cocktail hour in New York; he's in a bar, teaching the bartenders the right way to mix a martini. Scattering an armload of gaily wrapped presents, Nora is dragged into the place by Asta, their perky, nose-licking, wire-haired terrier, who's in a frenzy to greet his master. The headwaiter says the dog must leave; Nick explains that "It's okay—this is my dog. And my wife." Nora comments, "You might have mentioned me first," and says that Asta has tugged her into "every gin mill on the block"; Nick replies, "Yes, I had him out this morning." Throughout the script, there are memorable, gently barbed lines, including Nick's "I don't know anything. I've been in California for four years"; an exchange about newspaper reports of a shooting (Nick: "I'm a hero. I was shot twice in the *Tribune.*" Nora: "I read you were shot five times in the tabloids." Nick: "He didn't come anywhere near my tabloids."); and another exchange after he sends her sightseeing, against her will, to keep her out of danger: "How did you like Grant's Tomb?" "It's lovely. I'm having a copy made for you." Concerning the danger Nick is in, there's this:

> Nora: I think it's a dirty trick to bring me all the way to New York just to make a widow out of me.
> Nick: You wouldn't be a widow long.
> Nora: You bet I wouldn't.
> Nick: Not with all your money.[4]

In their screenplay, the Hacketts used Asta to liven up a necessary but potentially dull conversation by having Nick and Nora talk while dog walking: there are frequent halts while Asta is plainly, but out of the camera's view, relieving himself against trees and streetlights. "We got the idea," Albert said, "from seeing people walking dogs in New York and pretending so politely not to know them when they stopped."[5] (Albert enjoyed joking about dog walking, calling it "taking the dog out to empty it.") The script also got laughs out of Asta's personality: confronted by a crook, Powell threatened, "Don't make a move or that dog will tear you to pieces"—while the camera showed Asta cowering under a table.

*The Thin Man* was released in late July 1934 and was called "superlative cinema," "surefire entertainment," and "a picture you simply cannot afford to miss." "Dashiell Hammett's original story is by no means as clever as the film version," Louella Parsons wrote (she was then a reviewer, not a mudslinging columnist). "That's because of the amusing subtlety of the film delineations, the delightfully amusing portrayals and the smart dialogue. Albert Hackett and Frances Goodrich, adapters, come in here for our congratulations." Later commentators pointed out that the film "solved the Depression by completely ignoring it," and that, unless by choice, Nora never made herself subservient to Nick—"quite something in the days before woman's liberation was commonly accepted."

Soon after *The Thin Man*'s release, MGM started planning a sequel. The Hacketts did it plus a third picture; three more films followed, all starring Loy and Powell and with "thin man" in their titles. "The thin man" himself (the eccentric inventor, played by tall, skinny Edward Ellis) appeared in only a few scenes in the first film; to keep the series going, MGM kept using the words, and ultimately the public decided that Powell was "the thin man." Over the decades, the six films made many millions for MGM, but when the Hacketts wrote their three (and all of their subsequent pictures, except for their very last, in 1962), they were working on contract, like other screenwriters of that period, and got no part of the booty that piled up over the years—although in 1934 MGM gave them a $10,000 bonus.

*The Thin Man* was nominated for four Academy Awards—for Best Picture, Best Director, Best Actor, and Best Writing (Adaptation)—but didn't win in any category: all four awards went to *It Happened One Night*, with Clark Gable and Claudette Colbert, written by Robert Riskin. An odd result of *The Thin Man*'s popularity was that America fell in love with wire-haired terriers. Asta, featured throughout the series, sometimes aided the Charleses' sleuthing: in the first film, he sniffed out a body in a basement. His stardom—actually, the first dog to play Asta was a female—reportedly set off a craze for the breed; he was called the "best-known dog in the nation, with Franklin Roosevelt's Fala a close second." Asta also became famous abroad: on vacation in Denmark, the Hacketts found he had top billing at a movie house. "No mention of Loy or Powell at all!" Albert said. "They don't have many cats or dogs there, because of a high tax, and the cats and dogs that are there don't have much fun. There just aren't any smells. It is very pathetic to see the dogs running around wildly, not able to find a smell anywhere."[6]

In early September 1934, roughly two months after *The Thin Man*'s career-boosting reviews, Frances and Albert spent two weeks in Little Compton, playing tennis and softball, swimming in the surf, and going to parties. "Drank too many cocktails," my mother confessed to her diary during this time. "Feeling pretty rocky. Swim made me better." One evening, the Hacketts heard the monologues of an eccentric, English-born, sixty-five-year-old named Beatrice Herford, a long-time Goodrich family friend who had performed on Broadway, impersonating gabby boarding-house lodgers, prattling train passengers, and the kind of brat and addlepated mother "whose heads it would be a pleasure to crack together." "If there is a more entertaining woman extant," Alexander Woolcott once wrote about Beatrice, "someone has been concealing her from us."

For Frances and Albert, an important result of the success of *The Thin Man* was their friendship with Dashiell Hammett and his long-time companion, the outspoken, controversial playwright Lillian Hellman. "Dash and Lilly," Albert said, "were very satisfied with what we'd done, and that's how we got to know them."

The Hacketts' friendship with Samuel Dashiell Hammett spanned twenty-five-plus years. When they met him, he had already published the hard-boiled stories and novels—*The Thin Man,* of course, plus *The Dain Curse* and *The Maltese Falcon*—that rank him, some have said, among the most important American writers of the twentieth century. (Hammett's creative time, when he did his best work, was brief—1922 to 1934; after his Hollywood ventures, he tried another novel but ultimately aborted it.) Raymond Chandler, comparing Hammett's realistic style to genteel, British-influenced whodunits, once said, "He took murder out of the parlor and put it back in the alley, where it belongs." "He was a very good writer," Lillian Hellman said. "And while he was not of the very top level, he changed the face of much of American fiction."

Hammett felt that American life was far from perfect, and in his books he expressed a sense of confusion and dissatisfaction. A convinced Communist who refused to acknowledge the horrors of Stalinism, Hammett was also a man of integrity: in 1951, during "Commie-hunting" days, he went to jail for six months rather than give a federal court the records of an organization that provided bail for defendants arrested for political reasons. About his refusal, he said, "I have my own ideas about democracy. . . . I don't let cops or judges tell me what democracy is." He was intolerant of political dilettantes and jeered at the idea that Frances's Aunt Caro and two other "nice old ladies" had helped the *Daily Worker* through financial troubles. A lean, handsome former Pinkerton agent, Hammett was a fierce drinker, who squandered his large earnings on gambling, liquor, limousines, and whores. When he was drunk, he sometimes got into scrapes. Once, he asked Albert to send some money to a girl "in trouble." "I wondered if it was on the level," Albert said, "and Dash said, 'Ask her to describe the chandelier.'" On another occasion, at a party at Sid and

Laura Perelman's, Hammett hired a call girl as a joke and sent her up to the bathroom to strip. In Albert's words, "Sid went to the bathroom, and gee, he was gone a long time, and then Laura Perelman and whoever went up there and caught them *flagrante delicto*. That was a story. It ended with Laura going off to San Francisco with Hammett. . . . They were gone for days, and there was hell to pay all around."[7]

In the spring of 1938, the Hacketts figured in a notorious Hammett crack-up that was later described in various books in various ways. For many months, Hammett, then forty-three, had stayed sober. He was working desultorily on the third film in the *Thin Man* series, writing a treatment that the Hacketts were going to turn into a screenplay. Hellman was in New York, and Hammett was living at the Beverly Wilshire Hotel, in the spacious, gilded Royal Siamese Suite, which he liked because of its awful decor and corny name. He was unhappy with his work and had become reclusive. Although he wasn't drinking, he was growing steadily thinner and weaker—and in May, he started drinking again.

"[Dash wasn't eating]," Albert said. "We would try to get him to come to dinner now and again. . . . One day, a Sunday, I'd gone off to get a tennis lesson, and I came back and there was a note [from Frances, telling] me to come over to the hotel, that word had come [from Lillian Hellman] that Dash had said he'd do anything Frances said. Lilly had been trying to get him to go back to New York.

"I went over to the hotel. . . . I walked into the room and here was Dash asleep in a bed, and you know, he was about six feet two, and he weighed about a hundred and twenty-seven pounds then, so you could practically see through him. . . .

"Somebody said that Frances was down talking to the management. . . . I finally found out where she was and went in . . . and the manager was saying, 'Well, you're such a good friend of his, why don't you pay the bill?' And Frances was saying, 'I don't know anything about the bill, I just want to be sure he's taken care of.'

"Well, I had a feeling . . . if you owed a hotel a bill, they could attach your trunk or clothing and try to force you to pay. . . . And I couldn't figure out Frances saying that the money part had nothing to do with us. We'd been trying to get him to take some money, because we were afraid he wasn't eating. And he'd said, 'You can't give me money, I live flamboyantly.'

"So finally the manager went out of the room for a few minutes and I said, 'That money? We could—'

"She said, '*Shhhh*. His bill is eight thousand dollars! Eight thousand dollars!'

"Well, anyway, Frances and I got him out of the hotel and on a plane. We sent a wire to Lillian saying, 'We're putting him on a plane.' Lillian met him with an ambulance and took him to a hospital."[8] Albert's account raises a question: who found the $8,000—in those days a considerable sum? The record is unclear: one source says that the Hacketts "made an arrangement with the management"; another says that writer-director-producer Charles Brackett paid the bill.

Evidently, Frances and Albert were unaware of—or chose to ignore—Hammett's darker side, which occasionally led him to act cruelly, especially toward women. Albert once called him "a lovely man. Very amusing, very funny." To Albert, Hammett was an object of pity: "He wasn't well. . . . When he came out [of prison in 1951] he never really was the same. . . . They discovered that he had cancer. Lillian Hellman was wonderful. He stayed with her until he died [in 1961]. A lovely man."[9]

Frances and Albert were close to Lillian Hellman for roughly fifty years, and always in the relationship there were fondness and mutual respect—but also tension. Hellman was, in the words of her friend and lover Peter Feibleman, by turns "bombastic, opinionated, dazzling, enraging, funny, peevish, bawdy. . . . [She] was given to opposite extremes but the perversity was on a grand scale and somehow at her best she made it all work."[10] Albert reportedly once said, "The thing you've got to remember about Lilly is that she's basically contemptuous of most people."[11] Another time, he said, "Lilly never made any point of being kind to other women. There was a whole group that were ready to cut her head off. . . . Frances saw Lilly get rough with other women and said, 'If she ever let out on me like that, it would be the end.' But Frances was very admiring of Lilly and very vocal about it. I think Lilly knew there was a temper there too."[12]

When the Hacketts first met Hellman, she'd recently been divorced from Arthur Kober. She had worked at a book publishing house and as a reader for a theatrical producer but hadn't yet started the works that ultimately made her one of her generation's most original, most daring playwrights and a presence on the American scene. In addition to her dramas—including *The Children's Hour, The Little Foxes,* and *Watch on the Rhine*—and autobiographical books—*An Unfinished Woman, Pentimento,* and *Scoundrel Time*—Hellman became celebrated for her love affairs and political activism. (My father helped with one of those titles: in early 1973, he sent Hellman a definition of the word *pentimento,* and she wrote back, "I am acting my usual neurotic self about titles, but somewhere I am going to get in pentimento.") Though prickly, Hellman could also be generous—she helped the Hacketts greatly with *The Diary of Anne Frank*—and sometimes insightful and sensitive about other people. In 1977, after dinner with the Hacketts, who'd then been married for forty-six years, she said to Peter Feibleman (who described Frances and Albert as "spry and crackly and fun to be with"), "Did you see Albert's face when Frances tripped? . . . He turned white. He's more in love with her than he ever was. Imagine someone wanting you that long—just imagine."[13]

My wife, Patty, and I saw Lillian Hellman, expensively dressed and puffing cigarettes, at New York dinner parties given by the Hacketts, and the impression I got matched some of Feibleman's words (opinionated, bombastic, peevish). I seldom saw the dazzling, funny side; instead, she seemed, though a guest like the rest of us, to be grumpily holding court. Also at some of those parties was her old friend Sid Perelman, whose wife, Laura, had died in 1970 and who had grown morose and withdrawn. By this time, the Hellman-Perelman friendship had survived Laura's brief fling with Hammett, and the two seemed to enjoy each other's company. However, when they and the Hacketts shared a rented house in Sarasota, Florida, for several weeks in the winter of 1974, temperament reared its head.

The house had a housekeeper and a cook; on the cook's nights off, Hellman took over, with mixed results: Perelman wrote that she was good at spaghetti, boiled beef, and fish, but a pot roast "tasted like a shag rug." At first, Hellman and Perelman got along all right: in a letter to a friend, he merely reported that she was a

> curious mixture, part imperious yenta who throws her weight around and part amusing old friend when she and I and the Hacketts talk about old times in the movie biz and Broadway. She has a sense of her importance that frequently burns your ass. . . . We all get on together . . . though every so often I'm tempted to order Lillian to knock it off. (Should have said that I got here right in the middle of her being filmed by Bill Moyers . . .)

The only glamorous note supplied thus far consisted of a visit by Bill Blass, the dressmaker. L. H. spent the visit raving about some garment she had bought from Blass, and he indicated in seigneurial fashion that he would be pleased to make her a copy in corduroy or sisal or some recondite material. . . . He is very bronzed and (according to L. H. and Frances Hackett) good looking.[14]

So far, so good—but four days later, Perelman wrote to the same friend:

[I'm] in a cold rage at La Hellman, who I really think deserves to have her ass kicked roundly. Of all the imperious, arrogant spectacles . . . her behavior this evening takes the cake. . . . [The four of us] were dining at a supposedly chic restaurant-hotel. . . . Blass had told the hotel that she might be coming over . . . so there was a big tzimmas when we arrived. Swarms of fag headwaiters descended, we're swept to a table cheek to jowl with the Gulf of Mexico, and Hellman's beaming. . . . It emerges gradually . . . that the manager has presented our two bottles of second-rate Italian wine as freebies. . . . During the early ass-kissing of Miss H . . . the headwaiter told her that Senator Lowell Weicker was in the house and would join us at the end of the meal. Well, no Weicker shows up, and I suspect that this is what curdled Hellman's milk. . . .

So—we're . . . driving home and she in hoity-toity fashion declares that we should never have accepted the wine. "I *told* you we shouldn't be beholden—I make a point of never accepting anything in restaurants for free," etc., etc. Well, I stood it as long as I could, and at last I said, "Oh Lil, stop leaning on it, will you?" "I *will* lean on it," she snapped. "I don't want some fag going all over Florida telling people I accepted free wine" . . . she says with all the grandeur of Queen Isabella, Empress of Spain, and the Indies, Mexico, and the Iberian Air Line.[15]

# 7

## *Naughty Marietta* and *Ah, Wilderness!*

**H**ide-Out, released in August 1934, a month after *The Thin Man*, had a shaky beginning. "[Like] so many big studios," Albert said years later, "MGM was hoping to get quick pictures out, another picture every week for fifty-two weeks, because they had those theaters that had to be filled with something. And when they didn't have a product of their own, they had to take it from some other studio, which killed them. . . . So then word went out. . . . 'Every producer do a B picture quick.' . . . So we read [studio-owned] stories and found one that had an idea of a hide-out, and that was about all. . . . But we had [an idea] we had worked on once. . . . We blended the two stories. . . . But instead of being a B picture, it turned out to be an A picture. Robert Montgomery was in it . . . and Maureen O'Sullivan. And Mickey Rooney."[1] (Albert was mistaken in putting down the original story, by Mauri Grashin: it was nominated for an Oscar; the Hacketts' screenplay wasn't.)

As in *Fugitive Lovers*, in *Hide-Out* Montgomery again played a man on the run—in this case a New Yorker, Lucky Wilson, described in a *New York Times* review as "a pleasant, impertinent racketeer, whose affairs with women are many." Wounded by the police, Lucky takes refuge on a Connecticut farm complete with a farmer's daughter (O'Sullivan) and her younger brother (Rooney). Living on the farm among honest folk, doing honest work, hearing cocks crow and cows moo and crickets chirp—all these change Lucky's tough-guy outlook; when he's finally arrested, he goes to prison smiling because he knows O'Sullivan will be waiting when he gets out.

W. S. Van Dyke, who'd directed *Penthouse* and *The Thin Man*, also directed *Hide-Out*. Albert called his directing "strange. . . . He shot everything so fast. . . . There was an Irish actor in *Hide-Out* [Whitford Kane, from the Abbey Theater]. . . . He was used to days of rehearsal—there was no rehearsal with Van Dyke. Kane had to walk across the set with a teacup in his hand, and he shook so, and made such noise, that they had to cut the sound out. In the theater, when you had to walk with a teacup, you knew to put some water in the saucer, to keep it from rattling.[2]

"In one scene," Albert continued, "where Montgomery is wounded and in bed, Kane was told, 'Now you start right here at that doorway. When she answers the door, you take the cup and saucer, come down around the bed and carry it right off.' That was the rehearsal as far as Van Dyke was concerned. Kane says to someone 'What happens now?' 'They're going to shoot it.' 'Shoot it?' . . . He got back to New York so fast. . . . [He] couldn't understand how anyone could stand it. No rehearsal or anything."[3]

The reviewers' reaction to *Hide-Out* was mostly solid ("told with a pleasing naturalness and a certain subtlety. The dialogue is smartly written"), but it was also called perhaps too sweet: "achieves the feat of being decidedly pleasant saccharinity." To help theater owners promote the picture, MGM put out a wonderfully corny, twenty-page manual. "W. S. Van Dyke," it said, "who made *The Thin Man*, has caught the same spirit of swift drama, rollicking good humor—punch, sensation, and good clean fun. . . . Montgomery is swell. . . . Maureen O'Sullivan carries every scene she is in. . . . Montgomery is a ruthless night haunt habitué, the Romeo of the Rialto, the cause of many a female fluttering heart." The manual suggested that theater owners could run newspaper ads with lines like "[Montgomery] didn't like the farm but he followed a pair of pretty calves down the altar aisle." In the film, while milking a cow, Montgomery asked, "How're you, baby?"—surely one of Albert's lines—so the studio suggested a newspaper contest, with a prize of two free tickets, for "the most amusing answers from the cow!"

Van Dyke and the Hacketts teamed up again on *Naughty Marietta*, released in March 1935, a remake of the hardy, sentimental 1910 Victor Herbert operetta. Nominated for an Oscar as the year's best picture and now called a classic, this was Frances and Albert's first musical assignment; their job was to update the story, which dealt with a French princess (Jeanette Mac-Donald), fleeing from an arranged marriage and masquerading as a maid in eighteenth-century New Orleans, who's wooed by a gallant soldier (Nelson Eddy). The Hacketts did an outline; John Lee Mahin started the screenplay but then started drinking; they finished the screenplay. Again, the producer was Hunt Stromberg; he sent long, detailed memos concerning such questions as "Should MacDonald carry a purse?"

Working on *Naughty Marietta,* Frances and Albert got a taste of the control then exercised to ensure "wholesomeness." Joseph Ignatius Breen, an
ardent Catholic and the industry's official, all-powerful censor, sent six
single-spaced, typed pages of comments—for example, "The [italicized]
portion of the following lines should be dropped: 'yearning for the sound
of a sweet voice, *aching for the touch of a delicate hand*' and 'Surely in New
Orleans you have a place for a girl who doesn't wish necessarily to be a
housewife—*but who likes to be pleasant and charming?*'"⁴ (Sin-sniffing is, of
course, a job for the unenlightened, and Breen certainly was that. Although
the movies he drew his living from were almost all produced by Jews, he
could be venomously anti-Semitic: "Ninety-five percent of these folks are
Jews of an Eastern European lineage. They are, probably, the scum of the
earth." Breen once referred to Emile Zola as a "filthy Frenchman who grew
rich writing pornographic literature.")⁵

The songs in *Naughty Marietta*—Albert: "My God, those were famous
songs!"—included "I'm Falling in Love with Someone," "'Neath the
Southern Moon," and "Ah, Sweet Mystery of Life," and the critics loved
MacDonald and Eddy's singing, calling them "the queen of song-stars"
and "a thrilling thrush." This was the first of several tandem operettas; the
pair ultimately became known as the American cinema's greatest singing
duo. The MacDonald-Eddy films have since been called the pinnacle of
camp, but they were solidly entertaining. *Naughty Marietta* was revived in
1977, and the *New Yorker* commented, "It's an atrocity, of course, and one
of the most spoofed of all the Jeanette MacDonald–Nelson Eddy operettas,
and yet it has vitality and a mad sort of appeal. When the two profiles
come together as they sing, 'Ah, Sweet Mystery of Life,' it's beyond camp,
it's in a realm of its own."

Before its release, *Naughty Marietta* was tried out in the Los Angeles area,
and at one showing, Albert recalled, "[an audience reaction] card came,
saying, 'We saw the play in New York on our honeymoon and just now we
took our daughter, and everything was fine with the movie except when
Frank Morgan's fly was open.' [Morgan played the local governor.] Well,
this was an awful thing: we had to go back to the studio; none of us had
noticed. . . . We spent all day running the film, just looking for Frank Morgan's fly. . . . I think it was someone's idea of a joke. . . . We even looked at
film that hadn't been in the preview."⁶ Lillian Hellman told this same story,
which she may have heard from Albert, in one of her books—and added
her own punch line: "It was later discovered that the card had been written by a discarded mistress of a Metro official." Albert may also have told

the story to F. Scott Fitzgerald: in *The Last Tycoon,* the hero, the producer
Monroe Stahr (based on Irving Thalberg), tells one of his assistants, "Two
people at the sneak preview complained that Morgan's fly was open. . . .
I want that picture run over and over until you find that footage." Harold
Pinter also liked the story and used it in his screenplay for a 1977 version
of *The Last Tycoon,* which starred Robert DeNiro. The anecdote is plainly
immortal—and sometimes gets wondrously twisted: the *London Indepen-
dent's* 1995 obituary of Albert said it was he and Frances who, as a joke,
pseudonymously wrote the card reporting the open fly.

   (In show business, of course, people constantly borrow and change stories, and they also concoct them to enhance personal images. A friend of
the Hacketts whose mother acted in movies in the 1920s and 1930s told me
that her mother claimed she'd danced in the famous chorus line on the
wing of a plane, 10,000 feet in the air, in the Ginger Rogers–Fred Astaire
musical *Flying Down to Rio.* "My mother said she'd done that," the Hacketts' friend said, "but I've realized she probably didn't. But she wanted
to believe it—and after all, saying it didn't hurt anyone. A lot of Hollywood is like that—people pick up stories, and put themselves in them, to
build themselves up."[7] Interestingly, in its obituary of the mother, *Variety*
reported her wing-walking fantasy as fact.)

   *Naughty Marietta* was a favorite project of Louis B. Mayer, with a big
budget, sets covering many acres of the MGM lot, and over 1,000 actors
and extras; it premiered in Washington, D.C., reportedly in front of thirty-
five U.S. senators, several Supreme Court justices, and the Russian am-
bassador. Once again, the studio sent theater owners suggestions
concerning promotion; one was that "a sedan chair, of the type used as a
mode of transportation during the period of the story," could be rigged
up. "The [chair] may be empty and the windows mysteriously covered by
drapes, or a good-looking girl might be seated inside. A banner should
read, 'I'm on my way to see Jeanette MacDonald and Nelson Eddy in Victor Herbert's *Naughty Marietta.'*" The chair, MGM suggested, could be
"carried about town by two colored boys in costume."

Hunt Stromberg, the producer of *Naughty Marietta* (and of *The Thin Man*
and *Hide-Out*), was a former sportswriter and publicist, and an important
man at MGM. Tall and lanky, with untidy hair, wearing round-lensed
glasses, three-piece suits, and sometimes unlaced shoes, he looked more
like an eccentric professor than a Hollywood producer, and his story
conferences were held in clouds of pipe smoke. A workaholic, he was

interested in all kinds of story material; one of his colleagues called him "truly phenomenal, with a quick and prodigious intellect. . . . Everyone around him likes him so well that they can refuse him nothing." To the Hacketts, Stromberg was a hero: "It was wonderful working with him. . . . It was like the theater. He gave you the responsibility. You were consulted about casting and you saw all the rushes and you were part of the whole project."[8] Another time, they commented, "He was good, he encouraged us, he was darling to us. . . . [When] we brought a script in, he'd say—which very few people did—'This is just fine! Now we're off, now we're going!'[9] He had great plot sense—he always knew what was wrong with a story. He respected writers. He didn't tamper with our lines."

So strong was Frances and Albert's attachment to Hunt Stromberg that when their contract came up for renewal in March 1935, they signed for less than their Hollywood agent thought they should, just to keep working with him (the new contract gave them $1,750 a week the first year, and $2,000 the second). "If we go to another studio," Frances wrote to Leah Salisbury, "everything might go wrong. No credits, bad supervision. You have no conception of what other writers go through. And we never have any trouble at all. And we feel that our confidence and trust in Hunt, and our friendship, and our perfect relationship and ease and comfort with him, are worth the sacrifice of immediate money, which is all the other might be. We cannot work under adverse circumstances. We cannot work if we are not happy. We cannot work if we are fighting against a producer. . . . And those are the things every writer out here is up against. For these comforts, and even *necessities,* we are willing to sacrifice somewhat."

Plainly, Frances and Albert were nearly spellbound by Hunt Stromberg —but to some other writers, he was less enthralling. The Hacketts' good friend Donald Ogden Stewart reported that he would bring a "tender love scene" to Stromberg's office, where, after reading it, the producer would stride around waving a riding crop and "spitting freely as he moved and more fiercely as he talked. 'Son,' he would say, 'I like it (spit). I think it's a fine scene (spit). But how about that dumb Scranton miner? Would he understand it?' Hunt had never been in Scranton and I don't think he'd ever seen a miner, but every bit I wrote had to get the commendation of that mythic creature."[10] Dashiell Hammett also had a less-than-awed view of Stromberg. Frances remembered a time when Hammett upset him by taking a cat's-eye ring away from him. "Hammett said, 'Let me see that, Hunt,' and then wouldn't give it back, and Hunt pretended not to care, but . . . he was always calling, to find out how he could get that ring back—

he thought it was his good luck. Of course, Hammett gave it back eventually. Oh, he was so naughty."

From Hunt Stromberg, the Hacketts next got the job of adapting Eugene
O'Neill's only comedy, *Ah, Wilderness!* Years later, Frances said they welcomed the assignment—"That's when doing an adaptation is really wonderful, when you have a lovely thing like that to do"—but at the time she
and Albert were not enthused. "We are now trying to make a movie out of
*Ah, Wilderness!* with a little hokum and scenes on the beach and so forth,"
she wrote to my father. "I thought it was going to be an easy job, but . . . it
isn't . . . and in the end we'll be called 'over-zealous studio writers who
have spoiled O'Neill's masterpiece.'" Later, she wrote, "*Ah, Wilderness!* has
been postponed. . . . They . . . or rather *we* have all decided we've gone all
wrong. We've [stuck closely] to the play, and so it is so static it is terrible.
Perhaps now that we have written it, cut down to its very meat, we may
have the guts to depart from it. But it takes a lot of nerve." The Hacketts
found the nerve: when the film was released in December 1935, it got
splendid reviews, with particular praise for a high school graduation scene
that was their original work.

Set around 1905 in a small, picturesque Connecticut town (actually, it
was shot in Grafton, Massachusetts), starring Lionel Barrymore, Wallace
Beery, and Mickey Rooney, and centered around a closely knit family, *Ah,
Wilderness!* tells the simple, nostalgic story of a summer during which the
seventeen-year-old son first encounters the upsets of adolescence: infatu-
ation, frustrated idealism, learning the "facts of life" from his father. During the writing, Frances and Albert again got memos from Stromberg ("It
is all too casual now. Too thrown away. Too scattered and thinly sketched
to make much of a dent on the emotions. . . . We must . . . mirror a representative family of representative Americans in a representative American
town. The father in Oshkosh and the mother in Joliet must see themselves
on the screen"). Also, they again ran into censorship, "what you might call,"
Albert said, "the 'Catholic' viewpoint—twin beds and all that. . . . They
would not allow the man and his wife to be in the same bed, just to open
up a scene—the Fourth of July, firecrackers going off, and the husband getting up. [We] had to put in twin beds."[11] (Concerning censorship at that
time, Albert once joked that the only kind of marital infidelity that could
be shown was "one man taking another man's wife to lunch." Donald
Ogden Stewart, the writer of the 1939 picture *Love Affair,* said that because
the heroine, Irene Dunne, had sinned by living with another man before

meeting the hero, Charles Boyer, she "had to pay for it. . . . So Irene and Boyer were going to meet on the top of the Empire State Building, and . . . the censors suggested that I have her run over by a truck on her way there and that's what happened, she never got to the top. You dissolved to her in a hospital . . . realizing that God hadn't wanted her to meet Boyer until she was sorry for what she had done before. So finally she married Boyer, and all came out well.")[12]

In one of *Ah, Wilderness!*'s most moving scenes, the father and elder son discuss the previous evening, when the boy got drunk and was lured by a prostitute to her bedroom—where they simply talked. In the play, O'Neill had the father ask, "How about that tart you went to bed with?" According to Albert, George M. Cohan, who played the part in the original Broadway production, changed the line to "What about the woman last night?"—which was less shocking. Will Rogers was expected to play the father in the movie; before production started, he went on a road tour in the play and spoke the original words, which upset his prudish fans. As a result, he withdrew from the film. "Rogers," Frances wrote to Leah Salisbury, "talked to [a top MGM executive] and told him that the company was trying to force him to be a party to an OBSCENE, SENSATIONAL PICTURE! . . . Of course we have cleaned it up entirely in the [movie]script . . . had to, for the censors . . . [but Rogers is] definitely out." Instead of Rogers, Lionel Barrymore played the part. Albert thought he was "dreary and dull," but many critics praised his performance.

Will Rogers wasn't the only star who decided not to appear in the film version of *Ah, Wilderness!* Early on, W. C. Fields was set to play the part of hard-drinking Uncle Sid, and Albert said that was "very exciting. . . . We tailored the part and gave him a couple of special scenes." However, Fields dropped out and was replaced by Wallace Beery, who created problems. "[He] wouldn't say the lines," Albert recalled. "He wouldn't say O'Neill's lines! Anything that came into his head, he'd say, but not O'Neill."[13] Some critics rebuked Beery for his ego flexing: "Except for Wallace Beery, playing Wallace Beery as usual, the film has been beautifully cast." Albert remembered Beery as a "very nasty man around the studio. . . . [People said] that when a picture was over, he'd look at a piece of scenery—a chair or something that he liked—and he'd pick it up . . . [and they'd] say, 'Oh, wait a minute, we might have some retakes,' and he'd say, 'I'll have it. If you want to retake it, it'll be at my house.' . . . You know, actors are funny."[14]

The first Oscars were given out in 1929. For the next several years, the studios refrained from promoting their movies in the trade papers before the awards ceremony, but in 1935, for *Ah, Wilderness!*, MGM broke the un-written rule and ran an advertisement, a cartoon showing an Oscar stat-uette with the film's title around its neck standing next to Leo the Lion, MGM's trademark. The lion had its arms raised triumphantly, and the cap-tion said, "Leo, you've given so much . . . get ready to receive!" The ploy didn't work (or perhaps backfired): *Ah, Wilderness!* didn't get a single Academy nomination. All the same, the fine reviews—including "It is a film for the discriminating"—must have pleased Frances and Albert. What didn't please them was having their names left off the program of the film's New York opening. This problem—occasionally being given no recognition by the studio—persisted for some years, until (as we'll see) the Hacketts fought back.

Frances and Albert were now beginning to enjoy living in Southern Cali-fornia, among friends, with challenging work—but they didn't care for the endless summer. "We're having the strangest weather," Frances wrote in January 1934, during the writing of *Ah, Wilderness!* "Yesterday it was 88 in the sun. All wrong, and gives you Spring fever." She also missed going walking: "The greatest of luxuries out here, walks." About this time, she and Albert met Billy Wilder, the Austrian-born writer-director-producer whose pictures include *The Lost Weekend, Sunset Boulevard,* and *Some Like It Hot.* Once described as looking like a "libidinous owl," and famed as a raconteur, Wilder said about the Hacketts that he "liked them enormously. . . . When I came to Hollywood in '34, nobody knew me, nor did I know any English. . . . But they had seen a couple of pictures which I did in Ger-many, in the German language, and they liked them very much. . . . We met in the MGM commissary, and they dragged me all through MGM to all the producers [including Hunt Stromberg]. . . . They had a wonderful spiel. . . . They tried to sell me as hard as I've ever seen anybody trying. . . . My English was non-existent; we kind of spoke by sign language, or a word here or there, that I knew in English, or they knew in German. . . .
   "They were most sympathetic, and helpful—they kind of made a great big, European, deep-dish philosophical writer out of me. . . . Nothing re-ally came of it, but they spoke very well of me. That was very important, because they were just about on the top of the list of serious motion pic-ture writers.
   "I had many a dinner with Goodrich and Hackett with my [later] col-laborator, Mr. [Charles] Brackett. . . . They were wonderful, liberal people, much beloved in Hollywood."[15]

One of the reasons Frances and Albert tried to help newcomers like Wilder was that they knew success in the movie business wasn't easily attained—and could vanish overnight.

"In Hollywood," Albert once said, "they say, 'You're only as good as your last picture.' They are constantly looking at somebody and saying, 'Well, he's been up there a long time; any minute now they'll pull the rug out from under him.' In other words, he'll find that he no longer has an audience. When a picture goes out and it doesn't make money, then they become very suspicious that the man is slipping. . . .

"Hollywood can be very cruel. The moment they think somebody has no longer got that magic touch, they don't speak to him. Even the gateman won't speak to him. This is where they're really rough. The way they fuss over a director—or an actor or actress! And when they lose out, it breaks your heart. They're still dressing the same way, looking the same way, living the same way—and not making any money. It's very discouraging. You see so many people just destroyed, so quickly."[16]

Into the late 1930s, the Hacketts lived in Beverly Hills, on North Palm Drive and North Canon Drive, and worked hard, often not getting home until after dark—which required Albert to use a flashlight to check the vegetables in his lovingly tended gardens (although born a city boy, once he discovered Nature, he became highly skilled with rakes and hoes and pruning tools). "We tried not to get tired," he recalled. "That was the most important thing. . . . You know, when you're working against a [deadline], you're always scrambling around. . . . And then they make a change of some sort, and you have to go back and do something over—you were constantly trying to get something good or do better."[17] Frances and Albert spent some of their leisure time with James Cagney and his wife, Billie, once going on a weekend cruise to Catalina Island ("a grand rest," Frances wrote, "steamed around, and had a swim and a swell time") and also attending the Cagneys' parties. In his autobiography, Cagney described big Hollywood parties of the 1930s and later years as a "complete waste of good living time"; then he confessed that he and Billie *gave* "so-called big parties, but we always had people who were real fun, like George Burns and Gracie, Dick Powell and June [Allyson, Powell's second wife] and of course the Frank McHughs, the Hacketts, the Pat O'Briens."[18]

Cagney, O'Brien, and McHugh were part of the "1930s Hollywood Irish Mafia." While making their films, in the evening they entertained one another and friends like the Hacketts, and McHugh was sometimes the lead entertainer. Round-faced, with a "spunky snicker," McHugh once said his typical supporting part was easy to do: "I play a dumb cluck—there's nothing to it." Like Albert, he had started performing as a child and in the early 1900s had appeared often in a melodrama called *Human Hearts, An Idyll of the Arkansaw Hills.* This chestnut covered adultery, murder, and wrongful imprisonment and had wonderfully corny lines; McHugh's widow, Dorothy, said that in the late 1930s, McHugh came across a copy and took it to parties and suggested that everyone act out scenes after dinner.

"This was the Cagneys, the O'Briens, the Hacketts, and Dick Powell and Joan Blondell—they were married at that time—and Chester Morris," Mrs. McHugh said. "Frank would be the director, because he knew every word, every movement. . . . At first, everyone would say, 'I don't want to do it.' I don't know, maybe they didn't want to act in front of one another. But then they'd get carried away, and *want* to do it. . . . [Although I'd been an actress] I stuck to it—'No, no, no'—and I had a wonderful time watching it all."[19] Mrs. McHugh's pleasure is understandable. Imagine sitting alone, after dinner, an audience of one, with Pat O'Brien thundering, "Don't you dare to harm my child!" and Joan Blondell (or Frances) doing, "Will my Papa come back some day?" and Cagney snarling, "Now, you touch her if you dare!"

Albert also recalled those evenings—but according to him, they had a purpose beyond entertainment. At that time, he said, few of his fellow actors really believed that the movie business was going to prosper—and Cagney was particularly skeptical. "Once a week, a bunch of us would go over to Jimmy Cagney's house," Albert said. "Jimmy was already a big star, but he'd want us to put on a play with him—the first act of some melodrama—just so we'd stay fresh. Jimmy'd say, 'Look, when this picture stuff is over, we're going to have to go back to New York and *work,* so we'd better be ready.'"[20]

Together with memorable evenings, Frances and Albert also lived through great work pressures in the 1930s and fled east whenever possible. After the preview of one of their early films, they said to a man from the studio (probably Stromberg), "We're supposed to have a vacation. . . . Can we go now?"

"He said," Albert remembered, "'Well, I don't think there's anything more to be done, it looks fine to me.'

"I had a nickel in my pocket, so we went out and called Jim Cagney and got his wife. She always had money in a boodle bag around her neck—

they had played vaudeville, the two of them, when they were dancing together. . . . So I said, 'Have you got any money?' And she said, 'How much?' And I said, 'About three hundred dollars.' She said, 'Okay, I'll be in The Pig And Whistle.' . . . [that was] a little restaurant that was well-known around there. . . .

"So we went back and [packed quickly] . . . and picked up the Philippino boy who worked for us, and went over to The Pig And Whistle, got the three hundred dollars from Billie Cagney, and drove down to San Pedro and got on a boat. We needed the money to get on that boat. It left at one o'clock or something. . . . The next morning at eleven o'clock we woke up and we were off San Diego, on our way through the Canal up to New York. . . . That was how quickly we could get out of California."[21]

# 8

# Fighting for Writers' Rights

**A**s Frances and Albert saw during their early Hollywood years, the Golden Age's rapidly expanding film industry attracted writers in extraordinary numbers. Some, such as Dorothy Parker, F. Scott Fitzgerald, and Sid Perelman, were famous, and their movieland experiences have been described often; others are less well remembered today—but having them as friends and working alongside them added to the fun and stimulation of the Hacketts' Hollywood time. To digress for a moment and briefly mention four:

Samson Raphaelson was born in New York in 1896. After graduating from the University of Illinois, he worked at a Chicago ad agency and started selling short stories to magazines. One day he read a play script and decided to devote a weekend to adapting one of his stories to the stage; later, he rewrote it several times. In 1925, the play, titled *Day of Atonement*, was produced on Broadway, starring George Jessel. In 1927, the play was the basis for *The Jazz Singer*, starring Al Jolson and sometimes called "history's first talkie." (In fact, *The Jazz Singer* wasn't the first major picture that used sound, nor was it an "all-talkie": much of it was silent, and Jolson spoke only 281 words—but those words, and his singing of songs like "Mammy" and "Toot, Toot, Tootsie, Goodbye" changed the movie business forever. The advent of sound has been called "the most sensational event in motion picture history.") Raphaelson went on to write a dozen more plays and almost as many screenplays, several of which were directed by Ernst Lubitsch. He could be funny: "Once I wrote something called *The Wooden Slipper*, which lasted about three days on Broadway. . . . [Afterward], I dreaded to show myself on the street. I thought that everywhere I went people would be saying, 'There goes the man who wrote *The Wooden Slipper*.' I quickly found out that . . . nobody cared."[1] During the 1930s, when the Hacketts first met him, he lived in a Hollywood mansion complete with butler, but the "unaccustomed magnificence" made him uncomfortable, and he returned east; ultimately, he and his wife lived right around the corner from the Hacketts. For ten years before his death in 1983, he taught playwriting at Columbia University.

Chicago also figured in Maurine Dallas Watkins's history—in fact, her 1926 Broadway comedy hit—in which a red-headed showgirl, Roxy Hart, murders her boyfriend, confesses, and is acquitted by an all-male jury— was titled *Chicago*. Born in Kentucky and raised in Indiana, small and pretty and also strong and resourceful, Watkins in her mid-twenties be- came a crime reporter for the *Chicago Tribune*, where she found the back- ground for her play. In Hollywood, she worked on screenplays for MGM, and Frances and Albert remembered a "wonderful" handbag that held all of her important possessions, so that if she decided she'd had enough, she could walk right out of the studio. Sometime in the 1940s, Watkins *did* quit Hollywood, thereafter living reclusively in Florida with her widowed mother, turning to religion and astrology, and earning money by writing Hallmark greeting card messages. In 1959, hoping to do a stage musical version of *Chicago* with Gwen Verdon in the lead, the Hacketts wrote Watkins a warm letter, mentioning their accomplishments since the early days. Watkins sent a jokey, equally friendly reply, saying, in part, "Well. In 1927 Lindbergh carried across the Atlantic the world's least-needed letter of introduction—and 32 years later the Hacketts top it by listing their 'credits!' Where have You All been not to know Who You Are?" For years, Watkins had refused to authorize a musical adaptation; with the Hacketts, she stayed consistent. She died in 1969; four years later, without the Hack- etts' help, a Broadway musical was produced, starring—of course—Gwen Verdon; it ran for 923 performances and made everyone involved even richer than before, and in 1996 it was revived and was a hit again.

Raphaelson and Watkins used imagination and energy to start their writing careers; Nat Perrin added audacity. In late 1930, just out of law school but smitten by show business, Perrin sent one of his comic sketches, accompanied by an introductory note on the stationery of a leading agent, backstage to the Marx Brothers while they were performing in a theater in Brooklyn. Perrin had swiped the stationery and composed the note; he soon found himself in California, writing jokes for one of history's great- est comedy teams. It's been said that Chico Marx took a special liking to the phrase "Atsa fine, boss," which Perrin thought up, because he could mutter it whenever he forgot the actual line he was supposed to deliver. One of the Marx Brothers pictures Perrin worked on was *Monkey Business;* its director, a retiring fellow named Norman McLeod, used to say of him- self, "I'm as quiet as a mouse pissing on a blotter." Perrin went on to great success, writing many films for many other performers, and along the way, partly at bridge parties, got to know the Hacketts. He liked and admired them, calling them "very civilized," and when his daughter was applying to Vassar, he asked Frances if she'd write a letter of recommendation. "Most people," he told me, "would write a letter automatically, but Frances had to meet my daughter and be convinced she was a suitable candidate. . . . My daughter justified her belief in her: she was Phi Beta Kappa, class of 1961, and is now a judge here in California."

Philip Dunne was the son of Finley Peter Dunne, the political humorist who created the mythical Irish bartender Mr. Dooley ("Trust everybody— but cut the cards" was a famous Dooleyism). Philip grew up in New York—his father's friend Teddy Roosevelt often dropped by the house and urged the young Dunne to punch him in the stomach—and went to the "best" schools and Harvard. He got started in Hollywood as a script reader at Fox, and by the time of his death at eighty-four, in 1992, had written or cowritten thirty-six films—he was proudest of *How Green Was My Valley*—and directed ten. He took a dim view of movie critics, pointing out that one had said that in his script for *The Count of Monte Cristo*, "the Alexandre Dumas dialogue stood up with as much power and nobility as ever," but, in fact, the script contained exactly one line actually written by Dumas. One of the founders of Americans for Democratic Action, Dunne wrote articles and books, plus speeches for Franklin Roosevelt, Adlai Stevenson, and John Kennedy. He once recalled that his political activism had led to his being labeled everything from "crypto-fascist," "reactionary," "pseudo-liberal," "fellow-traveler," and "Communist stooge" to "radical Jew actor." The last label, he wrote, was stuck on him "in Adolf Hitler's journalistic outlet in Los Angeles, the *Weckruf und Beobachter*, whose reporter clearly had failed to do his homework: I am not now and have never been an actor." He called screenwriting "not so much an art as it is like fine cabinet-making. . . . We never claimed to be artists, but we thought we were good craftsmen." Asked if he considered writing more important in filmmaking than directing, he replied, "The writing is more important. The architect is more important than the contractor. I'm not saying the writer is more important than the director, I'm saying the writing is more important than the directing. Directing is only interpretation."[2] On two different occasions, listing the screenwriters he admired most, Dunne put Frances and Albert first: "They are *professionals* whose name on a script is a guarantee of its excellence."

These four people had satisfying careers, and earned good money, but as Frances and Albert saw when they first arrived in Hollywood, many younger, less experienced screenwriters were stuck at the bottom of the pecking order—far below stars, directors, and producers—and were mistreated in many ways, including having to write on speculation, being lent to other studios or laid off briefly without pay, and often getting low pay and no credit. An extreme example was a friend of theirs, William Ludwig, who as a member of MGM's Junior Writing Department turned out 1938's *Love Finds Andy Hardy*, starring Judy Garland and Mickey Rooney, in fifteen days, and got paid $74. "The previous Andy Hardy pictures hadn't done well," Ludwig recalled, "and the studio was looking for the cheapest screenwriter possible. They gave me a secretary, and I wrote a full, fade-in-to-fade-out screenplay, which they shot. Afterwards, they raised my pay to $50 a week. That movie took in $6 million domestic."[3] (Ludwig later became highly successful; in 1955, he received an Oscar for writing *Interrupted Melody*.)

In past years, Hollywood's screenwriters had tried to create an organization that could fight back but had failed. In the spring of 1933, new hope came with the birth of the Screen Writers Guild, and the Hacketts offered to help. Both of them cared about their fellow writers, believed in supporting underdogs, and were already members of the Dramatists Guild and Actors Equity, which had successfully fought management back in New York. In the summer of 1919, during the historic strike that forced producers to recognize Equity, Albert, who had a part in a play, walked out; with her actress friend Margalo Gillmore, Frances carried a picket sign outside a show called *The Better 'Ole*, "telling people not to go in. . . . That was one of the most exciting, stimulating times of my life."

During the stormy early years of the Screen Writers Guild, Frances and Albert worked hard, recruiting members, raising funds, and organizing meetings at home and elsewhere. Albert served on the executive board; in 1937 and 1938, Frances was secretary. (Albert, deadpan: "She was smarter than I and she's got dignity—and I don't have any. . . . They put me on the board because I drove her to the meetings."[4] Frances also gave time to the Motion Picture Relief Fund, which had been established in the 1920s to help movie industry employees of all kinds; she served on the Case Committee, which allocated sums to those in need.) In one way or another, the Hacketts stayed close to the guild for many years: in late 1959, for example, they served on one of the committees that organized an historic, eight-month-long strike which produced significant changes in writers' compensation.

The creation of the Screen Writers Guild was linked to the bank holiday Franklin Roosevelt ordered after his inauguration. Earlier in 1933, movie theater receipts had slumped as the depression deepened, and many studio-owned theaters had closed; the producers feared that, with the banks closed, the public would soon be short of cash, further deflating movie attendance. In response, the Academy of Motion Picture Arts and Sciences, nowadays best known for awarding the Oscars, but then, in effect, the producers' company union, recommended that all movie studio employees earning over $50 per week accept eight-week, 50 percent pay cuts.

At MGM, Louis B. Mayer called a meeting of stars, directors, writers, and department heads and made one of his typical, teary, impassioned speeches—he was a shameless manipulator—asking them to "help save the studio." He was reportedly red-eyed and unshaven and at the start broke down, "stricken," and held out his hands, "supplicating, bereft of words," saying that Metro had run out of money. Frances and Albert were there; when Mayer had finished, Lionel Barrymore spoke in favor of the pay cut. Ernest Vadja, a writer, questioned the cut, pointing out that Metro pictures were doing well at the box office and suggesting that everyone wait and see. Then Barrymore, Frances recalled, "said in that famous voice of his, 'You are acting like a man on his way to the guillotine waiting to stop for a manicure.' Everyone got very pious and scared about the possibility that the studio might shut down, so we took the pay cut. Most of us had never had so much money . . . and we preferred a few tough weeks instead of the end of the pastures of plenty."[5]

According to Samuel Marx, then MGM's story editor, after the meeting, which had exhausted the others, Mayer turned to an assistant and jovially asked, "So! How did I do?" Told about that, Albert made a comment that has often been quoted: "Oh, that Louis B. Mayer! He created more Communists than Karl Marx." Albert might have been even tougher on Mayer if he'd known that MGM's economic problems were caused partly by bloated bonuses; it's been reported that in that period, 20 to 25 percent of the net earnings of Hollywood's major studios went to a small handful of production chiefs, studio owners, and New York executives.

Obviously, Albert disliked Louis B. Mayer, and he showed that again in 1937, when he and Philip Dunne were sent by the Screen Writers Guild to plan anti-producer strategy with members of the newly formed Directors Guild. In his memoirs, Dunne wrote that, commenting half-jokingly on an auto workers' strike then under way in Detroit, the cocky Victor Fleming (who later directed *The Wizard of Oz* and *Gone with the Wind*) said he'd handle the strikers with a machine gun: "Poke it through the window,

and mow the bastards down." Then the directors learned that the producers had refused to recognize their guild—and Fleming suggested that
they stage their own strike: "Tomorrow morning we walk onto the set as
usual, sit down beside the camera—and that's it. We don't rehearse, we
don't roll the cameras, we don't do one goddamned thing."

"There was a moment of reverent silence," Dunne added, "and then Albert Hackett spoke up, with that air of wide-eyed innocence with which
he always camouflaged his often lethal wit. 'That's a great idea, Vic,' he
said, 'but what do you do when Louis B. Mayer pokes a machine gun
through the window and starts mowing *you* down?'"[6]

(Sid Perelman disliked Mayer, too—he disliked almost all Hollywood
moguls—and he also found him peculiar. Mayer, Perelman once told an
interviewer, "could have summoned any star to his bedside with the crook
of a finger. Instead, he had this fixation about rhumba dancers. So that
there should be no delay, they kept a bevy of them in a special house
nearby with a permanent rhumba band always tuning up.")[7]

The 1933 pay cut created problems for Mayer and the other producers:
it exposed the Academy's domination of the industry and the arrogance
and selfishness of the producers, causing agitation at the studios. Some
of it was pointless: on March 13, Albert wrote that there had been a rumor
that "a plane was to fly over the studio as a signal for all the union employees to walk out in protest against the cut. Crowds of supervisors and
executives stood out in the studio's main street and had their eyes glued
to the sky. Nothing happened. A gull flew over later but dropped no message." Although full salaries were eventually resumed, craft groups, including the Screen Writers Guild, were soon formed. Predictably, the
producers reacted with threats and harassment—but the Hacketts felt
secure.

"We were not afraid of losing our jobs," Albert said. "We didn't care if
they fired us—we would go back to New York and back on the stage. We
were on the [guild's] board because they didn't frighten us. . . . We just
avoided talking [to studio executives] about the guild, because . . . we
knew they had to be against [it. . . . Hunt Stromberg wasn't sympathetic to
the guild] but we were very, very close to him and very fond of him. And
he said to somebody, 'If the Hacketts are on that side, I'll stick with the
Hacketts,' or something like that."[8]

After Frances became the guild's secretary, she was subjected to great
pressure—at one point, the producers took her and her genial, urbane

friend Charles Brackett, then the vice president of the guild (who also happened to be a Harvard-trained lawyer), to court. "The studios," Albert recalled years later, "had a big powerful lawyer. . . . [He] was trying to get the names of all the members, saying to Frances [who was on the witness stand], 'You're the Secretary?' 'Yes.' 'How many members are there in the organization?' 'I don't know exactly.' 'Well, who are they?' 'I don't know that. I can't remember their names.' 'Certainly you know some of the names.' She kept saying she couldn't remember, couldn't remember. . . . Charlie Brackett kept smiling at this [lawyer. The lawyer] was so belligerent, and Charlie was so amused. . . . And the lawyer finally said, 'Your Honor, will you ask him to stop smiling at me?'"[9]

During its first three years, the Screen Writers Guild grew slowly in membership. In 1936, it asked for federal legislation protecting the ways an author's material could be used. The producers retaliated by forming another union, the Screen Playwrights, which has been called "spurious" — Frances called them "The Screen Playrats" — and threatening to blacklist writers who didn't resign from the guild. Among those who controlled the new union were Mayer and Jack Warner; Warner was famed for calling screenwriters "schmucks with Underwoods." Many writers caved in to the arm twisting; the Hacketts and others, including Dorothy Parker, responded by inviting writers to meetings in their homes and campaigning elsewhere.

"The pressure at MGM was relentless," Frances said. "[The studio had influential people] around all the time, day after day, talking to writers, particularly the young writers, the ones who were just starting. . . . So we proselytized, too. We walked around [the] lot, and so did Lilly Hellman, and we talked to the young kids . . . but only on our lunch hour, so that no one could ever say we had used studio time for union activities. And we couldn't do our proselytizing on the phone, of course, because [the studio] boys were always listening in."[10] One of the chief promoters of the Screen Playwrights was the writer John Lee Mahin; Frances called him "the man [Albert and I] had to . . . help out on three pictures, because he got drunk on the job."

Among the young writers who joined the guild, and experienced the producers' pressures, was Bill Ludwig (who, as mentioned before, was once paid $74 for fifteen days' work). "The studio had representatives outside guild meetings," he said. "They'd take down your name, and the next day you'd be called upstairs and asked, 'What do you want to get mixed up with those Communist bastards for? We'll take care of you—you're part of the family!'"[11] Another writer the guild recruited was Ring Lardner Jr., later a two-time Oscar-winner, for *Woman of the Year* and *M*A*S*H*.

"In 1937," Lardner said, "I was preempted into the guild [as a board member] to represent the young writers. . . . I was twenty-one. . . . It was a very distinguished board; Frances was secretary. . . . We would meet every Monday night. I was at Warner Brothers [and sometimes talked] to writers about joining the guild. There was one in particular, George Bricker, who was the ultimate hack. . . . He had more credits than anybody—sixty credits, all on B pictures. George was a very difficult, uncultured man who had joined the Screen Playwrights. I interviewed him and got the story of why he'd joined and how he felt about the guild, and the way he talked was so unusual that I wrote it down. I read my version at a guild board meeting, and Frances said, 'You're really your father's son.' I read this thing in Bricker's language, and she said, 'That sounds like Ring Lardner.' I was very flattered."[12]

When Catherine Turney, best remembered for cowriting the script of 1945's *Mildred Pierce,* first arrived in Hollywood, she was recruited into the Screen Playwrights by two older men who said "they were the ones to join with . . . all the big writers had signed with them. . . . It [sounded] like a good career move. . . . Then Frances Hackett [said to me], 'How could you sign with them? They're in with the producers.'" Turney resigned from the Screen Playwrights and joined the guild. A full fifty years after the battles between the unions, she observed, "The things that happened [then] . . . caused a great deal of bitterness. These wounds were never really healed. There are still people who, when they're invited to dinner, ask who's coming. They don't want to mix with their old enemies. It's very sad."[13]

One of the people who reacted with strong emotions during the Screen Writers Guild's troubled times was Lillian Hellman: at meetings, she would stand up and accuse the others of self-interest and timidity while facing "intolerable injustice." "While the rest of us considered various tactics against the studios and the dangers involved," Albert said, "Lillian would contemptuously brush such caution aside and say something like, 'They're bastards. Let's clean them out!'"[14] Albert's less-aggressive approach sometimes caused disagreements with Frances: "Frances was more liberal than I, so now and then we were not voting the same way. . . . I was going the other way on some things because I could see more fights coming up."[15] The author Nore Sayre said that at one meeting of guild executives, after Frances had voted with the "leftist" side on a certain issue, one of the more conservative members said to her, "very seriously, very formally, 'Mrs. Hackett, you have just fucked the guild.' There was an enormous gasp: the idea of saying that to Frances, who was such a lady!" Sayre added that, recounting the episode, Frances sounded "proud—quite pleased."[16]

Despite hard work by the Hacketts, Hellman, Dorothy Parker, and others, the lobbying efforts of the Screen Playwrights disrupted the guild and drastically shrank its membership. At one point, prospects were so bleak that the guild's organizers "went underground," keeping their activities clandestine. Then, in early 1938, they petitioned the National Labor Relations Board for a binding election in which writers would choose membership in either the guild or the Screen Playwrights by secret ballot.

The election was scheduled for late June; in the preceding weeks, supporters of both unions campaigned hard. A book by Nancy Lynn Schwartz quoted Frances concerning an afternoon recruiting party hosted by Dashiell Hammett in his Beverly Wilshire Hotel suite "that had been occupied by the President of Mexico, or some shah, or something like that": "It was a big place and [Dash] was about six feet two—as you got off the elevator and looked down the hall, he was standing in the doorway, and even he looked like a little boy because the place was so huge. Everybody was coming up there and ordering a drink, getting people to come in there and talk, getting them to join the [guild]. Lillian Hellman came out of a room where she'd been talking to a writer named Talbot Jennings, a big writer at MGM who did some additional dialogue for Shakespeare in *Romeo and Juliet*. And poor Lillian came out of the room and said, 'Well, if I get Talbot Jennings to join this thing, somebody's got to pay for the abortion.'" Albert added, "Dottie Parker was in another room talking to a writer named Everett Freeman, trying to get him to join the guild, and he said he didn't think any creative writer should belong to a union . . . and Dottie simply could not stand that and she lost her patience. 'That sonofobitch, telling me that *he's* a creative writer! If he's a creative writer, then I'm [Queen] Marie of Rumania.'"[17]

In their efforts to turn out voters, the Hacketts got mixed results. Herman Mankiewicz, an acerbic wit whose scripts included *Citizen Kane*, ridiculed highly paid writers who uttered working-class slogans ("Look at that son of a bitch Communist! Look at him driving his Jaguar!"); according to columnist-author Sheilah Graham, the Hacketts "stormed" at him, "You just don't care. You don't care what happens to the little people. But that is perhaps because you don't know any little people earning fifty dollars a week,"[18] but got nowhere. Frances and Albert were anxious to get the vote of their friend (and Graham's lover) F. Scott Fitzgerald, then writing scripts at MGM for Hunt Stromberg. In his case, they succeeded: "I promised I would deliver Scott to vote," Graham wrote, "'if I have to carry him there.' . . . Scott was recovering from a drinking bout and weak. He went on his own feet, rather shakily."[19]

On the day of the vote, both unions had checkers at the polling places, ready to contest unqualified voters. Frances was in the council chamber at Culver City Hall; she relished the moment when she jumped up and yelled "*Challenge!*" at Jean Harlow's mother, who was about to drop a ballot in the box. (Louis B. Mayer later insisted that Harlow's mother had, in fact, helped to write one of her films.) The final tally was 267 to 57 in the guild's favor. It was later said that the Screen Playwrights had blundered by not lobbying younger, lower-paid writers like the ones the Hacketts had approached, and that the producers hadn't seen how secret balloting would work against them: given anonymity, the writers expressed their deep feelings about past abuses.

Although the guild had won by an overwhelming margin and was designated the legal collective bargaining agency for writers, it took three more years before the producers capitulated and signed a contract. All in all, it had been a rough, unseemly battle. In 1941, Leo Rosten wrote:

> The obstinacy and indiscretion with which the producers opposed Hollywood writers in their fight for recognition, basic working conditions, and a code of fair practices, is one of the less flattering commentaries on the men who control movie production. The National Labor Relations Board charged that the producers had conspired to carry out "a plan of interference" with the writers' attempt to organize themselves and choose their bargaining representatives; that the producers had used pressure on writers in an effort to force their resignation from the . . . guild . . . that certain producers had made speeches . . . in which the leaders of the guild were mentioned in "opprobrious, vile, and defamatory" terms; that producers had threatened to fire and blacklist guild members. . . . They had hurled challenges, uttered threats, issued fiats, employed long and costly maneuvers of opposition. It would take years for the bitterness and suspicion (on both sides) to die away. . . . In their dealings with the writers . . . the producers demonstrated that they had no workable concept of employee relations.[20]

Running the Screen Playwrights wasn't the only way Louis B. Mayer tried to control people. He was the Republican State Committee vice chairman during the 1934 California gubernatorial campaign, when radical author Upton Sinclair's End Poverty In California (EPIC) crusade seriously challenged the state's Republican establishment, and he had a unique way of raising funds: he sent his employees unsigned checks.

"The check would be made out for $150 or $200," Albert said. "[The sum] was written in. It might be a day's salary, or whatever they decided. . . . They'd say, 'Here is the amount we think you should give. This is for the Republican candidate [Frank E. Merriam]. Date it and write in your name and the name of your bank; sign it and send it back.' This just came in the mail, delivered to you at your office at the studio. When a day or two [went] by and they had not received it, the telephone call would come. . . . So the telephone rang in our office, and they said, 'We have not got your check yet for Governor Merriam,' or something like that. [We heard people saying] 'If you [don't give], they make a note of it, and when your option time comes up, they fix you.' Well, since we had no options, it didn't bother us at all."[21] Frances also recalled the pressure—and, typically, her version was tougher: "You were warned that if you didn't send the check in . . . they might not pick up your option. But we were damned if we were going to give our money to the likes of Merriam, so we simply didn't send in our checks."[22]

The Hacketts weren't the only rebels: other writers, and a number of actors, including Cagney, refused to contribute to Merriam. However, a lot of money was raised, and some of it paid for a smear campaign against Sinclair, with billboards, leaflets, and radio broadcasts claiming his "maggot-like horde" intended to Sovietize California. MGM filmed short "newsreels," which were appended to their factual Metrotone newsreels, showing interviews with voters in which all the respectable-looking interviewees were for Merriam, and the others, who favored Sinclair, "scratched themselves, stammered, or rubbed their bleary eyes. A shaggy man with whiskers [and an accent] and fanaticism in his eyes favored Sinclair because 'his system vorked vell in Russia.'" It's been said that these "voters" were actors reading from scripts. Irving Thalberg once admitted making those "newsreels"; "Nothing," he said, "is unfair in politics." In the end, Merriam defeated Sinclair, 1,138,000 votes to 879,000.

# 9

# Rose Marie, Art Collecting, and Thin Man Struggles

To Frances and Albert, *Rose Marie*, based on the 1924 Otto Harbach–Oscar Hammerstein II operetta, might have seemed like a sequel to *Naughty Marietta*, because they, Stromberg, and Van Dyke were reunited, and the leading roles were again played by Jeanette MacDonald and Nelson Eddy. Again, another writer, Alice Duer Miller, shared the writing credits.

Supposedly set in the Canadian Rockies but in fact shot in California's High Sierras, *Rose Marie* tells the story of a famous opera singer (MacDonald) who treks into the wilderness to help a brother accused of murder and falls in love with the Mountie (Eddy) who's hunting the brother. The film was released in early 1936; of the eight MacDonald-Eddy films, it has been called the definitive one, the one that made the most money and that will be best recalled. Its songs include "Rose Marie," "Indian Love Call," "Dinah," and "Some of These Days." The movie had seven-hundred-plus extras; during the shooting, behind their backs, the stars were given nicknames. Because of Eddy's inert acting—"I've handled Indians, African natives, South Sea Islanders, rhinos, pygmies, and Eskimos and made them all act," Van Dyke said, "but not Nelson Eddy"—he was dubbed the Singing Capon. MacDonald was a notorious scene-stealer—John Barrymore reportedly once told her, "If you wave that loathsome chiffon rag you call a kerchief once more while I'm speaking, I shall ram it down your gurgling throat!"—so she became the Iron Butterfly.

Most reviewers liked *Rose Marie:* "as blithely melodious and rich in scenic beauty as any picture that has come from Hollywood . . . [MacDonald and Eddy] prove to be as delightful a combination here as they were in *Naughty Marietta.*" The two stars' popularity was confirmed when a recording of songs from the two films sold over a million copies. Frances and Albert went to a sneak preview of the film in Los Angeles. "It went well," Frances reported, "in spite of the studio Death Watch, all hoping that the other producer, and the other writers, and the other director, will have a flop. . . . There are lots of things in the picture that make me writhe. Of course, the public is crazy about . . . MacDonald and Eddy. You should have heard the yell that went up when their names were flashed on the screen . . . and the applause on their entrances . . . particularly Eddy."

Frances and Albert gave great help to one of the actors in *Rose Marie*. During a visit to New York, they saw the then-unknown James Stewart in a play, *Divided by Two,* and back in Hollywood, told MGM executives he was "a great bet for pictures." "I shall speak to Hunt [Stromberg] about Stewart," Frances wrote to Leah Salisbury, who was then Stewart's agent, "as I have such faith in the boy that I would like Hunt to have a chance to have him." Stewart was screen-tested and hired, and Frances and Albert met him, then suggested him for a part in the first *Thin Man* sequel. However, the sequel got delayed. Albert later recalled, "One day I saw Jimmy on the lot, and I said, 'How are things?' He said, 'Well, I'm leaving for New York tomorrow because they didn't pick up my option.' So I ran like hell up to the office. I said to Hunt Stromberg, 'Jimmy Stewart! They didn't pick up his option!' [Hunt said], 'Oh, my goodness, we've got to stop that.' To justify Jimmy's salary, Hunt put him into the musical we'd just written, *Rose Marie*."[1] Stewart played Jeanette MacDonald's wild-eyed, reckless kid brother—the murderer—and got fine reviews. When the sequel to *The Thin Man* was finally produced, Stewart gave another fine performance and was truly on his way. "So we helped to start Jimmy Stewart's career!" Albert said.

MGM's publicists jumped on the success of *Rose Marie* and ran articles in their house organ, *Studio News,* with titles like "Eddy Prefers 'Mountie' Role to Any Other," "D.A.R. Official Wires Praise of '*Rose Marie*,'" and "Whole Staff Given Credit for Film Hit." The last article angered Frances greatly. In it, Woody Van Dyke said that no one person was responsible for the movie's success, then talked, without mentioning actual names, about the "team members" who *were* responsible, starting with the producer ("It's up to him to select a good story, then to captain its passage . . . to the screen"), then the actors (they had to be chosen "wisely"), and on down to the cameraman, the soundman, and the art director ("the beauty of the picture comes largely from [his] work"), then to the cutter, members of the music, research, and wardrobe departments, and finishing with "the make-up expert" and "the men who supply the props."[2]

Frances first read this piece, which failed entirely to mention the writers, on a Saturday and thought it was "funny." Then, she said, on "Sunday, I got mad, and on Monday I was madder. [Albert and I] gave it to [columnist Sidney] Skolsky, hoping he would print it. . . . On Tuesday I boiled over to Hunt, and told him all I thought of the studio attitude to writers. . . . They always treat writers badly . . . just ignoring them. It is studio policy, although none of them will admit it, not to give writers any publicity. . . . And since then we have had two important newspaper interviews! Isn't it lovely? Maybe they were just studio stooges, not reporters at all, but Hunt must have done something. Of course Hunt says Van Dyke [wasn't to blame for the article], but I don't believe it. . . . If he [weren't], he would have called to apologize. . . . He is contemptuous of writers." Shortly after Frances's tirade, *Studio News* ran a five-inch piece that started, "Four smash hits in a row! This is the astonishing record of the screen's No.1 screen writing team of Albert Hackett and Frances Goodrich," then went on to mention the pictures they'd done with Stromberg and ended by pointing out "a feature much remarked in Hollywood writing circles— the dissimilarity of [the themes in these four films]."[3]

On September 14, 1936, Irving Thalberg died suddenly of pneumonia. Frances and Albert had hardly known him, but Stromberg insisted on giving them tickets to the funeral (tickets were probably needed to keep out gate-crashing movie fans). Thalberg had been greatly admired; MGM closed for the day, and a large crowd gathered outside the temple, watching the arrival of the stars. The ushers included Clark Gable, Fredric March, Moss Hart, and Douglas Fairbanks Sr.; the rabbi read a message from President Roosevelt. Like Stromberg, Thalberg had been popular among writers (he'd reportedly said they were "the most important people in film," then joked, "and we must do everything to keep them from finding out"),[4] so in addition to the Hacketts, Anita Loos, Talbot Jennings, Frances Marion, Herman and Joseph Mankiewicz, and George Oppenheimer were there. According to David Niven, the only sour note in the ceremony was "when some moron in the MGM publicity department saw to it that the child actor, Freddie Bartholomew, who had just completed the name part in the film, showed up in his black velvet *Little Lord Fauntleroy* suit."[5] Later, during the burial at Forest Lawn Cemetery, Wallace Beery flew over in his plane and scattered flowers on the mourners.

Describing long-past Hollywood events accurately today is sometimes hard because the reporting then was often slanted. Mayer evidently feared Thalberg's power at MGM, and one account says that, driving away from the temple, Mayer remarked, "Isn't God good to me?" It has also been written that, at the time, Mayer "cried very real tears." It has *also* been reported that, on the afternoon Thalberg died, Mayer visited his widow and "shed a few facile tears," then, that evening, danced "frenziedly" at a Hollywood nightclub, "almost as though he were performing some barbaric rite."

So which of those things did Louis B. Mayer actually do?

Maybe he did them all.

In Nutley and Little Compton, Frances had grown up knowing artists and visiting their studios, and her parents had had a modest picture collection. The best item in it, inherited from Frances's grandfather, William Winton Goodrich, was Winslow Homer's *The Brush Harrow,* which has been called "perhaps the most tenderly sensitive and perceptive of all of Homer's paintings of the Civil War." Henry sold it in 1921 for $3,150, and it's now at the Fogg Art Museum, at Harvard; in 1999, a Homer expert put its value at $4 to $5 million. In the mid-1930s, as their earnings rose, Frances and Albert started buying paintings, generally during visits to New York; most of the artists were American, but some were French or Haitian. Buying and selling paintings gave the Hacketts pleasure and profit—and sometimes pain: they once paid $500 at a Los Angeles auction house for a large pastel signed "Juan Gris" that turned out to be a fake. At one time, their collection grew too big: "We really haven't room to hang all our paintings. I think we'll have to build an ell." Many other Hollywood-ites had collections, some of which were first-class—Frances wrote that their good friend Edward G. Robinson had a "remarkable collection . . . some of the finest examples of Van Gogh, Renoir, Cezanne, and so forth"—and a few of which weren't: "Jim Cagney has been buying pictures out here," Frances wrote to my father, "and I wish there had been someone to advise him." Cagney, who painted and wrote poetry, was sincerely interested in American art. In early 1934, after my father published a book on the life and work of Thomas Eakins, Frances asked my father for a signed copy for Cagney. "He especially asked that you would autograph it. I wouldn't bother you, but he has been so sweet to us and is really terribly interested in the book."

Being involved in the movie business sometimes worked against art collectors. When Frances visited the New York gallery run by Alfred Stieglitz, the photographer husband of Georgia O'Keeffe, hoping to buy a painting by John Marin, the cranky, high-handed Stieglitz refused to sell her one because she earned her living in Hollywood and was "unworthy." The actress Anne Jackson said that once, when she admired a dress of Frances's, Frances replied, "I don't spend any money on clothes; I spend it on paintings" (the part about clothes stretched the truth: Frances was always beautifully dressed). Among the American artists whose works the Hacketts bought through the years were Max Weber, Beauford DeLaney, Lyonel Feininger, Ben Shahn, Yasuo Kuniyoshi, John Sloan, Raphael Soyer, and Alfred Maurer. Also, Frances had known Reginald Marsh since childhood—their families were neighbors in both Nutley and Little Compton—and liked the "brutality and ugliness" in his pictures, so she and Albert acquired a Marsh in 1934 and tried to persuade Cagney to buy one. The Hacketts' painting was titled *Negroes on Rockaway Beach;* they later gave it to the Whitney Museum, which often proudly displays it. Another friend whose work the Hacketts bought was theatrical caricaturist Al Hirschfeld. In 1958, a New York gallery showed Hirschfeld's drawings, and Frances and Albert wrote to my mother from California, "We want so much to have one . . . [but] if we say it to him he'll feel he has to give it to us. So will you buy one for us, and not tell [him] 'til afterwards?" My mother suggested drawings of George Bernard Shaw and Danny Kaye; Frances replied that she and Albert preferred GBS—and she would tell Kaye his image was for sale: "He might not know and might want to buy it himself." When he learned about the Hacketts' maneuvering, Hirschfeld wrote, "Delighted that you are delighted with your sneaky purchase of one of my doodles."

At various times, two of the Hacketts' painter friends hired other friends of theirs as nude models. Maureen Stapleton did her modeling before her acting career took off; in her memoirs, she wrote that she "worked for Reggie [Marsh] for quite a while. He passed me on to his friend Raphael Soyer. . . . I was zaftig, and that's what those guys wanted: a big, blubbery young dame."[6] Stapleton was sometimes interestingly uninhibited: a friend of the Hacketts said that at a small dinner party, she sought relief from the heat by taking off her clothes, which produced "suppressed smiles. . . . The men tried to ignore her." The photographer Nancy Rica Schiff, who was neither big nor blubbery, also posed for Soyer. One Christmastime in the early 1980s, Schiff appeared nude in a TV documentary about Soyer, and on a Christmas card Albert wrote, "We saw you in the film posing for Raphael Soyer. I stood up and announced loud and clear that I was going to write you this: The more I see of you, the more I want to see of you. Now I have done it."

The prize items in Frances and Albert's collection were two oils by Edward Hopper, a small painting of a six-day bicycle racer resting between races and the larger *A Woman in the Sun*, painted in 1961, which shows a nude woman with long reddish brown hair standing in a bedroom in a country house, holding a cigarette and staring out a window. The woman is young and slender, with large, upspringing breasts; the Hacketts had been told that Hopper's eccentric wife, Jo, insisted that he use only herself as a model, and since by 1961, Jo was no longer young, slender, or upspringing, the Hacketts always privately called the painting "Jo Glorified." Jo wrote to them that she and Edward called the picture "The Sorrowful Sinner," and said the woman seemed "triste," and it was too bad there wasn't a pair of men's shoes under her bed. The Hacketts paid $15,000 for the picture, using the profit from selling a Rouault; in 1980, they donated it to the Whitney Museum.

Frances and Albert first met the Hoppers in the 1940s, and saw them rarely when they lived in California. In 1963, after the Hacketts moved back to New York, Jo wrote, welcoming them with an artist's words (she was a painter, too): "I hope you both are going to be very happy. . . . It was such a long trek to get here, pulling up roots beside another ocean—a green ocean, not like our cerulean sky over the blue Atlantic." The Hoppers had visited the Hacketts' comfortable duplex New York apartment, and Jo invited them to the Hoppers' spartan, walk-up Washington Square apartment-studio. "We'd love to have you come to see where E. Hopper has lived for 50 years . . . [looking] out over the treetops . . . and working in the light of day under skylights," she wrote, but then she warned them that it was a long way up: "Not everyone can do those 74 steps." The Hoppers were an odd pair. He was tall and withdrawn, famous for his monumental silences; she was small and birdlike, chattering and fluttering. Even when Hopper became successful, they lived frugally. Into his old age, Hopper carried the coal up those seventy-four steps. One summer—Jo laughingly told this to many people—they took a stray cat into their house on Cape Cod and fed it with their leftovers. The cat stayed only a short time and, when it departed, left a dead seagull on the kitchen doorstep, obviously as a larder contribution. Jo did strange things, once addressing a letter simply "Mr. and Mrs. Albert Hackett, Authors of 'The Diary of Anne Frank,' Los Angeles, California." When it was returned marked "Insufficient Address," she wrote to my father, "Such a dumb cluck P.O. at Los Angeles. And Edward Hopper getting mail addressed only to 'New York, N.Y.'"

To some collectors, paintings are mere decor or status symbols, but Frances and Albert always enjoyed living with their pictures, and they were pleased to have others see them. Once, they opened their Bel Air house for a tour by the Los Angeles Vassar Club, and one of the less-bright ladies, having viewed the works by Hopper, Sloan, Kuniyoshi, Shahn, and others, asked Frances, "Now tell me, which one of you is the painter?"

In early October 1936, Frances and Albert visited for ten days in Little Compton. After they left, Aunt Caro felt "lonely . . . [the Hacketts] were very gay, and we were always going somewhere for lobsters or crabs or oysters, long drives, etc. They will have about two weeks in New York, and then back to that awful Hollywood grind. . . . They now must work on a sequel to *The Thin Man*. A desperate job."

Sadly, at this time, Caro herself was working at a truly desperate job: writing for the *Daily Worker*; as noted before, she ultimately became one of its nominal owners. Years later, I was told that "men in dark suits" came to Little Compton, bringing party-line-hewing writing assignments—and presumably asking for money. This routine evidently continued until late August 1939, when the Nazi-Soviet nonaggression pact was signed, dividing up Poland and granting Russia eventual sovereignty over the Baltic states. For many who believed in Communism, this was a shattering disillusionment; in the family, the story was that it "broke Caro's heart." True or not, she died, at age eighty-one, eleven months later.

The film Caro mentioned was *After the Thin Man*. Again, the producer was Stromberg, and the director was Van Dyke. The Hacketts' screenplay was based on a story by Hammett and, as Van Dyke pointed out, "it was not an easy task for the Hacketts to grope back through three years of time to catch the same characteristic idioms, voiced by Bill and Myrna in the first story."[7] Released on Christmas Day 1936, the film got high praise: "tight"; "arresting"; "few films this season have contained more risibles." Set in San Francisco, telling a complicated tale of deception and murder involving Nora's family, the picture gave Asta—"as engaging a canine personality as ever graced a screen"—a far larger role: at one point, he chewed up an important clue. James Stewart played the murderer, and in the climactic scene, toting a gun, he ranted at a woman who'd jilted him, "I want to see you go mad and madder and madder until you hang!" Once more, as with *The Thin Man*, the Nick-and-Nora, husband-and-wife relationship, which Frances and Albert understood so well, was praised. An English reviewer wrote:

> The air of married happiness which Mr. William Powell and Miss Myrna Loy contrive to convey . . . is of far more interest than the track-

ing down of the murderer. Too often cinematic love stories are stories of passions and improbabilities, quarrels and reconciliations, but here is the more genuine material of marriage—the private jokes shared together, the routine of daily life, the amused and affectionate tolerance each shows toward certain traits in the other. . . . [Nick and Nora] play into each other's hands . . . and it is the gaiety, the proper but never exaggerated sophistication, the charm and the irresponsibility, within limits, they bring to their lives which more than justify this sequel.[8]

Frances and Albert closed their three *Thin Man* pictures with intimate, emotionally charged—and funny—final scenes. In the first, they deftly caught the delicious, "naughty," "only-us" feeling of exciting sexual encounters—and did so without resorting to today's flesh shots and heavy breathing. In it, Nick, Nora, and Asta are aboard a train, headed back to San Francisco from New York; when they return to their compartment for the night, Nora suggests that Asta should share the lower berth with her, but Nick gives her a look, then says, "Oh, yeah?" and tosses the dog onto the upper berth, where, as the film fades out, Asta embarrassedly covers his eyes with his paws. At the end of the second picture, the Charleses are again in a sleeping compartment, now eastbound. Nick's in a bathrobe; Nora's in a nightgown; they're exhausted by their mystery solving and are cozily delighted to be alone. As usual, he's sipping a drink—and she's knitting. He grins at her, then, eyeing her handiwork, he murmurs, "What's that?" She smiles contentedly. He sips again, then says, "Mmmm, looks like a baby's sock." She's still smiling. Then realization hits, and his jaw drops. Then she speaks a line that particularly pleased Frances, because she wrote it: "And you call yourself a detective."

Frances and Albert had a pressing reason for making Nora pregnant: they were afraid they might be asked to write yet another sequel (as, of course, they later *were*), which would be boring and difficult: they would have to mine still more interest and amusement out of two characters they were growing sick of. The Hacketts thought that giving the Charleses a baby to care for might put an end to their adventurous life: "Two sophisticated people can't have a child and go through the things they went through." Actually, to forestall a third picture, the Hacketts wanted to do far more than just give Nick and Nora a baby: they wanted to kill them. "We wanted to kill both of them at the end [of the second picture] just to be sure," Frances wrote to Leah Salisbury, "but Hunt wouldn't let us." (Stromberg's refusal was surely no surprise: the series was a gold mine.)

Adding the Hacketts' negative reactions when they were assigned to the first picture to their feelings when they completed the second, maybe this book should be subtitled, "They First Wanted to Abort Two of America's Best-Loved Icons, Nick and Nora, and Then They Wanted to Murder Them."

# 10

# The Garden of Allah

In the 1930s, many talented people lived at the Garden of Allah, on Sunset Boulevard in Hollywood. There, twenty-five Spanish-style, tile-roofed bungalows and a main hotel building were set within walled grounds lushly planted with banana, orange, palm, and grapefruit trees, and a maze of narrow paths surrounded an enormous swimming pool shaped vaguely like the Black Sea. The Garden had been built in 1927 by Alla Nazimova, an eccentric, Russian-born silent film star. Sometimes called "the uterus of Flickerland," through the years (it survived until 1959) it was home to, among others, Ernest Hemingway, W. Somerset Maugham, Jascha Heifetz, Sergei Rachmaninoff, Greta Garbo, Marlene Dietrich, Katharine Hepburn, Errol Flynn, Beatrice Lillie, Laurence Olivier—the list goes on and on. Behavior at the Garden was quirky, jokey, uninhibited; there was no house detective, and men and women on interesting errands came and went freely through the unlocked side entrances. Many tales, some perhaps true, were told about the place. John Barrymore, a heavy drinker, frequently tumbled into the pool; while he was acting in *The Hunchback of Notre Dame*, Charles Laughton swam there wearing his costume hump. Tallulah Bankhead liked strolling naked around the pool in the moonlight. Robert Benchley, a longtime resident, was once visited in his bedroom by a doctor who'd predicted possible side effects from a new prescription, and Benchley showed him his torso, on which he'd glued feathers from a pillow. Evidently, the walls of the bungalows—which contained a bedroom, living room, kitchenette, breakfast room, and bath— were thin. "Arthur Kober stayed there once," Al Hirschfeld told me. "He came home around three in the morning, and couldn't remember where he was. . . . He fell on the bed and was wakened by this girl who said, 'Will you get me a glass of water, honey?' So he gets up, gets the water, comes back, and there's nobody there—she was next door. It was a crazy place."

During the 1930s and 1940s, when they weren't in one of the houses they owned or rented before finally settling down in Bel Air, Frances and Albert sometimes stayed at the Garden of Allah. Most residents prepared their meals in their bungalows, but since Frances didn't cook, she and Albert often ate in the hotel dining room; others called the food there "pretty bad," but Frances insisted that the steaks were good. The Hacketts' social life in Hollywood was always stimulating ("We had great fun," Frances said more than once, "a lovely, wonderful time"); at the Garden, it was evidently extra stimulating. There were many parties, a number of which the Hacketts threw, inviting such Garden neighbors as their playwright friend Marc Connelly, with whom Albert often sang songs from his vaudeville days.

"They knew all these wonderful old songs," Al Hirschfeld said. "They used to go on for hours, one topping the other. . . . The lyrics were absolutely marvelous—the old vaudeville routines. . . . Marc remembered them, and Albert was *in* a lot of them. . . . He knew them all. You could name the act, and he'd do the whole act." According to Faith McNulty, the widow of the Hacketts' friend, *New Yorker* writer John McNulty, Albert's repertoire included something called "Your Mother's Voice Rings in Your Ears": he sang it in sweet, sentimental tones while playing the piano—then crashed out a chord and yelled, "Albert, get off your sister!"[1] Among the routines Albert sometimes summoned up was a poem recited by married performers (whose names he'd forgotten) concerning the influences men had on women. The poem, Albert recalled, started with the husband claiming that women had always caused trouble and men had always got the blame. "At this point," Albert said, "all the men in the audience were applauding and cheering." Then the wife replied, saying that if women misbehaved, men had taught them how, so was it fair to knock them? "By now," Albert recalled, "the women were applauding, and the men were crying, '*Hoo, hoo!*'" The wife had the last lines, saying, "There never was a real bad woman / That wasn't made so by a man." "Now," Albert said, "the men were *hissing*."[2]

Among the Garden residents Frances and Albert saw often were Arthur and Gloria Stuart Sheekman. A slim, handsome, cigar-smoking ex-newspaper-columnist, Arthur was a collaborator on the scripts of Marx Brothers films, a cofounder of the Screen Writers Guild, and a funny storyteller who reportedly loved rerunning Cecil B. DeMille's *The Crusades* so he could hear Loretta Young, as Berengaria, say to her husband, Richard the Lionhearted, "Ya gotta save Christianity, Richard, ya gotta!"[3] Gloria was a blond, California-born beauty, a stage and film actress, and a liberal political activist. After her husband died, in 1978, she returned to acting, then

became a book illustrator and painter. In 1997, she played the chief supporting female role in the megahit *Titanic*, won several important awards,
and became the oldest person—age eighty-seven—ever nominated for
an Oscar.

Fortunately for Frances and Albert, Gloria Sheekman was also, on
top of her other accomplishments, an excellent cook. "I became the Den
Mother of the Garden of Allah," she wrote in her memoirs, recalling
wartime rationing. "Most of [the residents] gave me their ration tickets,
because not one of them, to my knowledge, could cook. But I could make
chicken in the pot with matzo balls, delicate buckwheat blini." In May
1944, the Hacketts were invited with sixteen others to a twenty-six-course,
rijsttafel-style dinner in the Sheekmans' bungalow. "I cooked," Gloria
wrote, "for three days on four different Garden of Allah stoves, hired two
professional waiters, [and] ran up fair imitations of Javanese turbans and
sashes for [the guests]."[4] (Among the diners that night was Robert Benchley. At one point, he occupied Garden rooms directly above the Hacketts
and kept them awake by drinking and talking all night with his crony
Charles Butterworth, a droll, highly successful film and stage comedian
famed for playing vacillating nonentities, "sub-average men suffering
from delusions of mediocrity.") Two nights before Christmas Eve that
same year, the Sheekmans served a Chinese dinner to, among others,
Frances and Albert, Groucho Marx and his wife, Lauren Bacall and
Humphrey Bogart, Dorothy Parker, Nunnally Johnson, Celeste Holm,
and Nat Perrin and his wife.

(Speaking of Christmastime during Hollywood's Golden Age, Frances
and Albert told me that before the holiday, small mountains of blatantly
expensive presents were displayed in the offices of leading producers, sent
by actors, writers, directors, and technicians—those lower in the pecking
order—as tribute, to curry favor. At the studios, where people worked
under great stress, holidays could be weirdly explosive. In 1935, Frances
wrote to Leah Salisbury that "Christmas started with a bang at the studio
at about twelve o'clock the day before. Albert and I sneaked out . . . around
three, avoiding the drunks. Heaven knows where they landed. Poor Ted
Healy [a comic actor who often appeared alongside the Three Stooges]
landed in jail, arrested for arson! He tried to burn down his ex-wife's
house! Started a pretty little fire in her stove, with all the Christmas wrap-
pings and excelsior. Millions of arrests for drunken driving, and acci-
dents." Frances didn't get the Healy story quite right. According to
newspaper reports, he forced his way into the apartment of his girlfriend,
then built a fire by breaking some of her furniture into kindling and adding

some of her dresses. One account said the police were "trying to dig out the facts, which were hazy in the minds of . . . the persons involved.")

Before the Garden of Allah, the Sheekmans had lived in grander style—but experienced occasional glitches caused by inexperienced servants. At a dinner party the Hacketts attended, a new couple was working in the kitchen. "We had finger bowls with flowers in them and lace doilies and all that," Mrs. Sheekman said. "After dinner we were all sitting in the living room and the new man walked in with fourteen brandy snifters filled to the brim with brandy. We fell off our chairs laughing."[5] Wherever the Hacketts and Sheekmans happened to be living, Albert—who was obviously very fond of the terrific-looking Gloria—always phoned her on her birthday. "*Tout le monde* celebrated my birthday," she told me. "It was July Fourth."

Another occasional tenant at the Garden of Allah was F. Scott Fitzgerald, whom Albert had met in New York some years before during rehearsals of Fitzgerald's play *The Vegetable*. In the spring of 1938, at age forty-two, Fitzgerald showed up in Hollywood; he was short of money, fighting alcoholism, and trying again, after painful failures in 1927 and 1931, to make it as a screenwriter, something he never truly managed to do: Albert said that screenwriting was a "curious kind of shorthand he couldn't catch on to." (In all his time in Hollywood, Fitzgerald got only one screen credit, for *Three Comrades*—and it was shared. That film's producer, Joseph Mankiewicz, said, "In a novel the dialogue enters through the mind. The reader endows it with a certain quality. Dialogue spoken from the stage enters through the ear. . . . It has an immediate emotional impact. Scott's dialogue lacked bite, color, rhythm. . . . When I rewrote Scott's dialogue, people thought I was spitting on the flag."[6] Fitzgerald resented Mankiewicz's changes and thereafter referred to him as "Monkeybitch.")

Added to these career difficulties was Fitzgerald's strong dislike of Hollywood: he once described it as a "dump . . . a hideous town, pointed up by the insulting gardens of its rich, full of the human spirit at a new low of debasement."[7] He also said that Hollywood studios were filled with a "strange conglomeration of a few excellent overtired men making the pictures and as dismal a crowd of fakes and hacks at the bottom as you can imagine." The result, he added, "is that every other man is a charlatan, nobody trusts anybody else, and an infinite amount of time is wasted from lack of confidence."[8]

All of these stresses may have been at work when Frances first saw Fitzgerald—formerly handsome, now faded, a man who, two years before, in *The Crack-Up,* had described himself as "a cracked plate, the kind one wonders if it is worth preserving . . . [even] to go into the ice box under the left-overs." He was seated alone in the MGM commissary and, Frances said, "he . . . sat there but he didn't order. What I noticed were his eyes. Never in my life will I forget his eyes. He looked as though he were seeing hell opening up before him. He was hugging his briefcase and he had a Coke. Then suddenly he got up to go out. I said to Albert, 'I just saw the strangest man.' He said, 'That's Scott Fitzgerald.'"[9]

Because Fitzgerald seemed, in their words, "shy and miserable, a jittery, beaten man [who] never stopped trembling," Frances and Albert felt sorry for him and later befriended him, urging him to join them and others—including S. J. Perelman, Dorothy Parker, Ogden Nash, and George Oppenheimer—at the writers' table in the commissary. The writers' table stood against a wall; in the middle of the room was another table, called the Big Table, where producers and other writers, their allies—"the finks, the ones who tried to break the guild," Frances called them—ate. That table had a cage containing dice, which was spun each lunchtime, with the loser paying the bill. "When [the producers] saw they wouldn't have to pay that day," Frances recalled, "they would order all kinds of things."[10]

Some accounts say that Fitzgerald overcame his shyness and joined the Hacketts at their table, but Albert said he never did. Perhaps Fitzgerald was frightened away by Groucho Marx: Ogden Nash said that Marx would sometimes arrive and "turn things upside down so that you couldn't have a coherent conversation—everything had to be a joke." In any event, whether at lunch or elsewhere, a friendship grew between Fitzgerald and the Hacketts, partly because Fitzgerald's daughter, Scottie, was then at Vassar; knowing that Frances had gone there, Fitzgerald occasionally dropped by the Hacketts' MGM office and read his letters to Scottie aloud. Frances called the letters "beautiful"; years later, a *New Yorker* article called them "among the most moving paternal letters ever written, far truer and more substantive than anything in [Fitzgerald's] later 'creative' work."[11]

Another experience the Hacketts shared with Fitzgerald was having worked for a producer named John Considine, whose pictures included *Boys Town* and *A Yank at Eton.* According to Frances, Considine "didn't know anything. Oh, that dreadful man! For Scott to be linked with him! . . . He read with a blue pencil in his hand ready to mark up the script. One day he was reading one of our scripts and he crossed out a line. 'That's not necessary,' he said. We said, 'Wait 'til you read the next page.' He had no conception of setting something up on one page to be developed . . . a page or two later. . . . We [suggested hiring] Fred Astaire to him. . . . When Considine saw Fred's [screen] test, he thought that Fred was the most awful thing he'd ever seen."[12]

Perhaps the strongest bond between Frances and Albert and Scott Fitzgerald was that, unlike many other people, they liked Sheilah Graham, the young, good-looking, English-born gossip columnist Fitzgerald was living with (at the time, his wife, Zelda, was in a mental ward in Asheville, North Carolina). Frances called Graham Fitzgerald's "salvation." Other people have agreed, pointing out that Graham supported Fitzgerald in many loyal, loving ways, helping him to drink less and pushing him to write *The Last Tycoon*. Fitzgerald didn't live to finish *Tycoon*, but some say it ranks among his greater works.

Sheilah Graham wrote often about her relationship with Fitzgerald and mentioned Frances and Albert. In one book, she said that when Fitzgerald was working on *Marie Antoinette* for Hunt Stromberg, and the Hacketts were living in one of their rented houses in Beverly Hills, he took her to a dinner party there. "I remember Joan Blondell [and] Dick Powell were there," Graham said. "In the middle of dinner, Scott received a call from . . . Stromberg, to come to his house to discuss the film. . . . Before he left, Scott had everyone on the staircase, which rose from the side of the living room. They were playing a game, mesmerized by Scott. I don't remember the game, only the laughter, and Scott at the top of the stairs, flushed with alcohol, but also with his magic that they were responding to."[13]

Fitzgerald wrote a poem, which he signed "for Frances and Albert" and gave to them, about his departure that evening; Graham later included the first half of it in four different books. (She was a notorious recycler of material and recorder of minutiae; Sid Perelman once observed, "It seems that while cleaning out a thimble she discovered still more revelations anent that tortured spirit Scott Fitzgerald".)[14] In the poem, titled "Les Absents Ont Toujours Tort," Fitzgerald misspelled Graham's first name, as he often did:

> Sing a song for Shielah's supper
> (Belly void of rye!)
> Gone before the cocktail
> Back for the pie.
> Stromberg sent for Papa
> (Tho' Papa hadn't et)

To do what Jesus couldn't—
Save Marie Antoinette.
Say, can famine-stricken whines
Ring the silver screen?
Oh, there will be some sour lines
To set before the Queen!
Sing a song of Hacketts
Thirteen at their dinner
But they should know these rackets
Yours—with groans
The Sinner[15]

The first two lines of the poem suggest that Fitzgerald hadn't been drinking, but Graham said he was "flushed with alcohol." Contradictions like this—plus errors, omissions, and falsehoods—were a regular feature of Graham's writings. Her son, Robert Westbrook, commented, "In the late fifties, my mother began what may best be described as a controlled experiment in truth—her autobiography, a task, constantly revised, which would occupy her on and off for the rest of her life."

Graham had a limited education and sometimes felt self-conscious about her lack of learning. According to her, she once told Fitzgerald she felt uncomfortable in the company of his brighter friends, such as the Hacketts and the Ira Gershwins: "I don't mind the parties at the homes of the stars, but I dread the ones given by your friends. I can't keep up." She said that one evening, as she and Fitzgerald were starting off for the Hacketts', he told her, "I'll give you something to hang on to. . . . When we get there, pretend that everyone bores you. That will give you just the right distance." "I tried it," Graham wrote. "All evening I [said] to myself, 'George S. Kaufman bores me. Oscar Levant bores me. Ogden Nash bores me.' It worked, after a fashion: I felt more relaxed. . . . Scott protected me. He mingled briefly with his friends and then found his place beside me in a corner . . . while the wit and repartee flowed around us."[16]

Around the time Frances and Albert met Fitzgerald, he started working for Hunt Stromberg on a screenplay titled *Infidelity*, based on a short story by Ursula Parrott. Stromberg had said the picture might star Joan Crawford, and Fitzgerald had strong hopes—but friends like the Hacketts suspected the film wasn't going anywhere: the censors would never tolerate honest writing about adultery. "We felt so desperately for Scott," Frances and Albert reportedly said, "because we knew it couldn't be done. They wouldn't allow it just because it was about infidelity. . . . We didn't tell Scott that it was impossible—we couldn't bear to break his heart. He was enthusiastic about his script; he wanted very much to do it. It was the first thing he really came to life on."[17]

Sometime in 1939, autographing the Hacketts' copy of *The Great Gatsby*, Fitzgerald dashed off another poem:

> When anyone dances
> It's liable to be Frances
> While a quiet and malicious racket
> Is liable to proceed from Albert Hackett
> (Writing this way is rash
> In the presence of Ogden Nash)[18]

In late 1939, Frances and Albert left California for an extended stay in the east. By then, their relationship with Fitzgerald had ripened—not into great intimacy but into strong affection. The same was true of their friendship with Nathanael West, who had become a friend of Fitzgerald's: it's been said that the two novelists were not only close but influenced each other's work. Certainly, when the Hacketts left California, they expected to be reunited some day with both men—but on December 21, 1940, in Sheilah Graham's apartment, Fitzgerald, age forty-four, was killed by a massive heart attack. (At that moment, he was underlining football games in the *Princeton Alumni Weekly*, and his pencil shot off the page in a squiggly line, the last mark he ever put on paper.) The next day, West, age thirty-six, and his wife, Eileen, were killed in an auto crash in the town of El Centro. It was a disastrous weekend for American literature; the bodies of the two writers were sent back east on the same train.

# 11

## A "Lovely Nervous Breakdown"

**A** writer-producer friend of the Hacketts, Robert Lord, once gave a speech in which he called the movie business in the 1930s "hectic, frenzied, hysterical, tough, exhausting, and man-killing" and said that most people in it suffered from "battlefield nerves. . . . The men curse, the women weep. Both sexes develop luxuriant crops of stomach ulcers." Almost all of Lord's words fit Frances and Albert's Hollywood experience from 1936 through 1939, when they got credit on four pictures, contributed to two others without credit, and almost certainly helped out on still more. They worked far too hard; they *did* curse and weep; they *did* experience battlefield nerves; and in the end they were hit by a health problem — not ulcers, but something Frances called "our lovely nervous breakdown."

Many of the films Frances and Albert worked on in this period were produced by their friend Hunt Stromberg, who was himself a frightening example of the negative side of the Hollywood studio system. In the mid-1930s, Stromberg became one of the industry's top producers and was listed by the Treasury Department among the ten Americans having the highest income — but, sadly, the man who'd once been the Hacketts' hero was a slave of his work. "His only life was motion pictures," Albert said. "He couldn't talk about anything else." Worse, Stromberg started behaving self-destructively: suffering from a slipped disc, he began getting heavy, addictive doses of morphine from an unscrupulous doctor, but he still insisted on holding meetings, in which he was often distracted and functioned poorly. During story conferences, the Hacketts said, Stromberg was "waiting for the doctor to come with the shot. . . . We couldn't work with him when he was on drugs."

The first released of the pictures the Hacketts worked on with Stromberg in the late 1930s was *Wife Versus Secretary*, which told the story of a wife (Myrna Loy) whose groundless suspicions about the rapport between her husband (Clark Gable) and his secretary (Jean Harlow) nearly destroy her marriage. Frances and Albert didn't do the original script but were called

in to make changes after the ever-vigilant Joseph Breen, the movie industry's chief censor, went to a screening and raised questions. For example,
Harlow was shown living in a luxurious penthouse; since she earned a secretary's wages, Breen asked, didn't that suggest she was making illicit
money on the side? The answer to that—the apartment should be shrunk
and deglamorized—was obvious, but other fixes weren't that easy: it took
sweat and ingenuity to think up alternatives to "off-color" dialogue that
would both satisfy Breen and preserve the film's story line and wit. With
the revisions in hand, the Hacketts sat with Stromberg and Breen while the
film was screened again; each time an "objectionable" scene appeared,
the projector was stopped, and Frances read the changes aloud. In the end,
the script was okayed by Breen—and pleased the critics: "excellently handled"; "The dialogue is brisk, and cleverly turned." James Stewart had a
small part in *Wife Versus Secretary,* and Frances reported to Leah Salisbury
that at the preview, she saw him "ring up another success. . . . He is splendid." Salisbury was so pleased by this note that she sent it to Stewart,
adding, "Thot [*sic*] you'd like to see this but please don't say I sent it—and
return it to me."

Frances and Albert got no credits for their contribution to *Wife Versus
Secretary,* but they did for Stromberg's *Small Town Girl,* which was released
in April 1936 to chilly reviews: "highly polished . . . but little shines beyond
the polish." At least two other writers worked on *Small Town Girl;* for the
Hacketts, it meant several weeks of laboring into the night ("It's eleven
thirty . . . and we're still at the studio. . . . Deadly work, because it is patch-
work"), and when it was done, they were "fagged." In the movie, Robert
Taylor and the quiet, gentle Janet Gaynor—who replaced the sexy Jean
Harlow at the last minute—wake up after a Saturday night of carousing
to find they're married. Taylor's from a grand Boston family; for the sake
of appearances, he agrees to let the union with his unsophisticated spouse
stand for six months, then get a quiet divorce. During that time, Gaynor
gradually wins him over, and he decides to stay married. (The *New York
Times* said that changing Taylor's mind wouldn't have taken Harlow that
long: she "could have done the job over the weekend.") Another review
noted the movie's "humorously-worked-in uncouth topics" and "convincingly boring small town talk spewed by the various hick residents."
Albert probably wrote some of those lines, which include an exchange between two patrons at the general store:

Mrs. Martin: Well, Agnes, how's Fred today?
Mrs. Hanes: Better, thanks, Florence. But that boil will not come to a
    head on his neck here.

Mrs. Martin: Oh—right on his neck?
Mrs. Hanes: Um-hum.

In *Small Town Girl,* James Stewart played the part of Elmer Clampett, a gangling bumpkin telephone lineman who pursues Gaynor. At one point, he laughingly says that, while up on a phone pole, he "sort of got some dust" in his throat and "without thinkin' . . . let fly right down on a girl's hat." Stewart's favorite phrase is "Keep your chin up," leading Gaynor to exclaim, "If Elmer Clampett says 'Keep your chin up' once more, I'll scream."

Another film the Hacketts scripted that was coolly received (in 1937) was *The Firefly,* a lavish revamping of the 1912 Rudolf Friml–Otto Harbach operetta in which Jeanette MacDonald, without Nelson Eddy, played a singer-spy in Spain in 1808. Early on, when the most basic decisions were being made about *The Firefly,* Hunt Stromberg dictated lengthy memos to the Hacketts; one sounded partly as though he'd just been stuck by the doctor's needle. Stromberg questioned whether the male lead should sing; wondered how certain songs would fit into the story; outlined the plot; and then began to *ramble,* saying the male lead's character might need changing, asking if soldiers' uniforms were attractive during the period of the film, and wondering if it might be better to lay the story "in [today's] Italy. . . . Would it give us more color . . . ? In listening to the score today . . . I [felt] there's plenty of 'wop' in the song 'Giannina Mia.' . . . Even the title song, 'The Firefly,' seems to suggest some Latin country—red blood, fiery emotions. Firefly. Fiery emotions. So . . . [if] we *do* lay the story in present day Naples . . . we get the returning soldier . . . by having him [be] one of Mussolini's officers returning from the Ethiopian encounter."

Hoping to protect its investment in *The Firefly,* MGM countered the negative reviews with wondrously worded newspaper ads: "New, brilliant, daring . . . for your eyes to behold, your heart to thrill to, your senses to revel in! Romance floods the screen! Drama throbs in tingling suspense! Music envelops the whole theater in divine beauty!" In an interview shortly before the picture was released, its director, Robert Z. Leonard, made some interesting comments about the changes then coming into moviemaking: mainly, audiences were beginning to relax their insistence upon realism and to accept filmmakers' embellishments. "There's a scene in *The Firefly,*" Leonard said, "in which Allan Jones, on horseback, sings to Jeanette MacDonald, who is riding alongside in a coach [in the middle of the desert]. The only accompaniment at the beginning of the song is from a guitar played by the coachman. But as Miss MacDonald and Jones join in the chorus we gradually swell into full orchestral accompaniment. . . .

Now, if we had a Spanish orchestra ride up on horseback and start sawing away to make that accompaniment realistic, the audience might [be] forgiven for walking out. As it is, they'll hear the song and, finding it greatly enhanced by the music, won't give a second thought as to its source."[1]

Several months before they started writing *The Firefly*, Hunt Stromberg told Frances and Albert that MGM had acquired a property set in Colorado during silver-mining days that needed a brand-new plot. Describing this assignment to a reporter, the Hacketts said, "Our title is *A Lady Comes to Town*. It isn't for Mae West. We'd have to rewrite the title for Mae. . . . We'd have to call it *A Lady Goes to Town*. . . . We've got one swell scene we can save from the original. It's a funeral. . . . [The heroine] and some other people are burying a guy. . . . The preacher is saying funeral offices when all at once everybody spots silver in the grave. . . . Then everybody deserts the corpse and races to town to stake a claim on the cemetery. Isn't it great?"[2]

There's no record of the Hacketts ever discussing this project again.

> *Reflections on Ice-Breaking*
>
> Candy
> Is dandy
> But liquor
> Is quicker

is, of course, one of the better-known gems crafted by the famed, reserved (Frederick) Ogden Nash, whom the Hacketts met during their work on *The Firefly* (he collaborated with another writer on an adaptation of Harbach's script; they turned the adaptation into a screenplay). Before he began to earn his living as a poet—actually, he called himself a versifier and said his subject was "the minor idiocies of humanity"—Nash worked as a bond salesman, copywriter, book editor, and (earlier) French teacher at a boys' boarding school, where he said he'd "lost [his] entire nervous system carving lamb for a table of 14-year-olds." He became a good friend of the Hacketts, although he didn't spend much time in Hollywood: he later said he "accomplished nothing to be proud of there," and he disliked the place as much as his friend Sid Perelman. (In an off moment, Hunt Stromberg— who called Nash, Dashiell Hammett, Scott Fitzgerald, Dorothy Parker, Alan Campbell, the Perelmans, and the Hacketts his "stable" of writers— assigned Nash and Perelman to do a screenplay based on Dale Carnegie's best-seller *How to Win Friends and Influence People*. "We spent six happy weeks," Nash recalled, "fooling around and talking about Sherlock Holmes"; in Albert's words, Nash and Perelman "looked at each other for a long time on that one. . . . It never got made.")

Nash once said that Frances and Albert were his best friends in Hollywood, and if it hadn't been for them, he probably would have left. Albert knew that Nash hated the place, and he said, "We hung onto him. He was a great lifesaver for everybody. . . . He was lovely and amusing and fun. . . . The people who came to our house were always hanging around him." To this, Frances added, probably recalling Nash's reserve, "I don't feel I ever knew him well . . . [but] I loved him well. I really loved him." Nash and Albert went to ball games, and Nash and his wife often came to dinner. Sometimes, Scott Fitzgerald was there, and they played cards; one evening, Nash won the then-soul-warming sum of $12, mostly from a screenwriter named Melville Baker, whom he described as "greener than ever." Frances and Albert felt protective toward Nash, mainly because of his diffidence at the studio. Frances said he should have spoken up more: "At a conference, I'm a screamer, and . . . here Ogden would be, shy and silent, and you thought, 'Oh, God, you are so good, you're so wonderful, you're worth all of us, why don't you yell?'"[3]

Frances thought Nash and his wife (also named Frances) had a "lovely relationship. . . . I've never seen two people who were lovelier together. . . . She was completely devoted to him, whatever he wanted, and he adored her." (Nash once wrote that his love for his wife was great enough "to fill infinite space and stick out over the edges.") The Hacketts later visited the Nashes in Baltimore; they recalled the turtle soup and going to a cotillion, with Albert wearing a tuxedo borrowed from Ogden's father-in-law. Albert remembered a time in Hollywood when Nash, whose eyesight was poor, went to a "very famous" ophthalmologist recommended by Aldous Huxley, who was then writing for MGM and had "very, very bad eyes." The doctor, Albert said, had people read a chart and recite what they saw, and then "he'd take a pin and put a hole through a card and say, 'Now look at it.' Well, with a pinhole you can see anything or read anything . . . so then [he'd] say, 'Throw the glasses away.' Well, a lot of people had done that, and Dash Hammett said when he found out that Ogden was going there, 'I can see Ogden looking through the thing and [throwing his glasses away], and then Ogden will come out, get in the car and turn around — and blackout.' It was a funny line, because it was terrifying, the idea of throwing Ogden's glasses away. Well, Ogden went . . . and came back with his glasses."[4]

Through the years, Nash sent inscribed copies of his books to Frances and Albert. In one, he wrote a poem that started with two lines whose meaning is hard to grasp:

A little stiff from wheeling,
Or westward the course of chlorine.
The tongues of the people are fashioned by the hands of an
all-wise potter.
In places where people say "wotter,"
The water tastes like wotter.

In another book, Nash wrote:

Hollywood is nothing but codfish and halibut
Compared to Frances and Alibert.[5]

Once, thanking Nash for his gift of a book, Albert wrote:

Such a lovely present. With a lovely inscription which we in no way deserve. And so many verses that we had missed. We keep it on the table between our beds where we can both get it at any hour of the night.

I suddenly found myself remembering something that happened in California years ago when we were all . . . in the Stromberg Stable. It was announced that you would autograph copies of your latest book at a small bookshop in Hollywood. I think it was on Vine Street. It was a very avant garde place with lots of liberals about. By the time Frances and I got there they had sold out the few books they had of yours. We ended up with an autographed copy of the play *Shadow and Substance*. The autograph read, "Stripsationally yours, Gypsy Rose Lee."

Albert once repeated to Nash a hideously corny line he'd had to speak in a play years before, and Nash put the line into a poem. Comparing different kinds of dramatic dialogue, the poem said that while some actors get to speak only flat things like "I love you Miss Scarlett, 'deed I do," other, luckier ones get to declaim things like "It's hell's fire in my veins, this desperate thirst for you." When Albert spotted his "hell's fire" line in Nash's poem, he commented that it was "wonderful to see it again and know that it hadn't been lost" and added that, at a dress rehearsal of the play, he'd been so embarrassed by the line that he spoke it softly. "The woman who wrote the play said, 'Mr. Hackett, I don't hear that,' and I said, 'You're not going to hear it.'"

Nash sometimes went around the country giving talks, and when he was in Los Angeles, he stayed with the Hacketts. "He hated lecturing," Frances said. "He hated it, I think. And he was so good. People were crazy about him. We went, of course, and heard him, and [he had] the most enthusiastic, loving audience, but he really, I think, being so shy, went through torment." Perhaps because of his difficulties with public speaking, when visiting the Hacketts, Nash stayed in the guest room a lot of the time. Concerning himself as houseguest, he once wrote:

> Have you hosted the wandering Nashes?
> They burn up their welcomes to ashes:
> Like some tropical shoot
> They arrive and take root
> And grow on their friends like moustaches.[6]

*Maytime,* adapted from a 1917 Sigmund Romberg operetta, reuniting Jeanette MacDonald and Nelson Eddy, was released in early 1937 and got fine notices, did excellent business, and is today sometimes seen on TV. When she and Albert were assigned to it, Frances wrote to Leah Salisbury, "We are about the twentieth writers that have been on it. But we start from scratch, with a new story. Last night I dreamt that the lover was killed in the first scene and that the whole of *Maytime* was a long cross-examination as to who did it. With the jury as a chorus and the principals as witnesses. You have a vague idea of my condition." Later, Frances wrote, "Terrible times on *Maytime,* which starts [shooting] in two weeks, and not a word written. But we'll get it somehow. The whole force of the office has been thrown into it, so that we don't know whose picture it will turn out to be . . . but that's all right with us." In the end, a young English writer, Noel Langley, was brought in and got sole credit. "He did the script," Frances wrote, "in three and a half days! Simply amazing! Took it right off our shoulders . . . for which we are tremendously grateful. We would have taken three and a half months to do it, and have been rotten at it, and have been slightly behind the cameras all the time. I tell Hunt that he doesn't need anyone but that one writer to turn out all his product for the year." (*Maytime* was Langley's first screenplay; his later writing included *The Wizard of Oz.*)

Next, working from a story by Hammett, Frances and Albert wrote *Another Thin Man,* the third picture in the series, for Powell and Loy—and Nick and Nora's infant son, Nicky Jr. When it was released, in late November 1939, it got almost unanimously bad reviews: "not as good as its predecessors"; "There is a noticeable lack of sparkle. . . . Nothing seems to click." In later years, the Hacketts agreed with the detractors, saying that the series had been getting "thinner and thinner" and "paler and paler." They hadn't *wanted* to write yet again about "the screen's most popular couple," Albert told a reporter. "You get a little punchy [doing] the same kind of thing. We thought the second *Thin Man* picture would be the last when we hinted they were going to have a baby . . . but the reviews [said] there must be a third picture planned, because they were going to have a baby. We just made it doubly hard for ourselves."[7] When Stromberg asked Frances and Albert to write the third film, Frances reported that he kiddingly sent her "a smock . . . with the message that it was to be worn while writing . . . to keep my clothes from being spoiled by Hackett's tears. And it isn't as much of a joke as [Stromberg] pretends." After the Hacketts had seen an unfinished version, Frances wrote to my father that it was a "very, very sick picture. Simply horrible. . . . Don't repeat [that]. . . . We haven't admitted it to anyone, not even talking about it at home, for fear the maids will spread the news."

By now, Frances and Albert weren't the only ones who were sick of Nick and Nora: even Hammett considered them silly and "insufferably smug" and called the third film a "charming fable of how Nick loved Nora and Nora loved Nick and everything was just one great big laugh in the midst of other people's trials and tribulations."[8] Hammett created the story when he was reclusive and often drunk in his ridiculous hotel suite, and working with him was no pleasure. He didn't show up for meetings with the Hacketts and Stromberg, and the Hacketts had to serve as go-betweens: once, when they were in Stockholm, Stromberg telegraphed from Biarritz, asking them to ask Hammett something about the story—so they had to cable Hammett in Los Angeles.

In his story, Hammett described Nicky Jr. as a "bored" baby. Albert later wrote, "[That] was funny to read but not to see—unfortunately, on the screen a bored baby looks like a sub-normal baby." Choosing other words, Frances and Albert introduced Nicky Jr. in their screenplay as a "fat, year-old boy who is interested in very little besides eating and sleeping. He eats anything that comes to hand and can sleep anywhere. He seldom laughs and never cries and doesn't think his parents are amusing." In one scene, Nora finds the baby sitting on the floor, chewing Asta's bone while the dog paces and whines, wanting his treasure. "What have you got?" Nora asks the child, then seeing what's going on, she scolds Asta: "You shouldn't leave it around. You're older than he is. You ought to have more sense!" In the script, the Charleses refer to the baby ironically. When a low-life friend asks Nick, "What's the idea [of having a baby]?" Nick replies, "Well, we had a dog, and he was lonesome." When Creepsie the Crook peers at Nicky and says he wants to see who he looks like, Nick asks, "Anyone I know?"

*Another Thin Man* may have been panned, but as they had for the earlier pictures, Frances and Albert wrote a terrific final scene—plagiarizing from themselves to create it. In its sexual tension, and the deadpan ignoring of interruptions, this scene is a close copy of the ending of *Up Pops the Devil*. After solving another mystery, Nick and Nora are in a bedroom, changing into evening clothes, waiting for friends to pick them up for a night out. Recently, they've had no time alone; sipping a drink as always, Nick asks Nora, seated before the dressing table mirror, when the friends will arrive.

Nora: They ought to be here now. They said they'd telephone up.

*(She rises.)*

They're going to take us to all of the new nightclubs.

*(She turns to him and starts to fix his tie.)*

Here. I'm crazy to go, aren't you?

Nick: Huh huh.

*(then)*

Of course, it's the first time we've been alone in days.

Nora: I know. But we can always be alone.

Nick: Can we?

Nora: Of course.

*(Nick looks at her dress.)*

Nick: New dress?

Nora: Huh huh.

Nick: When did you find time to get a new dress?

Nora: I telephoned, between murders. Like it?

Nick: Huh huh.

*(He looks at her lips.)*

And new lipstick.

Nora: Kiss proof.

Nick: Really?

Nora: It's not supposed to come off.

*(He leans over and kisses her. Then looks at her.)*

Nick: Did it come off?

Nora: *(smiling intimately)* It did for me.

*(The telephone rings. Neither of them looks at it.)*

Nick: What time were they supposed to call?

*(The telephone rings again. Again neither of them makes a move.)*

Nora: At ten.

*(The telephone rings a third time. Nick looks at his watch.)*

Nick: It's five minutes after.

*(The doorbell starts to ring. Nora looks at Nick's watch.)*

Nora: *(with worried concern)* So it is.

*(Both bells ring persistently.)*

Nick: Do you suppose they've forgotten?

Nora: *(smiling at Nick)* I'm sure they have.

*Added to the din of the doorbell and the telephone bell, there is a
determined knock at the door. Perfectly oblivious of the sounds,
Nick takes Nora in his arms. The shrill sounds of the bells and the
knocking at the door come to a crescendo as we* FADE OUT.

In the years 1936 to 1939, Frances and Albert did not, of course, spend every hour at their typewriters—and when they were on vacation, they enjoyed themselves: "That was a time when you could put a car on a boat for $125 *round trip* . . . so we would [drive around] England, France, Sweden." Frances carried a compass to help with finding the right roads; when selecting hotel rooms on overcast days, it showed where the sunlight would eventually come from. Years later, on a transatlantic flight from New York, after consulting her compass, Frances told Albert they were flying west, not east; he said she must be wrong, but she asked a stewardess, who admitted that engine trouble had forced the plane back toward the United States. Although she wasn't religious, aboard planes Frances also carried a small bronze medal, which Albert said was a gift from Myrna Loy; showing St. Joseph of Copercino, in long robes, with a halo, riding on the back of an eagle, the medal said, "Ye have seen how I bare [*sic*] you on eagles' wings."

To cite two years of the Hacketts' travels: in the spring of 1936, they went to the Kentucky Derby as guests of Hunt Stromberg, who was an ardent racing fan and a founder of the Hollywood Park and Santa Anita racetracks, then sailed on the *Normandie* with him to Europe. "We had planned,"

Frances wrote to Leah Salisbury, "to take a small, inexpensive boat, and then Hunt seemed so horribly disappointed that we changed to his boat. I thought he would be tickled to death to lose sight of us for a while, but he was genuinely hurt that we weren't coming on the same boat." Unfortunately, having reached France, Stromberg grew restless and cut short his vacation to return to work, forcing the Hacketts to do likewise. In 1937, Frances and Albert passed through New York in midsummer, staying at a hotel, inviting friends and relatives to dinner, and going to the theater with Hunt Stromberg. Then they toured in France and saw, close up, some of the results of the Spanish Civil War: "We drove down to the border. . . . We passed Spanish refugees . . . and they were living in tents and they were starving . . . the children of those refugees of the Loyalist Army."[9] This encounter spurred the Hacketts into trying to help the Spanish Loyalists— liberal-minded efforts that were later used against them. Back in New York, they gave more dinners and, with my parents, took James Cagney and his wife to lower Manhattan to watch Reginald Marsh painting his famous, highly detailed fresco murals, showing a ship's arrival in New York Harbor, in the rotunda of the Customs House.

My father was one of Reg Marsh's closest friends from childhood and had tramped around New England with him on walking trips and visited Europe with him. He later wrote a book about Reg's work, in which he called the Customs House creations "one of the great mural series in America." Marsh himself was once described as a "dashing draftsman" who "adored New York and its people . . . [and] found the city, even at its tawdriest, hopping with good spirits." During the visit to the Customs House, Reg and his paint-spotted assistants were working on a scaffold high above the desks of busily scribbling clerks. Cagney, Albert, and my father climbed a ladder to get a closer look; my father said later that "Reg explained the process of fresco painting. And somehow word got around that Jim Cagney [then at the height of his fame] was up there. So by the time we started down, about a hundred clerks were standing around with pads and pencils, saying, 'Jim, give us your autograph. Give us your signature, Jim.' The Collector of the Port learned that Mr. Cagney was there, so he sent word that he'd be honored to have Mr. Cagney . . . call on him. So we went in to meet the Collector of the Port, and Reg came along. And he'd been working there for about two months and the Collector [had] never even noticed him. And Reg comes in in a dirty old smock, and I think he was just as distinguished in his profession as Jimmy Cagney was in his."[10]

In the spring of 1938, Frances and Albert joined a mid-Manhattan club called the Elbow Room, which had expensive food and a membership that included Gary Cooper, William Paley, David Sarnoff, and the Hacketts' friends Brackett, Hammett, the Fredric Marches, Harpo Marx, Russell Crouse, and Marc Connelly. The dining room was narrow—hence the name—with a blue-tinted mirror covering one wall; *New Yorker* editor Harold Ross reportedly said, "This will make a beautiful swimming pool when they put the water in." The Hacketts probably didn't get there often: the place closed after six months.

*Society Lawyer*, released in March 1939, was a reasonably well-received remake of Frances and Albert's 1933 hit *Penthouse*. This time, the Hacketts shared script credit with two other writers, and Walter Pidgeon played the lead. The producer was the "dreadful" John Considine, for whom Scott Fitzgerald had also worked. Considine, who'd produced silent films, was a bold self-aggrandizer: he claimed to have a Ph.D. from New College, Oxford, but in fact had attended New College for only one term and had earned no degrees of any kind. His judgment could be bizarre. In 1940, he announced plans for an "aerial comedy-romance" starring James Stewart as a skywriting pilot whose career fizzles because he can't spell. Also, Considine felt that although *Gone with the Wind* was a "wonderful achievement," David Selznick, the producer, should have told the story in two short films instead of one long one.

Although their furloughs to New York and Europe gave Frances and Albert periodic relief, the longer they stayed in the Hollywood community, the more depressing they found it. In 1932, newly arrived, Frances had written, after a dinner party, "We are really having a nice time"; six years later, after a dinner party, she wrote, "We came home hating the world. And the awful thing was . . . [we were] with people we like . . . Dorothy Parker and Alan Campbell and the Norman Fosters and . . . the Cagneys. But we were all talked out with each other! We felt that they were bored to death with us, and our talk. You get feeling so horribly *dull* out here. And you see the same people and hear the same talk all the time." In other letters, Frances said, "We are fed up with this place. . . . It seems more and more like a squirrel cage," and "We do truly feel like the most awful backwoods people . . . in this prison life." Added to this was the grind at the studio. The pressure to pump out words, to produce page after page, exacted a physical toll to accompany the mental one. A few years before, to relieve the stress, Frances and Albert had hired an "ex-prize fighter" (obviously a masseur) to—as she joked—"soothe Albert and beat me." This regime, she added, was successful: "Albert has gained weight. . . . He has a pint of milk here at the studio every afternoon. So he is surviving this picture better than he ever did any other." Those measures had helped back then, but when—just after the release of *Another Thin Man*—Hunt Stromberg told them the studio expected them to write yet another picture in the series, plus more MacDonald-Eddy musicals, the result was alarming.

As noted before, Frances called their mutual problem a "lovely nervous breakdown." Concerning the experience, they said, "When we first went [to Hollywood], we popped with ideas. When they were right, we fought for them. But [later] we were flat. Not even a spark of fight in us. . . . They press you awfully hard there: we went to the studio every night to see the rushes. We were getting $2,500 a week as a team . . . [but when] they started to talk about another *Thin Man* and another Jeanette MacDonald, we started throwing up and crying into our typewriters. [We had gotten] to the point where we couldn't write anything. What we did write, we looked at and got awfully frightened. . . . We had the nervous breakdown together—this is a real team! Albert had lost a lot of weight, and we were punch drunk, slap happy, and on the ropes, [so] we said, 'Let's get out of here,' [and ] we quit."

The Hacketts described Hunt Stromberg's response when they told him they were taking time off from screenwriting: "He replied, 'That's fine, that's a wonderful attitude. I wish *I* could just pick up and get out.' We said, 'The trouble with you is, you've gone Hollywood.'"[11] Their shared problem made a lasting impression on Frances and Albert: when they returned to movie writing after their "sabbatical," they vowed they'd never overwork again. Mostly, they didn't. For example, when Samuel Goldwyn approached them years later to do the script of *Porgy and Bess*, they replied, "For a while we must not work. We remember with great foreboding the time we worked too hard and had to stop. . . . We were both crying into our typewriters in the morning." However, when they faced the biggest challenge of all, *The Diary of Anne Frank*, they threw that vow out the window.

# 12

## A Working Sabbatical: 1939–1943

**D**uring their years in Hollywood, Frances and Albert found a lot that they liked—chiefly their friends and their work, when it wasn't exhausting. However, they also found things they considered ridiculous. Compared to the comments of others (Sid Perelman, for example, called the place a "leprous, misbegotten kraal. . . . May a trolley-car grow in my stomach if ever again I put foot west of the Great Continental Divide,"[1] and the playwright Wilson Mizner reportedly said that being in Hollywood was like "a trip through a sewer in a glass-bottomed boat"), theirs were mild. Albert pointed out that "the street corner benches where the old people sit waiting for buses are printed with 'Donated by the McKinley Mortuary Parlor'"; Frances added, "They run an ad with a large picture of a bereaved wife gazing at the picture of her dead husband. The caption reads, 'It Was Such a Lovely Funeral—And So Cheap.'" The Hacketts were amused by remarks that denigrated the East Coast. "Someone heard a Californian say," Albert reported, "'I'd rather be in an earthquake here than in one of those electric storms they have in the East.'" Frances once commented to a Los Angeles woman that a certain building was "hideous," and the woman agreed, then said, "An eastern architect did that."

By December 1939, Frances and Albert had left all that behind for a time and had returned to a place they loved: they'd rented an apartment on East 54th Street in Manhattan and were—as they said to an interviewer who found them "as engaging in person as their creations, Nick and Nora, are on the screen"—"walking and walking all over the city. . . . We follow crowds round in department stores, and listen to what they are talking about. None of them are talking about moving pictures—and it sounds wonderful! . . . We're enjoying the nice cold weather. . . . We expect to see four seasons—spring, summer, autumn, and winter . . . and no writing for a year. We've had seven years of it. That's an awful lot."[2]

By "no writing," Frances and Albert meant "no *movie* writing"; once settled in Manhattan, they started revising their ten-year-old comedy *West-*

*ern Union, Please* again. Earlier revisions had resulted in a weeklong production in August 1937 at the Cape Playhouse in Dennis, Massachusetts, with Percy Kilbride in the lead; now, they had hopes of improving the play even more and having it done on Broadway. When summer came, continuing their new, relatively relaxed pace, they rented a bungalow in another place they loved, the Lakewood Theater community near Skowhegan, Maine. Here, life was relaxing, sometimes even boring; as Groucho Marx wrote to a friend, "This is a lovely spot . . . but it is inhabited mainly by octogenarians. . . . In the evening we sit around a fireplace with nothing to drink (unless it's my house), very little to smoke (unless it's my house) and nothing to eat (unless I buy it), and discuss what's the matter with the theater. Is it dead? . . . Then the clock tolls ten, and with a shout we all get up and beat it for bed as fast as our little legs will carry us."[3] (Marx was a prolific letter writer, and the Hacketts were on his list. For example, in early 1954, after they'd sent him a copy of the salacious 1748 English novel *Fanny Hill*, he replied, "Thanks for the Fanny Hill book. I have been over the hill for so many years that a rereading of this had no sexual effect on me at all. However [my wife] Eden seems quite interested and you may be sure that from here in I'll carefully bolt and double lock my bedroom door." Later that same year, from the Côte d'Azur, he sent a postcard showing a voluptuous, tanned young girl in a bikini, with the message, "This girl . . . may not be able to solve the Indo China problem, but she can solve many other problems for France, and frequently does.")

Among the people the Hacketts saw at Lakewood that summer was Owen Davis, the author of three shows — *Up the Ladder, The Nervous Wreck,* and *Whoopee* — that Albert had acted in. Davis told the Hacketts he was trying out a new comedy at Lakewood and hoped to move it to New York, and he offered Albert the lead. Years before, when the Hacketts first reached Hollywood, producers had occasionally approached Albert about acting jobs, and Frances had reacted fearfully: "Albert is to have another [screen] test. I am terrified of working alone . . . but at least I know I can talk faster and louder than Albert, and [producers] have to be shouted at." Now, in this less-pressured setting, with no script deadlines to meet, Frances, in an almost motherly way, encouraged Albert to accept Davis's offer.

"Frances felt it would be good for me to feel like an actor again," Albert said, "and I wouldn't have to worry about speeches and dialogue and things. . . . [I had begun] to envy actors. When they left the studio, they could have some fun. They could play golf, or fool around at parties, or just sit. They didn't have to think; all they had to do is remember. It's such a wonderful life when you don't have to think. [As writers], we had to think all the time. We had to get a better line for Myrna Loy. . . . Then we had to get a better crack for Powell. And so on. . . . But the actors, if a line wasn't any good they just had to say, 'Well, I don't see how they expect me to get anything out of that. Have Frances and Albert work out something better!'"[4]

The play Owen Davis offered to Albert was a mystery-comedy titled *Mr. and Mrs. North,* based on *New Yorker* stories by Frances and Richard Lockridge. In its opening scene, the attractive, scatterbrained Norths (her brain, a reviewer commented, was "so scattered that it can be virtually dismantled without interfering with what passes for thought") come gaily home to their New York apartment and open a closet—and a male corpse falls out, crashing shockingly onto the floor. The complications involve detectives, neighbors, and various suspects; one of the play's jokes is that murder becomes an ordinary social event, with Mr. North offering cocktails to the police. When they've finally solved the mystery, the Norths vow they'll move to an apartment with less closet space.

*Mr. and Mrs. North* opened at the Belasco Theater in mid-January 1941, with Albert playing the husband opposite Peggy Conklin, who'd been a major Broadway performer in the 1930s. Albert was well reviewed—"His air of ineffectual politeness and well-bred surprise is wholly entertaining"—and he enjoyed his work: "It's swell to be acting again. It's good to get back in the theater. . . . You have the sensation of returning to the source and being able to 'fill up' again. You get so empty in Hollywood."[5] The play ran for just over four months and might have done better if it hadn't been competing with the highly successful *Arsenic and Old Lace,* another mystery-comedy that opened two nights before. According to Albert, while he was onstage, Frances "walked around, taking off weight. . . . She had a fine time doing that."

When *Mr. and Mrs. North* closed, in late May, the Hacketts resumed work on *Western Union, Please.* Soon, investors came forward, including one whose message—"If your play is suitable, I will finance it"—was ignored because it was written on a penny postcard. In the summer of 1941, there were performances in New Jersey and on Cape Cod. Playing the leading role of the sixty-year-old messenger who'd left home ten years before, saying he was just going out for a loaf of bread, was the Hacketts' film-comedy-star friend Charles Butterworth, whose conversations with Benchley had kept them awake at the Garden of Allah. Butterworth put some of his own money into the production, and after poor reviews, he decided not to take it directly to New York, which pleased the Hacketts, who wanted to rewrite: "What we hope is that Butterworth will take it on the road for a run before [coming] into town with it. From the business he has done . . . sell-out and standing room at every performance, breaking house records . . . we are sure that he would do the same kind of business out of town. But when it comes to a New York opening, the critics would destroy us. Thank heaven he has had the same advice, so he is willing to try it in out-of-the-way places, then go into Chicago, hoping for a run there. . . . The consensus from the wise men of Broadway is that we have a good property for the road, and wonderful for stock and amateurs, but problematical for New York. . . . We have rewriting [to do] . . . spots that were flat . . . places that didn't play. So we are going to be busy."

Some of the Hacketts' revisions worked—up to a point. On October 6, when the play, retitled *Father's Day*, was staged in Cleveland, *Variety* called it "a rather amiable, daffy little farce . . . the lantern-jawed film comic makes the most of a juicy character role." Obviously, the play was improving; however, when it moved to Chicago, the reviews were thumbs-down ("so light that a Lake Michigan breeze might blow it away"). Still, *Western Union, Please* was worth the effort, later turning out to be, as *Variety* had predicted, "a made-to-order bet for stock companies and audiences that laugh easily" and producing satisfying royalties.

Roughly five years after he appeared in *Western Union, Please*, Charles Butterworth was killed in an early-morning car crash in Los Angeles; blood tests showed he'd been drinking. He wasn't the only Hollywood friend of Frances and Albert to die in an accident. Nathanael West has been mentioned; in addition, there were Paul Kelly's wife, Dorothy Mackeye (also an auto accident victim), and Edward E. Paramore Jr., who fell down an elevator shaft and fractured his skull. A poet, playwright, and journalist, Paramore covered the Russian Revolution, was a sailor before the mast, and was reportedly "run out of town in Santa Ynez because he dropped three flies in a baseball game [and] put in jail in Nicaragua during revolutionary troubles." Three of his plays were produced on Broadway; in Hollywood, he did many screenplays, one in collaboration with Scott Fitzgerald. He was an early member of the Screen Writers Guild; in 1936, Frances succeeded him as secretary.

In the summer of 1941, the Hacketts interrupted work on *Western Union, Please* and took the trip to Vermont previously mentioned in the introduction. The Green Mountain area around Rochester was beautiful, and land was inexpensive. Following long-distance negotiations, they bought two adjacent, mountainside farms covering roughly seventy acres, outside the village of Hancock, evidently thinking they might retire there some day. One of the farms had been abandoned, but a pair of reclusive bachelor brothers rented the other farmhouse; during various visits, the Hacketts got to know them. I was told that, a few years after the purchase, Frances and Albert saw James Cagney in New York, where he was promoting one of his films. He complained bitterly about being the center of attention—the fans, the interviews, the autographs. They said, "Come to Vermont and see our land." He agreed, and a female friend of the Hacketts went along, too.

When the four non-Vermonters got to the occupied farmhouse—lonely, isolated, high above the valley—the brothers were there: in their late fifties, unshaven, taciturn, and Yankees to the bone. Frances did the introductions. "This is Mrs. Smith" (or whatever her name was). "She's from California."

The brothers nodded.

"And this is James Cagney."

Silence, blank looks; then, "Where *you* from, Mr. Cagney?"

Cagney: "I'm from California, too."

After looking around, the four started down the mountain in the car. Cagney was livid: "Where am I *from*? Who're they trying to *kid, Where am I from?*"

The Vermont land wasn't the first the Hacketts had bought: in 1936, they'd acquired thirty wooded acres near the town of Madison, Maine, a few miles from the Lakewood summer theater community. A few years later, they had a one-room cabin built, and an outhouse. These primitive structures, which no longer exist, don't fit Frances's pearls-and-white-gloves image—but in fact she often called bathrooms "privies"; perhaps that was a holdover from her days in the Maine woods. A year after buying the Maine property, Frances and Albert bought close to three oceanside acres on Martha's Vineyard, outside the town of Gay Head, probably inspired by a visit to James Cagney, who'd owned a farm on the Vineyard since 1936 ("Everything about the land," he wrote, "charmed me right out of my shoes"). Although Cagney once wrote kiddingly that Albert should open a worm farm on the Vineyard property ("Albert could take his stud worm with him from California and cross him with the Island ones, and reap a small fortune supplying the mainland with Island-born [worms]"), the

Hacketts never developed the land and instead later rented houses elsewhere on the island. Having the Hacketts as neighbors pleased Cagney: "Good to hear that you are thinking about coming to the Vineyard again next year," he wrote in 1964. "We enjoyed your being there to the fullest, and hope you can make it. 'Tis the best kind of feeling to know that the people you love are hard by."

While Frances and Albert were buying their Vermont land, my father helped by inspecting the properties, talking to the owners, and drawing floor plans of the farmhouses. His taking time away from writing on American art bothered Frances: "[Your] effort meant a couple of pages in your book, and I was full of chagrin." Frances and Lloyd were always close, and she sometimes said he was "the smartest one in the family" and a "truer" writer than herself, because only those who wrote *books* could call themselves *real* writers. Frances's statements shouldn't be taken seriously, because she put a high value on the work she and Albert did.

Unlike his brothers and sisters, Lloyd didn't go to college—he was admitted to Amherst but then, still hoping to become a painter, went to the Art Students League instead—but he was later awarded four honorary degrees. He was intensely proud of Frances and called her "the most creative one in our family." It amused him that they both—can we call them scribbling siblings?—wrote near golf courses, thousands of miles apart. Frances overlooked the Bel Air Country Club, where she saw caddies surreptitiously improving certain players' lies; in the summer, Lloyd's study was close to the links in Little Compton, where he heard golfers crying, "Christ, what did I do *that* for?" Like Frances, Lloyd worked long and hard at writing, believing that success was earned partly through, in his words, "the constant application of the seat of the pants to the seat of the chair." "I probably rewrite every page," he once said, "at least ten times."

Both Frances and Lloyd were proud to have close relations who were also accomplished writers. Among them were Harvey O'Connor, whose refusal to answer Senator Joseph McCarthy's questions concerning his books, which were critical of the capitalist system and large U.S. family fortunes—*Mellon's Millions* was the best known—got him cited for contempt of Congress (he beat the rap); David Demarest Lloyd, grandson of the playwright of the same name, lawyer, novelist, and President Truman's speechwriter and administrative assistant, whose loyalty was questioned by Senator McCarthy (Truman silenced the senator by calling him a "pathological liar" during a press conference); and Clinton L. Rossiter III, a professor of American history and the author of *Seedtime of the Republic* and *The American Presidency*. A special favorite of Frances's was her cousin Beatrix Demarest Lloyd Dodd. Ten years older, Beatrix wrote short stories for leading magazines and published two novels. Frances once recalled that she lived for a while in the Nutley house—"I cried and cried when she left"—and used to draw pictures and make up verses. "I have never forgotten one of them," Frances wrote. "She drew a picture of a cart and wrote a limerick for us:

> How strange the workings of Art.
> Three elliptical wheels on a cart.
> They look very fair
> In the picture up there,
> But imagine the ride when they start!

In late May 1942, Frances and Albert decided to get back in the movie business and signed a contract with Paramount Pictures for $3,250 a week for six weeks to do the script of *Lady in the Dark*, the Broadway hit that had been created by an exceptionally talented team: writer-director Moss Hart, composer Kurt Weill, and Ira Gershwin, who collaborated on the lyrics. In committing themselves to this other studio, they were ignoring their long association with MGM. Their reasons seem to have included the fact that Charles Brackett was now a Paramount producer and was eager to work with them. "Dear Kids," he wrote, "I'm the first producer on the lot to start clamoring for you!" (Addressing the Hacketts, who were then fifty-two and forty-two, as "kids" was typical of those times, when producers often called screenplays "cute." On the title pages of scripts, the producers' names were preceded by "Mr.," while the writers were simply called "Frances Goodrich" or "Albert Hackett.") Another reason for choosing Paramount may have been that, since Irving Thalberg's death, MGM had begun to lose its momentum and its stars: Garbo, Crawford, and Norma Shearer had left, and James Stewart was in the Air Force. After the war, Stewart didn't return to Metro, accelerating the decline; in 1946, 1947, and 1948, MGM won no major Oscars.

When Frances and Albert began spending their days at Paramount, they discovered that, as at MGM, the writers occupied a special table in the commissary, but this one was in a smaller room to one side because at lunch the writers played something called the Word Game and, as one observer wrote, "were so quarrelsome over it that they were asked to go there." The Hacketts needed a new movie agent and were besieged by people wanting to represent them. "We have been hounded," Frances reported. "All of the agents in town have been after us. . . . We found that people were going around trying to sell us . . . entirely without our consent. We must have had at least fifteen agents who came not once, but often. . . . Phil Berg seemed the sanest and the best businessman, who would keep the wolves off and really protect us with some dignity out here, so in sheer desperation we took him." Phil Berg's partner was named Bert Allenberg, and through the following years, although they continued to correspond with Berg, the Hacketts grew to like Allenberg greatly and to depend on him more and more, ultimately considering him a close friend.

Paramount paid the then-enormous sum of $285,000 for the movie rights to *Lady in the Dark,* the first work that dramatized psychoanalysis for a mass audience. The story centered around a fashion magazine editor (played in the film by Ginger Rogers) who has three vivid dreams while undergoing analysis and finally understands herself, realizing she loves a man she thought she hated (Ray Milland). The film wasn't released until 1944; it did well at the box office but got many bad reviews. Kitty Carlisle Hart, the former actress and chairman of the New York State Council on the Arts, said that the show's author, her husband, Moss Hart, didn't like the film: "He told me not to see it. It's the only time I disobeyed him. . . . I went, and I thought it was awful."[6] Evidently, Paramount felt that the basic subject matter—psychoanalysis—might not appeal to audiences, so they rewrote Frances and Albert's script, which more or less followed Hart's story, taking out the more thought-provoking elements, stressing the elaborately costumed dream sequences, and replacing many of the Broadway show's songs with new ones. Also, they didn't mention psychiatry in the advertising or publicity. "The producers, and not Goodrich and Hackett, should be blamed for the superficiality," a critic wrote. "Their screenplay was inoffensively amusing, and the interplay between Ginger Rogers and Ray Milland benefited from Goodrich and Hackett's dialogue, with its usual good-natured banter."

(The people at Paramount were mistaken about the public's reaction to psychoanalysis as a subject. Within a few years, there was a flurry of films dealing with it, and analysts were hired as consultants, causing Sid Perelman to write in the *New Yorker,* "The vogue of psychological films started by *Lady in the Dark* has resulted in flush times for the profession, and anyone who can tell a frazzled id from a father fixation had better be booted and spurred for an impending summons to the Coast.")

Frances and Albert held two particular men responsible for *Lady in the Dark*'s damaging song changes and botched script. The first was Buddy De Sylva, the head of Paramount. Once described as "small and abrasive," he'd been a songwriter ("April Showers," "Somebody Loves Me"), and Albert said he was "very contemptuous of anyone [else] who wrote songs. . . . I think he said he could 'belch better lyrics than Ira Gershwin.'" The Hacketts' second villain was the director Mitchell Leisen, a former set and costume designer. Leisen, Albert said, "had been in analysis with a woman for six years, and they took [our] script and rewrote it. . . . We asked to have our name taken off, [but studio executives] said, 'No, you mustn't do that, because if we had to take the names of writers off all our scripts, so many would go out with no name at all on them.' Buddy De Sylva asked if we'd look at the picture and figure out how you could save it. Well, there wasn't any way."[7] Concerning the mishandling of the film, Frances wrote that she and Albert were "furious. . . . After they shot [the movie], they trimmed and trimmed (it ran three hours at first) and someone told us they were trying hard to trim it back to our script. But in the meanwhile they had put so much stuff in it that . . . they had hurt it tremendously. There were things in such bad taste. For instance, at the end of one [dream] sequence, Mitchell Leisen had a girl turn to the front, looking into the camera, and saying, 'It must be something she et.' It had nothing to do with the sequence, which we had ended on a very different note for Ginger Rogers."

Frances and Albert weren't the only writers to have problems with Mitchell Leisen. Preston Sturges reportedly considered him a "bloated phony, a fey and in some ways arrogant man"; Richard Maibaum called working with him "an ordeal." Billy Wilder said, "Brackett and I wrote three or four scripts for him. . . . He was a talented director, but actually he came to Hollywood as a set dresser, kind of a helper of a set designer, doing windows for Tiffany's or Lord & Taylor, or whatever. . . . I had a bad time with Leisen; he was counting the pleats in the skirts of the stars instead of looking for the jokes in the script. . . . I was on the set, and I was screaming bloody murder that they were omitting something, that he did not know where the joke was. . . . That was Leisen's specialty."[8] On the other hand, Leisen had his defenders. "He directed my first movie," Kitty Carlisle Hart told me, "and it was a very good movie. It was called *Murder at the Vanities*, and it still holds up." Also, Leisen's 1937 film *Easy Living* has been called a "classic screwball comedy."

While Frances and Albert were working on *Lady in the Dark,* and living in Beverly Hills, Sid Perelman and Al Hirschfeld visited. (The Hacketts' friendship with Hirschfeld was deep and strong. Years later, planning to return to New York, they looked at an apartment, then wondered about remodeling; Hirschfeld inspected the place and showed them sketches he'd made of possible changes. What an idea: to have Al Hirschfeld's inimitable pen laying out one's kitchen and laundry room and bathrooms!) Hirschfeld told me that one day, in Beverly Hills, they were all "out in the garden. Albert was putting in a walk of slate. Theda Bara lived next door, on one side, and Sam Spiegel was on the other side. The doorbell rang, and Frances answered. She came back redfaced, and said, 'You won't believe what just happened: a man asked me to sign a petition to keep Lena Horne from buying a house in the neighborhood.' Frances was so upset by this . . . and we looked at the petition, and Arthur Schwartz had signed it: he was a composer—Schwartz and Dietz ["Dancing in the Dark" and "You and the Night and the Music," among others]. Schwartz lived across the street. Frances said, 'We have to go over and confront Arthur with this.' So the four of us went across the street to Arthur's, and Frances said, 'Why did you sign this? You're supposed to be a great liberal, why did you sign?' And he said, 'Look, Frances, whatever money I have is tied up in this house.'"[9]

(Schwartz reportedly once told his son, "We're not Jewish, we're in show business." In her autobiography, Horne wrote about the petition, saying that Humphrey Bogart "threatened to punch anyone in the mouth who bothered me. Some of our other neighbors also rallied around. . . . Peter Lorre was suave and abusive [to the petition peddlers] and Vera Caspary, the writer, was indignant. Pretty soon the petitions stopped."[10] All her life, Frances cared deeply about people who suffered from injustice and persecution and wartime terrors. Nora Sayre recalled going to a Beverly Hills restaurant to have dinner with the Hacketts at the time of the school integration troubles in Arkansas. Albert was at the table, but Frances didn't appear for several minutes; when she did, she explained that she'd been in the ladies' room, crying about the horrors she'd seen earlier on TV: curses being thrown at black children. Anna Crouse, the widow of the writer Russell Crouse, remembered a time in the mid-1940s when her husband expressed doubts about the intentions of the regime in Russia. Recalling Stalingrad and the Russian people's wartime sacrifices, Frances "flew into a fit, and said, 'You have the blood of Russian babies on your hands!' Russell was as liberal as they come," Mrs. Crouse said, "but he was appalled at this, and stepped very gingerly with Miss Goodrich after that.")[11]

Around the time Frances and Albert were writing *Lady in the Dark,* Alexander King arrived in Hollywood to be Preston Sturges's assistant on *The Miracle of Morgan's Creek.* Small, slender, Austrian-born, a painter-illustrator-writer-editor-"idea man," King later wrote four witty, best-selling, autobiographical books, including *Mine Enemy Grows Older* and *May This House Be Safe from Tigers,* and became a popular TV raconteur, but he was then in bad shape.

"Alex had become addicted to the drugs he was taking for kidney stones," King's widow, Margie Barab, said, "and he hadn't yet written his best-sellers. He went to some of the Hacketts' parties and saw them at other places, and he said they were good to him at a time when being friendly meant a great deal to him. Alex called Hollywood a company town full of swivelheads who were always looking past you to see who was more important, but Frances and Albert weren't like that at all. They looked after Alex."[12]

Having finished their summer's work on *Lady in the Dark,* Frances and Albert quickly got back to their New York apartment on East 54th Street. The apartment was modest in size but comfortable, and they kept the lease for many years, sometimes subletting; they loved everything about it except the predawn crashing as empty bottles were collected from a next-door nightclub. The playwright-screenwriter Ruth Goetz, best known for her collaboration with her husband, Augustus, on *The Heiress,* recalled, "We played poker there every other Saturday night—the Perelmans, the Goetzes, the Hacketts, and the Willard Keefes [Keefe was a well-known theatrical publicist]. Very low stakes; Albert was a good gambler, and Frances was, too. We had hilarious evenings there. . . . We laughed all night—it was a lovely thing." Perelman recalled those evenings when he inscribed a copy of one of his books, "To Frances and Albert, two of the slickest customers at palming an ace who have ever stripped me down to my dainty underthings."

By early September 1942, Frances and Albert were at work on a new play, *The Great Big Doorstep.* Based on a novel by E. P. O'Donnell that hadn't sold well, it told the story of a shiftless, eccentric Mississippi Delta family who become ambitious after an ornate doorstep washes up near their shanty during a flood, giving them "something to live up to." It opened on November 26 at the Morosco Theater, starring Dorothy Gish and Louis

Calhern, and got both negative reviews ("some highly contrived incidents") and praise ("an engaging comedy . . . often hilarious"). Unfortunately, it closed after only twenty-eight performances; Brooks Atkinson
once theorized that the somber wartime climate helped to kill it. Atkinson
liked the play, calling it "pleasant, friendly, and droll . . . original, fresh,
and comic. . . . The Hacketts are popular authors, which prescribes a certain amiable comedy formula. And they also are modest and sympathetic
people who enjoy the mercurial temperaments of their characters and the
fundamental solidarity of the family. Without patronizing their river-bank
vagrants, they have written about their higgedy-piggedy lives with appreciation and relish."

Albert once said that Louis Calhern was drunk throughout the run
of *The Great Big Doorstep;* all the same, he got terrific notices: "the best role
in his distinguished career"; "a gigantic man. . . . When his soul is hurt
every quarter mile of him writhes in desperate agony." Calhern's alcoholism was no secret: Marlon Brando wrote that he was a "hard-drinking
old actor with a classic profile" and said that once, the afternoon before a
new play opened, to keep him sober, the producers locked him in a room
at the Lambs, the New York actors' club, but Calhern got someone to bring
him a bottle of whisky and put a straw through the keyhole. "[Louis] was
soon snockered," Brando wrote. "When the producers . . . came to get him,
they couldn't believe it. . . . It was like one of those English mysteries in
which a dead body is found in a drawing room but all the windows and
doors are locked. . . . Nonetheless, on opening night Louis got wonderful
reviews."[13]

Like *Western Union, Please, Doorstep* was later performed often by amateurs and stock companies; it was also produced twice on television in the
1950s. When Frances and Albert submitted it for publication to the Dramatic Publishing Company, of Chicago, in early 1943, they were asked to
eliminate one male character and turn four male characters into women
—because the Armed Forces draft had cut the number of available male
actors—and to prune swear words, respecting the feelings of large Catholic high schools, which mounted elaborate productions and paid high royalties. Albert evidently overcame his objections to "the Catholic point of
view": he and Frances made the suggested revisions.

The man who bought the dramatic rights to *Doorstep,* chose Frances and
Albert to do the adaptation, and produced and directed the play was the
highly successful Herman Shumlin. Arresting-looking, with a shaved
head, Shumlin was a crusty, autocratic perfectionist who produced and

directed several of Lillian Hellman's greatest hits and was, for a time, her
lover. Shumlin could be brusque and demanding; soon after *Doorstep*
closed, wanting to contribute to the war effort, the Hacketts went to work
for him at the Office of War Information (OWI) and got a firsthand
demonstration.

The main missions of the OWI, America's chief propaganda agency during World War II, were to explain the conflict to the American people and
their allies and to build a will to win. Many of its films were produced in
New York and written by unpaid volunteers like the Hacketts. Although
they'd never worked on documentary films, Frances and Albert were assigned to a project called *Doctors at War*, which was intended to reassure
Americans that their troops were being treated by doctors who were well
prepared for the battlefield.

"Shumlin was in charge of the picture," Albert said forty years later. "He
was a very emphatic, didactic kind of man, and running up against the di-
dactics of the Army was awful rough going. We went down to Washington, trying to find out where they trained these doctors, and no one
seemed to know. We ended up going to see a general, General Marietta.
He was very nice; he said, 'What do you want to see me about?' We said,
'We want to do a picture about the doctors in training for the war.' 'Pictures of doctors in training?' he said. 'I've got a drawer full of them right
here.' Shumlin was getting angry; he said, 'Moving pictures, a brand-new
discovery.' Well, the general didn't know where the doctors were and he
was getting angry with Shumlin, who was explaining things to him. . . .

"We found out that [the training] was in Carlisle, Pennsylvania," Albert
went on. "We went up there. . . . It was a regular Army camp, and the first
thing we saw were doctors—they were out for a march of two miles, followed by an ambulance. [We were told], 'Don't write that.' . . . We went
to [a classroom], and all the doctors had colds, and were coughing and
sneezing and blowing their noses."[14] In the end, *Doctors at War* turned out
to be ten minutes long; it was released in the United States in May 1943.
(While the Hacketts were doing their research in Pennsylvania, Albert got
a telegram offering him a part in a Marlene Dietrich musical to be produced by Cheryl Crawford. He replied that he didn't think he could "afford to do a show" but felt honored to be asked. His reply severed his
connection to acting; he'd now become totally a writer.)

While they were based in New York, Frances and Albert also contributed narration for OWI "News Reviews"—compilations of newsreel
footage that told the people of recently liberated countries what had been

going on in the world while they'd been under German or Japanese control—and condensed Lillian Hellman's anti-Nazi play, *Watch on the Rhine*, into a script for the Armed Forces Radio Network ("It's an extremely skillful job," Hellman said). Later, back in California, they worked briefly for the Army's 834th Signal Service Photographic Detachment, headed by Frank Capra, on the script of a film titled *Know Your Enemy—Japan*. While involved in this, unable to rent a house, they stayed for a while at the Garden of Allah, which had lost its glamor for Frances; she called it a "horrible, dreary, dirty pest hole."

*Know Your Enemy—Japan* was a puzzling and troubling assignment for Frances and Albert, mainly because they knew almost nothing about the Far East (and neither did the other writers from the 834th Detachment's "Typewriter Brigade," including John Huston and Carl Foreman, who also worked on the script). It's been reported that at one point, coming out of a projection room where they'd seen stock film about Japan as part of their research, the Hacketts had "tears streaming down their faces" and were saying, "How can we say bad things about the Japanese—did you see those wonderful, beautiful . . . little children?" Intended for viewing by both the armed forces and civilians, the film ran into many problems, chiefly centered around whom to blame for the war—the Japanese people or the emperor and the militarists. The Hacketts ended their script with words that indicted the militarists: "As surgeons, without hatred, we must eradicate this evil cancer of brutal, stupid, war-loving militarism that has caused the peoples of the world so much pain. And out of the bitterness and humiliation of crushing defeat, our hope is that the people of Japan will accept their rightful place among the peace-loving peoples of the world."[15] This passage wasn't used in the final film, and many other changes were made; in the end, the movie held the Japanese people ultimately responsible—because, it has been said, "higher U. S. echelons" had decided to placate Japan's leaders in order to ease the country's turn toward democracy. After many long delays, the film was released on August 9, 1945, three days after the Hiroshima bombing; it was soon withdrawn, because Japan was no longer, as the title said, an enemy.

# 13

## "Paramount's Lot Is Not a Happy One"

**F**rances was now in her mid-fifties—and her looks and style made a strong impression. Years later, my sister, Madeleine Noble, commented:

Frances I remember in a confusion of sharp details, all connected to a little girl's sensibilities. I remember thinking that she was incredibly glamorous. She and Albert would arrive "from the Coast" and be invited to our parents' New York apartment for dinner. Mother was always so pleased and excited to have them come, and their arrival is connected in my mind with Mother applying fingernail polish about when the doorman rang from downstairs to announce them. And when they did come through the door there was so much to look at, to smell, and to generally admire. And such vivacity, such warmth, such bursts of laughter. . . .

Frances wore really wonderful clothes, rather theatrical; I especially remember a stunning gold brocade dress with a fur-trimmed jacket which looked just beautiful with Frances's [reddish-dyed] hair and her lovely brown eyes. She wore bright red fingernail polish . . . and I recall her talking about spending the day at Elizabeth Arden's Red Door, having the works. I thought that sounded like the height of luxury. However, I don't think this glamor was connected with a personal sense of vanity. . . . It had to do with the period, when you dressed up as a matter of course for the evening (and "owed it to your audience")—and of course with the fact that she inhabited the theater world. She didn't like to be seen at a disadvantage, but joked about it when it happened, as when a local hairdresser in southern France once turned her locks, which she was then wearing a subtle Titian color, an incredible punk red, which she actually found funny. She never wore anything that could be called "sports clothes." In Little Compton or on Martha's Vineyard or in Provence, she would wear heels and a resolutely citified dress.

In her young acting days, Frances had displayed herself proudly before large audiences, but later she developed a hatred of being photographed. When she was in her midforties, MGM included her in a "trailer" promoting *After the Thin Man*, and she complained, "I look perfectly horrible . . . fat and a million years old." Al Hirschfeld said, "I remember trying to photograph her [in the 1960s] up on Martha's Vineyard, and she was *furious* that I aimed the camera at her."

While Frances and Albert were in New York finishing their OWI work, Paramount Pictures started sending suggestions for new projects. Since their contract allowed them to be choosy, the Hacketts turned them all down, including, to name just two, *Chicken Every Sunday*, a best-selling collection of anecdotes about a "typical American family," and *A Medal for Benny*, based on an outline by John Steinbeck. Concerning the latter, they telegraphed, "Story seems to have more trap doors than a magician's trunk. . . . May we stay out of this hand and wait for the next deal?"[1] (Both of those projects ultimately made it onto the screen.) Bert Allenberg, once called "the likable dean of agents," had now become the Hacketts' main representative in Hollywood, and he agreed with their decisions: "There is sufficient demand for your services so you should be able to pick and choose, and I want you to keep turning things down until you hit something you like."[2] Then Paramount asked them to write the script of a semidocumentary to be called *The Hitler Gang*, about the rise of the Nazi party. The idea was that the studio would contribute to the war effort by telling "the inside story of the gang that stole a nation . . . the authentic account of the rise to power of international political bandits who prevailed . . . not because they were themselves strong and worthy, but because they were in no way bound by the codes of civilization." The film, Paramount announced, would be made with the cooperation of the State Department and the OWI, and sixteen-millimeter prints would be smuggled into Nazi-occupied countries.

Frances and Albert felt this assignment was important and accepted eagerly. Back in Hollywood, they moved into an apartment at the Chateau Marmont Hotel (which was right across Sunset Boulevard from the Garden of Allah and, having been home to at least as many show business folk, has been called "Hollywood's Legendary Hotel of the Stars"). They soon set to work with the help of researchers from Paramount and Dr. Hermann Rauschning, an author of books on Nazi Germany. At first, their assignment was vague: "We have not the damnedest idea what we are to write," Frances commented. "[When] we got here, the news of what we were doing [appeared] in Louella Parson's column. I am still trying to find out what she said, so that I can know what we are doing." During the next five strenuous months, they read incessantly; coped with questions (Should the Nazis be called a "gang"? Yes: both Roosevelt and Churchill had used the word); took a course in documentary filmmaking from the famed Joris Ivens ("We learned [for example] that, to [get] a feeling of reality, we must have a 'reluctant' camera—close-ups would take away the feeling that you were witnessing a real scene"); and turned out two outlines, a treatment, a script, and a revised script. They wrote six days a week; on Sundays, they did volunteer work ("at least a relief from Hitler"), Frances at the Hollywood Canteen, Albert in various Victory Gardens, where he grew vegetables to compensate for wartime rationing. At one point, they went on vacation to Mexico but were recalled by a telegram concerning a casting problem: "We have Hitler. Come back." The actor, Robert Watson, was so convincing in looks, mannerisms, makeup, and uniform that during the filming he had to eat lunch in Paramount's kitchen because it was feared that if he ate in the commissary, he'd cause a riot. "As though this [banishment] weren't disgrace enough," Watson told an interviewer, "the cook kept reminding me of my sorry lot. My mashed potatoes would come in the form of a swastika."[3]

During the writing of *The Hitler Gang*, a heat wave hit: "I am sitting with my dress half off," Frances reported, "and the [office] door locked, so I won't be surprised in my nakedness." After the Hacketts thought they'd finished, people from the studio kept calling about details, then asked for another entire scene, which required "days of research, so we called in Allenberg, and he . . . made a deal . . . a week's salary for what we have been doing. We felt it wasn't right to our union to be doing these jobs for nothing." From New York, Sid Perelman wrote, asking when the picture would start shooting, then adding, "More to the point, when are you coming back here? . . . Why don't you write . . . telling us about your ideals and ideas, your aspirations, your hopes, your plans, your fears, your dreams, and anything else that occurs to you?"[4]

*The Hitler Gang*, directed by John Farrow, was released in early May 1944. Most of the reviews were favorable: "makes the facts of history vivid and significant"; "the most explicit and outspoken picturization yet . . . of the infamous junto of traitors, fanatics, sadists, industrialists, and militarists who in two decades brought Germany to its present stand against the rest of the world." Despite the reviews, Frances and Albert weren't pleased by the finished picture, evidently because the studio hadn't included German documentary footage. They had been deeply concerned about this project ("It was only after we really started to work that we realized . . . the tremendous responsibility we had taken on"), so it must have been a blow when an organization called the Society for the Prevention of World War III—the officers included such respected writers as Rex Stout, William L. Shirer, Clifton Fadiman, and Quentin Reynolds—called the movie "not only a bad picture but a very dangerous one. Germany— not only 'The Hitler Gang'—has occupied and oppressed most of the European continent. Millions of German soldiers are still fighting like lions. The German people still is united behind its Fuehrer—and Hollywood dares to show us this childlike picture of a 'gang that stole a nation.' Hollywood must come to . . . understand that this war has been brought upon the United Nations not merely by 'The Hitler Gang' but by the German people . . . the grave responsibility of the German citizens for what they have allowed has been neatly tossed on the shoulders of a few ruffians, officers, and industrialists."[5]

Frances and Albert had now written two scripts holding national leaders—not "the people"—responsible for historic tragedies, and their first indictment had been dismissed and their second severely criticized. Their feelings about these results aren't known, but when they took on *The Diary of Anne Frank*, they showed that their earlier experiences hadn't made them fearful of dealing with the evils of racism, militarism, and totalitarianism.

During their stint at Paramount, Frances and Albert had a hard time finding satisfying work. At one point, for Charles Brackett, they labored at adapting "a very, very bad play. . . . But it has a basically funny situation, and that is what we shall keep . . . and try to write up to it and over it and around it and beyond it." On Broadway, the play—*Oh, Brother!*, by Jacques Deval—had received scathing reviews ("an epic vulgarity"; "absolute trash . . . dreary, soporific, and inept") and had run for only twenty-three performances, but Paramount wanted Frances and Albert to try to shape it up because, before its Broadway opening, the studio had bought the movie rights for $75,000. The Hacketts' best efforts failed; eventually, the project was shelved. Also, Paramount asked them to write a fourth version of Owen Wister's classic Western, *The Virginian*.

The best of the three previous productions of *The Virginian*, released in 1929 and directed by Victor Fleming, had starred Gary Cooper and Walter Huston; the Hacketts' version, directed by Stuart Gilmore and starring Joel McCrea, Brian Donlevy, and Sonny Tufts, was released in 1946. It got tepid to cool reviews: "Joel McCrea [is nothing] special as the famous Virginian. . . . Sonny Tufts seems the victim of a practical joke. There is something unmercifully foolish about the sight of Mr. Tufts being hanged." When they started, Frances and Albert were told the picture was to be a musical, starring Bing Crosby, and, Frances said, "We were so enthusiastic. But Crosby refused finally and definitely to do it. He would not kill a man." The Hacketts weren't happy about their contribution. "The war was on and everybody was drafted," Albert said years later. "There were very few people around. . . . So [we were asked] to take the 'tarnations' out—the dialogue had a lot of 'tarnations,' and all kinds of curious expressions. . . . We just changed a little bit of it, to make it more like Owen Wister's story, a very famous story, that had the great line, 'When you call me that, smile.' . . . You couldn't take that out, because it was the whole [movie], but we took the 'tarnations' out."[6] Typically, Albert played down the extent of his and Frances's labors, which included a treatment, a script, and five revised scripts.

On November 27, 1931, Bob Ames, with whom Frances had remained friendly, had been found by a maid, in his pajamas, dead on the floor of a room at the Delmonico Hotel on Park Avenue. He'd come from Hollywood to work on a picture at Paramount's New York studio; around him were half-empty liquor bottles and photographs of his latest love, actress Ina Claire. Medical reports mentioned kidney problems; Frances was sure that his drinking had "done for him." Now, on March 11, 1944, at age sixty-two, Hendrik van Loon, just after writing a few pages of his autobiography ("I'll hand a copy to St. Peter," he once said, "and avoid filling out all kinds of entry forms") had a fatal heart attack in his home in Greenwich, Connecticut. By this time, the journalist-pedagogue, who "existed in the twentieth century but lived in the eighteenth," had become world famous through his books and his wartime broadcasts on behalf of his fellow Dutchmen. His funeral—Frances was in California—was attended by many distinguished people. President Roosevelt sent a telegram, and the *New York Times* editorialized: "His burning zeal for all his subjects gave him a kind of tidal force. . . . He was a hater of shackles on the mind and body, and a fearless voice against tyranny."

In early summer 1944, the Hacketts visited Little Compton again, and Frances sent Leah Salisbury their mailing address, in case "Max Gordon [a leading producer] wants us to do a musical with Cole Porter." One evening, they had drinks with my parents and the painter Isabel Bishop and her husband, Dr. Harold Wolff, an eminent neurologist whose books included *Headache and Other Pains in the Head*. According to my mother, Wolff had an odd habit: every evening, without fail, he brought his wife a single rose. "That," my mother said, "would drive me *mad*." Learning that my parents had no one to mow their lawn, the Hacketts bought a ewe and a lamb from a local farmer; the idea was, with the ewe tethered to a stake and the lamb gamboling gaily about, the two would crop the grass. The Hacketts then departed, leaving me, age thirteen, in charge: my father had returned to New York, and the ewe wouldn't let my mother near her. Talk about headaches! Every night, always at the darkest hour, the ewe managed to get hopelessly entangled in her tether and bleated deafeningly until I released her. Soon, my mother phoned the farmer.

More than once, Frances and Albert spent long hours on projects that were aborted; *The Flying Irishman* was one. In September 1944, Frank Capra, who'd recently joined a new production company called Liberty Films, hired them away from Paramount to write a screenplay based on Eric Knight's 1936 novel, *The Flying Yorkshireman*, which told the story of a man who discovered he could fly. Capra had approached Charlie Chaplin about playing the lead, but by the time the Hacketts got involved, Capra was pinning his hopes on Hollywood's ultra-Irishman, Barry Fitzgerald—hence the title change. The Hacketts finished a draft ("Nothing has ever given us more gray hair. . . . The studios out here are paved with the carcasses of those who died trying to do it") in late December 1944, but then came trouble. In Albert's words, "Barry Fitzgerald [was] a middle-aged character actor. When they gave him the script to read, he said, 'I wouldn't go up on one of those wires [to simulate flying] for all the money in the world!' That settled that!"[7]

In mid-January 1945, the Hacketts signed a new contract with Paramount. One of the main reasons for signing was that Albert was going to get a chance to direct; if that didn't happen within a year, they could break the contract if they chose. Evidently, Albert's main backer in this was an executive named Joseph Sistrom—but then Sistrom left the studio. With Albert's opportunity lost, he and Frances decided to stay at Paramount, where they next wrote an adaptation of *Alice-Sit-by-the-Fire*, a sentimental 1905 play by Sir James Barrie about a young Englishwoman who returns from a long trip abroad to confront problems created partly by her growing children. All along, the Hacketts had doubts about this job: "We did not know enough about English life to be inventive. . . . Consequently, we tiptoed through it."[8] It took several years for the film to get made; titled *Darling, How Could You?* and starring Joan Fontaine and John Lund, it was released in the fall of 1951 and got savage reviews: "feeble, sticky, and laboriously arch . . . lusterless flapdoodle . . . Paramount, how could you?" The Hacketts shouldn't be blamed: three different writers had redone their script—and the director was their *Lady in the Dark* nemesis, Mitchell Leisen, whose work the *New York Times* called "stuffy."

Wherever they lived during their three Hollywood decades, Frances and Albert always welcomed friends and relations into their home and gave exciting parties. Playwright-screenwriter-producer Julius Epstein, best known for the script of *Casablanca,* told me the Hacketts were "the greatest hosts in the world." That sounded a bit extreme, but Epstein topped it: "Their dinner parties were the most coveted in town. . . . They gave parties every other Friday evening—or so it seemed. . . . Invitations were highly prized. Without exaggeration, they were the most beloved couple in Hollywood."[9] Al Hirschfeld agreed that Frances and Albert "did a lot of entertaining. They had Abe Burrows before he was known. He sang and told jokes. He wrote his own material—songs like 'The Girl with the Three Blue Eyes.'"[10] Burrows, of course, went on to write *Guys and Dolls* and other Broadway hits; together, Albert and he dreamt up titles for songs they never wrote: "I'm Gonna Clean Out My Drawers and Forget about You, Honey" and—after seeing films of the punishment given to World War II female French collaborators—"Did They Bob Your Hair, Charlene?"

Hirschfeld recalled that Harry Ruby, Hoagy Carmichael, and Johnny Mercer also entertained at the Hacketts', as did a Minnesota-born painter and pianist named Hilaire Hiler. In Paris in the 1920s, Hiler had befriended Fitzgerald, Hemingway, Joyce, and other writers and had painted murals in Montparnasse nightclubs by day and served as piano player and bouncer by night. In the 1930s, in Los Angeles, he became a psychoanalyst—"He stuck out a shingle," Hirschfeld told me. "You didn't need a license"—and wrote about the visual arts in weird, confusing articles *(Art, Insanity, and Hatha Yoga)* and books *(From Nudity to Raiment).* The dancer Paul Draper and the harmonica player Larry Adler also performed at Hackett parties; their friend Cynthia Patten said that one evening the composer Johnny Green ("Body and Soul," among other songs) played the piano, and Draper "danced all over everything—over the backs of chairs, turning over the chairs, across the coffee table, all over the place."[11]

Naturally, other people invited Frances and Albert to *their* parties. Some featured square dancing, which Frances enjoyed because it was fun and good exercise. Bill Ludwig, their screenwriter friend, said that Albert was "one of the best dancers ever—he was like Nijinsky. We used to stand back and watch him in awe. . . . He always looked like a Princeton sophomore, and he was one hell of a square dancer." (Plainly, Albert still had "legs and feet that speak." Another observer said that, on or off the dance floor, he always seemed to be "bounding, bouncing—he had a kind of pneumatic quality." Ludwig said that at this time he found Frances "very impressive—like a galleon under full sail.")[12] Frances and Albert particularly liked the parties their friends gave during the spring and summer nighttime grunion runs. Grunion are fish, slightly larger than sardines, that spawn by the thousands on California beaches during certain high-tide periods; the Hacketts used to visit in Malibu, snatching up the fish after they'd come in on the waves, then feasting on the freshly fried catch.

Obviously, the parties the Hacketts gave and went to were very different from those at the gussied-up mansions of Hollywood's newly rich moguls. For example, at Samuel Goldwyn's house, he and his wife positioned themselves at the middle of their elaborately decorated table, facing each other, and held court, surrounded by the most famous names in acting and directing. "You always knew where your career stood," Katharine Hepburn reportedly said, "by where you sat at the Goldwyn table."[13] While the Hacketts didn't see this feudal side of Hollywood nightlife, they also missed the raunchy side. They were once asked if they'd attended any orgies and said no; Frances added, "I guess we were social failures." Albert added that the closest they got to an orgy was at a cocktail party when "some Whitney woman" coyly asked him, "Were you ever thrown into a swimming pool with your fur coat on?" "These horsey people," Albert explained, "were always being thrown into swimming pools with their fur coats on. This Whitney woman used to gallop around the countryside with nothing on but a fur coat."[14]

In addition to hosting parties, the Hacketts often had houseguests. Among them was John McNulty, the *New Yorker*'s small, merry, jauntily dressed chronicler of eccentric characters and odd happenings on Third Avenue and elsewhere. According to McNulty's widow, Faith, also a *New Yorker* writer, he "admired the Hacketts greatly" and during his brief time in Hollywood, in 1945, was as unhappy at Paramount as they were. Faith McNulty wrote:

In those days the movies wanted anybody who had appeared in the *New Yorker,* and seemed unable to discern that John's stories depended almost entirely on language. . . . [They] had no plots, no women, [no] sex, or much in the way of event. Paramount bought the rights to his collected works and hired him to turn them into a script.

He was lost in Hollywood. [He] had no idea how to write a screenplay, or even how to learn. . . . Billy Wilder said to him, kindly, "John, you look as though you are waiting for somebody to do something for you. You've got to understand that in Hollywood *nobody* is going to do anything for you." Somehow a movie was made of John's stories [*Easy Come, Easy Go,* starring Barry Fitzgerald]; it had been doctored up and was full of phony Irish sentimentality that set John's teeth on edge. He walked out of the screening and that was that.

When John first arrived in Hollywood he stayed with Ring Lardner, Jr. . . . As he was unpacking and wondering how long he should stay, one of the kids, hanging on the doorknob, watching, settled it for him. "This is my room," the child remarked. "I'm going to have it back in three days."[15]

Ring Lardner Jr. told me that after McNulty moved out, he visited Frances and Albert. "He'd been on the wagon a long time," Lardner said, "but he went off while living with the Hacketts. He stayed some weeks, I think. I remember hearing Frances say she didn't know how to handle this. . . . Here was this wonderful man—he was a sweet, nice man when he was sober, but when he was drunk he was very difficult. . . . Finally it became too much for them; I don't know what they did." (McNulty wasn't the only person who took advantage of Frances and Albert: a friend of theirs commented that people often visited too long because the Hacketts were "innocent and naïve.")

During McNulty's stay, he brought the Hacketts another *New Yorker* writer, E. B. White, who sent a letter from his home in North Brooklin, Maine:

> I may be wrong, but I think it is time I wrote you a note. That old refrain "Why don't you thank the Hacketts?" is beginning to repeat itself in my brain and reminds me of the time I got thinking of the phrase Wamsutta Percale (which I saw in an advertisement) and lived day and night with it for a long terrible stretch.
>
> I am the man McNulty brought in and you cared for so tenderly. The bed you so kindly let me sleep in felt awfully good to me that

night and I want to thank you for letting me use it . . . and for the green alligator pears and other courtesies. (The pears got back east in nice shape and we had them in a salad, of all places.)

It was a lucky thing for me that my one night in Hollywood was spent at your place, where people were kind to me. I am now at home, in my own place, and hope you will try our guest room here. . . . The beds are not comfortable but what the hell—it's out of the rain. And if you like lobster . . .[16]

John and Faith NcNulty were married in Hollywood in September 1945 and returned to New York in early 1946. She said that his parting remark—which seems to echo the Hacketts' feelings—was "Paramount's lot is not a happy one."

# 14

## It's *Not* a Wonderful Life

If movies could be given sainthood, a leading candidate would surely be *It's a Wonderful Life,* produced and directed by Frank Capra and released in late December 1946. It has been called "timeless," "a masterpiece," "a permanent part of American life," and "one of the 10 most popular movies ever made, and one of the best." It is the subject of a glossy, adoring coffee-table book. After its black-and-white images were colorized in the mid-1980s, its star, James Stewart, who often said it was his favorite film, denounced that sacrilege before a committee of the U.S. Congress. Each Christmas, millions of Americans gather before their TV sets to commune with it. All of this adds up to worship—but Frances and Albert had very different, bitter feelings about the movie because they found that Capra, undoubtedly a great producer-director, was nowhere near as worthy and likable as the heroes of his films but rather was unpleasant, shifty, and fiercely egotistical. For them, working on one of America's best-loved films was a long, long way from wonderful.

The idea for *It's a Wonderful Life* was born in February 1938 when Philip Van Doren Stern, a novelist and historian and the author of biographies of Lee, Lincoln, and John Wilkes Booth, drafted a short story about a small-town banker who thinks about suicide ("I wish I'd never been born!") and is rescued by his guardian angel, who miraculously shows him the difference he has made in the lives of his family and neighbors. Stern titled the draft *The Greatest Gift;* it was rejected by several magazines. Stern then revised the story and in 1943 printed two hundred copies and sent them out as Christmas cards. One went to his agent, who sold the story to RKO. Three distinguished writers—Dalton Trumbo, Clifford Odets, and Marc Connelly—drafted screenplays, but none was satisfactory. In September 1945, Capra bought the story and the various versions for his newly formed Liberty Films and hired Frances and Albert (he called them "perceptive, human writers") to do a script.

When Frances and Albert read the material, they soon saw what the problem was. "Those were fine, fine writers who had worked on it before us," Frances said, "but they had gone off the track. . . . They had gone off into stories of politics and other things. . . . But [basically] it was a simple story, so we went back to the Christmas card."[1] In their script, the Hacketts kept some scenes created by Odets—for example, the youthful hero, George Bailey (Stewart), telling a drunken druggist that he has mixed poison into his medicine and getting hit on the ear so hard that he's partially deaf from then on, plus the boyhood George rescuing his drowning brother, and the high school dance and subsequent moonlight walk taken by Stewart and his future wife (Donna Reed).

For many years, screenwriters admired Frank Capra. "I'd rather be Capra than God," Garson Kanin once said, "if there is a Capra."[2] "Any writer," Frances gushed in 1935, "would give his soul to work for [him]. He's so creative . . . you're pretty sure of a success." At first, on *It's a Wonderful Life*, the Hacketts and Capra got along smoothly: they told him what they planned to do, and he said "That sounds fine." However, relations soon soured.

"We were trying to move this story along," Albert said, "and then somebody told us that [Capra] and Jo Swerling [a highly successful screenwriter] were working on it together, and that sort of took the guts out of it. Jo Swerling was a very close friend of ours, and when we heard that he was working behind us all the time—which was supposed to be against the rules of the Screen Writers Guild—it was a very unpleasant feeling." Things worsened when, during a meeting, Capra called Frances "my dear woman." "He could be condescending," Albert said, "and you just didn't address Frances as 'my dear woman.' When we were pretty far along in the script but not done, our agent called and said, 'Capra wants to know how soon you'll be finished.' Frances said, 'We're finished right now.' We put our pens down and never went back to it. He's a very arrogant son of a bitch."

Frances called Capra "that horrid man" and said he kept pressuring her and Albert to finish; in her words, he "couldn't wait to get writing on [the script] himself." When the Hacketts handed it in, Capra quickly began making changes. Later, at a party while the film was being shot, the Hacketts were talking with Beulah Bondi, who had the role of Stewart's mother but didn't know the Hacketts had done the script. "She said," Frances recalled, "'The most miraculous thing happened. There is this scene which is just words, words, words, and it couldn't play. So Capra shut down for the day and told us to come back the next morning. He came in the next morning with a simple, lovely scene and it worked.' The point is, the scene that wouldn't work had been Capra's and the simple scene was the one we had done originally."[3]

In addition to Swerling, Capra brought in two others to work on *It's a Wonderful Life*. Michael Wilson did a "polish," and Dorothy Parker did a "dialogue polish." All of this created contention: following a Screen Writers Guild arbitration, Capra was given third-position credit after Frances and Albert, and Swerling got credit for "additional scenes."

According to Joseph McBride, the author of a 1992 Capra biography, Capra went into a "drastic creative decline" after *It's a Wonderful Life*, partly due to his insistence on getting credit for his writing. His need to deny the importance of screenwriters in his films had already dealt "a nearly fatal blow to his career by sabotaging his creative relationship with Robert Riskin [who wrote *It Happened One Night, Mr. Deeds Goes to Town*, and other Capra films], and from this point his need to be recognized as a writer himself would make it increasingly difficult for him to work with first-rate writers, finally throwing him back on his own limited resources. . . . Albert Hackett recalled telling his friend Riskin at the time of the '*Wonderful Life*' arbitration, 'Capra is now fighting for getting his name on the credits to beat the writers, not so much for the picture he's doing now but for all those pictures [you] did with him.'"[4] So bitter was the experience of working with Frank Capra that for some years Frances and Albert said they'd made a point of never seeing *It's a Wonderful Life;* however, they later contradicted that, saying they hadn't liked what they'd "seen at the preview" and adding that they'd later watched parts of the film on TV.

Although Frances and Albert seldom talked about the finished picture, many thousands of words have been devoted to it, some calling it the finest of Capra's generally sentimental works (sometimes called "Capracorn") and describing it as "heartwarming." More to the point in explaining its lasting appeal may be its darker aspects. George Bailey isn't merely a lovable guy who helped to save a town; he's a larger figure, a victim, a frustrated man who longed to escape from his narrow environment and do bigger things but never got the chance. *Wonderful Life* has been called "dark and despair-laden," a picture about suicide and reintegration into society, the story of a man who bears the burdens of his community's well-being and doesn't like it. "The enduring greatness of the film," this observer wrote, "is found in the conflicts that trouble [the hero], not in his comic and romantic grace notes."[5]

The fact that Frances and Albert could deal with the deeper elements in *It's a Wonderful Life* seems to show growth: they were no longer merely writing fluff like *Up Pops the Devil*. After *It's a Wonderful Life,* they went on to face stiffer challenges and earn greater rewards, but for Capra, the film was his last great achievement. In later years, he had trouble finding work, and he directed only three feature films. Although many of his collaborators had been Jewish, he blamed "the Jews" for his problems. He retired in 1966, then spent many years writing his autobiography, which, it has been said, was well salted with lies. When Capra died at age ninety-four, he'd been out of the movie business for twenty-five years and had not made a major picture for forty-five years. "No doubt," a journalist wrote, "many people who saw his obituary were taken aback, believing he had died long before. The truth is, he had."[6]

*It's a Wonderful Life* is now an American icon, but when it was first released, in December 1946, the reviews were mixed—many critics considered it overly sentimental—and box office receipts were slim. President Harry Truman was a fan: "If Bess and I had a son, we'd want him to be just like Jimmy Stewart." Then interest in the film began to grow, and in December 1996, its fiftieth birthday, the enthusiasm boiled over. Festivals and screenings were held around the country; high schools staged plays based on it; commemorative crockery and Christmas ornaments were produced; and perhaps the weirdest of all, Karolyn Grimes, who'd appeared briefly as the Baileys' cheery youngest daughter, Zuzu, revealed that she'd become the focus of a crazy little minicult, with its own newspaper and deranged followers, who clutched her hands and shared their sorrows with her, and begged her to repeat her line at the movie's end: "Look, Daddy, teacher says every time a bell rings, an angel gets his wings." James Stewart died in July 1997; by then, the many roles he'd played so warmly, plus his modesty and World War II military service, had made him a national hero. Again and again, obituaries called his a "wonderful life," and at his funeral, his daughter quoted the script of the movie: thanks to his many friendships, he was "the richest man in town."

Since their first days in Hollywood, Frances and Albert had occasionally stayed at the Garden of Allah and other hotels but mostly had shifted between Beverly Hills houses. At different times, they had owned or rented property on North Palm Drive, North Canon Drive, and North Crescent Drive, and in Coldwater Canyon, and Frances once said that whenever they sold, they took a beating: "We can't seem to make money in any way but by hard work. Every other way, we lose." In early 1946, they bought a handsome, stuccoed, red-tile-roofed house in Bel Air, at 10664 Bellagio Road; although they kept their New York apartment and often visited New England and Europe, for the next sixteen years this was the center of their lives. Built in the 1920s, the house stood on a south-facing, hillside half acre, above the sixth fairway of the Bel Air Country Club golf course; there was another house to the east, but none nearby to the west. The living room, library, dining room, breakfast room, kitchen, servants' rooms, garage, and a terrace overlooking the golf course were on the lower floor; upstairs were two guest rooms and the master suite: two dressing rooms, a "sewing room," and a spacious bedroom with a balcony above the terrace. The views were pleasant; visitors called the decor "warm and informal" and "tastefully done" and mentioned the art collection (plus a group of paintings done by children, evidently under the auspices of some charity) and the antique furniture.

"We'd go to auctions and get things," Albert said about the furniture. "In the rainy season, when I couldn't garden anymore, I'd spend the winter scraping and polishing." The Hacketts had large vegetable and flower gardens, specialized in fuchsias, and exchanged gift bags of manure with Gloria Sheekman, who was also a gardener (and sold the Hacketts, in her words, her "eight-burner, six-oven fabulous stove"). While Albert was gardening, the tourists on the sightseeing buses often mistook him, dressed in jeans and sneakers, for a workman. One Easter brought botanical thievery: someone dug up a white azalea given to the Hacketts by their 10601 Bellagio Road neighbor, Charles Brackett. They always had a cook-housekeeper; for thirteen happy years, the job was done by a Rumanian-born eccentric named Daisy, well-known for her skill in the kitchen, for her references to "President Eisenheimer," and for dressing her female dachshund, Pookie, in clown and Santa Claus costumes to parade her on Hollywood Boulevard (also, Daisy shoved Pookie into the oven on chilly mornings to warm her). The Hacketts treasured Daisy, even though, as Frances once reported, she grew "crazier and crazier every day," and they weren't always that lucky with housekeepers. They had one who quit right after returning from a paid vacation, claiming she was getting married (but the Hacketts knew she was already married), and another who was "really too much of a lady to work. She got more and more demanding, and [we called a halt] when she brought her son to live with us because she was afraid to be left alone at night."

In their comfortable Bel Air house, as they had before, Frances and Albert gave many parties. According to Gloria Sheekman, "Somebody would play the piano, they or we would sing. There was a great deal of [gossip about] studios, work, and personalities . . . lots of wonderful reminiscences of early days from Groucho and other 'poor boys from the New York ghetto' on their way up. . . . The guests were mostly writers."[7] Also, the Hacketts continued to have houseguests, including, in 1953, when she was making Alfred Hitchcock's *I Confess*, the actress Dolly Haas Hirschfeld, who, on the first morning she had to leave early for the studio, found a note on her breakfast tray saying, "Miss Dolly Haas is invited for dinner tonight and every night from now on." A few years later, the Hacketts invited a young English doctor, Patrick Woodcock, to spend time with them, and he saw some colorful corners of their life.

Frances and Albert had first met "Doctor Pat," as Frances called him, in London in January 1956, when he treated Frances for a painful, persistent case of shingles. She was confined to bed in their hotel for over three weeks and had a nurse who "fascinated" her, Dr. Woodcock wrote to me in 1994, because she was a member of the Communist Party ("not at all unusual in those days"). Normally, Frances distrusted doctors, but she liked Woodcock greatly. Then in his late thirties, he was witty and free spirited and, in his words, "absolutely nothing like a N.Y. or L.A. doctor. My medical expertise was rudimentary, but I had a quick brain and common sense. . . . Frances told me that if I'd been in L.A., I would have loaded her with useless medicine and sent her to a clinic. . . . I'd only just got a car (previously I'd done all my visits on a bicycle) and I loved visiting [patients], seeing [their] houses and how they lived."

Dr. Woodcock had never been to Hollywood and was delighted when Frances and Albert invited him: the place was "a world everyone in England of my generation knew about and in theory wanted to know—we were brought up on the films of the '30s." To pay for the trip, he sold a small Paul Klee drawing a friend had given him. On his way to California, he stopped in New York, where the Hacketts arranged for him to see *My Fair Lady* ("Dr. Woodcock," Albert wrote, "will be asking for a single ticket in the name of Albert Hackett—a friend of my wife's—at the box office"). On his second evening in the house on Bellagio Road, the Hacketts gave a party for him.

"Cars started arriving at 5–6," Dr. Woodcock wrote, "huge, shiny, and impressive. I later discovered they belonged to the [catering] staff." The caterers hung Chinese lanterns on the terrace overlooking the golf course and served cold salmon and hot risotto; Dr. Woodcock chatted with, among others, Christopher Isherwood and his companion Don Bachardy

—Isherwood later wrote that the party was "meaningless"—and director Lewis Milestone, actor Richard Conte, and writer-producer-director Norman Panama. On subsequent evenings, the Hacketts took Woodcock to other parties, where he encountered, he said, the same caterers, "the same lanterns, the same canapés, the same cutlery . . . and, alas, the same conversation." (The doctor's comments on some Hollywoodites—for instance, Olivia de Havilland, who was his dinner partner one night—could be rough: he cited their "silliness" and "lack of education." A few years later, at a studio outside London, he had lunch on the set of *The Road to Hong Kong* with the Hacketts, Bing Crosby, Bob Hope, and Dorothy Lamour and called the experience "lowering—Oh, how ill-informed they were. Not F. and A.")

At one evening party, Woodcock said, "a large man" offered him "a Japanese virgin. I was no prude, but my Quaker upbringing temporarily produced a *froideur*." Frances and Albert also took Woodcock to a studio where they watched some of the filming of *The Young Lions*, to "a Marx brother's house which had a pool half in and half out of the house," and to the Charles Bracketts' house, where they had lunch by the pool: "Small tables and an alcoholic Brackett daughter who came gingerly down the steps, slipped into the chair next to mine, and disappeared under the table. . . . No one paid any attention." Also, Dr. Woodcock got around on his own: Frances and Albert, who went to work every day, "typically lent me their car and hired one for themselves. It was my first automatic, and Tyrone Power, a friend [of mine] from London, had to come over and start it for me."

All in all, the Hacketts gave Doctor Pat a "wonderful, curious, magical, never to be forgotten holiday." Frances spoke to him, he said, in her "unforgettable voice, which I still hear." (He also remembered her "exquisite clothes.") "What did we talk about? Albert's wonderfully idiosyncratic theatre stories and Frances's getting me to talk, of course. It was only later that I realized what a beauty she had been, and still was. They were so exotic for me, and their world so unfamiliar. . . . [Thereafter] I saw them each time they landed in London: those huge luncheons in rented houses . . . with Frances becoming frailer and frailer but never losing her knife-edge intellect. . . . I fell under [the Hacketts'] spell. . . . they were unique."

Dr. Woodcock didn't say so, but Frances and Albert probably took him to dinner at Dave Chasen's restaurant in Beverly Hills. It had been started in 1936, not long after the Hacketts arrived in Hollywood, and they and their friends the Cagneys, Benchley, the Pat O'Briens, Dorothy Parker, and various Marx brothers went there often. Frances and Albert once took Laura and Sid Perelman, and Perelman fell in love with a dessert, Coupe Alexandre (vanilla ice cream rolled in roasted coconut and sprinkled with anisette), and raved about it in letters to the Hacketts: "One of the culminating points in my life. . . . I get limp in every nerve when I think of it. . . . The thought of that ambrosial sweetmeat has sustained me in some very trying periods."

When Dr. Woodcock visited, Bel Air was a fancy neighborhood (he called it "opulent"). Among the attractions were the Sunday afternoon parties given by Charles Brackett and his wife, Elizabeth. "The social life then," the producer David Brown told me, "was quite elegant, sort of like English country life. . . . People were well dressed. . . . You would see the Hacketts at the parties, with the writing and directing royalty—not the acting royalty—of Hollywood. . . . It was a grand kind of international atmosphere." (Incidentally, Brown called Frances and Albert "the ultimate class writing team of the Golden Age of Hollywood. . . . They worked only on the most select properties. . . . Virtually all their films were successful. . . . They were the epitome of elegance in writing.")[8]

According to Anna Crouse, the Bracketts' parties "always ended with people doing things. . . . Marc Connelly would recite *Spartacus* at the drop of a hat. . . . Howard Lindsay and Dorothy Stickney used to sing and act out a song called 'Mother,' a very sentimental, Victorian song, and [also] a commercial for a hotel, which was on the radio all the time—a ridiculous kind of jingle."[9] George Oppenheimer, the drama critic and playwright-screenwriter, called Charles and Elizabeth Brackett "two of the most civilized people in Hollywood" and said they "surrounded themselves not only with many of the most intelligent members of the movie colony, but they even invited 'civilians' [nonmovie people] to their house for Sunday lunch, an occasion to look forward to . . . and savor . . . a crucible of Western and Eastern culture with excellent Bloody Marys."[10] (Oppenheimer also wrote that on some evenings at the Beverly Hills home of Ira and Lenore Gershwin, "you might find Judy Garland singing to the accompaniment of Harold Arlen. . . . And if Judy tired of singing, Ethel Merman or Danny Kaye was there to carry on. In a corner that magnificent comedienne, Fanny Brice, would be playing gin with writer Arthur Kober. . . . Oscar Levant would be telling his ailments and neuroses with a devotion usually accorded to the beads of a rosary. Albert Hackett and Frances

Goodrich . . . the most devoted and friendliest couple in a town noted neither for its monogamy nor affability, would provide warmth and good
talk."[11] The Gershwin gatherings have been called "one of the town's ultimate salons"; the Gershwins and the Hacketts remained close even after
the Hacketts returned to New York. Ira once wrote, "If you think of, and
miss, Lenore and Ira a great deal, it's at least even money that Lenore and
Ira think of, and miss, Frances and Albert just as much.")

Another of the Hacketts' Bel Air neighbors lived in an enormous mansion, which some called a "Taj Mahal." The first time Sam Adams, a literary agent, was invited to the Hacketts' for dinner, not knowing what their
house looked like, he drove through ornate iron gates and up an intimi-
dating driveway. He suspected this wasn't the Hacketts' place—"It was
too pretentious"—but the doormat had an H on it, so he rang the bell,
which was answered by a liveried butler. "There was a marble floor inside," he told me, "and across it, carrying a drink and wearing a dinner
jacket, came Conrad Hilton."[12] Adams's word, "pretentious," isn't quite
adequate: Hilton's house had sixty-four rooms, twenty-six bathrooms, five
kitchens, laundry facilities for twenty-five families, two swimming pools,
badminton and tennis courts, and a staff of fourteen.

In these posh surroundings, Frances and Albert lived relatively mod-
estly. By now, they were highly paid—$4,500 a week. They gave a good
part of that to their mothers, other relatives, and friends. "They had an
enormous list of people they helped, for many, many years," Gloria Sheekman told me. "They gave regularly, every month. I don't know who was
on the list, and if I did, I wouldn't say, but everyone knew they had a list."
When I was at college, I was on the list: my father's museum salary was
then modest, and the books he wrote for the museum brought him no royalties; the Hacketts contributed part of my tuition. Their generosity toward
me and others may have shaped their career. More than once, Leah Salisbury urged them to "forget about all those dependents" and cut themselves free of movie earnings and return to writing plays. In the spring of
1933, from Hollywood, in a moment of discouragement, Frances wrote,
"We get so homesick, and we have to work so terribly hard, and we have
to give most of our money away, and it doesn't seem worth it." On the
other hand, there was sometimes joy in the giving. In January 1955, concerning tuition payments, Frances wrote to my mother, "Please, . . . let me
*really* help. I do so truly love to do it."

# 15

## *Easter Parade* and Other Judy Garland Hits

In early 1946, Frances and Albert returned to California after a stay in New York and, released from their Paramount contract, reentered the familiar embrace of MGM, where other writers were adapting their *Ah, Wilderness!* script for a musical version. Titled *Summer Holiday*, directed by Rouben Mamoulian, and starring Walter Huston and Mickey Rooney — who'd played the younger brother in *Ah, Wilderness!* and this time played the older brother — it opened in early 1948 and lost nearly $1.5 million, in those days an enormous sum. Judged a failure then, it has since been called a "milestone in the history of screen fare" thanks to innovations dreamed up by Mamoulian. The Hacketts were put to work on *Coquette*, a 1925 Helen Hayes play, unsuccessfully: "We could never find an ending to satisfy anyone." In August, they started on *The Pirate*, a fantasy-parody musical comedy based on the 1942 Broadway comedy by S. N. Behrman.

*The Pirate* had a fanciful plot (in the nineteenth century, on a Caribbean island, a young girl, engaged to a stuffy older man, imagines she's in love with a local pirate, whom she has never met; to pursue her, an itinerant actor poses as the pirate), a large budget, and a top-drawer cast, including Judy Garland and Gene Kelly. It also had songs by Cole Porter, most memorably, "Be a Clown," and was directed by the highly talented Vincente Minnelli.

As had happened with *It's a Wonderful Life*, several other writers had worked on the script of *The Pirate* before the Hacketts — in fact, there'd been *nine* of them, including Joseph L. Mankiewicz and Anita Loos. In the end, only the Hacketts got credit for the screenplay. In one of the pre-Hackett drafts, the premise of the play got totally switched around: instead of the hero being an actor impersonating a pirate, he became a pirate impersonating an actor. This horrified Minnelli, who felt that an actor could convincingly "become" a pirate, but how could a pirate possibly "become" an actor?

S. N. Behrman's play had had no music, so Frances and Albert had to integrate the score into the film's story. Minnelli felt their first draft was solid and workmanlike but didn't have the "outrageous" flavor of the play, so he suggested they go back to the Behrman work, and the Hacketts, he said, did the rewriting "with great patience and no displays of artistic temperament." They worked on *The Pirate* for four months and were paid $75,000. It was released in June 1948; in the South, the marvelous, dancing Nicholas Brothers were edited out of the "Be a Clown" number because they were black. The movie got excellent reviews—"best big-time musical show presented on screen or stage in years"; "eye-filling entertainment the stage can never match"—but it did poorly at the box office, losing over $2 million in its original release (it cost around $3.7 million to make). The failure has been explained many ways: the movie was "almost too fine for huge commercial appeal"; the merchandising was wrong; the picture was "20 years ahead of its time"; "the public didn't want to see Judy as a sophisticate."

At the time of *The Pirate*, Vincente Minnelli and Judy Garland were married and had produced their later-famous daughter, Liza, and Garland was beginning to show signs of the problems—drinking, pill popping, irrational outbursts—that afflicted her for the rest of her life. "We would see Judy Garland occasionally," Albert said, "and several times she came to dinner with us." During one evening at the Hacketts, Garland, "her eyes as big as saucers," put pills on a table and pointed, saying, "I'll have one of those, and one of those, and one of those." She also told a story that mocked her mother. "People who had contact lenses," Albert said, "had little suction things—you know, a stick with a little rubber thing on it, like a miniature toilet plunger. And Judy [said her mother was] poking this thing in her eye, trying to get [the lens] out, and then [realized] she didn't have the glass in there."[1]

During the filming of *The Pirate*, when Garland's paranoia worsened, she called her mother one of the people who had turned against her and were trying to ruin her career. She often failed to show up for work, sometimes locked herself in the makeup trailer, sometimes screamed that Minnelli was giving Kelly the major scenes. After the filming, she was sent to a sanitarium near Los Angeles; arriving in the dark, heavily sedated, she was moved across a lawn by two men and later said she was terrified that she'd gone truly mad because "something" kept "grabbing her feet"; the next morning, she saw that the "grabbers" had been croquet wickets.

In January 1947, in New York, Frances—"handsome in tailored black slashed with gold, radiating efficiency and humor"—and Albert—"slim, youthful-looking, giving the impression of scholarly calm despite a slight cold"—were interviewed by a columnist from a New Jersey paper, the *Newark Sunday News*, and Frances reported that the plight of screenwriters had improved greatly since the early days, in part because many had become producers:

> "Think what that means in terms of being able to control scripts from an artistic viewpoint. . . . This is a [big] step. . . . On the legitimate stage, no director or producer would dare trifle with an author's lines . . . yet, all screenwriters have the same complaint, that the studios have a phobia against leaving scripts untouched, and as a result some extremely silly things happen on the screen."
>
> Hackett said the introduction of Technicolor has meant one important change in musical films: "[Now the camera can] remain on a singer throughout the entire chorus of a song"—with black-and-white film, audiences got restive and the chorus had to be chopped up into little bits.
>
> "You see," said Mrs. Hackett, "films are improving all the time. As time goes by we—and that means everybody connected with films—will be able to eliminate all the other things that interfere with an audience's enjoyment. Admittedly, we still have far to go. But you would certainly be astonished if you knew how desperately everybody out there is always working to make pictures better and better."[2]

Not long after the *Newark Sunday News* interview, Sid Perelman visited Frances and Albert in Bel Air; he and his close friend Al Hirschfeld were starting the around-the-world trip they described in words and drawings in *Westward Ha!* The two enjoyed travel; Perelman once wrote that they first met in 1929 in Paris at a Javanese restaurant: "In no time at all—five minutes, to be exact—we were laughing and chatting as though we had known each other five minutes." In *Westward Ha!*, Perelman took still more potshots at Los Angeles—"the mighty citadel which [gave] the world the double feature, the duplexburger, the motel . . . and the shirt worn outside the pants"—and called himself and his 1930s coworkers a "splendid, devil-may-care band . . . ever ready to . . . lick a producer's boot . . . to sell out wife, child and principle to attain the higher bracket, the fleecier polo coat, the more amorous concubine." In a thank-you note after his visit, Perelman said that although he'd behaved "with the insolence of a freebooter," the Hacketts had been "marvels of forbearance, a monument of patience, in short, a duck."[3] The book was dedicated to Frances and Albert; Perelman gave a copy to my father, inscribed, "To Lloyd, this highly prejudiced and deplorably illiterate narrative of escapism, rascality, and double-dealing, from its remorseless progenitor." In January 1949, Perelman visited the Bel Air house again: he was circling the globe again, this time accompanied by his wife, Laura, their twelve- and ten-year-old children, Adam and Abby, many suitcases, and Abby's cello. (This strenuous voyage produced *The Swiss Family Perelman*, also illustrated by Hirschfeld.) During that visit, Frances and Albert often played poker with the children; one evening, to add to the fun, they appeared dressed as riverboat gamblers, Frances in a frilly dress, Albert wearing a fancy vest and a flat hat and smoking a cigar. During these trips, Perelman met many odd characters; one, an Indian journalist, later called on the Hacketts. He was touring the United States, searching for an understanding of the country, and told them, "I had been told that the problem in America was Communism, but I don't agree. I think it's parking."[4]

Frances and Albert's next screenplay was for *Easter Parade*. Like *It's a Wonderful Life*, the picture is often shown on television—and, also like *It's a Wonderful Life*, the project started smoothly but ended in bitterness.

*Easter Parade* was a tough job. Although Guy Bolton, P. G. Wodehouse's collaborator on many successful Broadway shows, had done a treatment, the major work was Frances and Albert's: they had to create a story that would plausibly link together sixteen unrelated songs—eight old and eight yet to be written—that MGM had leased from Irving Berlin. (Some songwriters might have sold the rights to their songs, but Albert later wrote that Berlin, always a shrewd deal maker, "leased—he did not sell"; Berlin was paid $600,000.) "We had [all these] songs," Albert said, "but one—'She loves him, and he loves *her*, and *she* loves *him*'—was supposed to be the idea this story was about. . . . We looked at that [triangular love affair], and we couldn't make anything out of it. But we could make a story out of 'Easter Parade,' which was one of the numbers."[5]

Frances and Albert quickly built a solid relationship with Berlin, often working with him in a fancy "Berlin Room" at the studio, where he had one of his famous transposing pianos (he could play in only one key, and the pianos—one is now at the Smithsonian Institution—enabled him to change keys by pushing a lever). Although it's been said that Berlin could be difficult, the Hacketts reported only good things: "We find him very nice and tremendously stimulating. Cole Porter, who did the songs for *The*

*Pirate,* was unyielding, gave us the songs and that was that. Berlin is so different—charming, anxious to help, and not wedded to any of his own songs. Willing to do new ones, to adapt them to our story, and to help us in every way. He is a truly gentle person, which is amazing in view of his phenomenal success over four decades. . . . He must be nearly sixty, and he is slender and tense and alive, and so enthusiastic and young in his vitality and energy. Now if we can only get a story for him, we'll be happy! They gave us a title and a cast and that was all." Frances and Albert had dinner at Berlin's Santa Monica beach house; Frances later called him "just the dearest man who ever lived." Berlin said he worked closely on the story of *Easter Parade:* "I didn't write any of the script, but I was very much involved in how they would develop their scenes. . . . I was anxious to get my songs done in the right atmosphere; the Hacketts were wonderful!"[6]

Albert felt that the story he and Frances constructed for *Easter Parade* "wasn't too good, but it served." The *New York Times* agreed that the script was marginal, saying that if it had been more than a conventional backstage romance, the film might have been not merely good but great. In the story, set in New York in 1912, the woman in a dance team walks out when she's offered a better deal; the man, angry and still in love, takes on a new partner, vowing to make her a bigger star than his ex-partner; after much effort and many fights, the new pair succeed professionally, fall in love, and wind up parading down Fifth Avenue. Gene Kelly was originally cast as the dancer but broke his ankle; to everyone's delight, Fred Astaire came out of a short retirement to replace him. The new partner was played by Judy Garland, and this time—perhaps because MGM took the directing job away from her husband—she made little trouble, and the film was shot in forty days.

Released in July 1948, *Easter Parade* pleased both critics and audiences—especially when Astaire and Garland, dressed as tramps, did their "A Couple of Swells" number. Other well-received songs included "It Only Happens When I Dance with You," "A Fella with an Umbrella," "Shakin' the Blues Away," and "Easter Parade." The film wound up making many dollars for MGM and has been called one of Hollywood's most memorable musicals. Despite Albert's negative feelings, the Hacketts won two Screen Writers Guild awards for their contribution—Best-Written American Musical (Screenplay) and Best-Written American Musical (Story)—but there was a sour note; once again, their work had been tampered with.

Frances and Albert finished their screenplay in September 1947, then went on another trip to Europe. While they were away, the film's producer,

Arthur Freed, decided that the script was "too authentic and harsh" and brought in Sidney Sheldon, later the money-coining writer of Sidney Sheldon–type TV shows and novels, to give it a lighter, more escapist tone (he shared the Screen Writers Guild award for screenplay). When the Hacketts learned what Freed had done, they reacted fiercely.

Arthur Freed was one of the most powerful producers in Hollywood. Before the *Easter Parade* changes, he had offered the Hacketts, as their next project, a prize package, Irving Berlin's *Annie Get Your Gun*, for which MGM had paid $650,000, the largest sum they had ever spent on a musical property. However, Frances and Albert were now angry and refused to work for Freed again. In a letter, Bert Allenberg urged them to change their minds. He was "outraged" at what had happened on *Easter Parade* because it was "so contrary to [Metro's] knowledge of your strongly expressed desires to have no one else touch your scripts," but he argued that both Freed and Berlin, with whom he'd talked, were "horrified" at the idea of losing the Hacketts and were "on bended knees. . . . [*Annie Get Your Gun*] should be one of the smash pictures of the year. . . . Why cut off your nose to spite your face? . . . Freed is so humble and abject about what happened on *Easter Parade* that he would be eating out of your hand."[7]

Frances and Albert had worked for Arthur Freed (once called "vulgar, crass, obsequious to superiors and often brutal to inferiors") before, when he produced *The Pirate*, and they weren't fond of him: in memos, others called him "Dear Arthur," but to them he was "Dear Mr. Freed" or "Dear Arthur Freed." Allenberg, whose clients included not only top-ranked writers but such performers as Danny Kaye, Clark Gable, and Frank Sinatra, was a famously persuasive man, but he failed to budge Frances and Albert. In the end, Sidney Sheldon wrote *Annie*, and the next picture the Hacketts did was another well-reviewed Judy Garland moneymaker — and, perhaps most important, for the next several years they had no more agony with interfering producers and no more anger caused by unexpected revisions.

The fights Frances and Albert had concerning the rewriting of *Easter Parade* and other screenplays might suggest that they were overly temperamental, or extra-sensitive, or even spoiled. After all, hadn't they themselves, back in the 1930s, praised the system that routinely involved many writers in a single project, and acknowledged that MGM's contract writers were expected to "take a fling at" scripts and "push them along"? Weren't they aware that in MGM's high-pressure Freed Unit, scripts *always* got revised? (It's been reported that of the forty-three musicals and musical comedies that Arthur Freed produced at MGM during a quarter of a century, *not one* was finally accredited to a single screenwriter.)

The answer seems to be, yes, the Hacketts understood the system; however, unlike some screenwriters of that period who'd previously been journalists or fiction writers, they'd come from the theater, where, as Frances told the *Newark Sunday News*, "no producer or director would dare trifle with an author's lines," and they simply couldn't shed that background. Also, they'd made those enthusiastic statements about team effort when they were beginners. Now that they'd proven themselves, their perspective had changed: as far as their own work was concerned, their attitude was, "Hands off, unless we're consulted." Finally, there was the ego factor: Frances and Albert had always taken greater-than-average pride in their work; other Hollywood writers might bite their tongues and kowtow to meddling, but by nature they were just plain feisty.

(Of course, Frances and Albert weren't the only writers who resented producers' revisions. Ben Hecht, who turned out some sixty screenplays—including *The Front Page*—once said, "I spent more time arguing than writing. . . . My chief memory of movieland is one of asking . . . why must I change the script, eviscerate it, cripple and hamstring it?"[8] Raymond Chandler, the novelist and screenwriter—*Double Indemnity*, *The Blue Dahlia*—wrote of his Hollywood experiences, "I personally had a lot of fun. . . . But how long you can survive depends a great deal on what sort of people get to work with. You meet a lot of bastards, but they usually have some saving grace. . . . The superficial friendliness of Hollywood is pleasant—until you find out that nearly every sleeve conceals a knife.")[9]

The screenwriter-turned-producer Dore Schary, who knew Arthur Freed well, once called him "not a lovable man." Schary also knew the producer Joe Pasternak well and said, "[He] is a lovable man . . . a sentimentalist and a romantic [who] lives in a highly original world that we used to identify even to him as the Land of Pasternaky. . . . His films [which included *The Student Prince* and *The Merry Widow*] were cute, gentle, and warm."[10] Pasternak's life story had a Horatio Alger flavor—born in Hungary, as a boy he punched holes in a belt factory in Pennsylvania and dreamed of having his own bathroom—and his deliberately schmaltzy pictures reflected his motto, "Keep the people nice." He produced a number of films starring Esther Williams, sometimes called the Chlorine Queen: "I used to keep her in the water 99 percent of the time—wet, she was a star."[11]

Schary's words "gentle, cute, and warm" could have been lifted straight out of the almost unanimously enthusiastic reviews of *In the Good Old Summertime*, the musical Frances and Albert wrote for Pasternak in the fall of 1948. For the third time, the star was Garland, playing a clerk in a 1911 Chicago music store who's exchanging increasingly ardent letters with an anonymous pen pal—who turns out to be her fellow employee Van Johnson, whom she heartily dislikes. Also in the cast were S. Z. "Cuddles" Sakal, Spring Byington, and Buster Keaton, whose crushing of a supposedly priceless violin during a dance was called "side-splitting." The songs, by various different writers, include the title number plus "Put Your Arms Around Me Honey," "Wait 'Til the Sun Shines, Nellie," and "Meet Me Tonight in Dreamland," which Garland sings while strumming a $29 harp, which she then sells for $99.50. At the picture's close, Garland's daughter, Liza, then eighteen months old, appears briefly as the product of Garland and Johnson's happy-ending marriage (in the words of *Variety*, in the windup the two principals "discover their postal amouring and clinch").

Frances and Albert's screenplay for *In the Good Old Summertime*—Ivan Tors, who did an earlier version, also got credit—was part of a long string of Hollywood-style recyclings. This particular story first appeared as a play in Budapest in 1937; it was set in a perfume shop. Margaret Sullavan and James Stewart starred in MGM's highly praised 1940 film, written by Samson Raphaelson and directed by Ernst Lubitsch and called *The Shop around the Corner*; in it, the shop sells leather goods. Before Frances and Albert began their script, it was suggested that they set it in a "lavish department store," but they ultimately put the hero and heroine in a music store. In 1998, Nora Ephron wrote and directed a third film version, *You've Got Mail*, in which Tom Hanks owns a chain of cappuccino-dispensing bookstores, threatening Meg Ryan's small children's bookstore; this time, the lovers communicate by e-mail.

The late 1940s and early 1950s have, of course, become notorious as a period of Cold War "Commie-chasing," with shameless, opportunistic witch-hunters and on-the-make politicians fanning public hysteria; Lillian Hellman aptly called it "Scoundrel Time." In the fall of 1947, the Special Committee of the House of Representatives on Un-American Activities, generally referred to as the House Un-American Activities Committee, or HUAC, held hearings in Washington and subpoenaed a number of Hollywood moviemakers, mainly directors, actors, and writers, taking testimony concerning possible Communist influence in the film industry. The committee, which never found any real evidence of that influence, heard first from "friendly" witnesses, some of whom named names, thereby gravely injuring careers and even lives. Later, another group of witnesses banded together and refused to testify on constitutional grounds. Most were writers, and the first question they were asked, right before the "big one" — "Are you now or have you ever been a member of the Communist Party?" — was, "Are you a member of the Screen Writers Guild?": obviously, HUAC was trying to link the guild with subversion and treason. Branded the Hollywood Ten, the "unfriendly" witnesses were cited for contempt. Ultimately, after various appeals, a Supreme Court ruling sent them to prison.

The jailing of the Ten was widely criticized — for example, Harold Ross, the editor of the *New Yorker,* wrote that asking "those Hollywood men what their politics were was unconstitutional"[12] — and it shook the Hacketts: almost all of them were friends. "We didn't belong to the Communist Party or anything of the sort," Albert once said. "The fact that these people were Communists didn't matter to us. We never bothered to ask [what] they felt [politically]. . . . The men who gave names, we don't speak to. . . . The people who went to jail still speak to us."[13]

A few years after the HUAC citations, the Hacketts were among the targets of another witch-hunt (fortunately, that one, though equally malevolent and brainless, had less damaging results); now, from the sidelines, they tried to be helpful. In 1948, as one of the twenty directors of the Screen Writers Guild, Albert joined some of the best-known figures in the movies and the theater in a lawsuit against three producers' associations and seven studios, charging that they had conspired to set up "a code which purports to govern the political views, actions, and associations" of screenwriters, "infringes on [their civil liberties]," and "establishes . . . the un-American principle of guilt by association." The suit was withdrawn five years later when the president of the Producers Association, Eric Johnson, stated under oath that the producers were not acting in concert. (Despite those words, discrimination based on political beliefs persisted. The producer Jack Warner reportedly once said to a director who complained that he'd been blacklisted, "There's no blacklist and you're not on it.")[14] Also, while some people in show business were treating beleaguered writers like lepers, Frances and Albert extended hospitality and tried to keep their spirits up.

In March 1952, Frances and Albert were in New York when Hy Kraft, the author of, among other works, the Broadway musical *Top Banana,* took the Fifth Amendment before Congress, in Washington; when Kraft reached New York that evening, the news media had spread the word concerning him, but he found a message: "Come right over for a drink." He went, and in his memoirs he later called Frances and Albert "fine people."[15]

Another friend the Hacketts helped was Ring Lardner Jr., their former fellow worker at the Screen Writers Guild. In 1947, Lardner became one of the Hollywood Ten when HUAC's chairman, J. Parnell Thomas—a New Jersey congressman who'd changed his surname, Feeney, because it was "too Irish," and was called a "professional anti-communist"—asked if he was a member of the party, and Lardner replied, "I could answer the way you want, but I'd hate myself in the morning." (Lardner told me his response wasn't premeditated but "kind of came out.") At the time, Lardner was, in fact, a party member; however, as he explained fourteen years later in a magazine article, he believed that the committee was demanding forced confessions or disavowals, which was an abuse of the legislative function that needed challenging. In the article, Lardner also wrote that in the Communist party, which he'd since left, he'd found not only some of the most thoughtful, witty, and generally stimulating men and women of Hollywood but also "a number of bores and unstable characters, [which] seemed to bear out Bernard Shaw's observation that revolutionary movements tend to attract the best and worst elements in a given society."[16]

Lardner's defiance of HUAC cost him nine and a half months in a federal prison in Danbury, Connecticut. At his sentencing, he told the court, "Everything I know about . . . history . . . confirms my conviction that there is only a minor difference between forcing a man to say what his opinions are and dictating what his opinions should be. Whenever men had been compelled to open their minds to government authority, men's minds have ceased to be free."[17] Before starting his sentence, he had to sell his ten-room Santa Monica beach house and advertised it under the heading "Owner Going to Jail." When he reached prison, one of the first people he saw was J. Parnell Thomas, who'd been sentenced to eighteen months for conspiracy to defraud the U.S. government by padding his payroll. "I recognized him," Lardner reportedly said, "and he recognized me, but we did not speak. It would have been hard to pick up the thread."

When Lardner was imprisoned, Frances and Albert couldn't help him directly, so they looked up Frances Chaney, his actress wife. "I fell in love with both of them," she told me, "when Ring went to jail, because they got in touch with me right away. . . . They sought me out; they found me— we had moved from our house in Santa Monica. . . . They'd call me up and say they had corn they'd grown or something they wanted to bring me and the children—you know, do something loving and sweet. . . . [Before that] they really hadn't known me very well."[18] After Ring Lardner was released from prison, he and his wife moved to New York, where, ultimately, they and the Hacketts lived only a few blocks apart. "Young Ring Lardner," Albert said in 1982, "lives right down the street, and we see him all the time, and he's an old, old friend of ours." The four also got together elsewhere: "We stayed with them on Martha's Vineyard," Lardner said, "and one evening Albert cooked a steak with great pride."

In the late 1940s and through the 1950s, Frances and Albert often went to parties at the home of Melvin and Anne Frank. Mel Frank, with his partner Norman Panama, was a successful producer of MGM romantic comedies; Anne, who had danced in films and done radio and movie writing, was witty: once, consoling her husband about professional problems, she said, "Mel, stop your worrying. This is just a film. Nothing is as important as your health. You are everything. If anything happened to you I wouldn't want to go on living, unless it was in the South of France."[19] Most of the Franks' guests were writers: Arthur Sheekman, Norman Panama, Julius Epstein, Michael Kanin and his wife, Fay. According to the Franks' daughter, Elizabeth—born in 1945, in 1986 a Pulitzer Prize winner for her biography of the poet Louise Bogan, since 1990 a professor at Bard College—the parties were "celebrations of wit. . . . People would tell anecdotes, tell stories, respond to each other's anecdotes, about projects they were on, characters they had met, actors they'd encountered."

"Many Hollywood writers' kids," Elizabeth Frank said, "have had the same experience I had—being lured by the sound of laughter out of their beds, and down the stairs, and you sneak behind a door and you listen to these stories. Then you go in in your nightgown, and you carry peanuts around, and someone puts an arm around you, and you sit on someone's lap while they're talking. . . . Everyone smoked in those days, and everybody drank, and they all wore beautiful, elegant clothing. . . . You'd be sitting in someone's lap, and hearing stories and one-liners, and it was absolute heaven—I completely adored that. The Hacketts were sweet and kind to me; their sophistication did not equal coldness.

"The writers' parties were intimate," Elizabeth Frank added. "Everyone was respectful of everyone else's humor. People knew not to interrupt one another, people were sensitive . . . . Every once in a while, someone's producer friend, who wanted to be in on the 'raconteuring,' would be there, and if he couldn't quite do it, everyone's behind got a bit fidgety. . . . These were writers-for-hire, who produced work on command, and were well paid, and were highly accomplished craftsmen, and they didn't pull 'artist's ego.' You very rarely saw anyone play the I Am an Artist Game—maybe Lillian Hellman did. . . . Once you entered the ranks of those who had earned professional respect, that respect was pretty much absolute. . . . [Their] stories transcended political difficulties: that was the [outside] world, and everyone had to make whatever compromises they had to. . . . They didn't sit in judgment of one another. . . . An ironic vision came through, and humor—although nobody *called* it that."

When Elizabeth Frank mentioned compromises made in the "outside world," she was referring to a dreadful problem that confronted her mother, Anne, during HUAC's Hollywood hearings. In the early 1940s, Anne Frank had been a member of the Communist Party; in 1952, no longer a member, she was subpoenaed by the committee. Her husband talked to people at MGM and asked what would happen if she refused to testify and was told—with regret but facing the facts—that he and his partner would never work in Hollywood again.

"And so," Elizabeth Frank said, "my mother did testify, to clear my father's name—otherwise, it would have been guilt-by-association. . . . I don't think my mother named anybody who hadn't already been named. I think she made a moral decision. I think it's just as moral to protect those you love as to protect those in your community. It was a very painful choice. . . . She did it out of complete love for her husband and children, not because she believed the government was right to do any of this. . . . Many writers were impassioned about their political beliefs and didn't speak later to those who testified, but the Hacketts spoke to my mother. They were part of our lives forever. The fact that my mother testified didn't cause bad feelings between my parents and Frances and Albert."

There's an odd postscript to this HUAC story. In 1992, Peter Viertel, the novelist-screenwriter, wrote in a book that one of the people Anne Frank cited as a party member was her own sister, Jigee—who was then Viertel's wife. Elizabeth Frank knew her mother hadn't done that, so she wrote Viertel, got him to admit he was wrong, then asked why he'd slandered her mother. Viertel replied that Anne Frank had once told his wife, Jigee, that he'd been spotted coming out of a motel with another woman. "My mother was naïve to say that," Elizabeth Frank said, "but to punish her forty years later by claiming she'd named her sister to HUAC seems a little excessive."

Another postscript: Elizabeth Frank stayed in touch with Frances and Albert. During a party at their New York apartment, she was seated with two of their screenwriter friends, Julius Epstein and Henry Ephron, and she told Ephron (a sometimes-sour man and the writer of, among other films, *The Desk Set*) that she found it curious that his daughter and Epstein's nephew had turned out to be writers—and so had she.

"I said," she recalled, "'Isn't it funny, Leslie Epstein is a wonderful novelist, and there's your daughter, Nora—everyone knows her work.'

"He looked at me and said, 'What have you written?'

"I said, 'A biography.'

"'Oh,' he said, 'anyone can write a biography.'

"I thought, 'Sure, anyone can be Boswell, anyone can be Lytton Strachey.' I didn't mention the Pulitzer Prize."[20]

# 16

## *Father of the Bride*

**A**s 1948 ended, Frances and Albert could look back with pride on scripting three lavishly produced MGM musicals starring Judy Garland, who was once called the greatest entertainer of her time. Plainly, they were on the highest-paid rungs of screenwriting success. However, they told Bert Allenberg and others that they weren't content: they were wary of getting pigeonholed as writers of musicals and wanted to get back into comedy. Happily for them, in early January 1949, they took on a best-seller titled *Father of the Bride,* by Edward Streeter.

Streeter was a New Yorker, a Harvard graduate who'd written a funny best-seller about World War I Army life called *Dere Mable,* then become a successful banker, turning out other books in his spare time. He was also a childhood pal of Frances's; when he learned that she and Albert were adapting *Father of the Bride,* he was delighted and wrote, "Could it be true? Could you by some fantastic chance be Frances Goodrich, friend of [a] jowly little boy . . . who visited you . . . at a great big house in Rhode Island?" For many authors, having their creations turned into movies is a mixed blessing—they love the cash but feel that the "vision" and "heart" of their works have been destroyed—but for Streeter, things were different. When he first read the Hacketts' script, he called it "wonderful." After seeing a preview in New York, he reported, "I went with fear in my heart and my fingers crossed. I came away exulting . . . that you . . . have caught the spirit of my little book so accurately. . . . It is really a great piece of work. Everything that you have added has been an improvement and all the cuts and omission have been to the good."[1]

The man who asked Frances and Albert to do *Father of the Bride* was Dore Schary, who'd become MGM's vice president in charge of production in 1948. The Hacketts liked Schary "tremendously" (he was, Frances wrote to her mother, "a Newark boy. . . . His family ran a catering establishment there . . . catered mostly to Jewish weddings. His stories are wonderful"), but they had fears about his future: "He has taken a tremendous task on himself . . . the really personal supervision of all the pictures. Everything must by read, okayed, discussed, re-written at his direction. . . . It is a heavy burden he has assumed. It killed one of his predecessors, Irving Thalberg." When Schary took the job, the Hacketts sent him a note: "You can never know what a comfort it is to think of you as the Boss." Not everyone was that admiring: Gore Vidal once called Schary a "kindly, good-natured, politically liberal man of endless sentimentality";[2] S. J. Perelman said he was "so constipated with his own importance that his smallest pronouncement sounds like Pitt the Elder."[3]

In his autobiography, Schary wrote that the Hacketts, as they often did when facing new projects, hesitated before committing themselves to *Father of the Bride*, calling the book "darling" but adding that they didn't know what to do with it. "I dosed them with my confidence," Schary wrote, "that they could do anything." Two weeks later, Frances and Albert reported that they had no idea how to write the screenplay, "and to prove it they came in with a few pages to illustrate their inadequacy. The pages were good, we discussed the story, and . . . they left, still in doubt, but— 'We'll see if we can put it together.' A few days later, they called, excited and happy, saying they 'had it,' and it was going to be wonderful. The Hackett-Goodrich syndrome appeared each time they went to a new screenplay."[4]

The Hacketts' screenplay told of the misadventures, upsets, and fun involved in the wedding of the daughter of well-to-do suburbanites, from her casual announcement that she's engaged, through awkward meetings with the future son-in-law and his parents, the engaged couple's temporary bust-up, comical conferences with haughty caterers, and the ceremony itself and the sometimes-raucous wedding reception. Throughout, the tone was gently satirical, with the main character commenting wryly while coping with crises, paying the ever-mounting bills—"What are people going to say when I'm in the gutter because I tried to put on a wedding like a Roman emperor?"—and hating the idea that he's losing his beautiful, beloved daughter.

This rich part was played by Spencer Tracy; Elizabeth Taylor, then seventeen, played the bride; Joan Bennett was the mother; and Vincente Minnelli directed. Tracy's performance has been called "magnificent"—but it almost didn't happen. When he was first approached, Tracy hesitated; then he learned that Jack Benny was also being considered for the part, and Tracy said he wasn't interested. Not until a screen test had shown that

Benny wasn't suitable and Minnelli had begged ("With you, this picture could be a little classic") did Tracy come on board. (During casting, Frances and Albert corresponded with Streeter about possibilities, and he expressed strong opinions: "March is obviously out, Laughton is my idea of nobody and as for Benny I would nominate Abbott and Costello. Better than that I would nominate myself.")

The idea of casting Jack Benny came from Dore Schary, not from the Hacketts or Minnelli or the film's producer, Pandro Berman. During the discussions about Benny, Berman made some interesting comments about the nature of the film. Benny was wrong for the part, Berman said, because the film was a "a comedy drama about a man whose heart breaks because he loves his daughter and is about to lose her. It's not a joke. It's not a funny thing. The laughs come out of sadness and reality."[5]

"Sadness and reality"—again, as in *It's a Wonderful Life,* Frances and Albert had helped to create a marvelous movie that has lasted not simply because of clever dialogue, but because it puts audiences in close touch with a likable, well-drawn character who's suffering in a way that's understandable and moving. It seems fair to say that, like *Wonderful Life, Father of the Bride* was another step away from comedy for fun's sake toward writing that had—and the Hacketts would almost certainly have flinched at the words—more "significance" and "deeper undertones."

In January 1950, while *Father of the Bride* was being filmed, Dore Schary wrote to Frances and Albert, who had again gone to Europe: "While you are out there somewhere on the briny deep, [the movie] is on the way. If it's anywhere near as cute and clever as that script of yours, it ought to be a knockout." Shary was right: everyone loved *Father of the Bride.* It was nominated for Oscars for Best Picture, Best Screenplay, and Best Actor and was seventh on *Variety*'s list of 1950's top-grossing films; the *New York Times* said, "Easily the funniest picture in town. . . . The customary exaggeration . . . in most comedies is almost completely absent. . . . There was no need for it here because there is . . . vast . . . latent comedy in family life, provided one has the capacity to recognize it." Feeling that the script reflected "the warmth and freshness that stem from spiritual inspiration," a Catholic group, the Christophers, gave the Hacketts an award of $5,000; they donated almost half to Vassar and to the Professional Children's School. MGM's advertising called the picture "the event of the season! . . . The bride gets the THRILLS! Father gets the BILLS!" During the shooting, Elizabeth Taylor got engaged to Nick Hilton, the son of Frances and Albert's neighbor, and MGM began a costly promotion campaign, giving

Taylor lavish gifts and issuing press releases concerning "the most note-worthy event in Hollywood's social history . . . Hollywood's most extravagant wedding ever." Taylor evidently entered this, the first of her many marriages, blissfully, and said that when she walked down the aisle when acting in *Father*, she looked radiant because she was thinking about becoming Hilton's wife, but trouble started during the honeymoon. Hilton, twenty-three, hated being married to a celebrity, and drank heavily and rejected Taylor's advances; seven months later, the two were divorced.

At the Oscars ceremony for 1950 (where the Hacketts' screenplay for *Father of the Bride* lost out to Joseph Mankiewicz's *All about Eve*), the newly divorced Elizabeth Taylor created the greatest stir among the bleacher sitters outside. The program featured many of Hacketts' friends. The host was Fred Astaire; the presenter of the writing awards was Ruth Chatterton, who held her glasses "regally" while reading her speech; Charles Brackett, the president of the Motion Picture Academy, somberly reminded the audience that 1950 had been "the year of Korea, Russian land grabs, [and] household bomb shelters." Backstage, Marilyn Monroe, scheduled to present the sound award, burst into tears because her dress was torn. The evening's tackiest moment came when Dean Martin and Jerry Lewis sang "Bibbidi-Bobbidi-Boo," with Lewis providing only the "Boo" and pantomiming that Martin had had a nose job.

The success of *Father of the Bride* demanded a sequel, and in early 1950, Frances and Albert started *Father's Little Dividend* — originally given the leaden title *Now I'm a Grandfather* — in which Elizabeth Taylor has a baby. The first film's sets were still up, the actors were under contract, and the Hacketts knew the characters intimately; all that was missing was a story. The one they invented includes Tracy's horrified reaction to becoming a grandfather ("I'm too *young!*"), another bust-up between daughter and son-in-law; the baby's irrational, terrified screams whenever it spots Tracy; and the climactic christening scene, in which the kid, by now Tracy's buddy, is named after him.

Like its predecessor, *Father's Little Dividend* proved to be relatively cheap and quick to make — twenty-two days of shooting, production costs reported at $971,437 — and it brought MGM a handsome profit and much praise, some cloying ("as tender as a baby's skin . . . as heartwarming as a baby's smile"), some straightforward ("the merriest movie of the year"), and some complimenting Frances and Albert ("[They] have projected Mr. Streeter's characters beyond their original boundary. . . . Once again the edge of witty social comment is oiled by good manners"). The next step, from MGM's point of view, was a sequel to the sequel, but some commentators worried about that, speculating that the logical title of the third picture would be *Father's Darling Divorcée* and hoping that the studio wouldn't be tempted to "go on working its father lode until the ore runs out."

Recalling their stressful *Thin Man* and MacDonald-Eddy days, Frances and Albert were worried about doing a third film: "We were back writing serials!" Nevertheless, they dutifully attended conferences to discuss the project and listened to story proposals. "[We were] told," Albert said, "to talk to Tracy — 'He's got an idea.' . . . So Tracy's [idea was that] since his daughter had a baby, and was sort of tired, and he had to go on business abroad, [he would take] her abroad to give her a rest, a little vacation. And . . . the men on board the boat to Europe would keep going after this beautiful daughter of his [and he would spend his time] trying to protect her from these wolves. . . . That was his idea."[6]

"Which meant," Frances said, "that Joan Bennett would be on the wharf to say goodbye and then hello when they got back. Bennett — out!"

"Then I went to dinner at [someone's] house," Frances added, "and sat next to [the producer] Walter Wanger, who was Bennett's husband at the time. He said he had a wonderful idea. . . . Elizabeth would say to Joan, 'Mummy, tell me, when did you fall in love with Daddy? When did you first meet him?' Well, of course, that [story line, going back to the past, would have eliminated] Spencer Tracy entirely — because Joan Bennett could play an eighteen-year-old and look lovely, but *he* couldn't."[7]

Frances and Albert laughed at this dinner-party backstabbing, but the threat of a third picture remained. Then, during breakfast one day, scanning the papers — they always got two copies of the *Los Angeles Times* and the *New York Times*, so they wouldn't compete for them — they found deliverance. For a long time, Walter Wanger had suspected that Joan Bennett was sleeping with Jennings Lang, her agent; on an afternoon in December 1951, outside Lang's office, Wanger showed up with a pistol and shot Lang.

"He shot him in the scrotum, in a parking lot," Frances said. "That was the end of the series."

"Yes," Albert said, "that saved us. . . . He didn't kill him, but I imagine he ruined the affair."

Wanger's bullet — some people claimed it wasn't aimed at Lang's private parts but at the pavement in front of him and ricocheted—ended his marriage; it also destroyed his wife's career. She'd made sixty-five pictures during the preceding twenty-three years; in the next ten years, she made only five. "It was painfully clear," she wrote, "that I was a professional outcast in Hollywood. . . . Suddenly I was the villain of the piece. . . . I might just as well have pulled the trigger myself."[8] Frances and Albert didn't know Bennett, but later they were seated next to her in a theater, and Albert felt "a strong coolness," probably because of the jokes he and Frances had made to Hollywood friends about the shooting. Wanger, a notorious womanizer who was often unfaithful to Bennett, made out far better than she. Originally booked on a charge that could have jailed him for fourteen years—assault with a deadly weapon with intent to kill—thanks to pressure from some of Hollywood's most powerful men, he was allowed to plead to a lesser charge; in the end, he served three months and nine days at an "honor farm," working as a librarian. "Only California," Albert said, "would do a thing like this." Soon, Wanger was again one of Hollywood's most successful filmmakers; concerning his shooting of Lang, he reportedly quipped to fellow producers, "You chaps just talk about agents. I'm the only one who ever did anything about them."[9]

In the summer of 1950, Frances and Albert joined a fund-raising group, the Citizens Committee for Candidates, whose mission included supporting Helen Gahagan Douglas in her senatorial run against Richard Nixon. Nixon's campaign tactics earned him his never-to-be-shed "Tricky Dicky" label; the committee included the Hacketts' friends Dore Shary, Billy Wilder, Philip Dunne, Groucho Marx, Vincente Minnelli, and Danny Kaye, plus—he hadn't yet turned conservative—Ronald Reagan. In August, not long after Frances and Albert finished the script of *Father's Little Dividend*, Dorothy Parker and Alan Campbell, who'd divorced in 1947 and then resumed living together, got remarried. The wedding reception was held at the Bracketts' house; the Hacketts were there, and the other guests included Frances and Ring Lardner Jr., Humphrey Bogart, Budd Schulberg, Howard Dietz, and James Agee. Reportedly, that morning, after waking up, Parker pulled the blanket up over her face and told Campbell not to look at her, the bride, because it was bad luck. At the reception, when someone said that a few of the guests had not spoken to each other for years, Parker commented, "including the bride and groom." The biographer Marion Meade said that Parker, carrying a bouquet of violets, "went around saying, 'What are you going to do when you love the son of a bitch?' . . . Alan was heard to remark brightly, 'Now we can have dinner parties again.' As the evening wore on, parlor games erupted. . . . All the guests . . . played, until Dottie got mad at Alan for guessing she was the wolf suckling Romulus and Remus when she was acting out the Brooklyn Bridge."[10]

# 17

## Seven Brides for Seven Brothers

In mid-April 1951, Frances and Albert turned in the script of *Too Young to Kiss* to MGM producer Sam Zimbalist; lightweight and music filled, based on a story by Everett Freeman, it told of a struggling concert pianist (June Allyson) who disguises herself as a thirteen-year-old, complete with braces, pinafore, and pigeon-toed walk, in order to get an audition with a prodigy-minded impresario (Van Johnson). The film, directed by Robert Leonard, was released in November 1951 and got mixed reviews: "chuckle-headed"; "a pleasant 89 minutes." The *New Yorker*'s critic had fun with the leads: "Miss Allyson is about as plausible in her role as Dame May Whitty would be as Cinderella. You have probably seen Mr. Johnson before, so I need say nothing about his inadequacies." In early October, in the company of another writer, two "starlets," and two actors—one of them Victor Jory—Frances and Albert spent several days in Oregon as part of a film industry public relations effort called MOVIETIME USA; a reaction to television's growing competition, (and probably also to Hollywood's liberal political reputation during the current McCarthy-tainted times), this campaign sent roughly forty-five groups of "filmland ambassadors" to different states to meet the public and demonstrate that motion picture people were "good solid citizens." Alongside their fellow goodwill campaigners, with Frances wearing white gloves and hats with veils, the Hacketts appeared onstage in movie theaters, spoke on the radio, went to cocktail parties, visited a veterans' hospital and a livestock show, and lunched with the state's governor, Douglas McKay. And on October 4, in Portland, they got a letter that ultimately involved them in a long, painful entanglement.

The letter was from David Merrick, later the producer of such Broadway superhits as *Gypsy, Oliver,* and *Hello, Dolly,* but then, at age thirty-nine, an almost-unknown beginner: he'd worked for a while as Herman Shumlin's assistant, then coproduced an English import, a slim farce called *Clutter-*

*buck,* keeping it alive with clever ads and stunts like having "Mr. Clutter-buck" paged in Manhattan restaurants and hotel lobbies. Merrick had recently secured the rights to three plays by the French author Marcel Pagnol—*Marius, Fanny,* and *Cesar*—and he asked if Frances and Albert would be interested in writing the script of a musical comedy based on them. The Hacketts' MGM contract allowed them to work in the theater, so they read the plays, then telegraphed that they liked them tremendously. Two days later, a letter came from Shumlin, calling Merrick, whom the Hacketts had never met, "a good person, an honorable and dependable person . . . a man of taste and discrimination," and urging them to "take hold of this project." Five days after that, perhaps influenced by Shumlin's message and ignoring a telegram from Leah Salisbury (DON'T MAKE A SINGLE MOVE UNTIL BUSINESS DETAILS FURTHER ALONG), leaving Sid Perelman residing at 10664 Bellagio Road ("I [am] alone in this chateau," he wrote to a friend, "except for Daisy, the maid, and her elderly dachshund, but the two of them have been cooking and sweeping for me devotedly"),[1] Frances and Albert made a big mistake, and got a leave of absence from MGM and flew to New York.

Through the years, many harsh words, including *mean, obnoxious, monster,* and *Abominable Showman* were thrown at David Merrick; the writer Larry Gelbart once said that Merrick's name "is on file at the U.S. Patent Office as one of the inventors of the slippery pole."[2] Judging from an eleven-page, single-spaced, typewritten account the Hacketts later created concerning their dealings with him between December 4, 1951, and December 29, 1952, Merrick deserved every bit of that opprobrium. After settling into a Manhattan hotel, Frances and Albert told Leah Salisbury they wouldn't sign a contract until they were sure they could produce a workable script and knew who the show's composer would be. They met Merrick—dark-haired, with an oversized mustache and large, limpid, brown eyes—and agreed to condense the three plays into a seventy-page outline. After a month of intense work, they showed this to him. A five-hour argument followed, with Merrick first insisting that the show's locale should be San Francisco, not Marseilles, then finally backing off. Regarding this, Frances said that she and Albert had wasted five hours, then added that, despite Merrick's argumentativeness, she and Albert had decided that it would be possible to work with him since they'd "soon be working with the director and others, and [Merrick] would be relegated to the position of manager."

That turned out to be wishful thinking at its most wishful. During the next eight months, David Merrick waffled, stalled, and equivocated about the script. To accommodate his shifting views, the Hacketts—who had finally signed a contract and received a token $2,000 advance—wrote five different versions, working themselves to exhaustion and battling often, sometimes bitterly. From the Hacketts' account:

> Feb. 14: Albert in grave doubt about possibility of material for a musical. . . . I am very enthusiastic and believe wholeheartedly in the project. Albert keeps saying, "What are they going to sing about?"
> . . .
> Feb. 19: Again the same crisis. The crisis we have always had on every story we have ever done. Albert thinks the story is too dour for a musical. I am desperate, as I believe so much in it, and know that we have our story line straight for the first time.

Frances later wrote Albert a note in which she said, among other things, "I have gone through hell this winter between [you] and David. I thought I was made of iron. I am not. I am at the end of my strength. I should be very happy if I were completely relieved of this job." In the midst of all this, hoping to find a star for the show, Frances and Albert went to see Judy Garland performing at the Palace Theater. "We, Merrick and ourselves," Frances wrote, "have agreed that she would be wonderful for the part of Fanny. We went backstage afterwards to see her, but did not get a chance to talk privately to her. Told her we were working on something that we thought would interest her."

Alongside the search for a star was the search for songwriters: at one time or another, Howard Dietz, Arthur Schwartz, Harold Arlen, E. Y. ("Yip") Harburg, Harold Rome, Ira Gershwin, and Burton Lane were approached by either the Hacketts or Merrick. In the end, Arlen agreed to write the music, and Harburg, the lyrics, but Merrick never actually offered either one a contract, and they grew disgusted with his shifts and vacillations and dropped out after fighting bitterly with him. A typical example of Merrick's neurotic indecisiveness came on June 10: Frances and Albert urged him to offer Harburg a contract, and in response he wondered what would happen if Harburg—a perfectly healthy man who lived thirty more years—wrote two songs and then died. "We urged him," Frances wrote, "to put it in the contract that Harburg couldn't die 'til he had completed the score. Merrick didn't laugh." Merrick's sense of humor was evidently odd. One year, his Christmas card showed a very dead, ugly Santa Claus suspended from a hangman's noose, with his eyes closed and his tongue dangling down his beard; the printed message was, "Season's Greetings."

In addition to their problems with Merrick, Frances and Albert had others with Harburg. At one point, Frances wrote to a friend that Harburg, a wonderfully talented lyricist—*The Wizard of Oz* and *Finian's Rainbow*—who often acted aggressively toward collaborators, invited them to a meeting. "He starts to tell us," Frances reported, "what he thinks of our script. I start to walk out, not thinking it is within his province. . . . He calls us 'kids,' pats my face, tells me nothing is worth getting upset about, tells us to make a deal, give up a little of our share and get out. Nice? Tells us first (before I stopped all that talk) that Merrick has handed around our script to [Joshua Logan], etc., and everyone has said how horrible and impossible it is." Another time, Frances wrote that Harburg "sent a notice to the *New York Times* which was about as damaging a little statement as you could make, saying that we hadn't handed in a perfect script and that he, who was such an expert, was going to step in and help us. He has wanted to get hold of the whole thing, script and lyrics, from the first. And he evidently won David Merrick over. I felt so terribly, I thought I wanted some revenge on David and then I suddenly thought, I have my revenge: David is going to have Harburg! There isn't a person who has ever worked with him who would do it again. So you see what David is in for."

One positive side of the *Fanny* experience was that Frances and Albert got to know the whimsical, free-spirited Harold Arlen, composer of more than five hundred songs, including the classics "Stormy Weather," "Blues in the Night," and "It's Only a Paper Moon." Arlen liked the Hacketts a lot and called them "the nicest people I ever met"; in his letters, he sometimes addressed them as "My dear Madame and Albert Hall"—probably a reference to the famous London concert hall. After they'd sent him a copy of their script of *Fanny,* he replied, referring to David Merrick, "I can assure you [that] D. M. (Doctor of Manuscripts) will not get his psychopathic hands on it."

In July, having spent eight months on the project, finally concluding they couldn't work with David Merrick ("I cannot express in decent language my feeling about him," Frances wrote), the Hacketts went back to California to do a movie for MGM. In late October, Merrick offered to settle their contract for $3,000, with no percentage of the show's profits. Naturally, they refused, and the question of compensation was scheduled for arbitration. The Hacketts needed a New York lawyer, so their friend (but not their agent) Irving ("Swifty") Lazar wrote to Lloyd Almirall of Breed, Abbott & Morgan that two friends of his were "in a hassle with a producer by the name of David Merrick. . . . The Hacketts are two of the nicest people I've ever known [echoes of Arlen!] . . . and they have rarely ever ventured to criticize anyone until they came in contact with the afore-mentioned David Merrick. And when they told me of his machinations and scheming ways, I was annoyed beyond words because they simply are not the kind of people you treat that way. . . . What is important is that no injustice be done them by this Merrick fellow."[3]

Frances and Albert admired Lloyd Almirall, saying that he was "Maurice Evans's lawyer, and a tougher man . . . has not been found. Tougher in the Harvard tradition." To show the arbitrators they had lived up to their contract by writing a more-than-satisfactory script, they sent copies to, among others, Russell Crouse, Alan Jay Lerner, Ogden Nash, and Lillian Hellman, who responded using such words as *professional, skillful,* and *competent.* Armed with these evaluations, Almirall felt "totally confident" of winning the arbitration but warned, Frances wrote, "that when we won we would end up with only our contract and David Merrick. Since we had had eight months of that horror, we compromised for a small percentage" (one-half of 1 percent of the weekly gross box office receipts, up to a total of $20,000).

Starring Ezio Pinza, Walter Slezak, and Florence Henderson, with a book by Joshua Logan and S. N. Behrman and songs by Harold Rome, *Fanny* opened in November 1954. It ran for 888 performances, so presumably the Hacketts got their share—but obviously it was far less than what they'd hoped for. When it came time for Almirall to be paid, he suggested in gentlemanly fashion that since "the whole situation has been one of loss to you," he "would be satisfied to settle our fee on the basis of the retainer already paid," but the Hacketts sent him $2,500 more ("We are deeply appreciative of your generous suggestion . . . but we cannot find it in our consciences to accept it"), to which he replied, "I feel, after more than twenty years' practice of law, completely unequipped to answer [your letter] adequately, much less appropriately. . . . I can only say that it has provided me with one of the most unique and . . . most heartwarming experiences of my entire professional career."[4]

When Frances and Albert, thoroughly fed up with David Merrick, returned to Hollywood in the summer of 1952, they were put to work on *Give a Girl a Break,* adapting a story by their novelist-screenwriter friend Vera Caspary, best known for *Laura.* The screenplay, which dealt with three chorus girls trying for the lead in a Broadway musical, was fluff, written to fulfill their MGM contract. (Frances and Albert were well aware that some of their projects were less than distinguished: once, traveling abroad, they used GOOD HACKS as their cable address; another time, asked if, as a writer, he had "any feelings of responsibility to the audience or society," Albert joked, "If we had any sense of responsibility, we wouldn't have written some of the things we wrote.")[5] The film's director, Stanley Donen, found the Hacketts' participation uncharacteristic. "I admired them so much," Donen told me, "that I was surprised, frankly, that they wrote that movie; it seemed so slight to me. . . . I thought they were so gifted as a writing team that it seemed . . . not worth their time. . . . I was very young when I did it—twenty-nine. . . . I had been directing for four or five years by then; I did it because there wasn't anything around that was better" (which was probably why the Hacketts also chose the project).

*Give a Girl a Break* was originally supposed to be a major production starring Gene Kelly, Fred Astaire, Judy Garland, and Ann Miller, but scheduling conflicts and illnesses forced MGM to put the dancers Marge and Gower Champion into the leading roles. Also in the cast were Bob Fosse and Debbie Reynolds, and the Hacketts' friends Ira Gershwin and Burton Lane did the lyrics and music. The cast changes set Frances and Albert against a deadline: MGM gave them ten days to rewrite the entire script. Also, they had to deal with artistic temperament: "They have put a new dance team in," Frances wrote to her mother, "and the girl has a million ideas how the script should be changed. This is really amusing, since we have written scripts for good actors and never had such a thing happen. But in order to help the director, whom we like a lot, we re-wrote. And then this week we had to go down on the set where they were rehearsing their dances, and explain to Marge Champion why what she wanted could not be done." Perhaps because it was put together under pressure, Frances and Albert's script was weak, and the film got trounced by the critics. The Hacketts agreed with the negative opinions, later calling the picture a "dud."

While Frances and Albert had been in New York working on *Fanny*, MGM had bought the rights to *The Long, Long Trailer*, a novel by Clinton Twiss about a newly married couple's funny foul-ups during a transcontinental trip in an enormous, unwieldy mobile home. As in the two Spencer Tracy *Father* pictures, the producer was Pandro Berman and the director was Vincente Minnelli, so the Hacketts were in familiar company, but the casting reflected the changes then taking place in American popular entertainment. The *Father* pictures had had recognized movie stars in the leading roles, and the films' success had inspired television networks to create imitations. This time, the stars were Lucille Ball and Desi Arnaz, from *I Love Lucy*, which during the 1951–52 season had a peak share of 71 percent of the TV audience, and the hope was that they would lure viewers out of their living rooms and back into movie theaters. Some highly placed MGM executives were doubtful ("Audiences won't pay to see actors they normally see for free"), but they were wrong: *The Long, Long Trailer* brought in many dollars.

Before starting their screenplay, Frances and Albert did some research. "God knows," Albert said, "we knew nothing at all about trailers, so we went to a place and pretended we were interested in buying one." The film had a slight plot but lots of wild comic action, particularly when Lucy tries to prepare dinner while the trailer's under way and winds up ricocheting off the walls of the bouncing kitchen, with food flying everywhere. Although most critics loved the picture—"hilariously funny"; "a wonderfully slaphappy farce"—and the Hacketts' screenplay was nominated for the Writers Guild of America's best-written comedy award (it didn't win), Albert wasn't keen on it: "It made a lot of money because [Lucy and Desi] were very popular, but it wasn't a particularly good picture, because there wasn't any *naturally* funny stuff in it. . . . The big thing in the story was that [Lucy and Desi] parked [their] long trailer and had to put money in all those meters. That was the big joke in the story."[6] While the Hacketts were finishing their script, Frances reported to my mother on the woes that new gimmickry had brought to Hollywood: "This business is in the most horrible dither. A Three-D dither. And all it needs is good pictures. . . . Production is at a standstill. They don't know which way to turn. I hope we never have to [write] anything in 3D. That is the one where you wear glasses. And they fall off my nose."

Frances and Albert cared about liberal political causes—she more than he—and made modest donations to them, and had some radically minded friends, but they never got deeply involved in political matters, and during the earlier, HUAC days, the headline-chasing Red-hunters had ignored them. (However, since 1947, the FBI had been making notes on their few, harmless affiliations: FBI documents I got thanks to the Freedom of Information Act describe Albert as an "associate of Communist Party members" because he and Frances belonged to something called the Hollywood Community Radio Group; another memo notes their involvement in the Screen Writers Guild and two other groups, the People's Educational Association and the Progressive Citizens of America; the last is called a Communist front organization in the FBI papers.)

In mid-1952, the Hacketts' immunity vanished, and their loyalty to the United States was questioned by the American Legion, which had gained great influence in Hollywood by picketing theaters that were showing movies said to be Communist tainted. The growth of TV was already cutting movie attendance, and the studios feared further losses if people didn't cross the picket lines, so studio executives told the Legion they wouldn't hire new people with leftist connections and would do loyalty checks on the people they'd already hired; the studios also asked to see the dossiers the Legion had put together on "suspect" employees. Frances and Albert first learned of their own problem on July 17, when a highly placed MGM executive named Louis K. Sidney called.

Then fifty-seven, dark-haired, fond of boutonnieres and loud ties, once described as "a large heavyset man who sat behind an enormous desk and issued pronouncements,"[7] "L. K." had mostly been a theater manager but was now a member of the studio's four-man executive committee. Frances and Albert knew about the Legion's picketing campaign, and they knew that many writers, actors, and directors had been asked to write letters to Nicholas Schenck, the president of Loew's Inc., MGM's parent company, answering questions about their connections to so-called subversive organizations and repenting their involvement, so the studio could "purge" itself. In a letter, Frances described her and Albert's first meeting with Sidney:

> Mr. L. K. Sidney calls. Will Albert come over to his office and will he bring his charming wife? We go over. . . . Mr. L. K. is very sweet. Tells us that they are being picketed. Cannot afford it. Trying to clear everyone. Will we write Mr. Schenck a letter. . . . He tells us what they want in the letter. Particularly names, names, names [of members of various organizations]. . . . I ask so so politely what Mr. Schenck will do with the letter? He tells me that when [groups like the Legion] come in protesting against a picture, Mr. Schenck will show our letter. Or he may give it out for publication. We will have no control whatsoever over the letter. Then he begins to read Albert's dossier, and you have no idea what an important fella Hackett is. He has practically saved the Communist party, swayed Supreme Courts, not to speak of foreign governments. My dossier is similar.[8]

Frances and Albert's page-and-a-half dossiers, compiled by the Legion, were indeed similar: for example, both said that they had "pioneered in and contributed freely to" the work of the Hollywood Writers Mobilization. Many screenwriters had belonged to this wartime organization, which created documentary films for overseas distribution by the OWI and arranged shows, from vaudeville skits to symphony orchestra concerts, for armed forces camps; there was nothing subversive about it. Mostly, the dossiers listed things the Hacketts had done, such as petitioning to lift the arms embargo imposed on the Loyalists during the Spanish Civil War and putting their names on a legal brief to the U.S. Supreme Court charging movie censorship instigated by HUAC. In many cases, the Hacketts recalled the documents and organizations that were mentioned, but in some, they didn't, because the Legion had blundered comically. Frances was confused with "one Fannie Goodrich, of Cayuta, New York" (who'd signed a Communist Party petition), and "one Frances Goodrich of 513 Herkimer Street, Brooklyn, New York" (who'd done the same), and —twice—with Francis Hackett, a politically active Hollywood screenwriter who just happened to be a man.

Carrying copies of their dossiers, the Hacketts, Frances wrote, "walked politely out" of L. K. Sidney's office—and ran into "the funniest thing of all." They had already decided they would never write to Schenck and knew that the result might well be dismissal, and now they met (probably in a hallway) two top MGM producers who hoped to have their services in the near future. "We first met Pasternak. [He] put his arms around us, [called us] 'his kids,' [asked] when we were coming to work for him, etc., etc. [Then we all] met Pan Berman. Big routine [between the two producers]: 'You took them away from me!' Pan says he hasn't got us—and when are we coming back to work with him? We look at them and die laughing inside."

After leaving Pasternak and Berman, Frances and Albert went to see their agent, Bert Allenberg, and told him that they wouldn't write the letter to Schenck and planned to send a very different one to Sidney. Allenberg said that was fine with him, but MGM would settle their contract immediately because the studio just couldn't keep them. "Everyone else, I gather," Frances wrote, "has conformed. I think [that, knowing what it would cost him], Bert is the only agent in town who would have encouraged us to do what our consciences told us." That evening, she and Albert went to a party at Melvin and Anne Frank's house and "had a good time. . . . Nothing seemed to matter any more. So we no longer have any problems here of who to invite with who and so forth. Just the problem of selling the house and breaking off our lives here." Concerning their situation, Frances wrote that if the studio wanted to give in to the Legion, "that's their hard luck. It's not going to be ours. Also we have been told by a lawyer that we have a good libel suit against the studio for passing around [our dossiers], if we want to be nasty."

In their letter to L. K. Sidney, dated July 21, Frances and Albert thanked him for his "tactful" handling of their situation, then dealt with the question of writing to Schenck, saying among other things:

> We feel that if we wrote such a letter we would be violating every principle of democracy and freedom in which we believe. . . .
>
> Our patriotism, our love and loyalty for our Country . . . [have] never been questioned, and cannot now be questioned. We will match our feelings and our actions in this respect against anyone, particularly our accusers.
>
> We are not Communists. We have never been Communists and never could be. We have never wavered in our devotion and loyalty to the United States.
>
> We have been employees of Metro-Goldwyn-Mayer off and on for twenty years. We love working here. . . . We shall continue to . . . give you the best of our abilities. . . .
>
> We hope you understand why we must refuse your request. Why we must adhere to our principles. After all, we must live with ourselves for many years to come.

Frances and Albert obviously hoped their letter would end the pressure, but on July 30, Sidney summoned them again, asking for changes in the letter: he wanted them to explain why they joined various organizations, who else was in them, and so forth—in short, he returned to the original demands. The Hacketts refused.

Three months later, on October 1, L. K. Sidney asked to see Frances and Albert a third time. Frances made notes to give to their lawyer:

> We discuss fishing and hunting for ten minutes. He has been on a vacation on the Rogue River and tells us how many salmon he caught. Then about the hunting trip he will take with [the actor, Robert] Taylor. . . . It finally comes to the discussion of our problem (interrupted by the news that Eddie Cantor is dead). . . . [Have we] changed our minds about writing the letter? He has a page of figures showing how much MGM has paid us. He admits we have earned it. But we owe an obligation to the company. . . . [Now] they report that Eddie Cantor is not dead. . . . [We return] to our problem. . . . We owe the com-

pany something. . . . Then he begins again to tell us what kind of letter we have to write . . . saying that we [belonged] to such and such
organizations and [made] donations . . . and that we did not know at
the time that they were Communist-dominated and if we had we certainly would never have joined. . . . [Then he said, in effect, if there's
no letter, our contract is canceled.] I laughed. "Oh, Mr. Sidney!" I got
up. Then he began pounding on [our July 21] letter and I began to cry
and Albert took me out. I didn't want to go out crying through the
front office so I asked where to go and kept howling "I want to get
out, I want to get out." And he showed me out.

After this third meeting, Frances and Albert's bosses finally realized
there was never going to be a "purging" letter, called off their dog, and
stopped making contract threats. The bosses might, in fact, have felt relieved about not firing them, because their pictures were often highly prof-
itable. The Hacketts had called the studio's bluff; however, the victory hurt
financially: caught between two attackers, the Legion and the studio,
they'd had to hire their own lawyer.

In December 1952, Frances and Albert spent a week at the big hotel at
Coronado Beach, not far from the Mexican border. Frances wrote that the
hotel was a "fantastic place . . . built about fifty years ago, in the period of
all the big Saratoga hotels, wood, balconies, mahogany bars, millions of
old ladies dripping with money. From there you drive seventeen miles to
Tiajuana, a real border town, honk-tonks, a million night clubs, people selling on the streets, sailors and soldiers reeling around, legal advice—which
means divorce done on the spot."

Happily, Frances and Albert's next job for MGM, after *The Long, Long
Trailer,* was the screenplay for *Seven Brides for Seven Brothers,* one of the
most memorable musicals of Hollywood's Golden Age, filled with fine,
rousing songs by Johnny Mercer and Gene de Paul and wonderfully energetic dances choreographed by Michael Kidd. The Hacketts' script was
based on a short story by Stephen Vincent Benét titled *The Sobbin' Women*—
which was based on *The Rape of the Sabine Women,* by Plutarch. The Hacketts knew the Benét story well: it had been "in and out of our lives for
about ten years. We first wanted to do it [with composer-lyricist Harold
Rome] as a musical for the theater, but we couldn't get the rights."[9]

As the Hacketts were nearing the end of their first version of the screenplay—in the 1850s in the Oregon Territory, a gang of lonely, horny brothers

kidnaps a group of women and takes them to a settlement in the woods—Frances wrote to her mother that it had been "a long, long haul" (seven weeks), and expressed relief that the "horror of that first draft" was over. She and Albert turned in their finished draft in late June 1953, then went on another European trip, driving through Austria, Switzerland, Italy, and France, eating picnic lunches in the woods and experiencing "not a day of rain in seven weeks. Along the roads and on the walls, one sees 'Yankee Go Home' every once in a while—but the French are charming to your face and that's all [we] care about. . . . Prices for food are very high in France—but what food!" "We were in Venice," Frances later said, "when we got a wire from Jack Cummings [the producer of *Seven Brides*] saying, 'Need you for one week re-write. Be here Monday.' We couldn't go, so they got Dorothy Kingsley to do it."[10]

The call for rewriting evidently came from the stars of the movie, Jane Powell and Howard Keel, who were unhappy with their parts: Powell felt she was too docile, and Keel felt he was unsympathetic. They persuaded Lillian Sidney, MGM's influential acting coach, to talk to Cummings and the film's director, Stanley Donen (the Hacketts' friend from *Give a Girl a Break*); Sidney suggested that Kingsley, a highly experienced script doctor, should be brought in.

"When the Hacketts came back from vacation," Kingsley's son, the actor-novelist Terry Kingsley-Smith said, "my mother was going to turn the project back to them, but they told her, 'No, we like what you've done, please stay with it,' and so she stayed 'til the last day of shooting, making changes all along. . . . My mother rewrote a lot of scripts at MGM, but usually she didn't take credit, but [this time the Hacketts] didn't want to go back on [the project] so she decided to take credit, because she knew it was going to be a good picture."[11]

Although Dorothy Kingsley had a solid reputation, Stanley Donen thought her participation was unnecessary and—as he told me—"stupid. [The Hacketts] had written a wonderful script. . . . My main function was trying to keep out the poor added material [Kingsley] was doing, and keeping what Frances and Albert had written." In the end, Kingsley rewrote 21 of the 113 pages, and unlike Donen, Frances and Albert found her contribution "wonderful . . . She was perfect [for the job]." Kingsley was, Frances once said, "the most wonderful little woman. She has a baby every year and it doesn't interfere with her writing at all. One week she'll be sitting at a table in the commissary, a little stout. Then she's gone for a week. The next week she's back, thin again. Another baby. I think she has eight."[12] Frances was mistaken about Kingsley's children—she had six, not eight—and it's doubtful that Kingsley would have cared for Frances's "most wonderful little woman" comment: she had grown up in Grosse Point, Michigan, and she traveled in so-called "high society" circles. In any event, the Hacketts and Kingsley became friends and sometimes had dinner together.

Stanley Donen overcame tough challenges in making *Seven Brides for Seven Brothers*. "The studio and the producer didn't want an original score to be written," he told me. "The producer wanted country songs—*real* ones. . . . I said, 'This movie can't be with "Turkey in the Straw." . . . [Also], all the brothers will be dancers.' Well, the studio was outraged, and so was the producer. . . . I'm afraid he said some very negative things about dancers and homosexuality: 'These are tough men in the back woods, and you're going to have them flitting all over the screen?'

"The studio wasn't with us in any way," Donen continued. "They were behind a movie Arthur Freed and Vincente Minnelli and Gene Kelly were doing called *Brigadoon*. . . . We were shooting at exactly the same time, and the studio spent I'd say more than twice the cost of our movie on *Brigadoon*, and *Brigadoon* was the one they were thrilled and excited about; *Seven Brides* was not considered to be *the picture*. . . . And when *Brigadoon* opened, it went into the toilet, and *Seven Brides* was the most successful musical I ever made, commercially."[13] (MGM, it has been reported, filmed *Brigadoon* in Hollywood rather than on location in Scotland because, after a scouting trip, Arthur Freed said, "I went to Scotland and found nothing there that looks like Scotland.")[14]

*Seven Brides for Seven Brothers* got marvelous reviews—the *New York Times* called the barn-raising scene "a combination of ballet, acrobatics and a knock-down and drag-out fight [that] should leave audiences panting and cheering"—and has often been shown on television. The advertising quoted President Eisenhower: "If you haven't seen it, you should see it." It was nominated for four Oscars, including Best Picture and Best Screenplay, and won one, for musical scoring. "The [Best Screenplay] nomination is very flattering," Albert wrote before the prizes were awarded, "but we have no chance of getting it. . . . Frances smiles and tries to look grateful, but each party has meant she has had to buy a new dress. She is going crazy." On the awards evening, the Hacketts and Dorothy Kingsley went to the ceremony at the Pantages Theater, then had dinner at Chasen's with the then-teenaged Terry Kingsley-Smith, who recalled that, although the Hacketts and his mother hadn't won, it was a cheerful occasion: "The people at the next table *had* won—I think they were songwriters. They had their Oscar wrapped in a napkin, like a toga. We all thought that was funny."

Evidently, *Seven Brides for Seven Brothers* was a big hit in Great Britain. "It plays there all the time," Stanley Donen said in the mid-1990s. "Somebody sent me one of those London tabloid newspapers, with a story about an English laborer named Balmy Bert. Every night, when Balmy Bert came home, he would run a video cassette of *Seven Brides*—every single night! His wife was going to divorce him unless he stopped looking at this movie."[15]

For Frances and Albert, writing *Seven Brides for Seven Brothers* was pleasant, nonstressful work, but then came the totally different, exhausting but ultimately fulfilling challenge of *The Diary of Anne Frank*.

# 18

## Writing *The Diary of Anne Frank*

**B**y the early 1950s, Frances and Albert had risen to the top of the exacting, highly paid profession of screenwriting, and with only a few exceptions, their work had been comedic. In 1953, when she was sixty-three and he was fifty-three, at a time in life when some people start thinking about slowing down or even retiring, they did something totally different from what they'd done before, taking on—purely on speculation, with no financial backup if they failed—the riskiest, most demanding job they'd ever faced. For the better part of two years, they labored almost continually, traveled thousands of miles across the United States and to Europe, and painstakingly wrote eight different versions of *The Diary of Anne Frank*, their play based on the words of the marvelously gifted Amsterdam teenager who was known around the world. During that time, they grew close to Otto Frank, Anne's father; fought between themselves; worked intensely with the director, Garson Kanin; and helped to shape every nuance of the final production. For both of them, the play became a "tremendous responsibility," a time-devouring mission, almost an obsession; for Frances —perhaps because she'd never had children and Anne "became her daughter" and because of her great sympathy for the victims of persecution—the project had, she said, a "terrible emotional impact." Writing *The Diary* turned out to be far and away the Hacketts' most important, most rewarding achievement, and it demanded a great deal more understanding of human nature than concocting wisecracking film scripts demanded: this 100 percent American, relatively sheltered, comedy-minded, lapsed-Catholic-and-Protestant couple had to turn the intensely personal observations of a hypersensitive, superbright, adolescent Jewish girl concerning herself and her family and their tormented friends, hiding under the threat of death in an Amsterdam garret, into a drama that could be performed convincingly and appealingly before an American audience. To do that, they had to think like Anne and the others, to feel like them, almost to "live inside them." The Hacketts would certainly have hated the clichés, but for them, writing *The Diary* was a journey to a world they'd never seen, a leap into the unknown.

In the summer of 1933, Otto Frank, a respected, forty-four-year-old businessman, who had always considered himself German (while serving in the army in World War I, he'd won the Iron Cross), moved with his wife and two daughters from Frankfurt to Amsterdam to escape anti-Semitic persecution. In Amsterdam, he started two new companies in one building, manufacturing pectin, a powdered fruit extract used to make jam, and selling special spice mixtures. For several years, the Franks lived freely and happily, but then the German invasion brought horrendous changes. Jewish businesses had to register (they were later confiscated); Jews were kept out of hotels, parks, and theaters; physical attacks began. Anne, the younger daughter, had to switch from public school to an all-Jewish school; the family was forced to wear yellow Stars of David on their clothes. On July 6, 1942, facing deportation to death camps and unable to flee, the four Franks went into hiding with another couple, Hermann and Auguste van Pels, and their teenaged son, Peter, in "the secret annex," a cramped attic above Mr. Frank's warehouse and office; later, they were joined by a cranky, middle-aged dentist, Friedrich Pfeffer. (When Anne wrote about the four others, she changed their surnames to Van Daan and Dussel.) For two years and one month, with gentile friends smuggling food and supplies to them, the eight escaped detection, but in early August 1944, they were seized. When Otto Frank, the only survivor, returned to Amsterdam after the war, he read, for the first time, the diary that Anne had started on her thirteenth birthday and kept through the time of hiding. While Nazi troops marched outside, and inside there was the hellish reality of eight people jammed into cramped quarters, always fearing discovery, Anne had set down, eloquently and movingly, with a precocious, insightful, sometimes humorous viewpoint, the routine of daily life (no trips outdoors; no washing or toilet flushing except at night; complete silence roughly ten hours a day while strangers were working downstairs), had wryly observed the good and bad sides of her annex mates, and had laid bare the innermost feelings of a teenager approaching womanhood. As Brooks Atkinson wrote:

> Thanks to the diary we know the homely details of this almost incredible example of the will to survive . . . [but] the diary would not have such a deep hold on the affections of the world if it were merely a record of events and techniques. Fundamentally, it is a portrait of

adolescence. . . . In the foreground is the figure of an enchanting girl. Her vitality rushes at the reader. Anne's inner life flourishes. . . . Her diary is an extraordinary mirror of a human being on the threshold of life—temperamental, impulsive, brash, but also intelligent, thoughtful, affectionate and aspiring. . . . Things that are irritating and things that are winning are tightly interwoven. . . . [She is] aware of the mysteries of life and eager to penetrate them. "Little bundle of contradictions" she calls herself in the last item in her diary before the dreadful day when the police raided the attic.[1]

Anne's skill as a writer, her keen reportorial eye, and the portrait of adolescence she painted were marvelous enough, but there's another element that observers have pointed to in wonder: her optimism, her believing "in spite of everything . . . that people are really good at heart." In her introduction to the American edition, Eleanor Roosevelt referred to Anne's optimism, saying that the diary made poignantly clear "the ultimate shining nobility of [the human] spirit. Despite the horror and the humiliation of their daily lives, these people never gave up." It is no exaggeration to say that Anne Frank's diary established her as one of the best-known, best-loved figures in human history.

After submitting Anne's diary to dozens of companies in Holland, Germany, England, and the United States without success, Otto Frank had it published in Dutch in 1947. It began to attract attention; the first American edition, titled *Anne Frank: Diary of a Young Girl,* came out in 1952; other editions soon appeared in other countries. Frances and Albert first got involved on November 26, 1953, when a letter arrived in Bel Air from Leah Salisbury, saying that Kermit Bloomgarden—then forty-nine and highly successful: his many productions included three of Lillian Hellman's best-known works plus Arthur Miller's *Death of a Salesman*—wanted them "to do a play from the book *Anne Frank*" (this quote, like many that follow, comes from a journal that Frances kept all through the project). The Hacketts responded quickly, saying they'd like to write the play but were under contract to MGM and would have to get a leave of absence. Four days later, having reread the book, they telegraphed Bloomgarden, confirming their interest and saying they wanted to talk with him, and began blocking out the play in scenes. On December 8, Bloomgarden telegraphed that he was coming to California.

During Bloomgarden's two-day visit to the house on Bellagio Road, the Hacketts and he "talked, talked, talked *The Diary*," and Frances and Albert learned that Lillian Hellman had been offered the job but had declined and had suggested them. According to Garson Kanin, who directed the Broadway production, Hellman said, "I think [the diary is] a great historical work which will probably live forever, but I couldn't be more wrong as the adapter. If *I* did this it would run one night because it would be deeply depressing. You need someone who has a much lighter touch." Frances and Albert also learned that other people had tried to create a play. In 1950, Meyer Levin, later well-known for *Compulsion*, his best-selling novel about the Leopold-Loeb case, persuaded Otto Frank to let him write a stage version, which turned out not to interest Broadway producers (as we'll see, Levin loudly claimed, in court, that he'd been the victim of a conspiracy). In 1952, Otto Frank and the producer Cheryl Crawford tried to interest Carson McCullers, but she passed, reportedly because reading the book produced a rash on her hands and feet, and she concluded that the emotional involvement would be too great. In addition, playwrights John Van Druten and George Tabori were queried, as were Ruth Goetz and her husband, Augustus; the Goetzes said no because Mrs. Goetz "thought it was a fake, a hoax. . . . When they gave it to me to read, I said to Gus, 'Forget it, it's absolutely a fake.' . . . But after Frances and Albert began to see the father, I knew it was true."[2]

From the beginning of their commitment to *The Diary*, Frances and Albert understood the importance of the material. They also saw the difficulties ahead: how could an audience be expected to sit through an evening that realistically re-created the tormenting experiences of the Franks and their friends, hiding in cramped, prisonlike rooms, forced to keep silent all day, constantly fearing death? And, of course, the audience would know that almost all of the people they were watching would ultimately die in German hands—Anne died at Bergen-Belsen of typhus and malnutrition a few weeks before British troops liberated the camp.

The answer, Frances and Albert realized early on, was to capture Anne's lighter, girlish side: without her natural humor and optimism, the play would be impossibly grim. "When we first talked [with Bloomgarden]," Albert said, "we said we had never done anything of that sort before, but [it might work] if we could get the spirit of Anne the way she was in the book. . . . We said we didn't think that anyone could stand it, if you tried a play that [was] wringing tears out of people. . . . And he said, 'Well, this is what I want. I don't want any breast-beating or anything of that sort. I want what Anna saw, what Anna did, and what she saw in these people. This is Anna, all Anna. . . . The only way this play will go will be if it's funny.' . . . So whenever anybody's [planning to perform in the play] we always say, 'Get [the audience] laughing. . . . That way, it's possible for them to sit through the show.'"[3]

By December 13, Frances and Albert and Bloomgarden agreed to go ahead, and they put him on a train. Back at home, Frances found a necktie in the room he'd occupied and mailed it with a note: "It is a lovely tie, and brown is Albert's color. But I suppose we had better start off right, so I am sending it to you. . . . We had a fine weekend. . . . We hope, we hope, we hope that we may do justice to this book." They asked Bert Allenberg to get them six months off from MGM, and (according to Frances's journal) they "made [the] guest bedroom into [an] office: two typewriters, card tables, chairs with back to view. Bought books on Holland, Jewish history, Jewish religion, Jewish holidays, teenagers. Wrote BBC in London asking for broadcasts of D-Day. Wrote Mr. Frank, introducing ourselves."

Frances and Albert needed the books on Jewish history and traditions because they feared that, out of ignorance, they might make "stupid, offensive mistakes." They also bought "Jewish prayer books and hymn books" and met with a rabbi to discuss the Hanukkah service. Also, they invited a couple named Meyer, friends of Mr. Frank who had been in Amsterdam during the German occupation, to dinner. (Frances's journal: "Anne was at their wedding! Showed us yellow Star of David, identity papers, underground newspaper, etc.") Another evening, Toni Von Renterghen, a Dutchman who had been in the underground, showed the Hacketts scrapbooks of photographs, faked identity papers, and ration cards, "none of which," Frances wrote, "may ever be mentioned in play, but all of which we must know. We are brazen about asking people for help, but we feel this play is a tremendous responsibility."

Frances's journal entry for December 15, 1953, reads: "Began play. Regular routine of work. Alarm at 7:30. Lunch 12–1. Knock off at 4:30." On December 23, Leah Salisbury wrote that Bloomgarden's contract called for initial payments of $1,000 upon signing and $1,000 upon delivery of a script *"if he is willing to accept it for production"* (Salisbury's italics). On January 21, 1954, Frances recorded, "Finished rough, very rough draft. Started back at beginning," and added a gem of understatement—"This is not like any other job we have done"—plus a note about her feelings: "Terrible emotional impact. I cry all the time." Frances's tears continued throughout the work on *The Diary;* Garson Kanin once asked why she wept so often, and she replied, "Guilt, guilt, guilt." According to Albert, "Anytime Frances talked about Anna, she cried. She kept saying, 'Where was I when this was happening? Why didn't we know about this, what was going on over there?' . . . Anytime she thought of Anna, she could hardly speak."

On February 26, 1954, Frances and Albert finished a second version, which Frances called "no good. So afraid of making people unsympathetic that we have not made them human. Started again." Two weeks later, they had a "bad fight over script"; a week after that, Albert had a cold: "Tried to work by myself. Didn't get far." On April 22, they "finished for third time. First 30 pages confused, lacking direction. Starting again from beginning." On May 10, during a party at the Nunnally Johnsons', Frances found herself "yelling that if we wanted a picture job we could get a picture job." She didn't say who she yelled at, but obviously she was frazzled by the pace she and Albert were keeping; he added a note that perhaps explains her agitation: "When you're writing a play in New York, you're treated like a playwright. In Hollywood, you're an unemployed screenwriter." Around this time, Frances wrote to my mother, "We are desperately trying to finish. . . . It is the hardest thing we ever tackled. And I am sure that no one is going to put it on at this time—not while [the United States is] trying to woo Germany! People's memories are very short. Only the Jews will remember that once there were . . . Nazis. And it is not only the Jews that we must reach. In fact we are likely to be told we are anti-Semitic, since we have tried to put comedy into the play."

On May 14, 1954, "a great day," Frances and Albert found "an ending for the play" and asked Bert Allenberg to get them another six-month leave from MGM. A week later, they finished the fourth version, and Frances wrote, "The play, if play it be, which I very much doubt, is now being professionally retyped." Anticipating a trip to New York, Frances started packing and sent my mother two blouses she'd never worn, saying, "I am trying to clear up my life—such accumulations. And I suddenly found, after this winter of working at home, how little I really need. It had all been to make an impression in the Studio."

On June 1, having mailed copies of the script to everyone involved in the project, Frances and Albert flew to New York, and the next day Frances "bought a new hat!" The pleasure was short-lived: "Lunch with Leah, conference with Kermit, drink with Lilly. All hate play. Devastating criticism. Kermit won't pick up option, but willing to read it again after re-writes."

Deciding to stay in New York during the rewriting, which was plainly going to be time-consuming, the Hacketts moved out of their hotel and into an apartment on Park Avenue. In a letter to Charles Brackett, Frances described summertime conditions in the city. "We have found out where all the people who have left Hollywood have gone," she wrote. "They are in Sardi's. Any night is old home week. George Oppenheimer, Harry Kurnitz, Arthur Kober, Emily Kimbrough, on, and on, and on. . . . But the air here is heavy and sticky, and there is no change at night. . . . I feel like a bad pupil who has failed all of the Spring exams and has to go to summer school and take all of the courses over again. . . . A dog, locked in for the weekend, barks in a nearby apartment. No one is on the streets. It is Sunday in New York City—a summer Sunday. I try to believe it is romantic, that it is a foreign city and I am learning about it. But it doesn't seem to work."

If working on a weekend in the steamy city near a barking dog was bad, the news from Amsterdam was worse. In her journal, Frances recorded: "Our blue Monday. Letter from Mr. Frank that he could not give his approval." In his letter (which he carried in his pocket for three days before mailing because he hated sending bad news), Otto Frank said he knew "how devoted [*sic*] you worked. . . . All your letters showed me your warm feelings, so that I feel a close relation to you even not knowing you personally. Therefore it is very difficult for me to answer . . . as I have to do." He then spelled out his reservations, saying among other things that the script didn't convey "Anne's wish to work for mankind, to achieve something valuable still after her death, her horror against war and discrimination" and didn't show her "moral strength and optimistical [*sic*] view on life." There were some more specific objections, then more regrets— "My heart aches in writing [this] way knowing that I must hurt your feelings"—and then a roundabout invitation to keep trying: "I beg you to answer me just as openhearted as I. . . . You wrote that it was your intention to come to Europe. . . . Perhaps it is not too late to do so. . . . I would be *delighted* to see you [and] discuss everything with you."

Frances and Albert lost no time in replying, and their answer showed the problems they were having—because they normally dealt with lighthearted material—in coping with this deeper subject: "We have prayed that we have conveyed the spirit of *The Diary*, but evidently . . . we went wrong. [Now] we have looked with a fresh eye, and [you] are right in the things that you criticized. . . . So we have started to re-write. . . . First we shall do the play more seriously. Anne had such a delightful humor, and said herself that she was determined to present only the humorous side of even dangerous moments. We are afraid that we tried to show too much the humorous side. . . . We are trying to show much more the terrible tensions, the ever-present danger, the constant battle against the spiritually degrading circumstances. . . . We hope to come abroad and see you. But first we must write a better play."

Frances and Albert started pushing hard on the fifth version: "July 24. Heat terrible. Bad fight with Hackett. He says I am killing us both with work." On August 19, they finished the rewrite; on the 24th "[Kermit] called. Enthusiastic. Wants definitely to do play, but has criticisms." Two days later, at lunch, Bloomgarden said he wouldn't go ahead "unless [the script has] more spiritual lift for Anne. I am down in depths. A. H. sure we can get it."

Since Lillian Hellman had suggested Frances and Albert for *The Diary*, and they'd shown her an earlier version, they sent her the latest one and arranged to visit her on Martha's Vineyard. On the way, they stopped for a supposedly brief stay in Little Compton but were marooned there for four days by a major hurricane named Carol. "They were at my parents' house," their niece, Frances Huntoon Hall, recalled. "During the storm, Albert ran around stuffing long underwear under the windows to keep the rain out. The roads were blocked by fallen trees, and there was no electricity, so we cooked in the fireplace." The Hacketts finally reached the Vineyard on September 4. Frances said in her journal she was "so blue about play I could cut my throat," but she later wrote, "Lilly was amazing. Brilliant advice on construction. Must hurry to catch N.Y. season." Getting off the Vineyard was almost as difficult as getting on because, Frances said, the airport was "struck by lightning."

There's no record of exactly what construction advice Hellman gave the Hacketts, but plainly it was useful. Back in New York, as the next three weeks passed, Frances noted, "Starting again. Feel Lilly's suggestions will work out," and "Work going quite well. Sold bonds," and "Hangover. Did nothing all day. Perhaps it is good to have break in routine?" By October 8, the sixth version was done, and Frances delivered copies to Leah Salisbury and Bloomgarden, then lost two others while doing some shopping, which upset her terribly: "When I got home Hackett told me that Kermit had called to say he is going to do play. I am too numb to take it in."

The day after Bloomgarden said yes, Frances and Albert's attitude changed: they realized the script still needed work, but now they started thinking about production details. They had lunch with Bloomgarden— "He wants to start right away. Discussed actors, directors"—then "cocktails with the Strasbergs. Saw Susan. Lovely." (Susan Strasberg ultimately opened as Anne in the play and later wrote, "The part changed my life; I would never be the same again"; her famous father, Lee, was artistic di-

rector of the Actors Studio.) On October 18, they asked for another three-
month leave from MGM and sent the script to Garson Kanin, who was in
London, where his wife, Ruth Gordon, was appearing in *The Matchmaker*.

At this time, Garson Kanin—small, slender, wiry, mostly bald, a self-
described "bundle of nerves"—was forty-two, with an outstanding writer-
director record: his plays and films, some written in collaboration with
Gordon, included *Born Yesterday, Adam's Rib,* and *A Double Life*. He and the
Hacketts had first met in Hollywood in the late 1930s. The Hacketts were,
he said, "very well-known . . . and much, much in demand. . . . The producers and directors at Metro used to kill each other to get them assigned
to their projects. . . . I knew them easily, I knew them in the lunch room,
and being from the theater myself, [I appreciated] their work." He also felt
that the Hacketts' experience as actors—unusual among screenwriters—
gave them a special understanding of their craft.[4]

Soon after he received the Hacketts' script, Kanin wrote some notes that
expressed doubts—and showed his ego:

> [I had] a good long talk with Ruth about plans. She feels I should go
> ahead and do Diary. . . . It is the first thing in a long time that appears
> to have captured my imagination and my interest. I point out that,
> suppose I do do it . . . and it is a success, will that be the sort of satis-
> faction for which I hunger? After all, it is just the putting on of a play,
> and that is not the direction in which my desires and ambitions lie.
> She says I am wrong to feel this, and that I will write a play when I
> have a play to write. In the meantime, I should use my talents.

Having calmed his doubts, Kanin turned enthusiastic and sent a cable
to Frances and Albert saying, TINGLING WITH EXCITEMENT AND HIGH
HOPES, then composed a seventeen-page, single-spaced, typewritten letter. It arrived on November 12 and set forth Kanin's thoughts and his commitment to the project ("I gave it everything within me," he once said).
Pulsing with (honestly earned) self-confidence, the letter said, among
other things, "When a manuscript is as good as this . . . there is bred a long-
ing to make it great. I feel that this is well within the realm of possibility.
I see and sense it thus, somewhere within me. The job now is to express
the detail, great and small, as best I can." Kanin next addressed the play's
title (*"The Diary of a Young Girl* seems . . . small. . . . I feel certain a better one
can be thought up") and then "stagecraft."

At this point, the Hacketts' script called for pauses between scenes when
the curtain came down, leaving the audience in silent darkness while the
set was changed, but Kanin said that kind of staging could be "disastrous"

(presumably because the audience's attention wandered). Instead, he suggested "bridges" between scenes, during which the lights would dim to darkness and Anne's voice would be heard, reading from her diary. "The material for these bridges," Kanin wrote, "should *not* refer to what we have already seen . . . but should provide further enriching detail. Whenever possible, dates should be used . . . as to the progress of the war. The hope of D-Day, the accomplishment of D-Day, the hope of imminent liberation, and so on. . . . [These bridges] would keep the play alive from the moment the first curtain rises. . . . Then, at the final curtain . . . we hear Anne's voice saying, 'In spite of everything, I still believe that people are good at heart.'" Kanin also said the play should have more "terror and suspense," and he suggested an "outside world" sound pattern to contrast with the silence of the hiding place: planes, sirens, whistles, church bells. "A military band goes by. Shots in the street. . . . In addition, there should be some sudden sounds now and then from below, which prove upon investigation to be nothing. And then, of course, the final one, which proves to be something."

In exhaustive detail, Kanin also took up the layout of the set, and the characters' language, and casting, and the choice of people to design the set and do the lighting, and Anne's outbursts against the artificial condition of her life ("[her] growth is being forced, as in a greenhouse"), and improving a line of the Hacketts' where Anne said, "I could not ride my bike" ("The diary tells us that all Jews were compelled to give up their bicycles . . . it seems far [stronger]"). "Our responsibility," Kanin wrote, "is to make every detail credible," and he even got involved with earplugs, which Anne made as a Hanukkah gift to protect her roommate, the dentist, when she cried out during nightmares. (In the finished play, with the hiding place dark and silent in the middle of the night, Anne suddenly, terrifyingly, starts screaming in her sleep, *"No! No! Don't . . . don't take me!"*) In their draft, the Hacketts said Anne had made the earplugs out of tissue paper, but Kanin asked, "Wouldn't it be better if [she] were more ingenious? Perhaps she has made . . . earplugs of absorbent cotton and wax . . . something more imaginative. (I just tried to make some earplugs out of tissue paper, and it can't be done.)"

Kanin's contribution to *The Diary* was immense, and he later said that Frances and Albert wanted him to be listed as collaborator. "I said, 'Now listen, that's one thing I won't do. . . . Most directors, by the time a play goes into production, feel that they should be credited, but I don't, because [I'm just doing] what a director does.'"[5] To show their gratitude, when Random House published the play, Frances and Albert dedicated it to

Kanin. Frances once wrote him saying she'd searched through shops in New York, London, and Paris for a gift to thank him with but had finally realized that no mere object could suffice. Albert put his thanks another way: "I know that if we spill over with love and gratitude you will probably snap your cookies all over that beautiful suite of offices you have. So we will try to contain ourselves."

At the close of his seventeen-page letter, Kanin said he was going to Amsterdam to study details of background, national characteristics, history, architecture, dress, and food. He also wanted to examine the Franks' hiding place and talk to people who'd known them, and to Otto Frank himself. He invited the "dear Hacketts" to come along, then ended on a note of optimism, saying he had "every faith that this play, properly cast, honestly produced, and faithfully directed, can be a notable and memorable success. It has, of course, lurking dangers, and deep pitfalls, but they don't frighten me in the least. I see and hear the whole thing with striking clarity."

Now that he was committed to *The Diary*, Kanin discussed it with friends, including Somerset Maugham, who, of course, had written plays as well as novels. "I tell Maugham," Kanin wrote in his 1954 notebook,

about my interest in the AF project. . . . He looks troubled and says, "Well, two things come to mind. The first is, isn't it likely to be a rather harrowing play, and second, now that Germany is being re-armed, is this the sort of thing they want to see in America?" I point out to him that forgetting is one thing, and forgiving another, and I argue that if . . . Germany is to be re-armed, and we are [supposed] to forget that there ever was such a thing as a world conflict involving [the Germans] it is asking too much. . . . Following this line of thought, I point out, Winston Churchill should stop publishing his memoirs. Willie seems impressed . . . although not decisively.

Somerset Maugham wasn't alone in questioning *The Diary*'s chances of success. According to Albert, one of his and Frances's friends, James Thurber, said their involvement was a "great shame, a great loss. . . . No one's writing comedy. . . . Why don't you stick to comedy?"[6]

To Frances and Albert, Kanin's seventeen-page letter was "inspiring," and they cabled that they were flying to London. Frances's journal said their work was wearing them down: "Did odd jobs. Sold rest of bonds. Got tourist flight for the 15th, traveler's checks, etc. Looked at passport picture. Couldn't believe we looked that good only a year ago." In London, they had a "big mix-up" at their fancy Park Lane hotel, Grosvenor House

("No reservation. There's a motorcycle show on and we had no motorcycle. So we went to a dreary hotel"), but soon they were given rooms at Grosvenor House and were "very comfortable."

The Kanins were staying nearby at Claridge's, and a routine soon developed: Frances and Albert worked from nine to five in their rooms, doing rewrites based on Kanin's notes, then, starting at 5:30, they and Kanin worked in his rooms, sometimes right through a room-service dinner. At 10:30, when the theaters let out, Kanin went to pick up Ruth Gordon. In a letter to Bloomgarden, Frances said that Kanin was "fine, just fine. A tremendously hard worker, indefatigable." (Kanin returned the compliment: "an enchanting couple, hard workers.") Frances added, "Our plan is to [continue] re-writing here, then go to Amsterdam together. . . . That is what [Kanin] wants to do . . . and he is so perfect for our play that we want to arrange our lives in any way that is right for him." The Hacketts' workload in London was, if anything, heavier than it had been in New York, and again there were consequences: "I am a little hysterical," Frances wrote in her journal on December 5. "Walking to Simpson's for dinner, took a running dive, landing in the middle of South Audley Street. Fortunately no traffic."

On December 6, 1954, Frances and Albert flew to Amsterdam; at the Amstel Hotel, they found presents from Otto Frank. They had talked to him on the phone from London but had never met him, and Frances observed, "He looks so much like Joseph Schildkraut [the Austrian-born stage and screen star who'd been offered the role of Anne's father], it is uncanny." Kanin felt that during their first meetings, Frank was "unhurried, casual, old-worldish," and "talked about the hide-out and the arrest without an ounce of emotion," and concluded—100 percent wrongly, as it turned out—that he was a "cold fish."

On December 7, Frances and Albert, Kanin, and Otto Frank spent the day meeting the people who had hidden the Franks and visiting, among other places, Anne's school, the Franks' prewar apartment, and the ice cream parlor that Jews were allowed to patronize during the Occupation. Most importantly, they went to the gloomy, four-story building on the Prinsengracht canal and inspected the confining spaces where the Franks and their four friends had lived. "Very harrowing," Frances wrote in her journal. "Stood in Anne's room, stretched out my arms, touched walls on either side. This is the room she had to share with the crotchety dentist. Saw Garson looking at one of the photographs Anne had pasted on her wall. It was Ginger Rogers in a picture he had directed, *Tom, Dick, and*

*Harry*!" One of Albert's memories was that the entire building smelled strongly of mace, one of the spices Otto Frank had used in his business.

During the next two days, Frances and Albert conferred with officials at the Netherlands State Institute for War Documentation, who checked the script for accuracy, and Kanin hired a photographer to take pictures in the hiding place of details like the doorknobs, stairs, sink, stove, and windows. They got recordings of Dutch children's games and a street organ, plus books on Amsterdam. Kanin also arranged for a tape recording of the Westertoren carillon, the tram cars that ran to the end of the line a block away, and canal sounds, street sounds, and bicycle bells. "And always," Frances wrote, Kanin asked "questions, questions, questions to Mr. Frank." The schedule was tight: the Hacketts had only twenty-five minutes at the Rijksmuseum to see Rembrandt's *Night Watch*.

From Amsterdam, Frances showed her faith in the project, writing to Kermit Bloomgarden that she wanted to invest in it. Albert, she said, wasn't joining her—"He says he can close any show by investing"—but she wanted, for herself, "a little unit. We both feel a little poor, particularly today, after giving lunch to the research workers. . . . So may I have one unit?" She added that Kanin never put any money into a play he was doing—"But, if you want money, he can get it. Do you want money?" In the end, the financing of *The Diary* came from one limited partner—Bloomgarden—and roughly sixty general partners, who put up an average of $1,500; among them were Frances ($1,400), and Joshua Logan and his wife, Howard Dietz, Lillian Hellman, Doris Vidor, Mrs. Marshall Field, Abe Lastfogel, and Ruth Gordon.

Being with Otto Frank in Amsterdam, discussing his painful history, put a great strain on everyone, and for Albert there was a bizarre twist. Some years before, Frances had abruptly quit smoking, declaring, "Cigarettes no longer exist for me" (but she later often said, "There isn't a day when I don't miss them"); Albert had recently made the same decision. Someone had told him he was going to cry a lot after quitting, but instead he "laughed a lot. . . . [In Amsterdam], Garson suddenly saw that I was a good audience for a joke . . . and we'd just met Otto Frank, and we'd be in the car, and Garson would turn around and say, 'Did you ever hear the one about . . .' Well, it didn't have to be too funny to just *kill* me. . . . [One of Garson's stories was], he went to a performance some place, for blind people. . . . They were looking over *here*, and the action was over *there*. . . . The program was on yellow paper, and they were trying to read it, and they had a little yellow on the ends of their noses. . . . Well, to me that was terribly funny. . . . Mr. Frank was looking around, wondering what was happening, and Frances said, 'He's given up smoking—that's what's happened to *him*.' . . . I don't know if he believed that—it was so awful. . . . I think he forgave me."[7]

Albert *was* forgiven: the meeting in Amsterdam was the start of a warm but occasionally strained friendship that lasted until Otto Frank's death in 1980. During their later trips to Europe, Frances and Albert always made a point of going to Basel, where Frank lived with his second wife, Fritzi, also a concentration camp survivor. They also saw the Franks in New York, and the Franks visited them in Bel Air. The Hacketts felt Frank was extraordinarily dignified and impressive, "a person of extreme integrity and warm, wonderful humanity," but they sometimes became annoyed with him. "He lives in the past," Albert wrote, "and gets talking about the diary, the play, or Anne, and very soon he has reduced Frances to tears." In ways, Frank perplexed the Hacketts: "He is a very frugal man in his own way [but] he gives his money away—scholarships in Israel, etc. But he is a smart cookie about business. [A] curious mixture of great emotion and business [sense]." Frank's frugality both annoyed and amused them. "I won a bet from Albert," Frances wrote in the spring of 1960, during a visit to Basel. "Otto Frank had dinner with *us* in his home town, not we with *him!*"

On December 11, 1954, the Hacketts and Kanin had lunch with Otto Frank, then returned to London for more rewriting. Soon, Kanin tried to telephone Frank but couldn't reach him. It turned out that, after Kanin and the Hacketts left Amsterdam, Frank collapsed and was put to bed for several days. "[Talking to us]," Kanin said, "he had been crushed, but he had not shown it. He had been as he had been in the days when the Gestapo was outside the door—a tiny, tiny modern miniature Moses. If he had shown a moment's fear then, the whole annex would have crashed down."[8] The Amsterdam visit was also terribly hard on the Hacketts. "Frances," Kanin said, "just had to be carried away. . . . She was destroyed." "I thought I could not cry more than I had," Frances wrote, "but I have had a week of tears."

In London, Frances and Albert worked on their eighth rewrite, putting in changes based on information gleaned in Amsterdam: "It is best to have complete agreement about every comma before we start production." Then, abruptly, Frances's journal entry for the 20th said, "Murder! Production postponed! Cables, transatlantic calls, conferences. Kermit and

Garson believe it's too late this season. Must wait for Fall." Needing money, Frances and Albert cabled Bert Allenberg, asking for a writing job in Hollywood, then went to Paris. They stayed for a week—it was their first vacation in a year—"just resting, and enjoying the fact that the alarm does not ring. . . . Always raining here, but when you've lived in California, you love rain. . . . We walk and walk and look at everything. Never such beauty in a city."

In Paris, with their script essentially finished, the Hacketts must have felt a glow of accomplishment. Although they had used many lines from the diary, the play was an original work in several ways. The diary was highly personal, but the Hacketts had to be objective and find ways of showing character traits that were merely mentioned in the diary. Also, they had to set the story against history and find a beginning, a middle, and an end. In addition to all that, there was the question of tone. As Brooks Atkinson later wrote:

> The play is neither heroic nor sentimental. Written in a subdued key, without pointing a moral, it chronicles . . . a strange adventure, some of it distressing, some . . . humorous, but all of it warm, simple and affecting. . . . Through every line . . . shines the spirit of Anne Frank. . . . By preserving it so delicately, [the Hacketts] have let a clean, young mind address the conscience of the world.[9]

# 19

## Getting *The Diary of Anne Frank* on the Stage

In early January 1955, Frances and Albert were in New York, preparing to return to California to work at MGM while awaiting *The Diary*'s startup in the fall. From the Sulgrave Hotel, Albert wrote to Garson Kanin, "We have been busy packing up, having our teeth cleaned of English tea stains and French wine stains, making ourselves pretty for Dore [Schary]. But to date Dore does not seem to care. We have heard nothing. We are flying out next Wednesday." When they arrived in California, the Hacketts had to stay at the Bel Air Hotel for a month because they'd rented their house while they'd been away. After the tenants left, Albert wrote, "It is nice to be back in the house again. We are still trying to find things. . . . When we got in, there were only two good electric bulbs left. . . . Somehow you got the picture of the people living in one room until the bulbs burned out and then moving to another room."

At first, all seemed wonderful at the studio. "The most fortunate thing happened," Frances wrote. "They offered us . . . a story that we liked. Usually it is months before we find what we want. . . . It is a remake of Robert Sherwood's [play] *Waterloo Bridge,* which was written long, long ago . . . and set in the First World War [in London]. We will put it in this war . . . put in a ballet, a couple of singers, some bombing, and stir. We hope it turns out right."

*Gaby,* the movie cooked from that recipe, told of the love between an English ballerina (Leslie Caron) and an American paratrooper (John Kerr), which goes unconsummated because he's called away for D-Day; believing he's dead, she "comforts" several lonely soldiers; when he returns, she's remorseful; ultimately, they work things out. Although Frances and Albert started the project on a positive note, setbacks soon developed, "the greatest of them a director [Curtis Bernhardt] who likes nothing that we write. He is a real pain, but a talented guy, so we are taking it and taking it. . . . We told our producer . . . that nothing mattered to us but our play in New York and nothing would keep us here if word came that we were needed."

Frances called Bernhardt a "real pain"—and he evidently agreed: he once signed a long, argumentative memo to her and Albert "Love, The Eternal Confuser." Probably because of the Hacketts' problems with Bernhardt, Charles Lederer finished the screenplay. The Hacketts got sympathetic letters from three different studio executives: "The Bernhardt syndrome is one that we have all had to cope with"; "I regret so much that the . . . picture was such an unhappy experience for you"; "I honestly believe all the unhappiness . . . will pay off with something very fine." The last prediction missed the mark: when the film was released, in the spring of 1956, the reviews included "merely a pedestrian, if occasionally tender, romance" and "a tremulous, tenuous, and somewhat over-extended idyll."

While working on *Gaby*, Frances and Albert remained involved in *Diary* affairs, chiefly, trying to find an actress to play Anne. Although they'd been impressed by Susan Strasberg when they met her in New York, Kermit Bloomgarden had had her read for him and hadn't been impressed, so the Hacketts corresponded with him and Kanin about other candidates and met with some who were in Hollywood. Joseph Schildkraut, nicknamed "Pepi," was on hand, and Frances and Albert were pleased by his enthusiastic help. (When the play opened in New York, Schildkraut was praised lavishly; in his memoirs, he called that day "the high point of my career and of my whole life.") "We are having auditions [for Anne]," Albert wrote, "that Pepi arranges. Whenever we or he hear of someone, we confer. Since we are at the studio all day we let Pepi manage everything. Then on a given night the people come to our house and read a scene with Pepi." Natalie Wood was among those who read; about her, Frances wrote to Bloomgarden, "Nice. No stage experience. Great picture possibility. Seventeen, beautiful eyes. This was really just as a courtesy to Pepi, since he was supposed to go into a picture with the director, Nicholas Ray, who is the 'patron' of Natalie Wood, according to Pepi." In another letter, Frances complained to Bloomgarden that another actress

came on Wednesday night to dinner. But she did not read. We had thought that she would. We had carefully paved the way by saying that [you had asked her to do so]. . . . We fed her braised celery with anchovies, filet mignon, fresh pineapple, petits fours . . . and she did not read. Her excuse was, she'd rather wait for Garson. She was far more interested in where her ex-husband, with whom, she said with downcast eyes, she was "reconciling," was. . . . He came. They sat 'til eleven, and left. . . .

Now there is another of your hopefuls out here. . . . She thinks she's going to play the part! She thinks she has no French accent. She calls us a great deal. We have been a little cruel, to someone so pregnable. . . . We have a little avoided her after the first cocktails and dinners, fearing that she might interpret it, not as a gesture to a friend of Dorothy Gish, a lonely friend, but as encouragement.

The search for Anne ended in late May. Susan Strasberg, then seventeen and a student at the Professional Children's School who'd appeared on TV and in films, was in Hollywood, preparing to go into *Friendly Persuasion,* starring Gary Cooper. Her agent called and told her mother to take her to lunch with Schildkraut and Frances and Albert at the Beverly Hills Hotel; Strasberg later wrote that she feared another rejection and went reluctantly. In the hotel's sunny, flower-filled garden, Schildkraut talked a lot about his famous actor father, Rudolph, and how difficult it had been to live up to his reputation—and added that the part of Otto Frank would close the gap. Strasberg said the Hacketts were "charming" and asked her about school and the filming of *Picnic,* her most recent movie. She was nervous throughout the meal, and then the five of them went into the "cave-like cool" of the hotel's downstairs ballroom. Someone turned out the lights and handed her the last scene in the play, a monologue of Anne's about her hopes for the future, her belief in the goodness of man. Although Strasberg almost knew the speech by heart from her previous reading, she clutched the script to keep her hands from trembling.

> The three of them sat at tables scattered around the dance floor. . . . I looked out the small window over the stage. I could see a hint of green and sky. As I began to speak the lines, I started to weep, for Anne, for her courage, her belief. . . . When I finished, there was a silence. Then I heard them whispering among themselves.

> "Hello, Anne," Pepi said. We all began to laugh.[1]

From the start, Garson Kanin had worried about the play's title, which was the same as the book's—*The Diary of a Young Girl*—and had suggested alternatives: *The Secret Annex, The Hiding Place, The Diary of Anne Frank.* On May 25, he wrote to Frances and Albert, addressing them as "Dear both" and saying he thought they "ought to stay simple" and choose the third. "You see," he wrote, "no matter what we call the play, it is always going to be referred to as 'the Anne Frank play' or 'the play about Anne Frank' or 'the dramatization of that Anne Frank diary,' and so on. So why not take advantage of our advantages?" Ever since the play's success, the title originally used on the book's American edition has been dropped, and the book itself is now called *The Diary of Anne Frank;* in effect, the play retitled the book. Also, because Anne's penultimate speech in the play ended with the words, "I still believe, in spite of everything, that people are really good at heart," recent editions of both the Oxford and Cambridge reference works on the American theater mistakenly say that that was the last line of Anne's diary—when, in fact, she wrote five or six more pages.

Boris Aronson, one of the best in the business, was given the job of designing the set for *The Diary* (Helene Pons did the costumes, and Leland Watson did the lighting), and he produced a representation of the hiding place, using authentic details thanks to Kanin's photos, which was highly praised by the critics: "glows with an elusive beauty"; "one of the finest my eyes have encountered in years of playgoing. Most sets are just something to be looked at and to keep the actors within bounds; this one looks as though it is being lived in." The "lived-in" appearance was achieved by making subtle changes in furnishings and decor during the darkened moments between scenes, so the space that started as nearly a bare attic was gradually transformed into an attractive (though cramped) home; at the same time, the Franks and the others appeared to grow steadily thinner and more shabbily dressed. Frances and Albert thought the set was "wonderful . . . so imaginative," and they grew close to Aronson: they went to his son's bar mitzvah and later bought one of his paintings (Aronson was a painter as well as a set designer).

In mid-July 1955, while they were still in Hollywood working on *Gaby,* Frances and Albert auditioned Dennis Hopper for the part of Peter Van Daan, the teenaged son of the other couple who shared the hiding place. They found Hopper a "beautiful young actor! . . . He is now under contract to Warner Brothers on the picture *Giant.* . . . He read the very first scene when he comes into the hiding-place, and suddenly we felt the whole thing. . . . He made you see his despair . . . and he made you see the four walls . . . and that he knew he was going to be there imprisoned. . . . He was sensitive . . . and a great find." The Hacketts tried to push Hopper for the part but failed: they "went all out, promising him his fare (ourselves) to New York for a reading. But the studio won't let him go. His agent says that James Dean (the star of *Giant*) is acting up, not appearing on the set for days, so they are thinking of shooting this boy in for a replacement."

Also in July, Sid Perelman visited again. His view of Hollywood was as tough as ever: he wrote a friend about "the usual interminable dinner parties, the same conversation about the same banalities," and said that the Hacketts had taken him to "a particularly ghastly [party] at Malibu, 135 people all eating in a rented marquee," where he saw "the survivors of my epoch out here, gray and twitching, as fatuous as they ever were, all of them heavy with annuities and real estate and Jaguars, and dreary beyond description. The Hacketts . . . are leaving here August 1st for N.Y., as their play . . . goes into rehearsal later in the month. They've spent almost two years of work on it, and if [God] isn't too busy . . . I'd like him to ensure the success of their show."[2]

By August 3, Frances and Albert were back in New York, conferring with Bloomgarden and Kanin about, among other things, the casting of some of the remaining parts. Kanin had already found Lou Jacobi and David Levin to appear as Mr. Van Daan and his son, Peter. After a series of readings, Eva Rubinstein, the daughter of the pianist Artur Rubinstein, got the role of Margo, Anne's sister; the parts of Mr. Kraler and a young girl named Miep, Dutch gentiles who risked their lives to help the annex's occupants, went to Clinton Sundberg and Gloria Jones. Jack Gilford was cast as the crotchety dentist. A highly skilled pantomimist and night club comic, Gilford had appeared two years before on Broadway in *The World of Sholom Aleichem,* speaking a line that became associated with him from then on: as a silent, long-suffering character who was told in heaven that he could ask for anything, he replied, "In that case, if it's true, could I have, please, every day, a hot roll with butter?"

Also put into *The Diary*'s original cast was a cat named Mouschi, the pet of Peter Van Daan. More than three years later, when *The Diary*'s U.S. touring company reached its last stop, the stage manager wrote to the Hacketts in Bel Air, saying he'd heard they might want to adopt Mouschi, and Albert wrote back, declining: "We would [break] his heart, I'm afraid. Our housekeeper has a dog. It is a sort of queer dog, but I do not think they would get along together. [Also], we close ourselves in a room and write and argue and type all day and I do not think a theater cat with Broadway experience could take that."

Rehearsals of *The Diary* began on August 22 in the Cort Theater; it was a wickedly hot day, and the air-conditioning was off. Garson Kanin addressed the company, giving—Frances wrote in her journal—a "wonderful talk. 'This is not a play in which you are going to make individual hits. You are real people, living a thing that really happened.'" Kanin's message—that this was a group effort, and they were all working for a noble cause—got across, and Frances wrote at one point that she had never seen a company "so dedicated, united, selfless." (Later, when Schildkraut and Strasberg *did* make "individual hits," some interesting tensions arose.) Following Kanin's talk, the cast read through the play, and it was immediately obvious that there was, in Frances's words, "something wrong in our second act. But what?"

*The Diary*'s schedule called for tryouts starting in Philadelphia in three and a half weeks. As rehearsals continued in New York, Frances and Albert sometimes dropped in. They still sensed a weakness in the second act, and they also knew the play was too long—in those days curtains went up at 8:30, and everyone knew it was hard to keep an audience's attention past 10:45. Cutting was needed, and Kanin suggested that instead of pulling out a few lines here and there—which might spoil the rhythm and design—a single, larger chunk should be eliminated; he suggested a "character-development" scene in which Anne and her father talked while he was cutting her hair. In plot terms, this could, in fact, be spared, but it was charming and intimate and was a favorite of Frances and Albert and of Schildkraut. Kanin said that during their time together on *The Diary*, he and the Hacketts had only one quarrel; it was about the haircut scene, and it was "bitter, tough. . . . It went on for some time, and it got to be a little bit acrimonious. . . . Although I adored them, it got to be very tight, and as I remember the climax, [Frances] just rose and stomped out of the room—she left the rehearsal. . . . Albert, who was a pussycat, stayed behind, and tried to patch things up. The next day, we met, and discussed the whole thing a little more calmly, and the scene was ultimately out of the play."[3]

During the rehearsals, Kanin worked closely with all of the actors, focusing especially on Susan Strasberg, who was making her Broadway debut. To prepare her, Kanin offered an insight into Anne's character. In Amsterdam, Otto Frank had told him that the last time he'd seen Anne—at a railroad station, where the men and women were being put, with Teutonic efficiency, onto separate trains for shipment to death camps—she was smiling. "Anne was on a moving train," Frank told Kanin. "She didn't see me, so she stood there smiling and waving [toward] the whole crowd of men, hoping I'd see her. That's the way I last saw her—smiling and waving. She never knew that I saw her."[4] Kanin repeated that story to Strasberg, saying, "That is the essence of Anne."

Everyone agreed later that Susan Strasberg was magnificent in the role, but during rehearsals, there was trouble. Kanin called her "a pain in the ass . . . and a spoiled child, terribly spoiled, with grandiose ideas about her importance. . . . I remember giving her direction in something, and she said, 'Well, I don't think I'd like to do that,' and I said, "Well, Susan, it isn't up to you—it's up to the playwrights, and me. . . . You are a servant of this project, you've got to do what we ask you to do' . . . and she said, 'Well, I don't want to, and if you want that done, why don't you get someone else.' . . . Frances wasn't there at the time, but I thought Albert was going to strangle her. . . . I talked to her [parents] and said, 'This is no longer my responsibility. . . . She's your child. . . . You have to explain to her that an actress is a servant. . . . I don't want to, because if I do, I'll probably wind up slapping her in the kisser.'"

On that occasion, Strasberg's parents were evidently helpful; however, according to Kanin, another time they created a problem. "[Susan's] mother—God help us—was at every moment of every rehearsal . . . and one time she asked me if it would be all right if Lee dropped in for just a few minutes: 'He'll sit in the last row, and he won't say a thing.' . . . I said, 'Listen, he's perfectly welcome to come to any rehearsal he wants to; he doesn't have to sit in the back where he cannot see' . . . and she said, 'I assure you, he'll never say a thing, he'll never say a word,' and I said, 'That isn't necessary: he's a teacher, he's a director, he's a force in the theater.' . . . The next day, at ten o'clock, Lee turned up, and at my invitation he sat right down front, and he sat through the whole rehearsal. . . . And the next day Susan came in and started giving a performance of such ghastly embroidery and detail and mix-up and curious reading that I was appalled, but what could I do? I brought it on myself. . . . Frances and Albert said, 'You've got to straighten her out,' and I agreed, and I did."[5]

Kanin also worked closely with Joseph Schildkraut, and there, too, the challenge was getting simplicity and believability, because Schildkraut was normally highly flamboyant. Schildkraut later said that he never worked so hard: the part was exactly the opposite of almost everything he'd done in the theater or the movies: "I had to forget I was an actor. . . . I would do a scene and think that I had achieved simplicity and realism—

that I had succeeded in being this man, Otto Frank. But Kanin would point out to me that I had been too graceful in this gesture, too theatrical in that crossing of the stage. And, always, he was right."

As Frances had noted in Amsterdam, there was a strong resemblance between Schildkraut and Otto Frank—except that Schildkraut had a full head of hair, while Frank was partly bald. During rehearsals, Kanin repeatedly asked Schildkraut to shave his head, but out of vanity, he refused and suggested a compromise: a makeup expert gave him a can of wax, which he smoothed down over his hair and painted with makeup. This fooled nobody, and Kanin kept urging the actor to shave. The stalemate lasted for weeks, and then one day while Schildkraut was holding the wax can, the makeup man's label fell off, revealing a smaller one that said, "For Morticians' Use Only." Schildkraut later wrote that he quickly said to Kanin, "Let's shave the head." He added that up to that point, he'd been unsure about his performance, fearful that he wasn't doing full justice to the part; however, after that, he "knew for the first time" that he had solved his problem. "This was more than an attempt to look like Otto Frank— the sacrifice, small as it was, somehow cured me of my vanity, my egotism, of my subconscious drive to be brilliant and startling, and helped me to achieve in my acting the simplicity and humility which this part demanded."[6]

As the September 15 Philadelphia opening drew closer, Frances and Albert got some bad news about *The Diary*'s financial future: "Haven't been able to sell any benefits for New York," Frances wrote in her journal. "Both Kermit and Gar talked their heads off. No good. 'Too serious.' We must count only on what comes in each night at the box office." Also, there was still the problem of the sagging second act: "Feeling more and more strongly that something needed. . . . Sit watching play, worried, scowling. Actors think we're scowling at them. Try to reassure them."

On September 8, after the rehearsal, a "big conference" was held at which Frances and Albert, Kanin, and Bloomgarden agreed that somehow tension had to be added midway through the second act—and found the solution: Mr. Van Daan would steal some bread. Already written into the script was the idea that Van Daan, a large man, was suffering from hunger even more severely than the others and was capable of selfish acts: he'd sold his wife's fur coat to buy cigarettes. The next step seemed logical, and Frances and Albert wrote a scene that hadn't been in the original diary: one night, Van Daan creeps eerily, in the silent darkness, to the communal food cabinet, takes out a half loaf, and then makes a noise that wakes the others. The reactions are violent: Mr. Dussel physically attacks Van Daan; Mrs. Frank insists that the Van Daans must leave the hiding place, which will surely mean their capture and death; Otto Frank observes, "We don't need the Nazis to destroy us. We're destroying ourselves." The tension in the scene, which is one of the play's most effective, is extreme, but it's broken by the arrival of Miep, joyously announcing that the Normandy landings have begun. At first buoyed by the news, the annex's occupants are then shaken with shame over their recent harsh words toward one another.

There's a curious footnote concerning this scene. As noted before, "Van Daan" wasn't the real name of the man whom Frances and Albert turned into a thief. Shortly after the play opened, a journalist learned Mr. Van Daan's real name, and Otto Frank began worrying that the actual man's surviving relatives might feel unhappy about being connected to a theft, even though it was fictitious. Frances and Albert were in Basel around that time, and, to relieve Frank's worries, they pointed out that in the play the theft is forgiven because, at bottom, the other characters love Van Daan. Frances wrote that, to illustrate their argument, Albert did "more acting for Otto [presumably demonstrating the forgiveness] than he has done since he was six."

It took Frances and Albert a couple of days to write the bread-stealing scene; the cast first rehearsed it on the train to Philadelphia. During rehearsals and preview performances there, Frances and Albert divided their time between the Walnut Street Theater and the Barclay Hotel, rewriting the new scene and others. After one preview matinee, which they missed because they were working, Bloomgarden told them, "You should have been there! It went marvelously! You never heard so many laughs!" —which was a good sign: the audience had caught the play's light side.

In Philadelphia, Garson Kanin got another audience reaction that told him the play would be a "real hit." "I wouldn't always watch the whole play," he told me. "I'd go out in the lobby for a little while, and I'd always find three or four of the audience standing there or sitting there, weeping . . . and I remember one woman indelibly who came up to me and said, 'How dare you do this to a theater audience? I paid for my ticket, and my husband paid for his ticket, and you bring me into the theater, and you destroy me—*how dare you?*' I said, 'Well, that's my job, that's what I do.'"

Frances wrote that the Philadelphia opening, with reviewers invited, "went well, in spite of terrible heat. Kermit gave company party afterwards." Among those at the performance and the party were Gloria and

Arthur Sheekman; Mrs. Sheekman said it was an "awesome occasion—[the play] so strong, so moving, so tender. We were sure it would be a tremendous hit, and were so happy for the Hacketts." The Philadelphia reviews were basically good, but there was still trouble in the second act—"There is a great deal of talk," the Associated Press critic said—and Frances and Albert did more rewriting: Frances's journal entry for September 17 read, "We have decided that we need more tension. . . . Worked all day and evening 'til 3 A.M.. Up again at 6 A.M.." On the 19th, she wrote, "Second act better. Only small changes now, tightening scenes, etc. New York stage crew came down. Garson rehearsing them all day, speeding up changes between scenes." The Associated Press critic also said something insightful, that no other critic said, calling the Hacketts' script a "labor of love."

When Frances and Albert's first successful play, *Up Pops the Devil*, had opened almost exactly a quarter of a century before, many of the offerings on Broadway had been, like the Hacketts' creation, lighthearted and detached—pure escapism. Now, the climate on Broadway was far more serious, and audiences could choose among several fine, thought-provoking, new plays—*A View from the Bridge, Bus Stop, Cat on a Hot Tin Roof, Inherit the Wind,* and *Witness for the Prosecution*—plus productions of plays by Shakespeare, Marlow, Giraudoux, Anouilh, and Wilder. It was the best theatrical season in years and promised to be formidable competition for the Hacketts' work.

On the evening of *The Diary*'s New York opening, October 5, 1955, a message from Otto Frank was posted on the backstage bulletin board in the Cort Theater: "You will all realize that for me this play is a part of my life, and the idea that my wife and children as well as I will be presented on the stage is painful. . . . Therefore it is impossible for me to come. . . . My thoughts are with every one of you . . . and I hope most ardently that the play will, through you, reach as many people as possible and awaken in them a sense of responsibility to humanity."[7]

Perhaps because her parents and her close friend Marilyn Monroe were in the audience, Susan Strasberg was "in a dither": "I couldn't eat; my stomach was playing strange tricks." Although he'd weathered many opening nights, Joseph Schildkraut was also agitated. "I went around to see the whole company," Garson Kanin said, "and I wished them well, and kissed the girls, and when I got to Pepi, he grabbed me, and held me, and squeezed me—I thought he was going to break my *back*—and he said, 'Gar, Gar, can you say something to me to get me through this evening—

say one word, say one word to help me, what shall I do, what shall I do?'
And I said, 'Less.'"[8] (In his memoirs, which are wondrously self-serving,
Schildkraut told a totally different, nonhysterical story: "Just before I went
on stage I found a little note which Kanin had left on my dressing table.
It read, 'Dear Pepi, thank you for you talent—thank you for your genius—
thank you for your patience. When in doubt—*less*. Please!'")[9]

Meanwhile, Frances and Albert had made their way up to the theater's
top gallery, where they sat "with dry mouths and twitching bodies," waiting for the curtain to rise, thinking about "all of the many people who had
helped us, of the company, of Garson Kanin, of the months and months
of work, of the miles we had traveled."

# 20

## After *The Diary*

**W**hen the curtain fell at the Cort Theater that night, there was total, stunned silence. It lasted and lasted—and then finally, hesitantly, applause began, and grew and grew. . . .

Almost all of the reviews of *The Diary of Anne Frank* were wonderful: "a fine drama, beautifully acted, directed, and mounted"; "a lovely, tender drama"; "There is . . . beauty, warm humor, gentle pity and cold horror in [the play]"; "By wisely shunning any trace of theatricality or emotional excess, the playwrights have made the only-too-true story deeply moving." Setting down the last item in her two-year journal, Frances wrote, "Every notice good! Walking on air! It was worth the tears, the months we worked, the miles we traveled. We only wish that Anne could have known."

The New York production of *The Diary* ran for almost two years—717 performances—and won all the major awards for 1955: the New York Drama Critics Circle Award for the best new American play, the American Theater Wing's Antoinette Perry (Tony) Award for the outstanding play of the year, and the Pulitzer Prize. (The last came with a check for $500; to Frances's amusement—and annoyance—it was made out only to Albert.) In the decades following its Broadway opening, in hundreds of productions in dozens of countries and dozens of languages, the Hacketts' play spread its universal message around the world, sometimes with curious overlappings: at one point, audiences in Buenos Aires could choose between productions in Yiddish and Italian; the latter was played by a repertory company visiting from Rome. The first foreign productions were in Europe, where opening-night reactions were even more extreme than in the United States. In Amsterdam (the king and queen of the Netherlands came), there were sobs and one strangled cry as the play reached its climax—the sound of the police hammering on the door. In Berlin (the play opened the same night in seven other German cities), the audience could hardly rise from their seats, would not permit applause, and left silently with bowed heads; one observer wrote, "For a full two minutes there was no sound in the theater. Then a spatter of hand-clapping began. It was hissed down immediately. Soon 700 sophisticated Berliners rose slowly and walked out of the theater. I saw tear stains on powdered cheeks and men walking as if they were very tired."[1] "This play," said another report, "appears to have burst from the bounds of the theater and become perhaps the most significant social fact of the year. . . . Every German has learned . . . that a play about the Jewish pogroms is shaking the emotions of all who see it."[2]

*The Diary of Anne Frank* brought in a lot of money, and Frances and Albert gave a lot of it to organizations that were keeping Anne's spirit alive and helping young Jewish writers—to name just four, the American Friends of the Hebrew University, Brandeis University, the American-Israel Cultural Foundation, and the Netherlands-America Foundation, which raised funds for the preservation of the Frank family's hiding place. The play was produced on TV in different countries (Frances and Albert wrote one of the American versions, and they also wrote the film version); perhaps in response to the rise of neo-Nazi groups, in the late 1990s the number of European productions of the stage version rose. And through the years, there were some commentators who felt that the play was flawed—for example, in 1955 *Commentary* magazine called it "false and shallow," and in 1989 Judith Thurman wrote in the *New Yorker* that Frances and Albert had "reduced Anne's . . . character . . . to that of a generic Hollywood ingenue. . . . Hackett and Goodrich [were steeped in Hollywood's] pieties and simplifications. In their hands, Anne's diary became the kind of domestic drama in which bad things happen to good people." (More about negative reactions later.)

When Susan Strasberg walked into the opening-night party for *The Diary* at Sardi's, a few blocks from the theater, the crowd—which included Marilyn Monroe—rose and applauded. She soon forgot her tricky stomach and like a normal teenager wolfed down fruit salad, ice cream, a chicken salad sandwich, steak tartare, and Franchot Tone's pizza. When she read the reviews of her performance, she got still more treats: "beautiful"; "warm, rich, at times with comedy overtones but always moving and real"; "She is a brat when she is brought to this prison, and by the time the Nazis come for her she has become a woman."

Roughly two months after the opening, Kermit Bloomgarden put Susan Strasberg's name, spelled out with 180 lightbulbs, above the title, making

her Joseph Schildkraut's costar. Schildkraut, who also got splendid reviews, said in his memoirs that this made him "especially happy," but in
*her* memoirs, Strasberg said he became intensely jealous and began a campaign of harassment and intimidation. Onstage, he pinched her, muffled
her mouth with his arm, killed her laughs and her lines, even kissed her
openmouthed. Frances and Albert heard about these "hair-raising" antics,
and Frances wrote, "What a horrible man! If only he weren't such a good
actor! But sometimes I feel that he destroys in the others more, much more,
than he contributes himself." Offstage, Schildkraut flirted with Strasberg;
once, trying to squelch him, she asked, "What would you do if I said yes?"
and he replied, "Oh, my dear child, you wouldn't do that to me, would
you?" Schildkraut was only kidding Strasberg, but he was serious about
other women. When the play moved to Los Angeles, a heat wave hit, and
he told his wife that on matinee days he was going to rest in his dressing
room between performances rather than come home. "Pepi is having a
heat wave all his own," Albert wrote. "A blond. . . . It seems [his wife] interrupted his 'rest' and chased the blond with her handbag around the
Huntington Hartford Theatre!"

In mid-November 1955, with *The Diary* well launched on Broadway,
Frances and Albert sailed on the U.S.S. *Constitution* to Naples. During the
voyage, they finally got some rest: "We sleep ten and twelve hours a night.
. . . We are gradually loosening up—don't re-write the play in our sleep
any more." Frances also wrote, "I am a little less irritable, Albert a little less
hysterical." In Rome, the Hacketts went to a four-hour performance of
Arthur Miller's *The Crucible*. The play had been produced in New York
by Kermit Bloomgarden, to whom Frances wrote, "The show was grand.
Couldn't understand a word, of course, but enjoyed it. . . . The house was
jammed, very dressy audience, lots of mink, every seat filled, and a lovely
theater. . . . The reason for the four-hour playing time is that there were
twenty and twenty-five minute waits between acts. . . . They all go out and
have coffee and food, and visit with each other, but it does not seem to
break their attention away from the play. They come back as excited as
ever." After visiting other Italian and Swiss cities, Frances and Albert met
Otto Frank in Basel. "As usual," Frances wrote, "I cried, [and] he cried."

By January 1, 1956, Frances and Albert were in London, staying at
Grosvenor House and going to the theater most evenings, partly in search
of an actress to play Anne in *The Diary*'s upcoming London production.
"Have seen *Waiting for Godot*," Frances wrote, "which I was mad about and
Albert slept through . . . [also] *The Reluctant Debutante* (which MGM wants

us to do and we don't want to do)." Their enjoyment ended when Frances was hit by the shingles. All that Dr. Woodcock could prescribe was bed rest and twice-daily changing of the dressings on the blisters. The disease is extremely painful—Dante put eternal shingles among the pains of hell—and often follows a period of intense stress: evidently Frances was paying a heavy price for her labors on *The Diary*.

With "Doctor Pat" urging that Frances would do best in a warm, dry climate, the Hacketts left London in mid-February and returned to Bel Air; many weeks of recuperation followed. In early March, the Writers Guild of America (which had been formed in 1954 by merging the Screen Writers Guild, the Radio Writers Guild, and the Television Writers Guild) gave them and their friends Julius J. Epstein and Philip G. Epstein—there was an unbreakable tie between the two writing teams—the Laurel Award for Screen Writing Achievement, bestowed annually upon "that member of the Guild who, in the opinion of the Screen Branch, has advanced the literature of the motion picture through the years, and who has made outstanding contributions to the profession of the Screen Writer." Because only fellow screenwriters vote on it, the Laurel Award is considered by many the profession's highest honor, more important than the Oscar. In May, Frances and Albert were visited by Frith Banbury, a witty, congenial, English-born, self-described "half-Australian Jewish homosexual," who was a good friend of Dr. Woodcock and had been chosen to direct the London production of *The Diary*. (Before Banbury arrived, Albert wrote to Garson Kanin concerning language changes needed for the London production—"tram" for "trolley," for example—and asked, "Have you some non-U words you'd like inserted? And where do you want them inserted?") The Hacketts had never met Banbury before, and they took to him instantly—"We had a lovely time when he was here. . . . He is so warm and friendly"—and gave a big party for him. "They were absolutely charming to me," Banbury said. "They had one of those parties where everyone including Harpo Marx is asked. . . . The world and his wife were at that party. *Hollywood* was there." The visit started a lifelong friendship: Frances and Albert saw Banbury in London, and he visited them in New York. "I used their apartment like a hotel," he said. "I sponged on them. I learned to make my bed before breakfast; if I didn't Frances rushed upstairs and made it."[3]

Thanks in part to *The Diary*'s success, in the winter of 1956 Frances and Albert were offered a number of best-selling books to adapt for the movies, including Irwin Shaw's *Lucy Crown* and Herman Wouk's *Marjorie Morn-*

*ingstar;* on behalf of his book, Wouk sent a hopeful letter: "Since you'll be getting this on Leap Year Day I think it's not inappropriate if Marjorie proposes to you. . . . I think we ought to have a lunch or a drink . . . and exchange notes on our detestable and enchanting way of making a living." Frances and Albert felt coolly toward Wouk's novel, and in any event, they were still under contract to MGM and couldn't act with total freedom. MGM had the right to loan out their services; in early July, they found themselves at Twentieth Century Fox, adapting Francoise Sagan's second novel, *A Certain Smile.*

An international best-seller that was then called amoral, *A Certain Smile* told the story of an affair between a young, Parisian female student and a married, middle-aged man. As always, Frances and Albert started by carefully studying the text and found, among other things, that in the American edition there was a sentence saying "He put his hand on my thigh and for the first time I was stirred"—and in the British edition the final word was "concerned." In an interview, Frances said, "She's a beautiful writer, the little Sagan, really poetic, a fine emotional quality"; nevertheless, because films dealing with adultery were still subject to pressure from watchdog groups, the screenplay made some changes of emphasis. "We have the girl really falling in love with the man," Frances said, "instead of just going off on a weekend. In the book, Sagan mentions that the girl's older brother was killed in an accident, and that her father spent all his time consoling her mother. To us, that was explanatory. The girl, rejected by her father, was looking for a father image in this man. Although Sagan didn't see it that way.

"Then we have a scene," Frances went on, "between the girl and the man's wife—not in the book—which explains a lot. Of course, just as in the book, he goes back to his wife. But we make it a lot tougher for him to go back. . . . It's a strange thing. Every middle-aged man who read that script said, 'This is the story of my life.' I can't believe that. I think they'd like it be the story of their lives." Rossano Brazzi played the middle-aged lover, and Jean Negulesco directed; the Hacketts reported that, at a "very funny" conference, the two men "were vying with each other as to which . . . was more really like [the lover]. This, each swore, was a perfect portrait of himself." Another conference concerning the film took place in March 1957, when the Hacketts were in Paris: "Twentieth [Century Fox] has had us to their offices looking over actresses. . . . All beautiful girls, and not a word of English among them, so it is all pretty silly."

While writing the screenplay, Frances, although now well into her sixties, was still worried about the reaction of a special viewer: her mother, Madeleine, the strictly raised minister's daughter. "The truth is now out," she wrote to my parents. "We are doing Francoise Sagan's *A Certain Smile*. But please, *please* buy Mother the September [*Woman's Home*] *Companion*, where it is condensed. The book will shake her to her roots! The mag. is censored." Frances's birthday came around during the writing of *A Certain Smile*, and my mother sent her some handkerchiefs; in her thank-you note, Frances asked that there be "never any more birthdays after this."

Frances and Albert were paid $100,000 for their twenty weeks of work on *A Certain Smile;* it was filmed mostly on the Riviera, contained beautiful shots of fantastic scenery, and in addition to Brazzi, starred Joan Fontaine, Bradford Dillman, and Christine Carere. Released in August 1958, it got mediocre to poor reviews: "essentially trite"; "a great deal of heavy moralizing"; "Frances Goodrich and Albert Hackett [faced a difficult task] in trying to be true to both the shibboleths of the Production Code and the author's original. They have not been able to serve two masters."

In August 1956, Frances and Albert stopped working on *A Certain Smile* and went to London to help with the casting and rehearsals of *The Diary of Anne Frank*. Finding an English actress to play Anne wasn't easy; Frith Banbury said he saw nearly three hundred girls before choosing (the Hacketts may have been present at some of those auditions), and the final choice "wasn't good enough."

Another time, the casting process was bizarre. *The Diary*'s London producer was the blond, elegant, smiling, hugely successful Hugh ("Binkie") Beaumont, the managing director of H. M. Tennant Ltd., Britain's major theatrical production firm. (Elia Kazan once called Beaumont "the best producer in London. He's the whole theater; he's the cream. A great guy and completely honest.") "There was a very big star, a flamboyant German actor, Anton Walbrook," Banbury said. "Binkie said to me, 'We better see [him] for Otto Frank.' I said, 'He'd be marvelous, but it's not perhaps as starry a part as he's used to.' . . . Walbrook was a very starry kind of star and created a great deal of fussation wherever he went. . . . He'd been a pain in the ass to Binkie over the years, and I think Binkie wanted to give him his comeuppance. . . . So it was arranged that Anton should come to the office at the Globe Theater and should meet Albert and Frances and myself. I thought Binkie would conduct the interview. . . . Frances and Albert were sitting on a couch, and I said, 'Where shall I sit?' And Binkie said, 'You sit here,' pointing to his chair . . . and I said, 'Where are you going to sit?' At that moment—it was all carefully timed—in came the secretary, saying, 'Mr. Walbrook is here.' 'Send him in,' says Binkie, and scuttles out of the room. . . .

"I was left in Binkie's chair. . . . I had never met Anton Walbrook. . . . He entered, very grand, and in a German accent said, 'Oh, yes, I'm very interested, but I sink zee part hass to pee consideraply rewritten. . . . Zee part iss not dominatink enough. . . . Anne's part goes on a lot.' I could feel the Hacketts bristling, and I realized this was the humiliation of Anton Walbrook—Binkie had planned that he would make a fool of himself in front of the director and the playwrights. I said, 'Well, thank you very much, it's interesting to know what you think, we'll discuss it'—and of course the moment he went out Frances and Albert said, 'Over our dead bodies,' which is exactly what Binkie wanted." (The next day, Frances wrote to Kermit Bloomgarden, "[Walbrook] seems reluctant to play it—but we are far more reluctant to have him play it. . . . He might throw the play out of balance. . . . He will never . . . be willing to sink his own personality enough to make himself part of a group.")

The London production of *The Diary* had a short run—only four months —which Banbury blamed partly on the actress playing Anne and on the fact that there was no star in the cast ("Anton Walbrook's name might very well have meant something") and on the size of the theater: "The Phoenix was too large." Most important, Banbury said, British audiences disliked the material. "The Germans regard the play as a service of antonement, almost a religious rite, but the British felt, 'Do we have to go through all of this? After all, *I* didn't persecute the Jews—why do I have to go and sit through it?'"[4]

Several months after *The Diary*'s London opening, Frances and Albert had a fight with Kermit Bloomgarden about the royalties from English repertory companies. Typically, it was Frances who stated their position: "We think we have done plenty for the English production! We went over twice, at our own expense. We wined and dined the British press, to get publicity for the play. We gave a party to the company, and their brothers and their sisters and their cousins and their aunts. We spent three of the precious seven days we had planned to be in Amsterdam, going back to London again for a *three minute* radio stint. . . . Altogether we feel we have done enough for the British. Now it's your turn! Okay?" Bloomgarden's answering letter started out, "I bow to your wishes regarding repertory rights," then moved quickly to other matters.

Through the years, *The Diary of Anne Frank* was performed in many different countries in many different languages. During a few hectic weeks in late February and early March 1957, Frances and Albert saw the productions in London, Amsterdam, Rotterdam, Berlin, and Rome. Almost everywhere they went, they were greeted with flowers, entertained, and interviewed for radio, TV, and the newspapers ("We hit the front pages in Amsterdam"). Summing it all up, Frances wrote, "We feel utterly exhausted . . . people, people, people." Although tiring, that experience was basically pleasant, unlike their dealings with the producers in Paris.

In mid-August 1957, just after they'd given a party for the forty-five-member company then presenting *The Diary* in Los Angeles ("[We] think they had a good time. [We] know they gave us one! Lou Jacobi . . . was a night club entertainer, and he can get everyone going"), Leah Salisbury sent Frances and Albert a copy of the script the French producers intended to use. The Hacketts had a man from Berlitz read it to them in English and were horrified by what they heard: the translator-adapter, Georges Neveux—André Maurois and Marcel Pagnol had earlier been suggested for the job—had rewritten many of the scenes, switched speeches between characters, and in the Hacketts' words, "made the people so unpleasant and disagreeable that an audience would welcome the Gestapo taking them." Among the alterations: when Mrs. Van Daan asks Otto Frank to help her son with his lessons, Neveux changed Mr. Van Daan's mildly sour comment on the request to "[My son] pays no more attention to me than a fart in the fiddle." Neveux also played with the text in minor ways, for example, switching the number of cigarettes Mr. Van Daan mentions in a speech from two to one. "[That]," Albert commented, "is the sort of thing that bad script writers used to do in an effort to get some credit." Worst of all, Neveux altered Anne's key line, "In spite of everything, I still believe that people are really good at heart" to the French equivalent of "In spite of everything, I believe that at the bottom of their hearts, men are not bad."

Frances and Albert reacted quickly: they cabled the French producers, protesting against the changes and telling them not to put the play into rehearsal. During the following weeks, they sent the French producers twenty-five pages of line-by-line corrections of the Neveux script and hired a Paris lawyer, Suzanne Blum, to make sure their version was used. The play opened in late October and was an award-winning success. The Hacketts particularly enjoyed the *Herald Tribune*'s review, which observed that "it is widely known that it is always best to tamper with hits as little as possible, and Georges Neveux has translated word for word rather than adapted the Frances Goodrich, Albert Hackett version." Visiting Paris in early May 1958, the Hacketts saw the play: "The girl is miraculous, fantastic. Silence for the rest." Hiring Suzanne Blum, an aggressive, fiercely bright attorney who represented many U.S. film studios in Europe, offended many people connected to the Paris production: Frances and Albert got "many terrible letters. . . . They considered it the most insulting and treacherous thing we could have done." However, they had no regrets; what mattered was defending the integrity of their work. (Blum was controversial, and not all of her clients made out well. She later took over the life of the increasingly gaga Duchess of Windsor, running her household, forbidding visitors, isolating her; a 1995 book called Blum "ruthless," "demented," and "a malignant old spider," and said she helped herself to some of the Windsor family treasures.)

As noted earlier, before Frances and Albert got involved with *The Diary*, Otto Frank gave the Chicago-born war correspondent and journalist-novelist Meyer Levin permission to write a stage adaptation. After it had been submitted to ten producers, some chosen by Levin himself, and they'd decided it wasn't stageworthy, Levin—who died in 1981 and has often been described as paranoid—concluded that he was the victim of a conspiracy: a cabal of powerful, theater-world Jews of German descent, he claimed, had suppressed his play because he wasn't like them (he was descended from Eastern European Jews) and because his play was "too Jewish." In 1954, Levin began litigation against Otto Frank, Kermit Bloomgarden, and the producer Cheryl Crawford, a suit that, by the time it came to trial in 1957, asked for $600,000 in damages. In 1959, the dispute was settled out of court, and Levin was paid $15,000 for agreeing to give up all claims and not to make the matter a subject of public or private controversy. Almost from the start of his relations with Otto Frank and everyone else connected with the stage production, Meyer Levin created dreadful problems.

Frances and Albert's first contact with Levin took place in December 1953, roughly two weeks after they took on the project: he wrote them in Bel Air, pointing out that he had done a version of the diary that hadn't yet been produced. They wrote back, saying, "When we heard that you had done a dramatization . . . as writers ourselves our first concern was for you. We asked Kermit Bloomgarden and he told us that an understanding with you had already been reached" and added that they could understand his frustration at not having his version produced. Their next contact came when they started doing research. Levin had run an emotional newspaper announcement challenging Bloomgarden to hold a test reading of his play before an audience and had aired his grievances in the press. When the Hacketts visited the Los Angeles rabbi to learn about the Hanukkah service and went to the Jewish bookstore for reference works, they got cool receptions. That bothered Frances: "I am afraid for the play," she wrote to Bloomgarden. "Will this man be able to marshall the Jewish people against us? . . . And the worst thing is that we can understand their resentment against two goys." (Frances and Albert's many Jewish friends realized they were in no way anti-Semitic. In August 1943, Leah Salisbury reported that B. P. Shulberg and another producer were going to film Budd Schulberg's novel *What Makes Sammy Run?* and were eager to have the Hacketts do the dramatization. "I told [them] I thought this book would never escape the anti-Semitism involved," Salisbury wrote, "but [they] disagree with me. They think, however, it should be dramatized by someone like yourselves who under no circumstances feel any anti-Semitism.")

While they worried about problems that Meyer Levin might create, Frances and Albert also heard some funny stories about him. Henry Ephron told them that Levin had once started to sue the writer Michael Blankfort for plagiarism, but then Blankfort had received a letter from Levin's wife, Tereska Torres, telling him not to pay any attention to her husband. Torres was also a writer; she ultimately came to feel that Levin's battle on behalf of his rejected Anne Frank script was futile and self-destructive and, according to a definitive 1995 book by Lawrence Graver, told him, "It is yourself you should be suing for damages."[5]

As the months went by, Meyer Levin, in his obsession, behaved more and more outrageously. "He is apparently immune to reason," one of his opponents said, "and totally unconcerned with the value of his word or commitment."[6] Also, his rantings and accusations grew louder and crazier—for example, Frances reported that he once told Otto Frank, his former friend, that by going along with the Bloomgarden-Hackett version, Frank had done "a worse thing to the Jews than Hitler ever did." Another time, according to Frances, he said that Otto Frank had managed to escape from his concentration camp, saving himself but consciously leaving the others to die. In his lawsuit against Frank and Bloomgarden, Levin didn't name Frances and Albert as defendants but charged that they'd plagiarized from his adaptation. Since they'd never seen the adaptation, that empty accusation probably didn't bother them all that much, but what did hurt was that in January 1958, a Manhattan jury decided that Levin's plagiarism charges were true. The Hacketts and Bloomgarden were shocked by that but realized that the jury was, in Frances's words, "completely incapable of judging such a technical thing as plagiarism." For one thing, the jury evidently couldn't understand that because the Levin and Hackett versions were based on the same text, there were bound to be similarities. Following an appeal, the judge agreed with the Hacketts and Bloomgarden and threw out the jury's finding. Many months later, after more contentious maneuvering by Levin, with both sides tired of the wrangling, Levin accepted the $15,000 settlement.

Throughout this bizarre battle, Levin insisted long and loudly that Bloomgarden and the Hacketts had "betrayed the Jewish people" by deemphasizing the Jewish elements in Anne's story and slanting the dramatization in order to tell a more "universal" tale. However, all along Levin knew full well that Otto Frank, who had ultimate control over the play's tenor, had said that Anne's story *should* be treated as a universal message. Lawrence Graver wrote that Frank often "emphasized his belief that the play should not be focussed on a distinctively Jewish situation but should emphasize the universal appeal of the girl's personality and growth, and 'propagate Anne's ideas and ideals in every manner' in order 'to show to mankind whereto discrimination, hatred and persecution are leading.'"[7]

During this prolonged, messy affair, a talented writer brought agony to Otto Frank, who'd once liked and trusted him, and to his own family, and blackened his own reputation. For Frances and Albert, this was a period of worry and anger, and it left them wary about projects offered to them thereafter. For example, in June 1958, having decided not to write the American adaptation of a successful play that had been translated from another language, they wrote to the producer that they were fearful about others making claims on the property: "We are burnt children who fear the fire. Our experience with Mr. Meyer Levin was so bitter that we cannot risk its happening to us again."

Meyer Levin's claims were aggressively reasserted in 1997 in *The Stolen Legacy of Anne Frank*, by Ralph Melnick, a fifty-six-year-old prep school librarian and instructor of religion, who argued that there *was* a conspiracy against Levin that Lillian Hellman had masterminded for "Stalinist" purposes, and that Frances and Albert were part of it. Some reviewers called Melnick's book, published by Yale University Press, "scholarly" and believed his conspiracy claims—a bad mistake, because the pages were rife with factual errors, misrepresentations, unproven conclusions, and character assassination.

When he first described Frances and Albert in detail, Ralph Melnick erred four times within eight lines concerning their writing career. Far more serious, he later slandered the Hacketts, whom he never met, and about whom he basically knew nothing. He called them "malleable," "safe," and "willing to follow Hellman's direction" — in other words, puppets; as their record shows, Frances and Albert were never anyone's puppets. In his most reprehensible blow, Melnick said they abandoned a friend for money — in effect, he called them Judases. After pointing out that they were unhappy about the legal position Otto Frank had assumed during Levin's lawsuit and were thinking about hiring their own lawyer, Melnick wrote:

> Abandonment of a colleague was apparently not at all unusual for the Hacketts. Six months earlier they had similarly forsaken Jack Gilford, the play's Dussel, when he sought to repeat his role in the film. Gilford's struggle to save his career from being destroyed in a HUAC-tainted Hollywood was apparently insufficient reason for the Hacketts to risk financial loss. "If he has been in trouble with pictures," they had written Salisbury, "I am afraid he may still be."[8]

The assertion that Frances and Albert might have lost financially if Gilford had been cast as Dussel is nonsense: they wrote the picture for a flat fee and had no share in possible profits. Gilford's widow, Madeline, told me that Frances and Albert "positively never" abandoned him and often invited the Gilfords to parties; she later described them as "amazingly decent people." The letter Melnick quoted is in the Rare Book and Manuscript Library at Columbia University; it was written by Frances on July 12, 1957, to Leah Salisbury, and the fourth and fifth paragraphs say this:

> About Jack Guilford [*sic*]. Of course we will do our best for him. But, if he has been in trouble with pictures, I am afraid he may still be. The scene has not changed enough to be optimistic about it.
>
> Of course we would want him. He was wonderful in the part. But, as you know, writers haven't got a gd [*sic*] things to say about casting in a picture.

Plainly, by quoting only that one sentence of Frances's letter, Ralph Melnick intended to turn her message from positive to negative. That's truly outrageous, and it's only one instance of misleading writing. For example, on page 208, Melnick stated that "months after the *Diary* opened on Broadway, Hellman . . . received a $10,000 check from the Soviet government for an unspecified reason." Clearly, he was trying to suggest that the $10,000

was a payoff for Hellman's services in somehow getting Meyer Levin re-
moved as the playwright so that she could shape the production along
what Melnick called her "Park Avenue Stalinist" lines. When the *New York
Times Book Review* called the suggestion about the $10,000 "gossip," Mel-
nick replied in a letter that documents among Hellman's papers, at the
University of Texas, proved that the payment had been made, and added,
"people do scheme with others to accomplish nefarious goals." What Melnick didn't realize, because he hadn't bothered to read the University of
Texas documents, was that the payment was for royalties on several of
Hellman's plays that had been performed in the USSR and was totally unrelated to *The Diary of Anne Frank*.

When Ralph Melnick concocted his book, he failed to do the most basic
checking, he almost never interviewed informed people, he committed numerous factual errors, and he slandered people. It is obvious that interest
in Meyer Levin's involvement in *The Diary* is going to be with us for many
years, so it is important to point out that Ralph Melnick's book is unreli-
able and irrelevant; it should carry a warning label in bright red capital letters: CONTENTS DANGEROUSLY DISTORTED.

When Frances and Albert started getting involved with the screen version
of *The Diary of Anne Frank* in the spring of 1956, they were in Bel Air and
had high hopes that Samuel Goldwyn, whose pictures they admired, and
who'd called the play "one of the finest dramatic presentations I have wit-
nessed in a considerable time," would buy the rights and produce, and
that William Wyler would direct. (Kanin said he was offered the directing job but passed: "I said, 'Listen, a year of my life is in that project, and
I have contributed everything that's within me; I have no more to give.'")[9]
The Goldwyn arrangement seemed to be shaping up—he made an offer
for the property and sent Wyler to New York to see the play—but then,
from Basel, Otto Frank told Goldwyn he wanted script approval.

The minute they heard that, on the morning of May 24, Frances and
Albert tried to phone Frank, but the lines were busy, so they sent a cable:
". . . beg you to accept this cinema offer without reservations. He is only
producer we all trust implicitly. He and director men of taste, integrity, and
devotion to Anne's message. Garson, Kermit and we willing to make financial sacrifice to get him. Insistence on approval of script will kill the
deal."

Later in the day, Leah Salisbury called Frances and Albert and said that
Goldwyn had withdrawn his offer, so they phoned him. According to
Frances's notes, he said, "I just got tired of it all. I used up three weeks of

my time—I've worked hard on this. They [Frank's representatives] asked me to sign things I've never been asked to sign before." On the phone, Frances and Albert tried to reason with Goldwyn, but he was obviously offended by the way he'd been treated, and they got nowhere, so they delivered a carbon copy of their cable to Frank to him. Four hours later, his chauffeur arrived with a note: "Dear Frances and Albert: Thank you for . . . the kind things you said. I . . . am sorry it had to turn out this way. With warmest regards, Sam."

In his definitive book on Goldwyn, Scott Berg wrote that he "lost the property because of his own vanity. . . . A short visit to Europe, a telephone call, even a letter explaining his intentions, would probably have won Mr. Frank over. Instead, Goldwyn rode away from the project on his high horse. . . . A few years later, looking back over almost 60 years in motion pictures, Goldwyn told his son his biggest disappointment had not been one of the films he had made; it was *The Diary of Anne Frank,* the one that got away."[10]

(A little over a year after Goldwyn said no to them, Frances and Albert said no to *him,* declining to do the script of *Porgy and Bess* because they needed to rest after *The Diary.* In their letter, they called the project—with some overstatement—"the greatest thing we shall ever be offered," but they were lucky not to be involved. The picture was plagued by problems: a fire destroyed the set, costumes, and props the night before the first dress rehearsal; Goldwyn fired the director, Rouben Mamoulian; and protests by the National Association for the Advancement of Colored People killed its chances of success. *Porgy and Bess* was Goldwyn's eightieth film—and his last.)

With Goldwyn having withdrawn, the movie rights to *The Diary* were bought by Twentieth Century Fox, and George Stevens was assigned as producer-director. Frances and Albert didn't know Stevens personally, but they admired his work, and after conferences in April 1957, they felt he was "very intelligent and sympathetic to the material." By late summer, they were trying to help out with the casting of the lead role: since the play's opening, Susan Strasberg had matured beyond the job. At one point, Frances suggested Elizabeth Frank (later the Pulitzer Prize winner) for the part. "I was a little girl with a wide-eyed look and brown curls," Elizabeth said. "Like all little girls in Hollywood, I had nourished fantasies of becoming an actress, but when the actual possibility of auditioning came up, it was terrifying. . . . Oddly enough, I did audition, and I wound up as one of the six contenders. . . . I remember going to the Hacketts' house in Bel Air to meet Otto Frank—a moving and touching experience."[11]

Concerning this search for a performer to play Anne, Albert wrote that "the girl need not be as fine an actress as we demand in the theater, as in [the picture] she will not have to sustain the part," and George Stevens said he wanted an unknown: "It makes it easier for the audience to believe they are seeing the real Anne Frank when they are not looking at a familiar face." In fact, however, for a time Stevens pursued Audrey Hepburn and even had Otto Frank visit her home in Bürgenstock, Switzerland, to try to persuade her. According to Albert, Stevens ultimately decided against using Hepburn because she "would only be available for so many weeks, and Stevens would have to get the picture finished hot or cold by a certain date. Because of her height he was thinking of using duplicate sets of everything . . . one set larger than the other so that she would look small at first. This was going to run into many weeks of work . . . and Stevens was not willing to risk the property." However, according to a 1996 biography of Hepburn, she turned down the role because it would be too demanding emotionally and because she realized that, at age twenty-seven, she was too old. In the end, the part went to Millie Perkins, an eighteen-year-old fashion model from Passaic, New Jersey.

George Stevens was a skilled, conscientious director. In the closing days of World War II, as the head of a U.S. Army camera team, he was with the troops who liberated the pitiful survivors at Dachau, an experience that affected him deeply, and he brought his feelings about injustice and suffering to the making of *The Diary*, working carefully, trying to capture nuances and authenticity. Stevens, Albert said, "tried to create some kind of tension for himself on the set, some kind of feeling that the war was [still] on, and even began to eat hardtack during the filming."[12] Mostly, Stevens succeeded in his quest for authenticity: many scenes effectively conveyed the essence of the claustrophobic Amsterdam hideout and the tensions between the people confined there.

Throughout their commitment to *The Diary*, Frances and Albert had had close relations with two strong-willed men, Otto Frank and Joseph Schildkraut, who portrayed Frank. Now, there was more contact. Before the filming began, Frank and his wife, Fritzi, visited in Bel Air. "We have the Franks [living with us]," Frances wrote. "They don't drive. We must chauffeur them everywhere. To the studio, to friends, to everything. I have to keep house, market, arrange their lives. And we [gave] a party for 100 people . . . to meet [them]. And we are working at the studio . . . worked all day Saturday, all Sunday. Home to dinner with their friends. It has been truly hectic. Just as bad, God knows, for them. The studio has worked them hard, seeing props, clothes, scenery, interviews, photographs with

Millie Perkins, with George Stevens." Frances and Albert's problems with Schildkraut started when the filming began: "Pepi will hardly speak to us. He says we loused up his part. It is exactly the same as it was in the play, but I think he has discovered that he is not 'on screen' for two hours as he was 'on stage' in the play. It must be that. Nothing else has changed."

When *The Diary of Anne Frank* was previewed in Los Angeles, Frances was obviously on edge: at a party, she introduced a woman to Otto Frank by saying, "My friend has a daughter, too." ("Mr. Frank was fine about it," the friend told me, "but Frances felt terrible.")[13] When it was released, in March 1959, the movie got generally good reviews, but Millie Perkins didn't. In Garson Kanin's opinion, "They did *The Diary of Anne Frank* without Anne. Perkins wasn't close to being Anne." The *New York Times* critic wrote, "In Joseph Schildkraut, Mr. Stevens has consigned the father role to one whose feeling and skill for this performance could not conceivably be surpassed. . . . Thus it is deeply unfortunate that Millie Perkins, a new and untried girl, does not rise to his level of spiritual splendor. . . . She is pretty, charming, and wistful . . . but there does not surge out of her frail person a sense of indestructible life, of innocence and trust that show no shadows, of a spirit that will not die."

The film version of *The Diary* was nominated for six Oscars, including Best Picture; it won one for Best Cinematography and another for Best Supporting Actress (Shelley Winters, as Mrs. Van Daan). Frances and Albert's screenplay won the Writers Guild Award for best-written American drama, but they weren't pleased by the picture: although originally they'd liked Stevens, they later decided he was a "difficult man." "Stevens liked to make a star," they said, "and that was the real problem. The girl, Millie Perkins, was someone no one could make a star. Stevens kept rewriting it and kept us there watching the rushes until Twentieth Century Fox got furious and we went off salary. Then we were on again, then off, and Stevens couldn't have cared less. It was a shame because it could have been an important picture."[14]

# 21

# Hollywood Finale

In early summer 1958, Frances and Albert traveled again to Europe and visited Russia, something few Americans did then. The tour they were on, Albert told a newspaper interviewer, was "the cheapest one. The eight day. We started from Helsinki and it was 12 hours to Leningrad. You could almost walk as fast. . . . It was a fascinating trip. Everyone is so interested in Americans and America. Their chief occupation is 'Beat America.' Everyone talks to you. . . . They have lapel trinkets, sputniks, Young Communist buttons, and they'll offer you one in exchange for something. A stick of gum will get you anything." Traveling with them were two American doctors who "went to watch an operation. . . . They were asked how long it took to remove a stomach in America. 'An hour and 45 minutes,' they said. The Russians said it took them only 45 minutes. 'That would be a miracle,' the Americans asserted. The Russian doctor said he himself could do it in 35 minutes. Everyone rallied around the man with the stomach, men in white, primitive surroundings, and he did it in 30 minutes. The American doctors had to admit they're ahead of us in some ways—we haven't got that sewing machine."[1]

According to Gloria Sheekman, during their Russian trip Frances and Albert were "amazed not to have any recognition from the government, the guides, or anyone" as the authors of *The Diary of Anne Frank.* "On their last night there," Mrs. Sheekman wrote, "a man who had [arranged] a meeting with them very hesitantly that afternoon . . . said the reason no one had approached them and that there were no copies of *The Diary* in Russia—or scripts of the play—was because the Russian government's official line was that the Franks hid and did not have the courage or integrity to meet the enemy and confront him!" (Mrs. Sheekman's recollection contradicts a newspaper item in which the Hacketts said, just before their trip, that they'd been told that *The Diary* was about to be staged in Moscow without the Russian producers' "having bothered to make a contract with us." In any event, the play *was* later produced in the USSR: in 1961,

Moscow State University put it on, and in 1963 a company from Rome—probably the same group that performed the play in Buenos Aires—did it in Italian; a Russian translation could be heard through earphones. The authorities allowed only two performances by the Italians, and both were enthusiastically received by the largely Jewish audience.)

Frances and Albert cut their 1958 European trip short because on July seventh, Albert's brother, Raymond, died in Los Angeles, age fifty-five, and on July 24, Frances's mother, Madeleine, died in Little Compton, age ninety-five. For years, the Hacketts had stayed close to both of them and tried to be helpful: for example, when Madeleine was ninety and growing feeble, they offered to hire an ambulance to take her from Nutley to Little Compton. Madeleine replied that she would take the (less expensive) train—whereupon, in my father's words, Frances successfully "put on the heat." Now, because Madeleine's family was large and could take care of things, Frances and Albert didn't go to Rhode Island but to California, to be with Raymond's widow, Blanche, who had no other family and was devastated by Raymond's death; Albert wrote that Blanche had been "splendid," but "the shock seems to get worse instead of better. . . . [Frances] has been a great help."

During 1958, Frances and Albert talked or corresponded with agents, producers, writers, and directors (including Saint Subber, Bob Fosse, Cheryl Crawford, Ray Stark, Richard Barr, Lawrence Kasha, Kermit Bloomgarden, Hillard Elkins, Lael Tucker Wertenbaker, and Frank Loesser) who were eager to have them adapt various properties for the stage in musical or dramatic form (including Jean Girudoux's *The Madwoman of Chaillot*, William Styron's *Lie Down in Darkness*, Paul Gallico's *Mrs. 'Arris Goes to Paris*, Jerome Weidman's *I Can Get It for You Wholesale*, and Colette's *Cheri*). They declined all of these offers, mostly because of the nature of the material: for example, they told Frank Loesser, concerning a book called *The Green Willow*, "We thought the book beautifully written, the story and characters enchanting. There is a . . . fairy tale quality that makes for the loveliest reading. . . . We could smell the meadow flowers, taste the sugar cakes hot from the oven. But we don't know how to translate that into theater." Another time, they blamed their tardiness in replying on ill health: "We have been laid low with a cold, which we passed back and forth between us until we finally gave it away to a friend." However, the main reason they kept saying no was that they were still under contract to MGM: "Unhappily, our past has caught up with us. . . . We have been under contract for years . . . and for the last three years we have refused all of the material they sent us . . . not feeling it was right for us. . . . But now they have sent us an unpublished book which we think we can do. At least we're having a fling at it. We hope we can do it . . . then get that monkey Metro off our back. They will now, after this picture, have to give us a little freedom."

The book Frances and Albert referred to, *Strike Heaven in the Face*, by Charles J. Calitri, told the story of a year at a New England high school during which the principal struggles to deal with a group of unruly students. From the start, the Hacketts were plainly not in tune with the subject. They began their first draft on September 2, 1958, and labored into 1959. Albert later wrote, "We were just no good on the story"; Frances wrote, "The story is perfectly horrible, but we have put our hand to it and we must finish. . . . We have had such sad times here. . . . Our agent, who was our dear friend, and such a wise counselor, died, and another friend, Sam Zimbalist, whom we had known for years and years . . . and two other deaths at the same time. I said to Albert, 'They're keeling over every day. . . . Let's drop everything and just have a good time and do exactly what we want from now on.' I asked what he wanted . . . and he said, as long as we'd started this script, he thought he'd rather finish it than anything else. . . . And we hate it! . . . It will take us weeks, and when it is done it will still stink."

In the end, following many lengthy conferences—including one in New York, in the Plaza Hotel suite of the producer, Pandro Berman, during which the book's author harangued them for an hour and a half, leaving them "completely bewildered, insulted, and humiliated"—Frances and Albert wrote to Berman that they could no longer be of value: "We have never worked so hard or so long or so unrewardingly on any picture, and we are sorry that we have been so unsuccessful." Berman replied that he, too, was sorry, and they were mercifully cut loose.

While working on *Strike Heaven*, Frances and Albert started thinking about a stage musical comedy based on the 1919 actors' strike in New York, which Frances recalled as one of the most exciting, stimulating times in her life. They felt this was a legitimate setting for songs and music since the striking actors had put on fund-raising shows at the Lexington Opera House, and in the fall of 1958, they discussed the idea with Kermit Bloomgarden, whose hit musicals included *The Most Happy Fella* and *The Music Man*. He was enthusiastic, and so was Leah Salisbury: "A wonderful idea, and period, and time—full of affection, love, enmity, characters . . . all that marvelous drama: George M. Cohan, Minnie Maddern Fiske refusing to join Equity . . . and Cohan resigning from the Lambs, actors refusing to play, hanging around corners."

All of this pleased Frances: "For the first time in a long time I am excited." She and Albert talked with the comedian Ed Wynn, who in 1919 was playing in the *Shubert Gaieties* and was the highest-paid actor on Broadway. "But," Frances wrote, "he was a musical and vaudeville star, not a legitimate theater actor, and he had not been approached to join Equity. He says that the night they were going to call the strike, J. J. Shubert was at his theater when he arrived. He said, 'You're not going to strike, are you Ed?' Mr. Wynn says he knew nothing about any strike. He told J. J. that he'd have to go to the Lambs Club and find out what it was all about. When he got [there] he was greeted with a great cheer, and the word went out, 'Ed Wynn's struck!' He said he hadn't at all, but then of course he did. He was tremendously active . . . passed the hat on Broadway, etc., and worked in the show at the Lexington Opera House."

The Hacketts' project started promisingly, but then came the challenge of finding a personal story to set against the historical background. They never did find one—"Albert has given up a dozen times," Frances wrote, "I only half a dozen"—and in early 1960 they admitted defeat. They weren't the only writers who did that. Ring Lardner Jr. and Burton Lane once talked about the idea, and Lardner interviewed Frances and got her recollections of the strike, but ultimately they also gave up.

During this time, Frances and Albert, in their words, "fell into another pit" while trying to turn Dorothy Parker's famous short story *Big Blonde* into a play. The plan was for Morton Da Costa to direct and coproduce with Kermit Bloomgarden; the Hacketts made a quick trip to New York and explained their ideas, and for a time, all seemed okay. What went wrong isn't totally clear, but later the Hacketts wrote, "We couldn't make a play of it . . . six and a half months work, and not a nickle . . . and not a line we could be satisfied with. . . . Our being unable to get a play . . . when we had been so definite, was a terrible blow to our self-confidence." (During all this, Albert suffered dentally: "[He] is having some drifting teeth anchored down," Frances wrote, "so we shan't be East 'til they're in port.")

Years before, Frances and Albert had made extensive notes for a play centered around Joe Hill, the radical labor organizer who was convicted of murder—wrongly, some said—and executed by a Utah firing squad in 1915. They didn't write the play, but that kind of subject still interested them (especially Frances, because of her heritage from Aunt Caro and Henry Demarest Lloyd). In the spring of 1959, they got involved with the director Fred Zinnemann, whose impressive credits included *High Noon* and *From Here to Eternity*, hoping to do a film for Columbia Pictures about the Sacco-Vanzetti case. The three corresponded enthusiastically and were encouraged when the lawyer Joseph Welch (who'd become famous during the Army-McCarthy hearings and believed that the two Italian-born anarchists, executed in 1927 in Massachusetts for murder, had been innocent) said he might serve as consultant—but then, by coincidence, in mid-April, the Massachusetts state legislature rejected a resolution to grant posthumous pardons. In the 1920s, many people had reacted passionately to Sacco and Vanzetti's conviction and execution, claiming that the trial had been unfair due to the defendants' radical beliefs; however, by 1959 America's political climate had changed, and the Hacketts began to have second thoughts about the viability of a film. In early May, Frances wrote a letter to Zinnemann that ended the project:

And now I must say something which may seem traitorous to you.

I have come to the conclusion that we haven't a chance of succeeding with this picture. This does not mean that my belief in its truth, my belief that it should be done, has changed. But I believe we have no chance of financial success—no audience.

My reason for this change is the attitude of the newspapers on that Boston hearing. Every one of them was biased, prejudiced. What hope would we have of getting people into the theater when we would start off with this terrible handicap. . . .

There was a time, during the trial, when wonderful people from all over the world were indignant and articulate about it. But no one seems to be indignant any more. I suppose it may be because the men are dead, and justice now is a little late.

In 1957, the Academy of Motion Picture Arts and Sciences had passed a bylaw barring Communists from the competition for Oscars, and Frances—but evidently not Albert—had resigned. Now, in January 1959, the academy repealed the bylaw, saying it was unworkable; since her "reason for resigning—discrimination against candidates on purely political grounds" was gone, Frances asked to rejoin, and the Board of Governors readmitted her.

Through all of 1959, as they had earlier, the Hacketts declined many proposed projects. Sometimes, the decisions weren't easy. Concerning one proposal, Albert wrote to Kermit Bloomgarden: "I have not been able to see anything [here] that sounds to me like a play, musical or otherwise.

This, as I say, is my own feeling about it. Frances does not agree with me, but says she has not the strength to argue with me any longer." In January 1959, they were asked if they were interested in writing the stage musical version of *Gone with the Wind*. They weren't, which was clearly one of their wiser decisions. Eleven years passed before the three-hour-long, lavishly produced show, with a book by Horton Foote and songs by the Hacketts' friend Harold Rome, opened in Tokyo, to mixed reviews: "As a hinterland attraction, the forecast is upbeat"; "Harve Presnell is less Rhett than wretched." In London, a horse defecated onstage on opening night ("EVEN THE HORSE HAD TO GO WITH THE WIND," a paper said). Noel Coward reportedly said that cutting was needed: the entire second act and the throat of the child actor playing Scarlett's daughter. The show never reached Broadway, and Frances and Albert often expressed sympathy for Rome, who called the undertaking "the world's longest out-of-town tryout."

Frances and Albert were still emotionally close to Garson Kanin and Ruth Gordon, but according to an October 1959 letter that Kanin sent from New York, getting *physically* close wasn't easy:

> We were here when you thought we were there and we were there thinking you were here. Where are you? We are here and on our way there which—the way things are going—means that you are doubtless on your way here. . . .
> Love to you both and hope to see you soon.

Having recently suffered setbacks, Frances and Albert must have hoped extra hard that 1960 would bring success, but . . .

The seed for *Carte Blanche*, intended to be a stage musical commenting on the ethical side of American life, was an article in *Life* magazine recounting the misdeeds of a young man who'd mistakenly been issued a credit card and used it to buy all kinds of things, including a car and a Puerto Rican vacation. Among those who read the article was Mary Rodgers, the daughter of Richard Rodgers and herself a composer: she'd recently written the music for a successful show, *Once upon a Mattress*.

"There was a two-page spread on this kid who had stolen all this stuff," Miss Rodgers said, "and a picture of him sitting on the car he stole, surrounded by his smiling family, and I thought, what's wrong with this picture, why isn't this guy in jail, why is everyone looking so happy? . . . I conceived of the show as slightly bitter, with a love interest—although the guy got away with everything, the girl turns him down; a very simple-minded little plot, but I thought it would be fun. . . . I think the Hacketts ultimately withdrew because it was too bitter for them. It was too bitter for most people. . . . And after they withdrew, Hal [Prince, who hoped to produce the show] approached S. J. Perelman, who said, 'This is the most disgusting idea I've ever heard; it's absolutely appalling.' . . . [The show] just never came together. . . . I wanted it to be like *Pal Joey* [but the Hacketts weren't] tough enough and mean enough and cynical enough to want to pursue it the way it needed to go."[2]

In May 1960, Frances and Albert visited Paris, where I'd been living for several months. We and a bright, beautiful friend of mine, Susan, shared a few fine days in the world's most beautiful city, then drove to Switzerland—an occasionally thrilling experience because Albert was a quirky driver, always keeping one foot on the accelerator and the other on the brake. In cafés and restaurants, Frances compulsively dashed off postcards. Once she wrote, "We are all together at Les Deux Magots. . . . David looks fine, Susan looks fine, Albert looks cold" (we were sitting outdoors), and Albert added, "Vive la Frances!" Later, from Geneva, Frances wrote that we were all again "sitting at drinks," and my brother-in-law, John Noble, made a note reflecting the widespread opinion, "Susan is gorgeous," to which Susan added, "Will success spoil Susan?" In Basel, we had dinner with Otto Frank and his wife, Fritzi; one could easily see why the Hacketts had been impressed by Otto Frank's strength and dignity.

In early July 1960, Frances and Albert started work on their last picture, *Five Finger Exercise,* based on the play by the English author Peter Shaffer, directed by Daniel Mann, and produced by Frederick Brisson. The story concerned a family—a pretentiously intellectual mother (played by Rosalind Russell, Brisson's wife); a bullying, insensitive father; and a neurotic son and daughter—who hire a young, German-born tutor who upsets the already shaky household balance and then tries to kill himself.

At first, Frances and Albert enjoyed being part of all this, especially because Brisson consulted them about casting. He was pleased that *they* were pleased that Alec Guinness was going to play the husband (but ultimately the role went to Jack Hawkins); he asked if they preferred Dirk Bogarde, Horst Bucholtz, or Maximilian Schell as the tutor. ("We know only Dirk Bogarde," they replied. "Is he a little old?" In the end, Schell got the part.) Peter Shaffer liked their adaptation ("I am impressed indeed. . . . [There is] a great deal that is excellent and moving and cruelly funny"), but when the picture was released (by Columbia), the critics hated it: *"Five Finger Exercise,"* one wrote, "is all thumbs." Frances and Albert agreed: "We had a good working relationship with Roz and her husband, but she was miscast and the play was really British and not easily adapted for an American locale. We feel it is the most embarrassing script we ever did. Of all the pictures we've written, this is the only one from which we get residuals. It is not very much money, but [we are] embarrassed even to cash the checks."[3]

Two notes: The Hacketts may have liked Russell's husband, but others didn't and called him "the Lizard of Roz." Also, although things were changing elsewhere, in 1960, when the Hacketts wrote *Exercise,* Hollywood's censorship system was still nearly as rigid as when they'd first arrived, three decades before. The new watchdog, Geoffrey Shurlock, said that while the script's basic story seemed acceptable, there was an unacceptable element: the suggestion that the son might be homosexual. "As you know," Shurlock wrote, "the [Production] Code forbids homosexuality or any *inference* of it. . . . It seems . . . that Philip's problem could quite easily be changed . . . to avoid the suggestion that he suffers from a distorted and unnatural sexual drive. . . . In addition, we direct your attention to . . . Page 71: we have received many and severe complaints about the use of the words 'hell' and 'damn' in pictures. . . . We ask that they be eliminated wherever possible. . . . Page 83 . . . The clauses 'she was half-dressed' and 'on the breasts' should both be omitted. . . . Page 86: Pamela's dialogue, 'Wouldn't it be wonderful if he was giving babies to all the girls on the Island?' is unacceptable."[4]

Frances and Albert had now worked on several stage projects that hadn't panned out, and at the same time, their screenwriting career had begun to falter. Their problem in Hollywood wasn't waning skills or energy, but changes in the movie business. In earlier years, luck and connections had helped them (for example, Hunt Stromberg undoubtedly gave them important assignments partly because he liked them); however, with the studio system breaking down, and television getting more of the focus, they were less tuned into the scene. Also, their light, sophisticated style was falling out of fashion, and soaring production costs and shifts in taste had made lavishly produced musical comedies—once their main income source—less viable. Their friend Henry Ephron spotted the trouble early on: after a dinner party at the Hacketts' where, except for the Cagneys, the guests were all veteran screenwriters and their wives, he pointed out to his wife, Phoebe, that only four of the writers—themselves and the Hacketts—were currently working. "This place," he said, "is ready to become a desert, which it was in the first place."[5] (In a December 1962 letter to Charles Brackett, the Hacketts reported another put-down of the current Hollywood atmosphere. Janet Gaynor, they said, had told them that "Selznick"—it isn't clear if Gaynor meant Myron or David—had told her, "My dear, it's Indiana out here now.")

In March 1961, the Hacketts traveled to Africa, staying at, among other places, Treetops, the informal Kenyan hostelry where up to two hundred elephants sometimes visited a nearby salt lick and baboons often wandered into the guests' bedrooms. In Nairobi, they got a cable releasing them from their long-standing contract with MGM; later, a studio executive, Milton Beecher, wrote that he felt "great sadness" at parting "after all these years." Beecher added that the severance could "only serve both our present interests, for unfortunately for us there is at the present time no 'quality' material of any kind worthy enough to offer writers like yourselves. It did not seem right to embarrass both of us by submitting the less than average material available at this time." In reply, the Hacketts wrote, "It was sweet of you to write us that note. It was nice to know that one person at least noticed our going. It was quite a shock to us. After such a long, long association. Like being served with divorce papers."

The area around Bel Air had often been hit by fires, and in early November 1961, the worst so far, driven by strong, shifting winds, did enormous damage, at one point reaching Bellagio Road, destroying several houses there, and giving Frances and Albert a bad scare. They had been in touch with Carson McCullers about adapting her novel *A Clock without Hands* for the stage, and when writing her about that (again, abortive) project, they said, "This letter would have been on its way to you yesterday, but the fires started here and swept around us all day. The skies were black and a curious poison yellow with smoke. The air was full of the roar of airplanes. One house, just a quarter of a mile from us, was afire. A dozen planes circled over our heads, swooping down to drop water bombs . . . and then circling around and back to drop them again. And the Fire Chief was in his plane, and the news men were in their planes. . . . We packed our car with paintings and a few clothes and our scripts—such as they are—and waited for the police to tell us to evacuate, but they never did and our house was spared . . . so far . . . unless the wind changes."

The wind didn't change; the beloved house Frances and Albert had lived in for seventeen years was safe. However, within a few months, realizing it was time to leave, they put the house on the market. Making fun of the selling process, Frances wrote, "People are coming in, sneering. And the agent said, 'Someone'll buy it and put some money in it, and it'll be really elegant, and you won't know it when it's done.'" In the end, Ray Milland bought the house, and the Hacketts gave their business papers to the Wisconsin Center for Film and Theater Research, and packed their belongings and said goodbye to the Movie Capital of the World.

Frances was now seventy-two; Albert was sixty-two. Mostly, their California years had been, as they'd often said, "wonderful." All along, though, they'd missed New York. Many of their friends were there, they had connections to the vitality and immediacy of the theater, and it was the place where they'd grown up and started their careers. In leaving California—obviously, not without regrets—they were coming home.

# 22

## Back in New York

For some theater and movie people, life's last years can be grim: their talents (and/or) looks are no longer in demand; their incomes fall; they no longer hear the all-important sound of applause. The case of Frank Capra has been mentioned; another—far more likable—person whose lengthy, reclusive old age wasn't great was Frances's "dearest man ever," Irving Berlin. Frances and Albert were happier because they mostly kept their health, worked occasionally at their craft, stayed close to their families and friends, traveled, and enjoyed new experiences.

In late May 1962, when Frances and Albert first arrived in New York from California, Albert told a reporter, "We're back in the theater; it may be just a little theater, but we're back." He was referring to an agreement he and Frances had recently reached with Kermit Bloomgarden to write the book of a Civil War musical comedy based on a magazine piece by Edmund G. Love, whose book *Subways Are for Sleeping* had been turned into a musical hit. Their show, Frances said, would center around the events in a small Virginia town called Waterford. "It was a Quaker town," she added, "and during the war it was caught between the North and the South. Most of the men left, and the story deals with three women who published a newspaper throughout the war."[1]

When Frances said that, she and Albert had strong hopes that their friend Burton Lane, whose Broadway successes included *Finian's Rainbow*, would do the music. Despite the confusion of settling into their new home, they plowed on through the summer and drafted a first act. Sadly, Lane, who once described himself as "very picky," saw problems ("The level of the writing should be real rather than musical comedy. . . . I would examine the basic story line and see whether there is enough motivation") and ultimately didn't commit himself, and the idea died. Coming after other failures, this seriously disappointed Frances: she often said she enjoyed life most when she was working. On the other hand, Albert, who'd been working since he was six, sometimes said they deserved a rest. In 1977, filling out identical biographical questionnaires, Albert answered "Yes" to the query "Are you retired?" and Frances—then age eighty-seven—answered "No."

Frances and Albert had always been strong and healthy, and during the next decades they mainly stayed that way. His hair turned gray, then white; her hairdresser kept hers pleasingly reddish brown. They both grew deaf and wound up wearing hearing aids; probably out of vanity, Frances resisted that for a time and during conversations carefully studied lips and expressions. To hear better at the theater—they went to almost every new production—they sat in the front row. Background noise worsened their hearing, and during dinner parties, some of their elderly guests, who were also deaf, shouted at one another, leaving Frances and Albert smilingly pretending to understand. Albert was twice hospitalized because of prostate troubles (he called catheterization "penal servitude") and at one point had heart surgery; happily, he had no problems thereafter. Both he and Frances were hit by aches and pains, which occasionally inhibited them during their trips abroad. Once, while they were staying at a friend's house in London, Albert developed a spastic back, "so for a week, a precious week," Frances wrote, "we did nothing. He lay on the floor, with little white Charley [the friend's dog] lying beside him, and me looking on." Two years later, in Paris, they occupied a hotel room "so small," Frances wrote, "that I can throw away my crutch and hop from bureau to bed to bath with not one inch to spare."

Inevitably, there were illnesses. In 1980, Albert got pneumonia, had to be hospitalized, and was sometimes delirious. "He had it bad," Frances said. "They were feeding him with penicillin. . . . At one point I said to the nurse, 'Have your lunch; I'll watch him. Take your time; have a little rest.' So I sit there reading. I'd only looked away for a moment; I look over and he's taken the penicillin needle out and he's writing. With *penicillin!*" Albert's comment on this was, "You see, writing's in my blood."[2]

Frances and Albert's new home—which they probably loved as much as the Bellagio Road house—was a handsome, airy duplex at 88 Central Park West, on the corner of 69th Street, overlooking trees and grass and open space. On the lower floor were the kitchen, maid's room, and dining room plus a large foyer and extra-large living room, both decorated with their art collection; in the living room were a piano and, in one corner, a table on which Frances and Albert, who'd given up gin rummy, now competed fiercely at Scrabble. On the upper floor—in time, the staircase came to have a chairlift running alongside it—were two bedrooms and a study with walls lined with books, many written by friends. The building's spacious lobby was guarded by uniformed doormen, one of whom once asked me, "You know what Mrs. Hackett has? Class!" This doorman thought Albert also had class: the two talked baseball, and Albert gave him a ball autographed by famous players. The address, 88 Central Park West, was one of the area's most desirable; through the years, the residents included others involved in show business: Celeste Holm and her actor husband, Wesley Addy; actress Joan Copeland (sister of playwright Arthur Miller); broadcaster-critic Pia Lindstrom; actor Robert Ryan; and singers Paul Simon and Sting. For Frances and Albert, being on the West Side had one big advantage—they were near the theater district—but many of their friends were on the East Side, and so were Frances's hairdresser and most of her favorite shops; she complained that there was "nowhere to buy decent stationery" on the West Side. As cook-housekeeper, they hired a large, jolly, warmhearted lady from Guiana named Vivian Mix; when extra help was needed, Vivian's shy, soft-spoken mother, Mrs. Dublin, would don a uniform and wait on table. The apartment impressed many of the Hacketts' friends; after a visit, Charles Brackett wrote, "Everybody asks me about your apartment. I hope I describe it adequately. It fair knocked me speechless."

Frances and Albert's apartment was welcoming and comfortable in the cooler months, but when summer's heat came, they escaped. Sometimes, as we've seen, they went to London or Paris. In Paris, they stayed in hotels, but in London they often rented flats or houses and took Vivian along. In June 1966, they rented a house on Cheltenham Terrace that was four stories tall but so narrow that they spent days "wondering how to get two typewriters in here! We finally arranged to get some [furniture] sent to storage for the summer. [In] the dining room . . . one cannot have more than two guests for dinner." There was a trapdoor in the dining room floor; Vivian would load the dumbwaiter, then knock to warn of the food's arrival. The house overlooked a walled garden next door; one evening, while a party was under way in the garden, the Hacketts watched the Queen Mother climb out of a limousine and, concealed by the wall, down a glass of champagne before joining the others. In the spring of 1967, Frances and Albert rented the Montpelier Square residence of the author Arthur Koestler. When they met to make final arrangements, Frances said the Koestlers must of course put away anything particularly precious; when the Hacketts moved in, there wasn't a plate or glass in sight, and they had to buy their own. (In March 1983, Koestler and his wife committed suicide in this house: he because he was gravely ill, and she evidently because she couldn't bear to live without him.)

Frith Banbury thought the Hacketts' London visits were odd: "They entertained Americans. . . . I used to [invite them to my house], and not ask other Americans, but a few British people instead, because I felt, 'If you're coming to London at vast expense, why don't you fraternize with the natives more?'" (Frances may have wondered the same thing: in a letter from London in July 1967, she commented, "Weather lovely here. Millions of California friends. Oh dear.") "Sid Perelman [who briefly lived in London] came to my house once with the Hacketts," Banbury continued. "I remember him sitting there, and I felt he was terribly lost. He was among a lot of rich people he didn't really know; he'd decided to give up New York—and I think he was thinking, 'This isn't working out . . .' I remember thinking, 'Now what can I do for him, as the host?' I never came in for Sid Perelman's being very funny."[3]

From London, Frances and Albert traveled around Britain. In August 1964, they went to Barmoor Castle, in Berwick-on-Tweed, where their American actress friend Joan Castle was living with her husband, William Reresby Sitwell, a cousin of the famous Sitwell siblings, Osbert, Edith, and Sacheverell. ("We're all a little crazy," her husband once told Joan, "because so many cousins married cousins.") Barmoor Castle dated back to the eleventh century and had roughly sixty-five rooms; when the Hacketts visited, Joan and her husband were living in twenty-five of them. In the music room, which had an enormous glass dome, a sound system played Fats Waller and Jelly Roll Morton. During a walk on the castle's vast lawn, Joan remarked that she'd never found a four-leaf clover—and then, to her great annoyance, Frances spotted one. In the guest book, Frances wrote fairly conventional thanks for "four beautiful, unforgettable days," and Albert added, "Ah, Joanie, Joanie, just another Castle in the Sitwell chain."[4]

During some summers, Frances and Albert rented houses in the south of France, where they entertained, among others, the writers Emily Kimbrough and Cornelia Otis Skinner and Al and Dolly Hirschfeld and their daughter Nina, whose name Hirschfeld regularly hid in his *New York Times* drawings. Again, Frances sometimes felt overwhelmed: "Millions of guests . . . People say they couldn't possibly come—and now they're coming!" One of the better rentals was outside the handsome Provencal village of Seguret: "It is lovely here. We look over a valley of vineyards and behind us lovely pines. But it is hot! The only relief is the pool." The house belonged to the owner of the vineyards, who offered a special deal on his delicious *rosé*; also, according to my sister Maddy, the gardener supplied "an extremely powerful, homemade—and of course entirely illegal—*pastis*, which didn't affect Albert's Scrabble in the least. Frances and Albert used to enjoy going into the village to do the grocery shopping. They were a real hit at the market. . . . They were truly hospitable, but sometimes it got to be too much. They decided to give up Seguret when they heard that someone they didn't particularly care for said that her summer plans included 'a few weeks in Provence at the Hacketts' villa.'"

In the spring of 1965, Frances and Albert took an eight-week round-the-world trip (Sid Perelman called it a "global dash"); in Hong Kong, the *China Mail* ran an interview under a three-column headline, "Famous Writers Visit Colony." A year later, during another trip, Frances reported that Vienna looked "lovely," but "poor Budapest" was "having a subway built. The whole town dug up and a fine sand dirt over everything. . . . Cook's got us a seventh-rate hotel . . . no bath. This never happened to me on one-night [touring] stands." In the summers of 1967 and 1968, they joined Emily Kimbrough and others on barge trips in France and Ireland. The barges were comfortable but cramped (Albert said he once had to change his clothes in a corridor "behind his hand"). Kimbrough wrote books about these floating houseparties; although those on board—for example, Frances's fellow 1919 striker, actress Margalo Gillmore; Cornelia Otis Skinner; lawyer Lloyd Garrison and his wife; and Hollywood agent Sam Jaffe and his wife—were articulate, the books were bland, reporting little of the spirited dinner-table conversation. In her book on the French trip, Kimbrough also didn't report that it rained often, nor that Albert and Sam Jaffe got manic about laundry. "Every morning," a fellow passenger said, "they washed their underwear and socks, and hung them out on the railing so they could get a little wetter." Kimbrough implied that the Hacketts relished barge travel, but before the first trip Frances said she was "dreading" it, and she found the second one tiring: "A long drag. Too long."

In the spring of 1968, Frances and Albert were in Paris when rioting and a general strike erupted, sparked by student protests over conditions at the University of Paris. "All transportation stopped," Al Hirschfeld said, "railroads and everything, and the Hacketts got the last bus out of Paris, the last one to leave, and just before they got on, Frances said, 'Albert, do you think we should leave? This might be our last chance to see a revo-

lution.' It was typical of Frances—she thought it might be a great opportunity to see a revolution."[5]

When they weren't in Europe, Frances and Albert rented houses in the
Martha's Vineyard town of Vineyard Haven. During their first summers,
they sometimes worked on theatrical projects and, being newcomers,
hoped to find friends. "We work from 9:30 to 12:00, 1:30 to 4:00, have a
swim, have a drink, have dinner, go to a movie. We know a few people
here, but most of them hate each other, so we have a tough time getting a
group together." Starting around 1968, when they were more "into" Vineyard life, they rented a large, rambling house—Perelman called it "an absolute dream"—from Kingman Brewster, then the president of Yale. Later
owned by broadcaster Mike Wallace, it overlooked Vineyard Haven harbor, where racing sailboats dodged the lumbering, mainland-based ferries;
in one room was a bright-red telephone that served as the emergency line
from the university. This was a time of campus unrest, and Albert said that
if it rang, he'd put on an authoritative voice and command, "Send in the
Marines!"

In the Brewster house, the Hacketts had many houseguests—the Fredric
Marches, the McHughs, the Perelmans, the Lardners, and others—and
many dinner guests: Garson Kanin and Ruth Gordon, the Cagneys, Lillian
Hellman, Patricia Neal, the director Margaret Webster, and on at least one
occasion, Katharine Hepburn. With Vivian and Mrs. Dublin on hand,
Frances often read in the shade of a tree; Albert pruned the trees and
shrubs and every morning walked a mile into town to get the *New York
Times*. This leisurely life didn't suit Frances: "How I wish we could get
back to work. But right now pruning seems to be Hackett's metier." Occasionally, Albert went fishing with Hellman and author John Hersey.
Hellman loved trolling for bluefish. While waiting for strikes, and even
while reeling in her catch, she puffed on cigarettes; since her eyesight was
poor, Albert lit them for her. If another boat came too close, rocking them
with its wake, Hellman would rise from her chair, grab the rail, and give
the offending skipper the finger, meanwhile yelling at him to keep his
distance.

A lot of Frances and Albert's Vineyard time was spent among high-
strung personalities. One of their houseguests was Frith Banbury, who
later said he "didn't form a very good opinion of Miss Hellman, partly because she ignored me [at first]—quite obviously, she thought, 'Who's this
old fool, I'm not really interested in him' . . . and then Frances obviously
tipped her the wink who I was. Not that I'm making any claims, but

Frances told her what my accomplishments were, and I was incredibly embarrassed the next time we saw Lillian, by her being all over me and frightfully forthcoming and polite." Banbury was surprised when he met Cagney: "You think of Jimmy Cagney as this sort of little lithe creature, and here was this portly old boy, who seemed not quite with us."[6] One evening, Frances and Albert invited the Cagneys and Garson Kanin and Ruth Gordon to dinner, and then realized that the two couples were diametrically opposed politically: the Kanins on the left, the Cagneys (through the years, Cagney had turned conservative) on the right. Frances told Banbury she hoped he'd serve as a buffer, but, mercifully, politics weren't discussed. (Albert had a theory that Cagney's swing to the right started in the 1930s when Ella Winter, the wife of Donald Ogden Stewart, angered Cagney by putting his name, without his permission, on a fund appeal for a Communist front organization.)

Blanche Sweet visited on the Vineyard—and created yet more tension. A friend of the Hacketts recalled an evening when Lillian Hellman and Blanche, who evidently weren't on the best of terms, were vying for attention at the dinner table, and then Hellman, whose health and eyesight were poor, announced that she had to go to the bathroom, whereupon Blanche leapt up and escorted her, a kindness Hellman accepted reluctantly, "smoking and swearing." Blanche, this observer said, was "a wonderful swimmer, off the beach in front of the house, but when she came out of the water, you saw that she walked like a land crab, because she was bent over—probably by osteoporosis."[7]

During several of Frances and Albert's Vineyard summers, my wife and I and our daughter, together with my sister, Maddy, and her husband, John Noble, and their three sons, paid daylong visits. While Frances, in a summer dress and straw hat, looked down from the lawn above, and Albert hovered watchfully, the rest of us would swim; then Albert, assisted by Vivian, would grill hamburgers. Sometimes there would be, in Maddy's words, another guest "guaranteed to appeal, such as James Cagney." Maddy's eldest son recalled a visit in his teens when, during the adults' prelunch drinks—S. J. Perelman was also there—he and his younger brother played energetic Ping-Pong nearby and accidentally smacked Cagney on the head with the ball; Cagney "was a good sport about it." "We were invariably sent home," Maddy continued, "with the world's densest chocolate cake, made by Vivian. The Hacketts were wonderful to the kids. One of the last times we saw them on the Vineyard the kids as usual all settled around Frances so they could have a good chat and be

heard—Frances was growing deaf—and she said, 'Now you're all probably being nice to me because you think I'm going to die soon, *but don't
count on it!*"

By the time Frances made her joke, two of her siblings—Will and Connie—were already gone. Will died in the fall of 1976; during his burial,
Frances, who then had serious hip problems, stubbornly defied advice and
walked painfully across muddy, uneven ground at the cemetery to stand
beside his grave. Constance's final years were passed in a nursing home,
but her mind never weakened; the last time I visited her, when she was
eighty-seven, she asked me to send her some detective novels in German
so she could practice the language. Both my father and Caroline Huntoon
outlived Frances, dying in 1987 and 1988, respectively.

In early 1966, surely to Frances's delight, she and Albert went briefly back
to work: ABC commissioned them to write a two-hour TV version of *The
Diary of Anne Frank*. To the producer David Susskind, the reason for tele-
vising the play was simple: "Man may not have progressed much since the
Nazi era, Vietnam being one example, but at least we are not pushing
people into incinerators. The concentration camps were humanity's ultimate horror, and I think we need to be reminded of them periodically."
The production was broadcast in November 1967 with a cast including
Max von Sydow, Lilli Palmer, Vivica Lindfors, Donald Pleasance, and
Theodore Bikel, and evidently pleased Frances and Albert: speaking for
them, Leah Salisbury told Susskind it was "first-rate. . . . We are indeed
grateful for your overall stamp of good taste." Through the years, TV
adaptations of *The Diary* have been done in many foreign countries, and
in 1980 NBC did a second U.S. version, starring Maximilian Schell, James
Coco, Joan Plowright, and Melissa Gilbert.

Later in 1966, surely to Frances's even greater delight, she and Albert
got involved in a project that was far more challenging than the TV script:
adapting the French author Marguerite Duras's play *Days in the Trees* for
the New York stage. This started in July, when they were in London: Kermit Bloomgarden was interested in the play, so they saw it, and Frances
wrote to him that they were "tremendously enthusiastic." The Hacketts
also went to *A Song at Twilight*, by Noel Coward, and Frances liked it:
"Nice, beautifully played, old-fashioned. But I like that old-fashion." Another evening, they saw two of Coward's one-act plays, and Frances wrote,
"If we had not paid rent for the whole summer, I would have left England.
The second play is the most outrageous caricature of an American woman,
played by Irene Worth. And the London audience roared with delight at

every horrible thing that Coward had written. Albert tried to soothe me: 'A vaudeville act,' he said. But it was deeply offensive to me."

Because Frances liked *Days in the Trees*, she and Albert kept working sporadically on it, and by August 1970 they had a finished script and a list of possible leading ladies, starting with Lynn Fontanne. It's not clear why, but from then on the project lost momentum. In August 1971, Elizabeth Bergner declined the role, and Ingrid Bergman did the same a year later, and that was the end. Later, Albert revealed that he'd never had much confidence in the play: "We were never really satisfied. We couldn't figure out how to make it better. We made it better than it was, but that wasn't good enough. . . . Nothing happened in the play, nothing changed. It [concerned a woman] who lived in a French colony and came back to France to see her son. . . . Frances was a lot more optimistic than I was."[8]

As noted before, Frances and Albert had extraordinary gifts for friendship. All their lives, wherever they lived, whatever field they worked in, they preserved the relationships they'd grown up with while meeting new people and establishing warm connections. That talent was a key to their happiness during their last years: being close to others was *sustenance*.

Among the friends Frances and Albert saw in New York was Patric Farrell, a Brooklyn-born admirer of Irish culture who had once been director of the Irish Theater and the Museum of Irish Art. Farrell had long hair and a mustache and goatee, and carried a blackthorn walking stick given to him by William Butler Yeats. For fifty years, he lived with Elsa de Brun, a Swedish-born painter, without marrying her and boasted about defying convention; in 1985, he married her and said that now *marriage* defied convention. In 1960, he made headlines when, following his advice, an Irish scholar memorized lengthy sections of some important, restricted papers at the New York Public Library and published them; before sheriffs seized the books, Farrell hid nine copies, which he kept after a legal battle. In the spring of 1979, Farrell's landlord tried to force him and de Brun, who'd recently broken her hip, out of their fifth-floor, walk-up apartment; to get them through the summer, the Hacketts lent them their own apartment. At Hackett dinner parties, Farrell enjoyed dominating the conversation and chatting up young female guests, some of whom he phoned the next day. A reporter once asked him to describe himself, and he replied, "I can do it in one word: outrageous."

Another friend the Hacketts spent time with was tall, ruggedly handsome Robert Ryan, who had an apartment at 88 Central Park West and had starred in such films as *Crossfire*, *The Wild Bunch*, and *The Dirty Dozen*. An energetic, articulate liberal, Ryan had worked for the World Federalists and the American Civil Liberties Union; Montgomery Clift once asked him why he hadn't been blacklisted, and Ryan replied, "I'm a Catholic and an ex-Marine. [J. Edgar] Hoover wouldn't touch that combination."[9] In the early 1970s, Ryan was hit hard by the death of his wife, Jessica, and the knowledge that he, too, had cancer. Then he met the actress Maureen O'Sullivan, and a romance started. "Maureen fell madly in love with Robert," Albert said, "and I think they were going to get married, but Robert wanted to wait a respectable period of time after Jessica died." Later, at a dinner party at Frances and Albert's, Ryan seemed happy and did a song and dance. "Robert was in a joyous mood," Albert said. "It looked like he was getting ready for the big moment when the year was up, and he and Maureen would be married."[10] That didn't happen: Ryan died July 11, 1973; Frances and Albert were among those at his private memorial service.

In New York and on Martha's Vineyard, Frances and Albert stayed close to their prickly friend Lillian Hellman. In the early 1980s, with her eyesight gone, Hellman's health began declining. In the summer of 1983, the Hacketts took her to a Vineyard dinner party given by Ben Kaplan, a retired law professor and judge, and his wife, the poet Felicia Lamport; the guests included John Hersey and his wife and the biographer Joseph Lash. Another guest, the author and journalism professor Michael Janeway, wrote to me that "the question of the evening was whether Miss Hellman, frail and failing, would be strong enough to come to dinner. If so, the now quite ancient Hacketts would be driving her from Vineyard Haven. . . . As we waited, the conversation turned to physical complaints. Felicia Kaplan was prone to falling, John Hersey had strained a nerve or muscle . . . Barbara Hersey had severe arthritis, and Joe Lash had sprained or broken something and wore a cast.

"The Hacketts' car rolled up," Janeway continued, "and Frances and Albert emerged, followed by Hellman—carried by her young male nurse. 'Enough,' said Felicia, 'here they come—and [she's] so much sicker than we are!' [The dinner was] dominated by Hellman. Quite blind, she flirted with the men, including Albert, and smoked non-stop. John Hersey, to whom she was particularly close, would feed her; to get her to take her cigarette away from her face he'd say, 'Here comes a bite, Lilly.'" (Hellman, whose physical problems included emphysema, continued to smoke heavily; Peter Feibleman said she consumed four packs on the day she died, roughly a year after the Kaplans' evening. Feibleman also said that shortly before she died, he asked how she felt, and she said, "Terrible! I have the worst case of writers' block I've ever had in my life." Albert often repeated that: he thought it showed the right priorities for a writer to have at the end.)

In New York, Frances and Albert often entertained at home but also saw their friends elsewhere. In 1962, Frances joined the Cosmopolitan Club, organized in 1909 "for purposes of entertainment, social intercourse, and the inter-change of opinion among women of artistic and intellectual interests." Despite those heavy words, the several-hundred-member club, occupying a handsome building on East 66th Street, was congenial and stimulating. By now, Albert had resigned from The Players and joined the Lambs Club, where he spent much time with fellow actors; also, he often had lunch at a midtown restaurant, the Lobster, with Sid Perelman, Brooks Atkinson, Joseph Mitchell, Al Hirschfeld, and Philip Hamburger. Mrs. Marshall Field, an enthusiastic supporter of the arts and liberal causes, invited Frances and Albert to her posh plantation near Ridgefield, South Carolina, where the staff hustled guests' soiled clothes off to the laundry the instant they stepped into the shower. In New York, the Hacketts gave a talk at a girls' school, Chapin, about writing *The Diary*. "I spoke first," Albert said, "and when I introduced Frances I said, 'At some point, she's going to cry.' And of course she did, and the little girls loved it." Almost every Christmas, the Hacketts went to Dorothy Stickney's East Side townhouse; a friend said those parties were "marvelous, with everyone in the theater there."

Frances and Albert enjoyed seeing their 88 Central Park West neighbors. Joan Copeland, who'd understudied in *The Diary*'s New York production ("It's frustrating to be an understudy, but [the Hacketts] were gracious. . . . I was as important to them as the stars of the play") had them to dinner twice with her brother, Arthur Miller. "Arthur tends to be a bit stiff-backed when he first meets people," Miss Copeland said, "[because] people tend to be in awe of him, but Frances was very secure in her intellect and her capacity."[11] Albert was surely secure, too: feeling it was exploitive, he privately called Miller's 1964 play, *After the Fall*, which mostly concerned his marriage to Marilyn Monroe, "After the Money."

*After the Fall* wasn't the only play—or movie—that the Hacketts disliked. Although I don't recall their saying so, I suspect they didn't care for that time's male frontal nudity (sometimes called "noodle frontity"). In 1984, a journalist wrote that since much of their own writing had been "sound and dynamic and humanistically clear and feelingful," he guessed

—and he was right—that the Hacketts "scorned [much of] the obscuran-
tist, cocaine-befuddled nonsense that Hollywood writers are turning out
now."[12] Sometime before, Albert said that in Hollywood's great years, he
and Frances had written for adroit actors—"Bill Powell and Myrna Loy, a
wonderful team, good foils"—in sophisticated comedies, and then added
gloomily, "Nobody can find anything funny to write about any more. It's
all so terrifying, the news of the day and the atmosphere. There's such a
feeling, it seems, of restlessness. There seems to be more of a feeling for
violence now . . . than there is for comedy."[13]

As they grew older, the Central Park West apartment became more and
more the center of Frances and Albert's social life. Sometimes, their dinner guests came formally dressed: Joan Copeland recalled Albert in his "elegant, snappy, burgundy velvet smoking jacket." Emily Kimbrough and
her former collaborator Cornelia Otis Skinner were there often; one
evening, seated between them, I was dazzled by those two witty friends
of many years. During another dinner, William Saroyan told a young female guest that he was having an affair with "a very attractive woman
who's got a wonderful-looking daughter—but it wouldn't be right to
screw both the mother and the daughter . . . (pause) . . . Well, why, not?"
On some evenings, Frances and Albert consoled depressed widowers, including S. J. Perelman and Henry Ephron; at other times, after dinner, their
friends played the piano, performing their own songs: Harold Rome sang
"Sunday in the Park" and "Sing Me a Song with Social Significance"; Burton Lane sang "Look to the Rainbow" and "How Are Things in Glocca
Morra?" "Albert always liked that [last] one," Lane's wife, Lynn, said. "He
was a bit leprechaunish himself."

In January 1974, my wife and I gave a party to celebrate my parents' fiftieth wedding anniversary. The Hacketts were there, and when someone
asked Frances if *she'd* been married for fifty years, she said she had—if you
added all three of her husbands together.

In early 1983, Nancy Rica Schiff published *A Celebration of the Eighties*, a
book of photographs of sixty-two talented octogenarians. Several of
Frances and Albert's friends (and my father) were included: Lillian Gish,
Al Hirschfeld, Samson Raphaelson, Raphael Soyer. Frances and Albert
were shown seated close together in their New York living room, grinning
at each other, with her hand on his wrist. Giving Schiff her age, Frances cut
off five years. "Being with this couple," Schiff wrote, "is like watching a

comedy team." Frances was quoted as calling her spouse "Hackett" because "'Albert' never suited him. . . . In order to see all our films, you would have to be an insomniac. . . . We can't work with other writers. . . . Being polite is too much of a strain."[14]

In late fall 1983, Frances fell ill and was hospitalized. The original diagnosis, a bad case of flu, was changed to inoperable lung cancer. When she came home to the Central Park West apartment, she talked often with friends and family on the phone but didn't want visitors. She died on the evening of January 19, 1984, at age ninety-three. When my father and I got to the apartment to try to help Albert, Vivian and her mother and two nurses were there, and Albert was wandering around in a daze; several times he said, "She could always make me laugh." When friends started phoning, he repeated again and again, "Yes, yes, isn't it awful, isn't it awful?" (Later, writing to a friend, he said, "The advice I get from people who have suffered the same shock seems to be to hang on—hang on and keep going and after a while it doesn't hurt so much.") One of Frances's nurses, Agatha, told me that in midafternoon, Frances had said, "I would like to rest, and you get some rest, too"—the same words she'd spoken to another nurse four years before, while visiting Albert in the hospital. Just before she died, Frances said, "You have all been wonderful—Albert, Vivian, everyone. Thank you for everything. I am ready to go now. Goodbye."

A year after Frances's death, Albert married Gisella Svetlik, the bright, funny, high-spirited, young widow of one of his and Frances's friends (perhaps he recalled Samuel Johnson's words: "By taking a second wife he pays the highest compliment to the first, by showing that she made him so happy as a married man, that he wishes to be so a second time"). During the next decade, there were trips to Europe, and evenings at the theater and with friends, and even dancing: Gisella—good-looking, dark-haired, slender—had danced in shows on Broadway and elsewhere (she often laughed about the fact that she'd once been banned in Boston), and at parties she and Albert got to their feet and moved well. Twice, they came to visit Patty and me in Little Compton; Albert pruned trees and sometimes sat up late over drinks, laughing and talking with us and my father (my mother had died in 1984). After one of those trips, Albert typed a thank-you note on a narrow piece of paper. It started, "That visit of ours was just right. It was wonder"—but then he reached the paper's edge. Starting again, he typed, "Felt I was getting into trouble, so I stopped to put the light on. Just in time." Sadly, in his last years Albert lost touch to a degree—but his wit stayed with him: when I told him at his ninety-fifth birthday party that he looked good, he replied, "It must be something I picked up coming here." He died—suddenly, of pneumonia—on March 16, 1995. One of his obituaries said, "Hackett was a bon viveur, an enthusiastic traveler and a courtly man; and his learning sat easily on one born in the proverbial trunk." Albert would have liked that.

# Epilogue

**M**any of the movies Frances and Albert wrote during Hollywood's Golden Age are still with us at film centers, on TV, and on videocassettes. Some of them have been given second lives thanks to new technology, or rewritten and updated, or used as grist for new projects. Taking them in the order that the Hacketts wrote them:

In 1991, *Nick and Nora,* a big-budget musical based on the *Thin Man* films, opened on Broadway and flopped disastrously. The composer and lyricist reportedly wrote fifty songs to get the sixteen that were finally used, but the script was unsprightly (meaning "unHackettslike"); admitting her errors, the producer said, "You don't take beloved characters and change them. The public was hungry for a musical, and they loved the characters of Nick and Nora, the zaniness, the fun and the mystery. They didn't want messages. . . . They were hopelessly disappointed."

As noted before, *It's a Wonderful Life* got colorized. It also got imitated twice on TV: in 1977, when Marlo Thomas played the Jimmy Stewart part in *It Happened One Christmas* ("monstrous, horrible," one commentator said), and in 1990, in *Clarence,* which centered around the angel who saved Stewart's life. In the early 1980s, a musical version was put together, but it never reached Broadway. (Some years before, Hal Prince had talked with Frances and Albert about doing a musical version. "They were very cooperative," he said, "but I couldn't figure out how to do it. . . . The big problem with [adapting] a great movie is, unless you can make [the musical] better than the movie, there's not much point in doing it.")[1]

In 1991 and 1995, Steve Martin starred in films based on *Father of the Bride* and *Father's Little Dividend.* About the first, a critic wrote, "Back in 1950 . . . MGM told this story sharply and beautifully. . . . [This version cannot] match the original film's grace or wit" (nevertheless, it reportedly grossed around $100 million). The new version didn't just lack the original's grace and wit; it was frequently oversentimental and had new "action" scenes that groped for laughs. The remake reflected the ongoing dumbing down of American popular entertainment, where, for example, the tunes of songs have become mere ear-shattering noise, and lyrics are grunted obscenities.

In 1978, a touring stage version of *Seven Brides for Seven Brothers* was put together; four years later, it reached Broadway but closed after four performances. Over the years, the original color negative of the film deteriorated; in 1996, Turner Entertainment created a restored print and started showing it on TV.

Implausible as it may sound, *The Diary of Anne Frank* served as the basis of a musical. Titled *Yours, Anne,* the show had a short off-Broadway run in 1985 and was later revived in a couple of other cities; the tunes, book, and lyrics ("No more talking, no more walking in shoes. They are listening, they are looking for Jews") have been called feeble, tedious, and obvious.

In early December 1997, a new, thoughtfully produced version of *The Diary* opened on Broadway. The director was James Lapine; Natalie Portman played Anne; the text, rewritten by Wendy Kesselman, laid heavier emphasis on Jewish elements and included franker material concerning Anne's "sexual awakening" and her conflicts with her mother. It seems safe to say that Frances and Albert would have welcomed some of the new material in the play, because it tended to make Anne more "human," and because, in their earliest drafts, they had included a good many references to Judaism and the plight of the Jews that were later cut. The production, which got mixed reviews, revived the charge that the Hacketts' play had universalized Anne too much; the most extreme comments came, in the *New Yorker,* from novelist-essayist Cynthia Ozick, who damned Otto Frank and the "Anne Frank industry" created around the diary and suggested that Otto Frank should have burned the diary. (Three years later, in a collection of her essays, realizing that many readers of the *New Yorker* piece had concluded that she had meant the suggestion about burning seriously, Ozick unconvincingly claimed she hadn't.)

Two pieces of real estate the Hacketts loved have undergone traumas. Their isolated, starkly simple Vermont farmhouse (where the two reclusive brothers didn't recognize Cagney) has been replaced by a jazzy, circular dwelling with a swimming pool on the first floor and an elevator to the second. In 1997, their wonderful, modest-sized Bel Air house was torn down, and excavation began for a French chateau–style structure with seven bedrooms, nine bathrooms, a screening room, an exercise room, a wine cellar, and a twelve-car garage. Scheduled to be painted aqua, this obscenity was originally designed for one of the world's richest men, the

Sultan of Brunei, but he backed out; in 1999, the lot and house foundation sold for $3 million.

The work of truly fine writers—and, as pioneers and perfectionists in their special craft, Frances and Albert were certainly that—lives on after their deaths. The Hacketts' work, which energized so many highly popular films and *The Diary of Anne Frank,* has left a lasting mark on American and world culture. And their deeds—the actions and support that affected so many others—will always be remembered. They weren't churchgoers, so there were no memorial services for them, but a few days after Frances died, fifty of her friends, including many people mentioned earlier, signed an announcement in the *New York Times:* "We, as friends of Frances Goodrich, are deeply moved by her death and wish to express our love and sympathy to Albert Hackett." Shortly after Albert died, friends and relations gathered for an evening of remembrance. Since there were no formal eulogies for Frances and Albert, we can turn instead to the words of "Doctor Pat" Woodcock:

> I was amazed that a couple who had obviously reached the heights of their profession spent so much of their time thinking of other people: with imagination, with total lack of negative judgement, with colossal generosity, with humor. They both had, in entirely distinctive ways, that mysterious "complicity" that makes personal relationships so intoxicating—"me and you." . . . What an extraordinary feat to achieve such success and never make enemies; and be surrounded by affection and respect.

Filmography

Notes

Select Bibliography

Index

# Filmography

| Date | Title | Director |
|------|-------|----------|
| 1930 | *Up Pops the Devil.* Based on their play. Dialogue director: Albert Hackett | Edward Sutherland |
| 1933 | *The Secret of Madame Blanche.* Adaptation. | Charles Brabin |
|      | *Penthouse.* Adaptation | W. S. Van Dyke |
| 1934 | *Chained.* Uncredited contribution. | Clarence Brown |
|      | *Fugitive Lovers.* Coscript. | Richard Boleslawsky |
|      | *The Thin Man.* Script. | W. S. Van Dyke |
|      | *Hide-Out.* Script. | W. S. Van Dyke |
| 1935 | *Naughty Marietta.* Coscript. | W. S. Van Dyke |
|      | *Ah, Wilderness!* Script. | Clarence Brown |
| 1936 | *Rose Marie.* Coscript. | W. S. Van Dyke |
|      | *After the Thin Man.* Script. | W. S. Van Dyke |
|      | *Small Town Girl.* Coscript. | William Wellman |
| 1937 | *The Firefly.* Coscript. | Robert Z. Leonard |
| 1939 | *Society Lawyer.* Coscript. | Edwin L. Marin |
|      | *Another Thin Man.* Script. | W. S. Van Dyke |
| 1944 | *Lady in the Dark.* Script. | Mitchell Leisen |
|      | *The Hitler Gang.* Script. | John Farrow |
| 1946 | *The Virginian.* Script. | Stuart Gilmore |
|      | *It's a Wonderful Life.* Coscript. | Frank Capra |
| 1948 | *The Pirate.* Script. | Vincente Minnelli |
|      | *Summer Holiday.* Remake of *Ah, Wilderness!* Script. | Rouben Mamoulian |
|      | *Easter Parade.* Story, Coscript. | Charles Walters |
| 1949 | *In Good Old Summertime.* Coscript. | Robert Z. Leonard |

| Date | Title | Director |
|------|-------|----------|
| 1950 | *Father of the Bride.* Script. | Michael Curtiz |
| 1951 | *Father's Little Dividend.* Script. | Vincente Minnelli |
|      | *Too Young to Kiss.* Script. | Robert Z. Leonard |
| 1953 | *Give a Girl a Break.* Script. | Stanley Donen |
| 1954 | *The Long, Long Trailer.* Script. | Vincente Minnelli |
|      | *Seven Brides for Seven Brothers.* Coscript. | Stanley Donen |
| 1956 | *Gaby.* Coscript. | Curtis Bernhardt |
| 1958 | *A Certain Smile.* Script. | Jean Negulesco |
| 1959 | *The Diary of Anne Frank.* Based on their play. Script. | George Stevens |
| 1962 | *Five Finger Exercise.* Script. | Daniel Mann |

Plays produced on Broadway include *Up Pops the Devil, Bridal Wise, The Great Big Doorstep, The Diary of Anne Frank.*

Academy Awards include an Oscar nomination for adapting *The Thin Man* in 1934; that same year, the original story for *Hide-Out* by Mauri Grashin earned a nomination (the script was by Goodrich and Hackett); a nomination in 1936 for the screenplay of *After the Thin Man;* a nomination in 1950 for the screenplay of *Father of the Bride;* and a nomination in 1954 for the co-screenplay (with Dorothy Kingsley) of *Seven Brides for Seven Brothers.*

Writers Guild awards include the Best Comedy of 1948, *Easter Parade,* cowritten with Sidney Sheldon; the Best Comedy of 1951, *Father's Little Dividend;* the Best Musical of 1954, *Seven Brides for Seven Brothers,* cowritten with Dorothy Kingsley; and Best Drama of 1959, *The Diary of Anne Frank,* based on their own play. In 1955, they received the Laurel Award for Achievement; they were chosen by their fellow screenwriters.

# Notes

Throughout this book, there are many quotations from letters written to the Hacketts as well as letters written by the Hacketts to their friends, relations, coworkers, and particularly their agent, Leah Salisbury. The personal correspondence is in the author's files; the Salisbury correspondence is at the Rare Book and Manuscript Library at Columbia University. Many review quotations from various newspapers and periodicals also appear in these pages. Because the quotations are so numerous, in most cases there has been no attempt to include their sources in the endnotes.

## Introduction

1. *New York Times*, 30 Apr. 1956.
2. Garson Kanin, interview by author, 7 Dec. 1992.
3. George Oppenheimer, *A View from the Sixties* (New York: David McKay, 1966), 141.
4. Patrick McGilligan, *Backstory: Interviews with Screenwriters of Hollywood's Golden Age* (Berkeley: University of California Press, 1986), 199.
5. *New York Times*, 30 Sept. 1956.
6. Frances Hackett, letter to Sam Goldwyn, 7 Oct. 1956.

## 1. Frances, the Lawn Child

1. Ron Chernow, *Titan: The Life of John D. Rockefeller* (New York: Random House, 1998), 339.
2. Barbara Hogensen, *Reminiscences of Albert and Frances Hackett* (New York: Columbia University Oral History Research Office, 1983), 29.
3. Charles Francisco, *Gentleman: The William Powell Story* (New York: St. Martin's, 1985), 22.
4. Burns Mantle, *Contemporary American Playwrights* (New York: Dodd, Mead, 1938), 237.
5. *Vassar College Class of 1912, Class Bulletin*, May 1920.
6. *Hartford Daily Courant*, 28 Nov. 1926.
7. Hogenson, 36.

8. Hogenson, 37.
9. Hogenson, 37.
10. *The Players Club Yearbook*, 1908.
11. *New Yorker*, 9 Sept. 1996, 82.
12. The letters between Frances and van Loon can be found at the Kroch Library, Cornell University, and in Gerard van Loon's biography of his father.
13. Emily Kimbrough, *Time Enough* (New York: Harper and Row, 1974), 13.

## 2. Albert, the Nickelodeon Child

1. Hogenson, 1–2.
2. Ruth Goetz, interview by author, 13 Nov. 1992.
3. Hogenson, 83–84.
4. *Pittsburgh Post*, 14 Jan. 1910.
5. "A Playwright's Cradle Days," *Variety*, 4 Jan. 1961.
6. Hogenson, 24–25.
7. Hogenson, 58.
8. Joan Franklin and Robert Clyde, untitled interview of the Hacketts (New York: Columbia University Oral History Research Office, 23 June 1958), 8.
9. Franklin and Clyde, 2.
10. Program of the *New York City Ballet*, spring 1965.
11. Sally Dixon Wiener, untitled conversation with Albert Hackett, Nov. 1984, 2. Property of David L. Goodrich.
12. Wiener, 1.
13. Hogenson, 74–78.
14. Hogenson, 80.
15. Wiener, 5.
16. Franklin and Clyde, 18.
17. Wiener, 12.
18. Wiener, 3.
19. Wiener, 5.
20. Nora Sayre, interview by author, 14 Apr. 1994.

## 3. Working, Fighting, and Living Together

1. Wiener, 2.
2. *New York Herald Tribune*, 3 June 1956.
3. Wiener, 4.
4. The quotes in this paragraph are from Hogenson, Wiener, and the *Los Angeles Times*, 16 Dec. 1956.
5. Gisela Svetlik, interview by author, 17 Dec. 1999.
6. Frith Banbury, interview by author, 18 May 1994.
7. Elizabeth Frank, interview by author, 3 Nov. 1995.
8. Wiener, 13.
9. William Ludwig, interview by author, 26 Oct. 1992.
10. Hogenson, 34.

11. Sayre, interview.

12. *Philadelphia Inquirer,* 28 Nov. 1982.

13. Harlan B. Phillips, *Lloyd Goodrich Reminisces* (New York: Archives of American Art and Brandeis University, 1963).

14. A. Scott Berg, *Goldwyn: A Biography* (New York: Knopf, 1989) 201.

15. *New York Herald Tribune,* 12 Jan. 1941.

16. Hogenson, 90.

17. Anna Crouse, interview by author, 16 Dec. 1996.

## 4. Hollywood 1931: A Hopeful Baptism

1. Hogenson, 119.

2. Paramount press release, undated.

3. Hogenson, 50.

4. Hogenson, 50, 41.

5. Hogenson, 47.

6. *New York Herald Tribune,* 12 Jan. 1941.

7. Franklin and Clyde, 34.

## 5. Entering Hollywood's Golden Age

1. Neal Gabler, *An Empire of Their Own: How the Jews Invented Hollywood* (New York: Anchor, 1989), 210.

2. Franklin and Clyde, 21.

3. McGilligan, 203.

4. McGilligan, 202.

5. McGilligan, 203.

6. David King Dunaway, *Huxley in Hollywood* (New York: Harper and Row, 1989), 98.

7. Note made by Albert Hackett, probably in 1962, on a file copy of the *Madame Blanche* script.

8. Wiener, 9.

9. Hogenson, 94.

10. Hogenson, 95.

11. Conference notes, 30 June 1933.

12. McGilligan, 207.

13. Ben M. Hall, *The Golden Age of the Movie Palaces* (New York: Clarkson N. Potter, 1961), 179.

14. McGilligan, 205.

15. Franklin and Clyde, 22.

16. Hogenson, 122.

17. Gabler, 326.

18. Leila Hadley, interview by author, 1 Mar. 1993.

19. S. J. Perelman, *Don't Tread on Me: The Selected Letters of S. J. Perelman,* ed. Prudence Crowther (New York: Viking, 1987), 173.

20. Perelman, 173.

21. Perelman, 138.

22. Philip Hamburger, letter to author, 7 Dec. 1992.

23. Gerta Conner, interview by author, 20 Jan. 1994.

24. Jay Martin, interview by author, 12 Dec. 1993.

25. Ian Hamilton, *Writers in Hollywood* (New York: Heinemann, 1990), 98.

26. Goetz, interview.

27. Marion Meade, *Dorothy Parker: What Fresh Hell Is This?* (New York: Villard, 1988), 209.

28. Meade, 264.

29. *St. Louis Post-Dispatch,* 19 Apr. 1987, 36.

## 6. *The Thin Man*

1. Hamilton, 255.

2. *Guardian,* 9 May 1995.

3. *New York Times,* 23 May 1999.

4. James Robert Parish and Ronald L. Bowers, *The Golden Era: The MGM Stock Company* (Westport, Conn.: Arlington House, 1973), 215.

5. *New York Post,* 1 Mar. 1941.

6. *New York Post,* 1 Mar. 1941.

7. Diane Johnson, *Hammett: A Life* (New York: Random House, 1983), 123.

8. Hogenson, 125.

9. Hogenson, 126.

10. Peter Feibleman, *Lilly: Reminiscences of Lillian Hellman* (New York: William Morrow, 1988), jacket copy.

11. William Wright, *Lillian Hellman: The Image, The Woman* (New York: Simon and Schuster, 1986), 25.

12. Carl Rollyson, *Lillian Hellman: Her Legend and Her Legacy* (New York: St. Martin's, 1988), 55.

13. Feibleman, 195.

14. Perelman, *Don't Tread on Me,* 287.

15. Perelman, *Don't Tread on Me,* 288.

## 7. *Naughty Marietta* and *Ah, Wilderness!*

1. Hogenson, 98.

2. Hogenson, 123.

3. McGilligan, 206.

4. Joseph Ignatius Breen, memorandum, 4 Dec. 1934.

5. *New York Times Book Review,* 28 Nov. 1999.

6. Wiener, 6.

7. Frank, interview.

8. *Films in Review,* Oct. 1977, 464.

9. Franklin and Clyde, 33.

10. Donald Ogden Stewart, *By a Stroke of Luck: An Autobiography* (New York: Paddington, 1975), 72.

11. Franklin and Clyde, 36.
12. McGilligan, 343.
13. McGilligan, 209.
14. Hogenson, 189.
15. Billy Wilder, interview by author, 23 Sept. 1993.
16. Franklin and Clyde, 3.
17. Hogenson, 197.
18. James Cagney, *Cagney by Cagney* (New York: Doubleday, 1976), 98.
19. Dorothy McHugh, interview by author, 29 Apr. 1994.
20. Billy Altman, *Laughter's Gentle Soul: The Life of Robert Benchley* (New York: Norton, 1997), 295.
21. Hogenson, 197.

## 8. Fighting for Writers' Rights

1. *New York Herald Tribune,* 1 Sept. 1940.
2. McGilligan, 166.
3. William Ludwig, interview by author, 3 June 1997.
4. Hogenson, 110.
5. Nancy Lynn Schwartz, *The Hollywood Writers' Wars* (New York: Knopf, 1982), 10.
6. John Gregory Dunne, *The Studio* (New York: Bantam, 1970), 104.
7. *London Sunday Times,* 10 Nov. 1968.
8. Hogenson, 104.
9. Hogenson, 105.
10. Schwartz, 65.
11. Ludwig, interview, 3 June 1997.
12. Ring Lardner Jr., interview by author, 1 Dec. 1992.
13. Lee Server, *Screenwriter* (Pittstown, N. J.: Main Street, 1987), 231.
14. Wright, 118.
15. Hogenson, 116.
16. Sayre, interview.
17. Schwartz, 124.
18. Sheilah Graham, *The Garden of Allah* (New York: Crown, 1970).
19. Graham, *The Garden of Allah,* 184.
20. Leo Rosten, *Hollywood: The Movie Colony, the Movie Makers* (New York: Harcourt Brace, 1941), 318.
21. Franklin and Clyde, 22.
22. Schwartz, 37.

## 9. *Rose Marie,* Art Collecting, and *Thin Man* Struggles

1. *St. Louis Post-Dispatch,* 19 Apr. 1987, 36.
2. *Studio News,* 11 Jan. 1936.
3. *Studio News,* 11 Jan. 1936.
4. *New York Times,* 25 Apr. 1997, 12.

5. David Niven, *The Moon's a Balloon* (New York: Putnam, 1972), 228.

6. Maureen Stapleton, *A Hell of a Life* (New York: Simon and Schuster, 1995), 38.

7. Gary Fishgall, *Pieces of Time: The Life of James Stewart* (New York: Scribner, 1997), 100.

8. *London Times,* 5 Apr. 1937.

## 10. The Garden of Allah

1. Faith McNulty, interview by author, 8 Dec. 1992.

2. Wiener, 2.

3. Philip Dunne, *Take Two: A Life in Movies and Politics* (New York: McGraw-Hill, 1980), 36.

4. Gloria Stuart, *I Just Kept Hoping* (New York: Little, Brown, 1999), 144.

5. Nora Johnson, *Flashback: Nora Johnson on Nunnally Johnson* (New York: Doubleday, 1979), 78.

6. *New York Sunday News,* 23 May 1971.

7. Gene D. Phillips, *Fiction, Film, and F. Scott Fitzgerald* (Chicago: Loyola University Press, 1986), 12.

8. A. Scott Berg, *Max Perkins: Editor of Genius* (New York: Dutton, 1978), 342.

9. Aaron Latham, *Crazy Sundays: F. Scott Fitzgerald in Hollywood* (New York: Viking, 1971), 7.

10. Latham, 9.

11. *New Yorker,* 3 Jul. 2000, 82.

12. Latham, 55.

13. Graham, *The Garden of Allah,* 188.

14. Dorothy Herrmann, *S. J. Perelman: A Life* (New York: Simon & Schuster, 1986), 118.

15. A copy of the poem, in Fitzgerald's handwriting, is among the Hacketts' papers at the State Historical Society in Madison, Wisconsin.

16. Sheilah Graham and Gerald Frank, *Beloved Infidel: The Education of a Woman* (New York: Holt, 1958), 218.

17. Latham, 152.

18. Latham, 14.

## 11. A "Lovely Nervous Breakdown"

1. *New York Herald Tribune,* 21 Nov. 1937.

2. *United Press,* 29 Jan. 1936.

3. David Woods, interview with Frances Goodrich and Albert Hackett (Hanover, N.H.: Special Collections, Dartmouth College Library, 9 Mar. 1976), 7.

4. Woods, 3.

5. Woods, 8.

6. *Century Association Yearbook,* 1972.

7. *Providence Journal,* 22 Dec. 1939, 9.

8. Richard Layman, *Shadow Man: The Life of Dashiell Hammett* (New York: Harcourt Brace, 1981), 168.

9. Hogenson, 184.

10. Lloyd Goodrich, interview by Elizabeth Frank, 21 Jul. 1982.

11. Franklin and Clyde, 33.

## 12. A Working Sabbatical: 1939–1943

1. S. J. Perelman, *Westward Ha! Or Around the World in Eighty Clichés* (New York: Simon and Schuster, 1947), 23.

2. *Providence Journal*, 22 Dec. 1939, 9.

3. Groucho Marx, *The Groucho Letters* (New York: Simon and Schuster, 1967), 186.

4. *New York Herald Tribune*, 12 Jan. 1941.

5. *New York Herald Tribune*, 12 Jan. 1941.

6. Kitty Carlisle Hart, interview by author, 26 Oct. 1993.

7. Hogenson, 139.

8. Wilder, interview.

9. Al Hirschfeld, interview by author, 23 Feb. 1993.

10. Lena Horne with Richard Schickel, *Lena* (New York: Doubleday, 1965), 156.

11. Crouse, interview.

12. Margie Barab, interview by author, 15 Apr. 1996.

13. Marlon Brando, *Songs My Mother Taught Me* (New York: Random House, 1994), 236.

14. Hogenson, 130.

15. *Sight and Sound*, spring 1983, 128.

## 13. "Paramount's Lot Is Not a Happy One"

1. Frances Goodrich and Albert Hackett, telegram to William Dozier, 21 Jan. 1943.

2. Bert Allenberg, letter to Frances Goodrich and Albert Hackett, 10 Feb. 1943.

3. *New York Herald Tribune*, 7 May 1944, 4:1.

4. Perelman, *Don't Tread on Me*, letter dated 25 June 1943.

5. *Variety*, 28 June 1944.

6. Hogenson, 195.

7. Albert Hackett, script notes, 21 Dec. 1944.

8. Albert Hackett, script notes, Aug. 1943.

9. Julius Epstein, interview by author, 4 Apr. 1993.

10. Hirschfeld, interview.

11. Cynthia Patten, interview by author, 16 Dec. 1996.

12. Ludwig, interview, 26 Oct. 1992.

13. Berg, *Goldwyn*, 247.

14. *Vineyard Gazette*, 2 Aug. 1963.

15. Faith McNulty, letter to author, 20 Jan. 1993.

16. E. B. White, letter to Frances Goodrich and Albert Hackett, 10 June 1943.

## 14. It's *Not* a Wonderful Life

1. *Films in Review,* Oct. 1977, 464.

2. *New York Times,* 14 Mar. 1999, 47

3. *Films in Review,* Oct. 1977, 464.

4. Joseph McBride, *Frank Capra: The Catastrophe of Success* (New York: Simon and Schuster, 1992), 511.

5. *Village Voice,* 30 Dec. 1986, 57.

6. *New York Times Book Review,* 3 May 1992, 3.

7. Gloria Sheekman, letter to author, 11 Jan. 1993.

8. David Brown, interview by author, 10 Feb. 1993.

9. Crouse, interview.

10. Oppenheimer, 105.

11. Oppenheimer, 140.

12. Sam Adams, interview by author, 11 Feb. 1994.

## 15. *Easter Parade* and Other Judy Garland Hits

1. Hogenson, 194.

2. *Newark Sunday News,* 27 Jan. 1947.

3. Perelman, *Don't Tread on Me,* letter dated 11 Feb. 1947.

4. *New York Post,* 16 Aug. 1954.

5. McGilligan, 208.

6. Hugh Fordin, *That's Entertainment!* (New York: Doubleday, 1975), 223.

7. Bert Allenberg, letter to Frances Goodrich and Albert Hackett, 31 Oct. 1947.

8. *New Yorker,* 21 Mar. 1994, 112.

9. Raymond Chandler, *Raymond Chandler Speaking.* Ed. Dorothy Gardner and Kathrine Sorley Walker (New York: Houghton Mifflin, 1977), 123, 138.

10. Dore Schary, *Heyday: An Autobiography* (Boston: Little, Brown, 1979), 181.

11. John Gregory Dunne, 50.

12. Thomas Kunkel, ed. *Letters from the Editor: The New Yorker's Harold Ross* (New York: The Modern Library, 2000), 328.

13. Hogenson, 182–83.

14. David Brown, *Let Me Entertain You* (New York: William Morrow, 1990), 53.

15. Hy Kraft, *On My Way to the Theater* (New York: MacMillan, 1971), 174.

16. *New York Herald Tribune,* 10 Oct. 1961, 10.

17. Larry Ceplair and Steven Englund, *The Inquisition in Hollywood* (New York: Doubleday, 1980), 349.

18. Frances Cheney, interview by author, 1 Dec. 1992.

19. *New York Post,* 27 Jul. 1973, 20.

20. Frank, interview.

## 16. *Father of the Bride*

1. Edward Streeter, letter to Frances Goodrich and Albert Hackett, 3 May 1950.
2. Gore Vidal, *Palimpsest, a Memoir* (New York: Random House, 1995), 288.
3. *Nation*, 15 Aug. 1987, 129.
4. Schary, 217.
5. Vincente Minnelli with Hector Arce, *I Remember It Well* (New York: Doubleday, 1974), 217.
6. Hogenson, 158.
7. McGilligan, 207.
8. Joan Bennett and Lois Kibbee, *The Bennett Playbill* (New York: Holt, Rinehart and Winston, 1970), 306.
9. Brown, 140.
10. Meade, 339.

## 17. *Seven Brides for Seven Brothers*

1. Perelman, *Don't Tread on Me*, 121.
2. Larry Gelbart, *Laughing Matters* (New York: Random House, 1998), 130.
3. Irving Lazar, letter to Lloyd Almirall, 15 Dec. 1952.
4. Lloyd Almirall, letter to Frances Goodrich and Albert Hackett, 27 May 1956.
5. Wiener, 6.
6. Hogenson, 196.
7. William Murray, *Janet, My Mother and Me* (New York: Simon and Schuster, 2000), 121.
8. Frances Goodrich, letter to Reata Kraft, undated.
9. Albert Hackett, script notes, 16 Sept. 1953.
10. *New York Post*, 16 Aug. 1954.
11. Terry Kingsley-Smith, interview by author, 14 Dec. 1997.
12. *New York Post*, 16 Aug. 1954.
13. Stanley Donen, interview by author, 25 Aug. 1994.
14. Halliwell, 101.
15. Donen, interview.

## 18. Writing *The Diary of Anne Frank*

1. Frances Goodrich and Albert Hackett, *The Diary of Anne Frank* (New York: Random House, 1956), viii–ix.
2. Goetz, interview.
3. Hogenson, 171
4. Garson Kanin, interview by author, 7 Dec. 1992.
5. Kanin, interview.
6. Franklin and Clyde, 28.
7. Wiener, 11

8. *New York Times,* 2 Oct. 1955, A1.
9. Goodrich and Hackett, x, xii.

## 19. Getting *The Diary of Anne Frank* on the Stage

1. Susan Strasberg, *Bittersweet* (New York: Putnam, 1980), 49.
2. Perelman, *Don't Tread on Me,* 173.
3. Kanin, interview.
4. *New York Times,* 2 Oct. 1955, A1.
5. Kanin, interview.
6. Joseph Schildkraut, *My Father and I* (New York: Viking, 1959), 235.
7. Strasberg, 55.
8. Kanin, interview.
9. Schildkraut, 235.

## 20. After *The Diary*

1. *New York Sunday Times,* 26 Nov. 1967, 5:38.
2. *New York Times,* 14 Oct. 1956.
3. Banbury, interview.
4. Banbury, interview.
5. Lawrence Graver, *An Obsession with Anne Frank* (Berkeley: University of California Press, 1995), 135.
6. Graver, 149.
7. Graver, 78.
8. Ralph Melnick, *The Stolen Legacy of Anne Frank* (New Haven, Conn.: Yale University Press, 1997), 172.
9. Kanin, interview.
10. Berg, *Goldwyn,* 477.
11. Frank, interview.
12. *St. Louis Post-Dispatch,* 19 Apr. 1987, 36.
13. Patten, interview.
14. *Films in Review,* Oct. 1977, 464.

## 21. Hollywood Finale

1. *New York Post,* 4 Aug. 1958, 26.
2. Mary Rodgers Guettel, interview by author, 10 Sept. 1994.
3. *Films in Review,* Oct. 1977, 464.
4. Geoffrey Shurlock, letter to Samuel J. Briskin (of Columbia Pictures), 8 Nov. 1960.
5. Henry Ephron, *We Thought We Could Do Anything* (New York: Norton, 1977), 175.

## 22. Back in New York

1. *New York Herald Tribune,* 24 May 1962.

2. McGilligan, 211.

3. Banbury, interview.

4. Joan Sitwell, interview by author, 2 Feb. 1994.

5. Hirschfeld, interview.

6. Banbury, interview.

7. Margaret Brooks, interview by author, 11 Aug. 1998.

8. Hogenson, 200.

9. Patricia Bosworth, *Montgomery Clift: A Biography* (New York: Harcourt Brace, 1978), 144.

10. Franklin Jarlett, *Robert Ryan: A Biography and Critical Filmography* (Jefferson, N. C.: McFarland, 1990), 173.

11. Joan Copeland, interview by author, 20 Aug. 1994.

12. *Quirk's Reviews,* Mar. 1984, 15.

13. Franklin and Clyde, 28.

14. Nancy Rica Schiff, *A Celebration of the 80s: Portraits* (New York: Harry N. Abrams, 1983), 36.

## Epilogue

1. Hal Prince, interview by author, 15 Sept. 1994.

# Select Bibliography

## "Oral History" and Other Recorded Interviews

Franklin, Joan, and Robert Clyde. Untitled interview of the Hacketts. New York: Columbia University Oral History Research Office, 23 June 1958.

Hogenson, Barbara. *Reminiscences of Albert and Frances Hackett*. New York: Columbia University Oral History Research Office, 1983. (For the sake of clarity, some of the excerpts from this interview have been lightly edited.)

Phillips, Harlan B. *Lloyd Goodrich Reminisces*. New York: Archives of American Art and Brandeis University, 1963.

Wiener, Sally Dixon. Untitled conversation with Albert Hackett. November 1984. Property of David L. Goodrich.

Woods, David. Interview with Frances Goodrich and Albert Hackett. Hanover, N. H.: Special Collections, Dartmouth College Library, 9 Mar. 1976.

## Books

Altman, Billy. *Laughter's Gentle Soul: The Life of Robert Benchley*. New York: Norton, 1997.

Bennett, Joan, and Lois Kibbee. *The Bennett Playbill*. New York: Holt, Rinehart and Winston, 1970.

Berg, A. Scott. *Goldwyn: A Biography*. New York: Knopf, 1989.

———. *Max Perkins: Editor of Genius*. New York: Dutton, 1978.

Berman, Avis. *Rebels on Eighth Street: Juliana Force and the Whitney Museum of American Art*. New York: Atheneum, 1990.

Blotner, Joseph. *Faulkner: A Biography*. New York: Random House, 1984.

Blum, Daniel. *A Pictorial History of the Silent Screen*. New York: Putnam, 1953.

Bosworth, Patricia. *Montgomery Clift: A Biography*. New York: Harcourt Brace, 1978.

Brando, Marlon. *Songs My Mother Taught Me*. New York: Random House, 1994.

Bronner, Edwin. *Encyclopedia of the American Theater, 1900–1975*. New York: A. S. Barnes, 1980.

Brown, David. *Let Me Entertain You*. New York: William Morrow, 1990.

Bruccoli, Matthew J. *Some Sort of Epic Grandeur: The Life of F. Scott Fitzgerald.* New York: Harcourt Brace, 1981.

Cagney, James. *Cagney by Cagney.* New York: Doubleday, 1976.

Cannom, Robert C. *Van Dyke and the Mythical City, Hollywood.* New York: Garland, 1977.

Capra, Frank. *The Name above the Title: An Autobiography.* New York: Macmillan, 1970.

Carr, Virginia Spencer. *The Lonely Hunter: A Biography of Carson McCullers.* New York: Doubleday, 1974.

Caspary, Vera. *The Secrets of Grown-Ups.* New York: McGraw-Hill, 1979.

Ceplair, Larry, and Steven Englund. *The Inquisition in Hollywood.* New York: Doubleday, 1980.

Chandler, Raymond. *Raymond Chandler Speaking.* Ed. Dorothy Gardner and Kathrine Sorley Walker. New York: Houghton Mifflin, 1977.

Chernow, Ron. *Titan: The Life of John D. Rockefeller.* New York: Random House, 1998.

Cole, Lester. *Hollywood Red.* Palo Alto: Ramparts, 1981.

Corliss, Richard, ed. *The Hollywood Screenwriters.* New York: Discus Books, 1972.

Crichton, Kyle. *Total Recoil.* New York: Doubleday, 1960.

Crowther, Bosley. *Hollywood Rajah: The Life and Times of Louis B. Mayer.* New York: Holt, Rinehart and Winston, 1960.

Curtis, James. *Between Flops: A Biography of Preston Sturges.* New York: Harcourt Brace, 1962.

Dewey, Donald. *James Stewart: A Biography.* Atlanta: Turner Publishing, 1996.

Douglas, Helen Gahagan. *A Full Life.* New York: Doubleday, 1982.

Dunaway, David King. *Huxley in Hollywood.* New York: Harper and Row, 1989.

Dunne, John Gregory. *The Studio.* New York: Bantam, 1970.

Dunne, Philip. *Take Two: A Life in Movies and Politics.* New York: McGraw-Hill, 1980.

Ephron, Henry. *We Thought We Could Do Anything.* New York: Norton, 1977.

Farber, Stephen, and Marc Green. *Hollywood on the Couch.* New York: Morrow, 1993.

Feibleman, Peter. *Lilly: Reminiscences of Lillian Hellman.* New York: Morrow, 1988.

Finch, Christopher. *Rainbow: The Stormy Life of Judy Garland.* New York: Grosset and Dunlap, 1975.

Fishgall, Gary. *Pieces of Time: The Life of James Stewart.* New York: Scribner, 1977.

Fordin, Hugh. *That's Entertainment!* New York: Doubleday, 1975.

Francisco, Charles. *Gentleman: The William Powell Story.* New York: St. Martin's, 1985.

Frank, Anne. *The Diary of a Young Girl.* New York: Doubleday, 1952.

Frewin, Leslie. *The Late Mrs. Dorothy Parker.* New York: Macmillan, 1986.

Gabler, Neal. *An Empire of Their Own: How the Jews Invented Hollywood.* New York: Anchor, 1989.

Gelbart, Larry. *Laughing Matters.* New York: Random House, 1998.

Goodrich, Frances, and Albert Hackett. *The Diary of Anne Frank*. New York: Random House, 1956.

Graham, Sheilah. *The Garden of Allah*. New York: Crown, 1970.

———. *Hollywood Revisited: A Fiftieth Anniversary Celebration*. New York: St. Martin's, 1985.

———. *The Real F. Scott Fitzgerald: Thirty-Five Years Later*. New York: Grosset and Dunlap, 1976.

———. *The Rest of the Story*. New York: Coward-McCann, 1964.

Graham, Sheilah, and Gerald Frank. *Beloved Infidel: The Education of a Woman*. New York: Holt, 1958.

Graver, Lawrence. *An Obsession with Anne Frank*. Berkeley: University of California Press, 1995.

Guiles, Fred Lawrence. *Joan Crawford: The Last Word*. New York: Birch Lane, 1995.

Hall, Ben M. *The Golden Age of the Movie Palaces*. New York: Clarkson N. Potter, 1961.

Hamilton, Ian. *Writers in Hollywood*. London: Heinemann, 1990.

Hammett, Dashiell. *The Thin Man*. New York: Knopf, 1934.

Harmatz, Aljean. *Round Up the Usual Suspects*. New York: Hyperion, 1992.

Harvey, Stephen. *Directed by Vincente Minnelli*. New York: Harper and Row, 1989.

Hellman, Lillian. *Scoundrel Time*. Boston: Little, Brown, 1976.

Herrmann, Dorothy. *S. J. Perelman: A Life*. New York: Simon and Schuster, 1986.

Hilton, Conrad. *Be My Guest*. New York: Prentice Hall, 1956.

Horne, Lena, with Richard Schickel. *Lena*. New York: Doubleday, 1965.

Jablonski, Edward. *Gershwin: A Biography*. New York: Doubleday, 1987.

Jarlett, Franklin. *Robert Ryan: A Biography and Critical Filmography*. Jefferson, N.C.: McFarland, 1990.

Johnson, Diane. *Hammett: A Life*. New York: Random House, 1983.

Johnson, Nora. *Flashback: Nora Johnson on Nunnally Johnson*. New York: Doubleday, 1979.

Kimbrough, Emily. *Better Than Oceans*. New York: Harper and Row, 1976.

———. *Time Enough*. New York: Harper and Row, 1974.

Koestler, Arthur, and Cynthia Koestler. *Stranger in the Square*. New York: Random House, 1984.

Kraft, Hy. *On My Way to the Theater*. New York: Macmillan, 1971.

Kunkel, Thomas, ed. *Letters from the Editor: The* New Yorker's *Harold Ross*. New York: The Modern Library, 2000.

Latham, Aaron. *Crazy Sundays: F. Scott Fitzgerald in Hollywood*. New York: Viking, 1971.

Layman, Richard. *Shadow Man: The Life of Dashiell Hammett*. New York: Harcourt Brace, 1981.

Loy, Myrna. *Being and Becoming*. New York: Knopf, 1987.

Mantle, Burns. *Contemporary American Playwrights*. New York: Dodd Mead, 1938.

Martin, Jay. *Nathanael West: The Art of His Life*. New York: Farrar, Straus, 1970.
Marx, Arthur. *Goldwyn: A Biography of the Man Behind the Myth*. New York: Norton, 1976.
Marx, Groucho. *The Groucho Letters*. New York: Simon and Schuster, 1967.
Marx, Samuel. *Mayer and Thalberg: The Make-Believe Saints*. New York: Random House, 1975.
Marx, Samuel, and Joyce Vanderveen. *Deadly Illusions*. New York: Random House, 1990.
McBride, Joseph. *Frank Capra: The Catastrophe of Success*. New York: Simon and Schuster, 1992.
McCreedie, Marsha. *The Women Who Write the Movies*. New York: Birch Lane, 1994.
McGilligan, Patrick. *Backstory: Interviews with Screenwriters of Hollywood's Golden Age*. Berkeley: University of California Press, 1986.
Meade, Marion. *Dorothy Parker: What Fresh Hell Is This?* New York: Villard Books, 1988.
Mellen, Joan. *Hellman and Hammett: The Legendary Passion of Lillian Hellman and Dashiell Hammett*. New York: Harper Collins, 1996.
Melnick, Ralph. *The Stolen Legacy of Anne Frank*. New Haven: Yale University Press, 1997.
Minnelli, Vincente, with Hector Arce. *I Remember It Well*. New York: Doubleday, 1974.
Morley, Sheridan, *Tales from the Hollywood Raj*. London: Weidenfeld, 1983.
Morse, Frank P. *Backstage with Henry Miller*. New York: Dutton, 1938.
Murray, William. *Janet, My Mother and Me*. New York: Simon and Schuster, 2000.
Nash, Jay Robert, and Stanley Ralph Ross. *The Motion Picture Guide*. Chicago: Cinebooks, 1985.
Navasky, Victor. *Naming Names*. New York: Viking, 1980.
Niven, David. *The Moon's a Balloon*. New York: Putnam, 1972.
Nolan, William F. *Hammett: A Life at the Edge*. New York: Congdon and Weed, 1983.
Oppenheimer, George. *A View from the Sixties*. New York: David McKay, 1966.
Parish, James Robert, and Ronald L. Bowers. *The Golden Era: The MGM Stock Company*. Westport, Conn.: Arlington House, 1973.
Parish, James Robert, and Gregory W. Mank. *The Best of MGM*. Westport, Conn.: Arlington House, 1981.
Perelman, S. J. *Don't Tread on Me: The Selected Letters of S. J. Perelman*. Ed. Prudence Crowther. New York: Viking, 1987.
———. *Westward Ha! Or Around the World in Eighty Clichés*. New York: Simon and Schuster, 1947.
Phillips, Gene D. *Fiction, Film, and F. Scott Fitzgerald*. Chicago: Loyola University Press, 1986.
Rivkin, Allen, and Laura Kerr. *Hello, Hollywood!* New York: Doubleday, 1962.
Rollyson, Carl. *Lillian Hellman: Her Legend and Her Legacy*. New York: St. Martin's, 1988.

Rosten, Leo. *Hollywood: The Movie Colony, the Movie Makers*. New York: Harcourt Brace, 1941.

Sayre, Nora. *Previous Convictions: A Journey through the 1950's*. New Brunswick, N. J.: Rutgers University Press, 1995.

Schary, Dore. *Heyday: An Autobiography*. Boston: Little, Brown, 1979.

Schiff, Nancy Rica. *A Celebration of the 80s: Portraits*. New York: Harry N. Abrams, 1983.

Schildkraut, Joseph. *My Father and I*. New York: Viking, 1959.

Schwartz, Nancy Lynn. *The Hollywood Writers' Wars*. New York: Knopf, 1982.

Server, Lee. *Screenwriter*. Pittstown, N.J.: Main Street, 1987.

Stapleton, Maureen. *A Hell of a Life*. New York: Simon and Schuster, 1995.

Stewart, Donald Ogden. *By a Stroke of Luck: An Autobiography*. New York: Paddington, 1975.

Stickney, Dorothy. *Openings and Closings*. New York: Doubleday, 1979.

Strasberg, Susan. *Bittersweet*. New York: Putnam, 1980.

Stuart, Gloria. *I Just Kept Hoping*. New York: Little, Brown, 1999.

Teichman, Howard. *Smart Aleck: The Wit, World, and Life of Alexander Woolcott*. New York: Morrow, 1976.

Thomas, Lawrence B. *The MGM Years*. New York: Columbia House, 1972.

Thomson, David. *The Biographical Dictionary of Cinema*. London: Secker and Warburg, 1975.

van Loon, Gerard Willem. *The Story of Hendrik Willem van Loon*. New York: Lippincott, 1972.

Vidal, Gore. *Palimpsest: A Memoir*. New York: Random House, 1995.

Walker, Robert. *Intimate Lies: F. Scott Fitzgerald and Sheilah Graham: Her Son's Story*. New York: Harper Collins, 1995.

Wiley, Mason, and Damien Bona. *Inside Oscar: The Unofficial History of the Academy Awards*. New York: Ballantine, 1993.

Wright, William. *Lillian Hellman: The Image, The Woman*. New York: Simon and Schuster, 1986.

# Index

David L. Goodrich is the nephew of Frances Goodrich and Albert Hackett. He was born in New York City and lives there with his wife. A Yale graduate, he has published magazine fiction and nonfiction plus two other nonfiction books and a novel.